HISTORIC PLACES OF BUFFALO & WNY

INFORMATION ABOUT HISTORIC LOCATIONS, BUILDINGS, HOMES AND PLACES

by Rick Falkowski
with
Doreen Gallagher Regan
& Ellen Mika Zelasko

History Books

Copyright 2025 © by Rick Falkowski

All rights reserved. No part of this book may be used or reproduced in any manner whatsoever without the written permission of the author, except in the case of reviews or brief quotations in articles, where the source is properly credited.

Published by:
BuffaloHistoryBooks.com
rickfalkowski@aol.com
Facebook: Historic Places of Buffalo & WNY

Historic Places of Buffalo & WNY – Information about Historic Locations, Buildings, Homes & Places

ISBN number 979-8-9869824-4-1

1. Buffalo, NY
2. Local History
3. Historic Places, Nonfiction

Written by: Rick Falkowski, Doreen Gallagher Regan and Ellen Mika Zelasko
Edited by: Mike Buckley
Proof Readers: Mike Reid, Nancy Wise-Reid, Marsha Falkowski
Interior Design by: Nancy Wise-Reid/WiseBookDesigns
Front Cover Design by: Paul Marko/Digital Design
Front Cover Photo of Grand Island Bridge: Marsha Falkowski
Photo Enhancement by: Gene Thompson

First Edition: August 2025
Second Printing: February 2026
Printed in the U.S.A.

TABLE OF CONTENTS

Table of Figures _____ i

Historic Markers _____ ix

Acknowledgement & Dedication _____ xiv

Introduction _____ xv

    Town of Newstead _____ 2

1. PERRY'S ICE CREAM _____ 4
   - 1 Ice Cream Plaza, Akron _____ 4
2. RICH-TWINN OCTAGON HOUSE _____ 5
   - 145 Main Street, Akron _____ 5

    Town of Evans _____ 7

3. CRADLE BEACH CAMP _____ 9
   - 8038 Old Lake Shore Road, Angola _____ 9
4. EMBLEM BICYCLE FACTORY _____ 10
   - LaSalle Street, Angola _____ 10
5. WHITE CITY – CONNER'S POULTRY FARM _____ 11
   - Grandview Bay, Angola _____ 11
6. GRAYCLIFF _____ 12
   - 6472 Old Lake Shore Road, Derby _____ 12
7. LOCHEVAN- THE KELLOGG SUMMER ESTATE _____ 13
   - 7200 Lake Shore Road, Derby _____ 13
8. STURGEON POINT MARINA _____ 14
   - 618 Sturgeon Point Road, Derby _____ 14
9. SUNCLIFF MANOR - ST. COLUMBAN CENTER _____ 15
   - 6892 Lake Shore Road, Derby _____ 15
10. WENDT BEACH PARK _____ 16
    - 7676 Lake Shore Road, Derby _____ 16

    City of Buffalo _____ **18**

11. 800 WEST FERRY _____ 20
    - 800 West Ferry Street, Buffalo _____ 20
12. A&P WAREHOUSE _____ 21
    - 545 Swan Street, Buffalo _____ 21
13. ADAM MICKIEWICZ LIBRARY & DRAMATIC CENTER _____ 22
    - 612 Fillmore Avenue, Buffalo _____ 22
14. ADULT LEARNING CENTER _____ 23
    - 389 Virginia Street, Buffalo _____ 23
15. ALBRIGHT KNOX ART GALLERY _____ 24
    - 1285 Elmwood Avenue, Buffalo _____ 24
16. AM&A'S – JN ADAM'S DEPARTMENT STORES _____ 25

377 Main Street, Buffalo	25
17. AMERICAN RADIATOR COMPANY/ INSTITUTE FOR THERMAL RESEARCH	26
1807 Elmwood Avenue, Buffalo	26
18. ANCHOR BAR	27
1047 Main Street, Buffalo	27
19. ANNA KATHARINE GREEN HOUSE	28
156 Park Street, Buffalo	28
20. ASBURY DELAWARE AVENUE METHODIST CHURCH	29
339 Delaware Avenue, Buffalo	29
21. BELT LINE RAILROAD	30
10 Starin Avenue and Stations Circling Buffalo	30
22. BLOCHER MAUSOLEUM	31
Forest Lawn Cemetery, Buffalo	31
23. BRISBANE BUILDING	32
403 Main Street, Buffalo	32
24. BROADWAY ARSENAL, ARMORY, AUDITORIUM & BARN	33
201 Broadway, Buffalo	33
25. BROADWAY MARKET	34
999 Broadway, Buffalo	34
26. BUFFALO & ERIE COUNTY BOTANICAL GARDENS	35
2655 South Park Avenue, Buffalo	35
27. BUFFALO & ERIE COUNTY PUBLIC LIBRARY	36
1 Lafayette Square, Buffalo	36
28. BUFFALO ATHLETIC CLUB	37
69 Delaware Avenue, Buffalo	37
29. BUFFALO CENTRAL TERMINAL	38
495 Paderewski Drive, Buffalo	38
30. BUFFALO CITY HALL	39
65 Niagara Square, Buffalo	39
31. BUFFALO CLUB	40
388 Delaware Avenue, Buffalo	40
32. BUFFALO ELECTRIC VEHICLE COMPANY	41
1219 Main Street, Buffalo	41
33. BUFFALO GAS LIGHT COMPANY	42
249 West Genesee Street, Buffalo	42
34. BUFFALO HISTORY MUSEUM	43
One Museum Court, Buffalo	43
35. BUFFALO MAIN LIGHTHOUSE	44
Buffalo Harbor, Buffalo	44

36. BUFFALO METER COMPANY – BETHUNE LOFTS _____ 45
    2917 Main Street, Buffalo _____ 45
37. BUFFALO MILK COMPANY _____ 46
    885 Niagara Street, Buffalo _____ 46
38. BUFFALO SEMINARY _____ 47
    205 Bidwell Parkway, Buffalo _____ 47
39. BUFFALO STATE COLLEGE _____ 48
    1300 Elmwood Avenue, Buffalo _____ 48
40. BUFFALO VETERANS' ADMINISTRATION HOSPITAL _____ 49
    3495 Bailey Avenue, Buffalo _____ 49
41. BUFFALO WATER INTAKE _____ 50
    Buffalo Harbor, Buffalo _____ 50
42. BUFFALO ZOOLOGICAL GARDENS _____ 51
    300 Parkside Avenue, Buffalo _____ 51
43. C.W. MILLER LIVERY STABLE _____ 52
    73 West Huron Street, Buffalo _____ 52
44. CALUMET BUILDING _____ 53
    46-58 West Chippewa Street, Buffalo _____ 53
45. CAMPANILE APARTMENTS _____ 54
    925 Delaware Avenue, Buffalo _____ 54
46. CANALSIDE _____ 55
    44 Prime Street, Buffalo _____ 55
47. CANISIUS COLLEGE _____ 56
    2001 Main Street, Buffalo _____ 56
48. CANISIUS HIGH SCHOOL - RAND MANSION _____ 57
    1180 Delaware Ave, Buffalo _____ 57
49. COIT HOUSE _____ 58
    412 Virginia Street, Buffalo _____ 58
50. COLORED MUSICIANS CLUB _____ 59
    145 Broadway, Buffalo _____ 59
51. CONNECTICUT STREET ARMORY _____ 60
    184 Connecticut Street, Buffalo _____ 60
52. CORNELL MANSION _____ 61
    484 Delaware Avenue, Buffalo _____ 61
53. CURTISS AIRCRAFT – CONSOLIDATED, BELL, M WILE _____ 62
    2050 Elmwood Avenue, Buffalo _____ 62
54. CURTISS BUILDING – CURTISS HOTEL _____ 63
    210 Franklin Street, Buffalo _____ 63
55. CYCLORAMA BUILDING – GROSVENOR LIBRARY _____ 64

    369 Franklin Street, Buffalo _____ 64
56. D'Youville College _____ 65
    320 Porter Avenue, Buffalo _____ 65
57. Darwin Martin House _____ 66
    123 Jewett Parkway, Buffalo _____ 66
58. Delaware Midway Rowhouses _____ 67
    Delaware Avenue between Virginia & Allen, Buffalo _____ 67
59. DL&W Terminal & Train Sheds _____ 68
    29 South Park Avenue, Buffalo _____ 68
60. Dun Building _____ 69
    110 Pearl Street, Buffalo _____ 69
61. E & B Holmes Machinery Company Building _____ 70
    55 Chicago Street, Buffalo _____ 70
62. E.M. Hager & Sons Company _____ 71
    141 Elm Street, Buffalo _____ 71
63. Edward M. Cotter Fireboat & Icebreaker _____ 72
    155 Ohio Street, Buffalo _____ 72
64. Ellicott Square Building _____ 73
    295 Main Street, Buffalo _____ 73
65. F.N. Burt Company Factory _____ 74
    500 Seneca Street, Buffalo _____ 74
66. Forest Lawn Cemetery _____ 75
    1990 Main Street, Buffalo _____ 75
67. Fosdick-Masten Park High School–City Honors _____ 76
    186 East North Street, Buffalo _____ 76
68. Foster Mansion _____ 77
    50 Tudor Place, Buffalo _____ 77
69. Foster Mansion – DeRose Foods _____ 78
    981 Delaware Avenue, Buffalo _____ 78
70. Francis Fronczak House _____ 79
    806 Fillmore Avenue, Buffalo _____ 79
71. Garret Club _____ 80
    91 Cleveland Avenue, Buffalo _____ 80
72. General Electric Tower _____ 81
    535 Washington Street, Buffalo _____ 81
73. Goodyear Mansion _____ 82
    888 Delaware Avenue, Buffalo _____ 82
74. Great Lakes & Paramount Theaters, Nemmer Furniture and The City Centre Condos _____ 83
    600 Main Street, Buffalo _____ 83

75. GUARANTY BUILDING - PRUDENTIAL BUILDING	84
140 Pearl Street, Buffalo	84
76. HOLY ANGELS CHURCH	85
348 Porter Avenue, Buffalo	85
77. HOTEL LAFAYETTE	86
391 Washington Street, Buffalo	86
78. HOTEL LENOX	87
140 North Street, Buffalo	87
79. JAPANESE GARDENS OF BUFFALO	88
One Museum Court, Buffalo	88
80. KLEINHANS MUSIC HALL	89
3 Symphony Circle, Buffalo	89
81. KNOX MANSION	90
800 Delaware Avenue, Buffalo	90
82. LAFAYETTE HIGH SCHOOL	91
370 Lafayette Avenue, Buffalo	91
83. LAFAYETTE SQUARE	92
Main at Court Street, Buffalo	92
84. LINDE AIR PRODUCTS FACTORY	93
155 Chandler Street, Buffalo	93
85. MARGARET WENDT HOUSE	94
570 Richmond Avenue, Buffalo	94
86. MARKET ARCADE	95
617 Main Street, Buffalo	95
87. MAYFAIR LANE	96
North Street, Buffalo	96
88. MCDONNELL & SONS – GRANITE WORKS	97
858 Main Street, Buffalo	97
89. MENTHOLATUM COMPANY	98
1360 Niagara Street, Buffalo	98
90. MICHIGAN AVENUE BAPTIST CHURCH	99
511 Michigan Avenue, Buffalo	99
91. MONROE BUILDING – RECORD THEATRE	100
1786 Main Street, Buffalo	100
92. NASH HOUSE MUSEUM	101
36 Nash Street, Buffalo	101
93. NIAGARA SQUARE	102
Downtown Buffalo	102
94. NIETZSCHES, MULLIGANS BRICK BAR, THE OLD PINK	103

Allen Street, Buffalo	103
95. NORTH PARK THEATRE	104
1428 Hertel Avenue, Buffalo	104
96. OLD COUNTY HALL	105
92 Franklin Street, Buffalo	105
97. OSCAR MEYER MOTOR CORP – COLES RESTAURANT	106
1104 Elmwood Avenue, Buffalo	106
98. PACKARD MOTOR CAR SHOWROOM	107
1325 Main Street, Buffalo	107
99. PALACE BURLESK, STUDIO ARENA, SHEA'S 710 THEATRE	108
710 Main Street, Buffalo	108
100. PARADE/HUMBOLDT/MARTIN LUTHER KING, JR. PARK	109
Olmsted Park System, Buffalo	109
101. PARKSIDE CANDY	110
3208 Main Street, Buffalo	110
102. PEACE BRIDGE	111
1 Peace Bridge Plaza, Buffalo	111
103. PIERCE ARROW FACTORY	112
1695 Elmwood Avenue, Buffalo	112
104. PIERCE ARROW SHOWROOMS – VERNOR BUILDING	113
752-8 Main Street and 2421 Main Street, Buffalo	113
105. RAND BUILDING	114
14 Lafayette Square, Buffalo	114
106. RICHARDSON OLMSTED CAMPUS – BUFFALO STATE HOSPITAL	115
444 Forest Avenue, Buffalo	115
107. RICHMOND – LOCKWOOD HOUSE	116
844 Delaware Avenue, Buffalo	116
108. ROBERT T. COLES HOUSE & STUDIO	117
321 Humboldt Parkway, Buffalo	117
109. ROSWELL PARK COMPREHENSIVE CANCER CENTER	118
665 Elm Street, Buffalo	118
110. SATURN CLUB	119
977 Delaware Avenue, Buffalo	119
111. SCHENCK HOUSE	120
Grover Cleveland Golf Course, Buffalo	120
112. SENECA INDIAN CEMETERY	121
Buffum Street, Buffalo	121
113. SHEA'S BUFFALO THEATRE	122
646 Main Street, Buffalo	122

114. SHEA'S SENECA ___ 123
    2178 Seneca Street, Buffalo ___ 123
115. ST. JOSEPH'S CATHEDRAL ___ 124
    50 Franklin Street, Buffalo ___ 124
116. ST. LOUIS CHURCH ___ 125
    35 Edward Street, Buffalo ___ 125
117. ST. PAUL'S EPISCOPAL CATHEDRAL ___ 126
    139 Pearl Street, Buffalo ___ 126
118. ST. STANISLAUS ROMAN CATHOLIC CHURCH ___ 127
    123 Townsend Street, Buffalo ___ 127
119. STATLER HOTEL ___ 128
    Washington and Swan Streets, Buffalo ___ 128
120. SWANNIE HOUSE ___ 129
    170 Ohio Street, Buffalo ___ 129
121. TEMPLE BETH ZION ___ 130
    805 Delaware Avenue, Buffalo ___ 130
122. THOMAS MOTORS/CURTIS AEROPLANE/RICH PRODUCTS ___ 131
    1200 Niagara Street, Buffalo ___ 131
123. TICOR TITLE BUILDING – UNITARIAN CHURCH ___ 132
    110 Franklin Street, Buffalo ___ 132
124. TIFFT NATURE PRESERVE ___ 133
    1200 Fuhrmann Boulevard, Buffalo ___ 133
125. TIMES BEACH ___ 134
    11 Fuhrmann Boulevard, Buffalo ___ 134
126. TOWN CASINO ___ 135
    681 Main Street, Buffalo ___ 135
127. TRI-MAIN CENTER ___ 136
    2495 Main Street, Buffalo ___ 136
128. TRICO PLANT #1 ___ 137
    628 Ellicott Street, Buffalo ___ 137
129. TRINITY CHURCH ___ 138
    371 Delaware Avenue, Buffalo ___ 138
130. TWENTIETH CENTURY CLUB OF BUFFALO ___ 139
    595 Delaware Avenue, Buffalo ___ 139
131. ULRICH'S TAVERN ___ 140
    674 Ellicott Street, Buffalo ___ 140
132. UNION SHIP CANAL ___ 141
    Outer Harbor Drive, Buffalo ___ 141
133. UNITARIAN UNIVERSALIST CHURCH ___ 142

	695 Elmwood Avenue, Buffalo	142
134.	University of Buffalo - South Campus	143
	3435 Main Street, Buffalo	143
135.	War Memorial Stadium	144
	285 Dodge Street, Buffalo	144
136.	Weed Block Building	145
	284 Main Street, Buffalo	145
137.	Werner Photography Building	146
	101-103 Genesee Street, Buffalo	146
138.	Wilcox Mansion – Theodore Roosevelt Inaugural Site	147
	641 Delaware Avenue, Buffalo	147
139.	William Conners Mansion	148
	1140 Delaware Avenue, Buffalo	148
140.	William Dorsheimer House	149
	434-438 Delaware Avenue, Buffalo	149
141.	Williams-Butler Mansion	150
	672 Delaware Avenue, Buffalo	150
142.	Wurlitzer – Tent City Building	151
	674 Main Street, Buffalo	151
143.	YMCA Building, Olympic Towers	152
	45 West Mohawk, Buffalo	152
	Counties of Cattaraugus and Chautauqua	**154**
144.	Athenaeum Hotel	155
	3 South Lake Drive, Chautauqua	155
145.	Chautauqua Institution	156
	1 Ames Avenue, Chautauqua	156
146.	Lewis Miller Cottage	157
	24 Whitfield Avenue, Chautauqua	157
147.	Fredonia Gas Light & Water Company	158
	Canadaway Creek at West Main Street, Fredonia	158
148.	Sunset Bay Beach Club	159
	1028 South Shore Road, Irving	159
149.	Thomas Indian School	160
	Cattaraugus Reservation, Irving	160
150.	Lily Dale Assembly	161
	5 Melrose Park, Lily Dale	161
151.	J. N. Adam Memorial Hospital	162
	10317 County Road 58, Perrysburg	162
152.	Barcelona Lighthouse	163
	8234 E Lake Road (Route 5), Westfield	163

153. WELCH GRAPE JUICE FACTORY _____ 164
    101 North Portage Street, Westfield _____ 164
    Town of Cheektowaga _____ **166**
154. BUFFALO NIAGARA INTERNATIONAL AIRPORT _____ 168
    4200 Genesee Street, Cheektowaga _____ 168
155. CHAPEL OF OUR LADY HELP OF CHRISTIANS _____ 169
    4125 Union Road, Cheektowaga _____ 169
156. GEORGE URBAN MANSION _____ 170
    280 Pine Ridge Road, Cheektowaga _____ 170
157. REINSTEIN WOODS NATURE PRESERVE _____ 171
    93 Honorine Drive, Cheektowaga _____ 171
158. ST. STEPHEN'S EVANGELICAL LUTHERAN HOME _____ 172
    3350 Broadway, Cheektowaga _____ 172
159. WAR OF 1812 CEMETERY _____ 173
    Aero Road, Cheektowaga _____ 173
    Town of Clarence _____ **175**
160. ASA RANSOM HOUSE _____ 177
    10529 and 10897 Main Street, Clarence _____ 177
161. CLARENCE TOWN PARK CLUB HOUSE _____ 178
    10405 Main Street, Clarence _____ 178
162. HISTORICAL SOCIETY OF CLARENCE & GOODRICH-LANDOW CABIN _____ 179
    10465 Main Street, Clarence _____ 179
163. SPAULDING LAKE _____ 180
    Development in Clarence _____ 180
    Village of East Aurora _____ **182**
164. FISHER-PRICE TOY COMPANY _____ 184
    636 Girard Avenue, East Aurora _____ 184
165. GLOBE HOTEL _____ 185
    711 East Main Street, East Aurora _____ 185
166. HAMLIN VILLAGE FARMS _____ 186
    100 North Willow, East Aurora _____ 186
167. KNOX FARM STATE PARK – KNOX FAMILY ESTATE _____ 187
    437 Buffalo Road, East Aurora _____ 187
168. MILLARD FILLMORE HOUSE & MUSEUM _____ 188
    24 Shearer Avenue, East Aurora _____ 188
169. ROYCROFT CAMPUS _____ 189
    Main and South Grove Streets, East Aurora _____ 189
170. ROYCROFT INN _____ 190
    40 South Grove Street, East Aurora _____ 190
171. VIDLER'S 5 & 10 _____ 191

676-694 Main Street, East Aurora	191
172. MARILLA COUNTRY STORE	192
1673 Two Rod Road, Marilla	192
Town of Grand Island	**194**
173. BEDELL HOUSE	196
1437 Ferry Road, Grand Island	196
174. GRAND ISLAND NIKE BASE	197
3278 Whitehaven Road, Grand Island	197
175. LEWIS ALLEN VILLA AT RIVER LEA	198
Beaver Island State Park, Grand Island	198
176. WBEN RADIO: TRANSMITTER BUILDING	199
1791 Bush Road, Grand Island	199
Town of Hamburg	**201**
177. PENN DIXIE FOSSIL PARK & NATURE RESERVE	203
4050 North Street, Blasdell	203
178. WOODLAWN BEACH	204
S-3580 Lakeshore Road, Blasdell	204
179. IDLEWOOD ASSOCIATION	205
West Arnold Drive, Lake View	205
180. LAKE VIEW HOTEL	206
1957 Lake View Road, Lake View	206
Village of Kenmore	**208**
181. EBERHARDT MANSION	210
2746 Delaware Avenue, Kenmore	210
182. HUNTLEY POWER PLANT	211
3500 River Road, Tonawanda	211
City of Lackawanna	**213**
183. BETHLEHEM STEEL	214
Route 5, Lackawanna	214
184. HOLY CROSS CEMETERY	215
2900 South Park Avenue, Lackawanna	215
185. JOHN B. WEBER MANSION	216
1619 Abbott Road, Lackawanna	216
186. OUR LADY OF VICTORY BASILICA	217
767 Ridge Road, Lackawanna	217
Village & Town of Lancaster	**219**
187. HULL HOUSE & GIPPLE CABIN	220
5976 Genesee Street, Lancaster	220
188. LANCASTER OPERA HOUSE	221
21 Central Avenue, Lancaster	221

Town of Lewiston	**223**
189. ARTPARK	225
450 South 4th Street, Lewiston	225
190. BENJAMIN BARTON HOUSE	226
210 Center Street, Lewiston	226
191. FRONTIER HOUSE	227
460 Center Street, Lewiston	227
192. OUR LADY OF FATIMA NATIONAL SHRINE	228
1023 Swann Road, Lewiston	228
City of Lockport/ Town of Newfane	**230**
193. VAN HORN MANSION	231
2159 Lockport-Olcott Road, Burt	231
194. COLONEL WILLIAM BOND/JESSE HAWLEY HOUSE	232
143 Ontario Street, Lockport	232
195. OLCOTT BEACH AMUSEMENT PARK	233
5979 Main Street, Olcott	233
City of Niagara Falls	**235**
196. ADAMS POWER PLANT TRANSFORMER HOUSE	237
1501 Buffalo Avenue, Niagara Falls	237
197. CASTELLANI ART MUSEUM	238
5795 Lewiston Road, Niagara University, Niagara Falls	238
198. CAYUGA ISLAND	239
Niagara Falls	239
199. DEVEAUX COLLEGE	240
3100 Lewiston Road, Niagara Falls	240
200. DEVIL'S HOLE STATE PARK	241
3120 DeVeaux Woods Drive, Niagara Falls	241
201. FORT SCHLOSSER	242
Niagara Falls	242
202. GREAT BEAR MARKET	243
1801 Pine Avenue, Niagara Falls	243
203. LOVE CANAL	244
Niagara Falls	244
204. NIAGARA FALLS STATE PARK	245
332 Prospect Street, Niagara Falls	245
205. NIAGARA UNIVERSITY	246
5795 Lewiston Road, Niagara Falls	246
206. OAKWOOD CEMETERY	247
747 Portage Road, Niagara Falls	247
207. PETER PORTER MANSION	248

6 4th Street, Niagara Falls	248
208. SCHOELLKOPF POWER PLANT	249
Niagara Gorge, Niagara Falls	249
209. WHITNEY MANSION	250
335 Buffalo Avenue, Niagara Falls	250
City of North Tonawanda	**252**
"The Lumber City"	252
210. CANTILEVER BRIDGE	254
Erie Canal near Sweeney at Oliver Street, North Tonawanda	254
211. CARNEGIE LIBRARY	255
240 Goundry Street, North Tonawanda	255
212. DEGRAFF MANSION	256
273 Goundry Street, North Tonawanda	256
213. GATEWAY HARBOR PARK	257
Erie Canal between Tonawanda and North Tonawanda	257
214. HERSCHELL CARROUSEL FACTORY	258
180 Thompson Street, North Tonawanda	258
215. NIAGARA FALLS POWER TRANSFER STATION	259
Twin City Highway & Robinson Street, North Tonawanda	259
216. NIAGARA POWER BUILDING	260
2-6 Webster Street, North Tonawanda	260
217. NORTH TONAWANDA ERIE RAILROAD STATION	261
111 Oliver Street, North Tonawanda	261
218. REMINGTON RAND BUILDING	262
162-184 Sweeney Street, North Tonawanda	262
219. RIVIERA THEATRE	263
67 Webster Street, North Tonawanda	263
220. WURLITZER BUILDING	264
908 Niagara Falls Boulevard, North Tonawanda	264
Town of Orchard Park	**266**
221. CHESTNUT RIDGE PARK	268
6121 Chestnut Ridge Road, Orchard Park	268
222. JOHNSON-JOLLS HOUSE	269
4287 South Buffalo St., Orchard Park	269
223. ORCHARD PARK BUFFALO, ROCHESTER, PITTSBURGH STATION	270
395 South Lincoln Avenue, Orchard Park	270
224. OLMSTED CAMP	271
12820 Benton Road, Sardinia	271
Village of Springville	**273**
225. BUFFUM INN	274

8335 Boston-Colden Road, Colden	274
226. SPRINGVILLE-GRIFFITH INSTITUTE	275
290 North Buffalo Street, Springville	275
227. WAITE BUILDING	276
25 East Main Street, Springville	276
228. WARNER MUSEUM AND DYGERT FARM	277
98 East Main Street and 206 Elk Street, Springville	277
City of Tonawanda	**279**
229. BENJAMIN LONG HOMESTEAD	281
24 East Niagara Street, Tonawanda	281
230. TONAWANDA ARMORY	282
79 Delaware Street, Tonawanda	282
231. TONAWANDA RAILROAD STATION	283
113 Main Street, Tonawanda	283
Town of West Seneca	**285**
232. CHARLES E. BURCHFIELD NATURE & ART CENTER	287
2001 Union Road, West Seneca	287
233. CHRISTIAN METZ HOUSE	288
12 School Street, West Seneca	288
234. LEIN'S PARK	289
810 Union Road, West Seneca	289
235. MALECKI MANSION	290
2544 Clinton Street, West Seneca	290
236. MAYER BROTHERS	291
1540 Seneca Creek Road, West Seneca	291
237. SCHWABL'S	292
789 Center Road, West Seneca	292
Town of Wheatfield	**294**
238. BELL AIRCRAFT	296
Niagara Falls Boulevard, Wheatfield	296
239. DAS HAUS – GERMAN HERITAGE MUSEUM	297
2549 Niagara Road, Wheatfield	297
240. SAWYER CREEK HOTEL	298
3264 Niagara Falls Boulevard, Wheatfield	298
Village of Williamsville/ Town of Amherst	**300**
241. BUFFALO NIAGARA HERITAGE VILLAGE	304
3755 Tonawanda Creek Road, Amherst	304
242. COUNTRY CLUB OF BUFFALO	305
250 Youngs Road, Williamsville	305
243. EAGLE HOUSE	306

5578 Main Street, Williamsville	306
244. GLEN PARK	307
5565 Main Street, Williamsville	307
245. PARK COUNTRY CLUB	308
4949 Sheridan Drive, Williamsville	308
246. REFORMED MENNONITE CHURCH	309
5178 Main Street, Williamsville	309
247. SAINTS PETER & PAUL CHURCH	310
5480 Main Street, Williamsville	310
248. WILLIAMSVILLE MEETING HOUSE	311
5658 Main Street, Williamsville	311
Village of Wilson	**313**
249. WILSON HOUSE	314
300 Lake Street, Wilson	314
250. FORT NIAGARA & THE FRENCH CASTLE	315
102 Morrow Plaza, Youngstown	315
Source Notes	316
Bibliography	353
History & Music Presentations available from Rick Falkowski	**364**
Index	366

Properties that have been listed in the **National Register of Historic Places** by the U.S. Department of the Interior have been identified on their profile page by the official Historic Marker sign or the historic marker at the site.
See **Historic Markers** for larger versions of these signs _____ ix

Every effort was made to correctly acknowledge each photo included in this book. The author apologizes if any copyright photo was considered public domain (**PD**) or if a photo was not properly credited. Any unintentional errors or omissions, upon notice, will be corrected in future printings or editions of this book.

Table of Figures

Front Cover Photo of Grand Island Bridge: Marsha Falkowski
Back Cover Photo of author: Mike Reid

Figure 1 This Marker will be found next to all of the Registered Historic Places in this book ------- xiii
Figure 2 Historic Marker Ely Parker in Akron ------- 2
Figure 3 Newman Flouring and Cement Works in Akron New York PD ------- 3
Figure 4 Perrys Ice Cream photo courtesy Brian Perry ------- 3
Figure 5 Historic Marker Russell Park ------- 3
Figure 6 Perry's Ice Cream 1 Pearl Street Akron photo courtesy Perry's Ice Cream ------- 4
Figure 7 Rich Twinn House photo credit Rick Falkowski ------- 5
Figure 8 First Church of Evans PD ------- 7
Figure 9 Historic Marker Aaron Salisbury War of 1812 Evans ------- 7
Figure 10 Bank of Angola early Business District PD ------- 8
Figure 11 Historic Marker First Church of Evans ------- 8
Figure 12 Cradle Beach vintage postcard ------- 9
Figure 13 Emblem Bicycle Factory photo Company Archives PD ------- 10
Figure 14 White City - Ducks at Conners Poultry Farm early 1900s postcard courtesy Evans Historical Society Donna Nagel ------- 11
Figure 15 Graycliff: A Lakefront Masterpiece by Frank Lloyd Wright photo credit Matthew Digati ------- 12
Figure 16 Lochevan Kellogg Estate photo credit Doreen Gallagher Regan ------- 13
Figure 17 The Willows George Pierce Estate ------- 14
Figure 18 Suncliff on the Lake photo credit Daniel Regan ------- 15
Figure 19 Wendt Beach Mansion in 1960s photo credit Doreen Gallagher Regan ------- 16
Figure 20 1798 Drawing of Buffalo Peninsula near current location of Times Beach photo Picture Book of Earlier Buffalo ------- 18
Figure 21 Eagle Tavern, Main & Court Streets 1825 Picture Book of Earlier Buffalo ----- 19
Figure 22 800 West Ferry photo credit Ellen Mika Zelasko ------- 20
Figure 23 Ap Lofts at Larkinville photo aploftsatlarkinville.com ------- 21
Figure 24 Adam Mickiewicz Library Dramatic Circle photo credit Patra Mangus ------- 22
Figure 25 Adult Learning Center ------- 23
Figure 26 Albright Knox Art Gallery photo credit Rick Falkowski ------- 24
Figure 27 AM&A's 377 Main St. Still JN Adams Store PD ------- 25
Figure 28 American Radiator Company 9-1-1915 photo American Radiator Company PD ------- 26
Figure 29 Anchor Bar photo credit Rick Falkowski ------- 27
Figure 30 Anna Katharine Green House photo credit Rick Falkowski ------- 28
Figure 31 Asbury Delaware Avenue Methodist Church photo credit Rick Falkowski ----- 29
Figure 32 Belt Line Railroad Central Park Station PD ------- 30
Figure 33 Blocher Mausoleum photo credit Rick Falkowski ------- 31
Figure 34 Brisbane Building photo early 1900s postcard of Lafayette Square ------- 32
Figure 35 Broadway Auditorium postcard from 1914 PD ------- 33
Figure 36 Broadway Market postcard late 1800s PD ------- 34
Figure 37 Botanical Gardens photo credit Marsha Falkowski ------- 35

i

Figure 38 Original 1887 Library being demolished in front of New Library constructed in 1963 -------- 36
Figure 39 Buffalo Athletic Club - 69 Delaware Avenue photo credit Rick Falkowski ---- 37
Figure 40 Buffalo Central Terminal photo credit Patra Mangus -------- 38
Figure 41 Buffalo City Hall photo credit Rick Falkowski -------- 39
Figure 42 Buffalo Club photo credit Rick Falkowski -------- 40
Figure 43 Buffalo Electric Vehicle Company photo credit Rick Falkowski -------- 41
Figure 44 Buffalo Gas Light Company in 1920s photo Forgotten Buffalo PD -------- 42
Figure 45 Buffalo History Museum back entrance photo credit Rick Falkowski -------- 43
Figure 46 Steamship passing Lighthouse when entering Port of Buffalo in 1900 photo National Archives -------- 44
Figure 47 Buffalo Meter Company 1920s PD -------- 45
Figure 48 Buffalo Milk Company Home of the Queen City Dairy 1911 PD -------- 46
Figure 49 Buffalo Seminary Bidwell Parkway facade Buffalo Express 1906 drawing by Architect -------- 47
Figure 50 Buffalo State College Original 1931 Campus buffalostate.edu -------- 48
Figure 51 Buffalo VA Hospital old postcard PD -------- 49
Figure 52 Colonel Ward Pumping Station vintage postcard PD -------- 50
Figure 53 Water Intake PD -------- 50
Figure 54 Buffalo Zoo photo credit Marsha Falkowski -------- 51
Figure 55 CW Miller Livery Stable before/after photos credit photo restoration by Gene Thompson -------- 52
Figure 56 Calumet Building photo credit Ellen Mika Zelasko -------- 53
Figure 57 Campanile Apartments photo credit Ellen Mika Zelasko -------- 54
Figure 58 Canalside Boardwalk with Naval Park and Apartments photo credit Ellen Mika Zelasko -------- 55
Figure 59 Old Main at Canisius College photo camisius.edu -------- 56
Figure 60 Canisius High School Rand Mansion photo credit Ellen Mika Zelasko -------- 57
Figure 61 Coit House photo credit Ellen Mika Zelasko -------- 58
Figure 62 Colored Musicians Club construction in progress photo credit Rick Falkowski 59
Figure 63 Connecticut Street Armory shortly after construction PD -------- 60
Figure 64 Cornell Mansion photo credit Rick Falkowski -------- 61
Figure 65 Consolidated Aircraft 2050 Elmwood Avenue 9/9/1927 PD -------- 62
Figure 66 Curtiss Hotel photo credit Rick Falkowski -------- 63
Figure 67 Cyclorama Building in 1890 photo Library of Congress -------- 64
Figure 68 Koessler Administration Building at Holy Angels School 1887 -------- 65
Figure 69 Darwin Martin House photo credit Mike Shriver buffalophotoblog.com -------- 66
Figure 70 Midway Rowhouses photo credit Ellen Mika Zelasko -------- 67
Figure 71 DL&W Train Shed 1919 postcard -------- 68
Figure 72 Dunn Building PD -------- 69
Figure 73 E.& B. Holmes Building in 1876 PD -------- 70
Figure 74 EM Hager & Sons - Planing Mill photo credit Rick Falkowski -------- 71
Figure 75 The Edward M Cotter photo credit Ellen Mika Zelasko -------- 72
Figure 76 Ellicott Square Building Late 1890s photo restoration by Gene Thompson --- 73
Figure 77 F.N. Burt Company 500 Seneca St. PD -------- 74
Figure 78 Forest Lawn Cemetery photo credit Marsha Falkowski -------- 75
Figure 79 Original Masten Park High School 1905 postcard -------- 76
Figure 80 50 Tudor Place photo credit Ellen Mika Zelasko -------- 77
Figure 81 Foster Mansion photo credit Mike Shriver buffalophotoblog.com -------- 78
Figure 82 Francis Fronczak House photo credit Patra Mangus -------- 79
Figure 83 Garret Club photo credit Rick Falkowski -------- 80

Figure 84 Electric Tower in 1927 photo Company Archives --------------------------------81
Figure 85 Goodyear Mansion photo credit Ellen Mika Zelasko --------------------------82
Figure 86 Buffalo Theatre District 1963 postcard-------------------------------------83
Figure 87 Guaranty Prudential Building photo credit Ellen Mika Zelasko-----------------84
Figure 88 Terra Cotta Design of Guaranty Building photo credit Ellen Mika Zelasko ----84
Figure 89 Holy Angels Church photo credit Ellen Mika Zelasko --------------------------85
Figure 90 Hotel Lafayette photo credit Ellen Mika Zelasko-----------------------------86
Figure 91 Lenox Hotel early 1900s original entrance PD -------------------------------87
Figure 92 Japanese Gardens in Delaware Park photo courtesy Buffalo Olmsted Parks
    Conservatory--88
Figure 93 Kleinhans Music Hall photo credit Ellen Mika Zelasko ------------------------89
Figure 94 Knox Mansion photo credit Rick Falkowski -----------------------------------90
Figure 95 Lafayette High School early 1900s postcard ---------------------------------91
Figure 96 LaFayette Square 1907 with German Insurance Co. and original Lafayette
    Theater historic postcard PD ---92
Figure 97 Linde Air Products Chandler Street Factory National Register of Historic
    Places Submission 2017 ---93
Figure 98 Wendt Family Home 570 Richmond courtesy Wendt Foundation ----------------94
Figure 99 Market Arcade Interior photo credit Ellen Mika Zelasko ----------------------95
Figure 100 Mayfair Court photo credit Marsha Falkowski-------------------------------96
Figure 101 McDonnell & Sons Co. photo enhanced by Gene Thompson ------------------97
Figure 102 Mentholatum Company - mid-1900s photo Company Archives ---------------98
Figure 103 Michigan Avenue Baptist Church photo credit Petra Mangus ------------------99
Figure 104 O'Neill Motor Company later became Record Theatre photo enhanced by
    Gene Thompson -- 100
Figure 105 Jesse Nash House photo credit Rick Falkowski ----------------------------- 101
Figure 106 Niagara Square Buffalo in 1920s PD ------------------------------------- 102
Figure 107 Mulligans Brick Bar photo credit Steve Cichon----------------------------- 103
Figure 108 North Park Theater early photo PD ------------------------------------- 104
Figure 109 Old County Hall photo credit Ellen Mika Zelasko -------------------------- 105
Figure 110 Cole's Restaurant in 1934 PD--- 106
Figure 111 Packard Building photo enhanced by Gene Thompson---------------------- 107
Figure 112 710 Main Street Palace Theater under construction ----------------------- 108
Figure 113 Martin Luther King Park Parade Pavilion Picture Book of Earlier Buffalo
    photo restored by Gene Thompson --- 109
Figure 114 Parkside Candy Main & Oakwood watercolor by Dr. V. Roger Lalli--------- 110
Figure 115 Peace Bridge photo credit Ellen Mika Zelasko ----------------------------- 111
Figure 116 Pierce Arrow Factory 1921 brochure PD--------------------------------- 112
Figure 117 Pierce Arrow Showroom PD Detroit Public Library photo restored by Gene
    Thompson --- 113
Figure 118 2421 Main Street watercolor by Dr. V. Roger Lalli ------------------------- 113
Figure 119 Rand Building photo credit Ellen Mika Zelasko---------------------------- 114
Figure 120 Richardson Olmsted Campus photo credit Marsha Falkowski--------------- 115
Figure 121 Richmond Lockwood Mansion photo credit Mike Shriver
    buffalophotoblog.com--- 116
Figure 122 Robert T. Coles House photo courtesy National Trust for Historic
    Preservation Jalen Wright--- 117
Figure 123 Roswell Park entrance photo credit Rick Falkowski ----------------------- 118
Figure 124 Saturn Club photo credit Ellen Mika Zelasko----------------------------- 119
Figure 125 Schenck House photo courtesy Erie County Parks, Recreation & Forestry - 120

Figure 126 Schenck House Restored photo courtesy Erie County Dept. of Parks, Recreation & Forestry --- 120
Figure 127 Seneca Indian Cemetery photo credit Mike Buckley -------------------------- 121
Figure 128 Shea's Theatre Grand Opening 1926 photo sheas.org------------------------ 122
Figure 129 Shea's Seneca 2019 photo credit Katie Schneider Photography--------------- 123
Figure 130 St. Joseph Cathedral photo credit Ellen Mika Zelasko ------------------------ 124
Figure 131 St. Louis Church late 1800s PD --- 125
Figure 132 St Paul's Episcopal Church photo credit Rick Falkowski ----------------------- 126
Figure 133 St. Stanislaus Church photo credit Patra Mangus--------------------------- 127
Figure 134 Statler Towers photo credit Rick Falkowski ----------------------------------- 128
Figure 135 Swannie House during early 1900s photo contributed by family PD -------- 129
Figure 136 Temple Beth Zion photo credit Rick Falkowski------------------------------- 130
Figure 137 Thomas Motor Company in 1905 Buffalo of Today PD ---------------------- 131
Figure 138 Ticor (Austin) Building PD photo restored by Gene Thompson -------------- 132
Figure 139 Tifft Nature Preserve photo credit Doreen Gallagher Regan ------------------ 133
Figure 140 Times Beach Wilkinson Pointe before development PD --------------------- 134
Figure 141 Town Casino --- 135
Figure 142 Ford Motor Company at 2495 Main St. PD ------------------------------------ 136
Figure 143 Trico Apartments photo credit Rick Falkowski-------------------------------- 137
Figure 144 Trinity Church photo credit Rick Falkowski ---------------------------------- 138
Figure 145 Twentieth Century Club photo credit Rick Falkowski------------------------ 139
Figure 146 Dobmeier's Hotel in 1900 photo from Ulrich's Tavern Archives restored by Gene Thompson -- 140
Figure 147 photo early 1900's courtesy of the Steel Plant Museum of Western New York Facebook page --- 141
Figure 148 Unitarian Church early 1900s photo buffalouu.org PD ----------------------- 142
Figure 149 UB in 1950s Foster Crosby & Hayes Hall archplan.buffalo.edu -------------- 143
Figure 150 Civic Stadium historic postcard --- 144
Figure 151 Weed Company Building 1857 PD --- 145
Figure 152 Werner Photography Building block photo credit Rick Falkowski ------------ 146
Figure 153 Wilcox Mansion Circa 1900 PD -- 147
Figure 154 Conners Mansion photo credit Rick Falkowski-------------------------------- 148
Figure 155 William Dorsheimer House 1965 photo Library of Congress ----------------- 149
Figure 156 Williams-Butler Mansion photo credit Ellen Mika Zelasko ------------------- 150
Figure 157 Poppenberg Motor Car 674 Main Street PD ---------------------------------- 151
Figure 158 Wurlitzer Store 674 Main Street PD -- 151
Figure 159 YMCA Building Library of Congress 1908 Detroit Publishing Co. ---------- 152
Figure 160 Olean High School 1935 Olean Historical Society PD ------------------------ 154
Figure 161 Athenaeum Hotel Chautauqua Institution -------------------------------------- 155
Figure 162 Docks at the Chautauqua Institution --- 156
Figure 163 Chautauqua Institution Gymnasium -- 156
Figure 164 Lewis Miller Cottage from the Library of Congress website------------------ 157
Figure 165 Historic Marker - First Gas Well in Fredonia ---------------------------------- 158
Figure 166 Burghardt Sunset Bay Beach Club in the 1940s photo courtesy Sam Bova -- 159
Figure 167 Thomas Indian School Iroquois Genealogy Society PD ----------------------- 160
Figure 168 Lily Dale Forest Temple photo lilydaleassembly.org PD ----------------------- 161
Figure 169 J.N. Adams Hospital Artvue postcard PD -------------------------------------- 162
Figure 170 Barcelona Lighthouse 1900 photo courtesy Patterson Library Archives ----- 163
Figure 171 Welch's Grape Juice Company vintage postcard ------------------------------- 164
Figure 172 Liberty Park 1949 Cheektowaga Historical Museum ------------------------- 167
Figure 173 Gardenville Union Garage Union & Losson Bell Helicopter ------------------ 167

Figure 174 Buffalo Airport Art Deco Terminal Built in 1939 -------------------------------- 168
Figure 175 Our Lady Help of Christians Chapel photo courtesy Cheektowaga Historical Society -- 169
Figure 176 Res of George Urban, Jr. Pine Hill Town of Cheektowaga Erie County NY PD --- 170
Figure 177 George Urban House photo credit Rick Falkowski ---------------------------- 170
Figure 178 Reinstein Woods - former Reinstein Family Summer Building photo credit Marsha Falkowski --- 171
Figure 179 St. Stephens 1898 PD History of Germans of Buffalo & Erie County ------- 172
Figure 180 From the War of 1812 Cemetery photo credit Rick Falkowski -------------- 173
Figure 181 National Gypsum Company on Roll Road in Clarence Center photo courtesy Clarence Town Historian --- 176
Figure 182 Ransom House at 10897 Main Street photo courtesy Clarence Historical Society -- 177
Figure 183 Clarence Country Club photo courtesy AAA ---------------------------------- 178
Figure 184 Clarence Museum photo courtesy Clarence Historical Society ------------- 179
Figure 185 Goodrich Landow Log Cabin photo courtesy Clarence Historical Society -- 179
Figure 186 Undeveloped Spaulding Lake photo courtesy Historical Society Town of Clarence -- 180
Figure 187 Historic Marker The Middle Road East Aurora ------------------------------ 182
Figure 188 Jewett Farms Covered Mile Horse Racetrack photo Aurora Historian ------- 183
Figure 189 Fisher Price Girard Avenue facility fpclub.org ----------------------------- 184
Figure 190 Globe Hotel 1890 photo courtesy Archives of the Aurora Town Historians Office --- 185
Figure 191 The Judge's Stand -- 186
Figure 192 Knox Farms Ess Kay Farm Fox Hunt PD ------------------------------------- 187
Figure 193 Millard Fillmore House photo credit Marsha Falkowski ----------------------- 188
Figure 194 Roycroft Campus Chapel Library 1973 photo National Register of Historic Places --- 189
Figure 195 Roycroft Inn in early 1900s photo courtesy Roycroft Archives --------------- 190
Figure 196 Vidler's 1930 Center Store 2 aisles with 900 Sq. Ft. vidlers5and10.com ------ 191
Figure 197 G.C. Monchow & Co. Store photo Marilla Country Store Archives ---------- 192
Figure 198 Whitehaven Settlement photo courtesy Grand Island Historical Society ---- 194
Figure 199 Grand Island Bridge photo credit Marsha Falkowski -------------------------- 195
Figure 200 Bedell House Annex when opened in 1877 photo courtesy Grand Island Historical Society --- 196
Figure 201 Grand Island Nike Base and Golden Age Center photo courtesy Grand Island Historical Society -- 197
Figure 202 Lewis Allen House on Grand Island photo credit Rick Falkowski ------------ 198
Figure 203 WBEN Transmitter Site photo credit Rick Falkowski -------------------------- 199
Figure 204 Hamburg Water Works 1913 Hamburg Historical Society PD --------------- 201
Figure 205 Bank of Hamburgh Hamburg Historical Society PD ------------------------- 201
Figure 206 Saints Peter & Paul Church Hamburg PD ------------------------------------- 202
Figure 207 Hamburg Grange in 1930 Hamburg Historical Society PD -------------------- 202
Figure 208 Penn Dixie photo credit Marsha Falkowski ------------------------------------- 203
Figure 209 Woodlawn Beach 1896 PD -- 204
Figure 210 Bridge Over 18 Mile Creek Schoellkopf Tannery 1906 ------------------------ 205
Figure 211 Lake View Hotel 1908 PD --- 206
Figure 212 St. Peter's Evangelical Church built 1849 photo courtesy Tonawanda-Kenmore Historical Society -- 208

Figure 213 Adam Zimmerman House at 785 Delaware Road photo courtesy Tonawanda-Kenmore Historical Society --- 209
Figure 214 St. John's RC North Bush Chapel photo courtesy Tonawanda-Kenmore Historical Society --- 209
Figure 215 Eberhardt Mansions photo courtesy Tonawanda-Kenmore Historical Society 210
Figure 216 Huntley Power Plant photo credit Marsha Falkowski --- 211
Figure 217 Limestone Hill late 1800s St. Patrick's Church and St. Joseph's Orphanage PD --- 213
Figure 218 Early Photo of Lackawanna Steel PD --- 213
Figure 219 Bethlehem Steel Plant during WWII showing Ships being built --- 214
Figure 220 Holy Cross Cemetery Entrance photo courtesy Holy Cross Cemetery --- 215
Figure 221 John B Weber Mansion photo credit Rick Falkowski --- 216
Figure 222 Our Lady of Victory in 1920s photo courtesy Our Lady of Victory Charities 217
Figure 223 Central Avenue in 1908 Lancaster Historical Society PD --- 219
Figure 224 Hull House photo credit Rick Falkowski --- 220
Figure 225 Lancaster Opera House In 1906 Lancaster Historical Society PD --- 221
Figure 226 Kelsey Tavern at 625 Center Street in 1800s PD --- 224
Figure 227 Freedom Crossing Monument photo credit Rick Falkowski --- 224
Figure 228 Artpark Concert Stage with Niagara George --- 225
Figure 229 Benjamin Barton House --- 226
Figure 230 Frontier House photo Library of Congress --- 227
Figure 231 Our Lady of Fatima Shrine photo credit Marsha Falkowski --- 228
Figure 232 Erie Canal Locks at Lockport PD --- 230
Figure 233 Van Horn Mansion photo Newfane Historical Society --- 231
Figure 234 Jesse Hawley House niagarafallsusa.com --- 232
Figure 235 The Rialto Amusement Park early 1900s PD --- 233
Figure 236 Frozen Niagara Falls in 1903 PD --- 235
Figure 237 Niagara Falls 1882 Map PD --- 236
Figure 238 Adams Power Plant photo Library of Congress --- 237
Figure 239 Castellani Art Museum photo courtesy Castellani Art Museum of Niagara University --- 238
Figure 240 Mckinley Pan Am Stake Lasalle Island Buffalo Times PD --- 239
Figure 241 Schoellkopf Hall is the only building still standing in DeVeaux Woods State Park --- 240
Figure 242 Devil's Hole photo credit Ellen Mika Zelasko --- 241
Figure 243 Old Chimney & Falls photo credit Rick Falkowski --- 242
Figure 244 Great Bear Market PD --- 243
Figure 245 Children's protest at Love Canal photo courtesy Rob Neubauer --- 244
Figure 246 Niagara Falls photo credit Marsha Falkowski --- 245
Figure 247 Seminary of Our Lady of Angels Niagara University niagara.edu --- 246
Figure 248 Oakwood Cemetery Mausoleum photo courtesy Oakwood Cemetery --- 247
Figure 249 Peter Porter Mansion photo credit Rick Falkowski --- 248
Figure 250 Schoellkopf Power Plant PD --- 249
Figure 251 Whitney Mansion photo Library of Congress --- 250
Figure 252 Long Bridge Collapsed with Buildings --- 252
Figure 253 Tonawanda Paper Mill on Tonawanda Island photo taken from River Road PD --- 253
Figure 254 Bascule Bridge in North Tonawanda photo credit Marsha Falkowski --- 254
Figure 255 Carnegie Library with NT Football Hall of Fame photo credit Dennis Reed Jr. nthistory.com --- 255
Figure 256 DeGraff Mansion in 1900 photo courtesy Maria Aurigema --- 256

Figure 257 Gateway Harbor Park Tonawanda/NT photo credit Dennis Reed Jr. nthistory.com --- 257
Figure 258 Allan Herschell Factory in 1919 photo courtesy Allan Herschell Carrousel Museum --- 258
Figure 259 Niagara Falls Power Transfer Station photo credit Dennis Reed Jr. nthistory.com --- 259
Figure 260 Scanlon House State Bank Sweeney Building --- 260
Figure 261 Erie Railway North Tonawanda Station 1910 PD photo Library of Congress 261
Figure 262 Remington Building 2008 photo credit Dennis Reed Jr. nthistory.com --- 262
Figure 263 Riviera Theatre with remodeled lobby & ticket office 2025 photo credit Rick Falkowski --- 263
Figure 264 Wurlitzer Events Center 2025 photo credit Rick Falkowski --- 264
Figure 265 Lincoln Street in Orchard Park 1908 PD --- 266
Figure 266 Friends Meeting House Orchard Park 1911 PD --- 267
Figure 267 Orchard Park Country Club in 1920s PD --- 267
Figure 268 Original Casino Building (late 1920's) before it burned --- 268
Figure 269 Eternal Flame Chestnut Ridge Conservancy --- 268
Figure 270 Johnson Jolls House photo courtesy Orchard Park Historical Society --- 269
Figure 271 Orchard Park BR&P Train Depot photo courtesy Western New York Railway Historical Society --- 270
Figure 272 Olmsted Camp --- 271
Figure 273 Springville Railroad Depot 1910 postcard PD --- 273
Figure 274 Buffum Inn PD --- 274
Figure 275 Griffith Institute old postcard PD --- 275
Figure 276 Waite Building Springville photo credit Paige Miller --- 276
Figure 277 Warner Museum photo credit Dave Ploetz --- 277
Figure 278 Transition Lock from Erie Canal to Tonawanda Harbor photo courtesy Historical Society of the Tonawandas --- 279
Figure 279 Kibler High School photo courtesy Historical Society of the Tonawandas -- 279
Figure 280 Niagara/Main/Young Traffic Circle before Urban Renewal photo courtesy Historical Society of the Tonawandas --- 280
Figure 281 Long Homestead in 1920 photo courtesy Historical Society of the Tonawandas --- 281
Figure 282 Tonawanda Armory museum.dmna.ny.gov PD --- 282
Figure 283 New York Central Railroad Station in 1920 photo courtesy Historical Society of the Tonawandas --- 283
Figure 284 Ebenezer Home now West Seneca Historical Society photo courtesy West Seneca Historical Society --- 285
Figure 285 Leydecker Covered Bridge photo courtesy West Seneca Historical Society - 286
Figure 286 Charles Burchfield Home photo credit Mike Buckley --- 287
Figure 287 Christian Metz House 1903 photo courtesy West Seneca Historical Society 288
Figure 288 Lein's Park Welcome Arch PD --- 289
Figure 289 Malecki Mansion photo credit Rick Falkowski --- 290
Figure 290 Mayer Brother Cider Mill 1900s photo from Company Archives --- 291
Figure 291 Semlitsch Tavern 1940 photo courtesy Schwabl's Restaurant --- 292
Figure 292 Schwabl's Restaurant 2025 photo credit Rick Falkowski --- 292
Figure 293 6230 Baer Road photo courtesy Justin Higner --- 294
Figure 294 Kohler Homestead photo courtesy Wheatfield Facebook page --- 294
Figure 295 Wa-ha-kie Hotel on River Road Wheatfield photo courtesy Town of Wheatfield --- 295
Figure 296 Bell Aircraft photo courtesy Justin Higner --- 296

Figure 297 Das Haus photo courtesy Justin Higner --- 297
Figure 298 Sawyer Creek Hotel photo courtesy Justin Higner --- 298
Figure 299 Glen Falls early 1900s photo Eastern Mill & Tannery edyoungs.com PD --- 300
Figure 300 Williamsville One Room Schoolhouse 72 South Cayuga PD --- 302
Figure 301 Amherst Toll Gate at Getzville Road managed by the Fry Family in 1880 PD 303
Figure 302 Buffalo Williamsville Electric Glen Falls PD --- 303
Figure 303 Bigelow Farmhouse photo courtesy Buffalo Niagara Heritage Village --- 304
Figure 304 Country Club of Buffalo Entrance photo credit Rick Falkowski --- 305
Figure 305 Eagle House PD --- 306
Figure 306 Glen Park Amusement Rides photo courtesy Susan Fenster --- 307
Figure 307 Park Country Club photo credit Rick Falkowski --- 308
Figure 308 Reformed Mennonite Church PD --- 309
Figure 309 Reformed Mennonite - Evans Bank --- 309
Figure 310 Saints Peter & Paul photo credit Ellen Mika Zelasko --- 310
Figure 311 Williamsville Meeting House PD --- 311
Figure 312 Wilson House Inn --- 314
Figure 313 French Castle at Fort Niagara photo credit Marsha Falkowski --- 315
Figure 314 Mike Buckley (Editor), Ellen Mika Zelasko (Author), Nancy Wise-Reid (Interior Design), Doreen Gallagher Regan (Author) and Rick Falkowski (Author) photo credit Mike Reid --- 362
Figure 315 Buffalo History Museum Presentation photo credit Nancy Wise-Reid --- 364

Historic Markers

Here are larger versions of the Historic Markers found at the tops of the pages of many profiles, listed by page number.

Historic Marker
Ely Parker in Akron Town of Newstead
on page 2

Historic Marker Russell Park Town of
Newstead on page 3

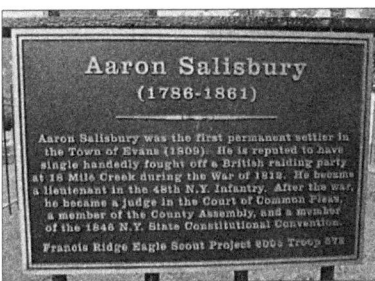

Historic Marker Aaron Salisbury War of
1812 Evanson page 7

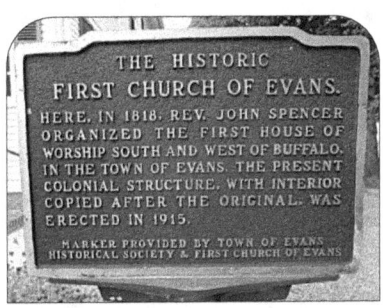

Historic Marker First Church of Evans
Town of Newstead on page 8

Welcome to Cradle Beach Camp sign
on page 9

Buffalo Seminary on page 47

Canisius College on page 56

D'Youville College on page 65

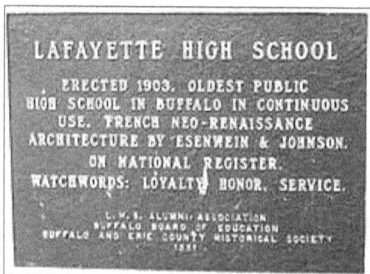

Lafayette High School on page 91

Richardson Olmsted Campus – Buffalo State Hospital on page 115

Coit House on page 58

Holy Angels Church on page 85

Michigan Avenue Baptist Church on page 99

Seneca Indian Cemetery on page 121

Thomas Motors/Curtis Aeroplane/Rich Products on page 131

Tifft Nature Preserve on page 133

Weed Block Building on page 145

Sunset Bay Beach Club on page 159

Fredonia Gas Light & Water Company on page 158

Welch Grape Juice Factory on page 164

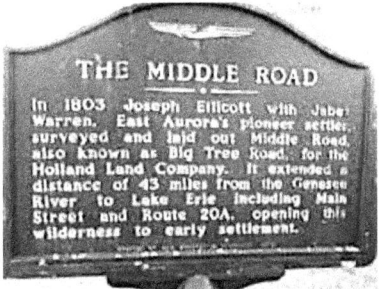

Village of East Aurora on page 182

Bedell House on page 196

Idlewood Association on page 205

John B. Weber Mansion on page 216

Benjamin Barton House on page 226

Van Horn Mansion on page 231

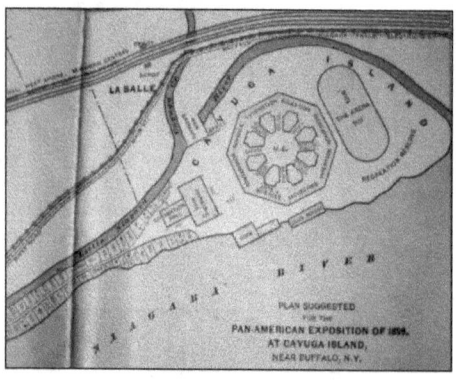

Cayuga Island on page 239

Oakwood Cemetery on page 247

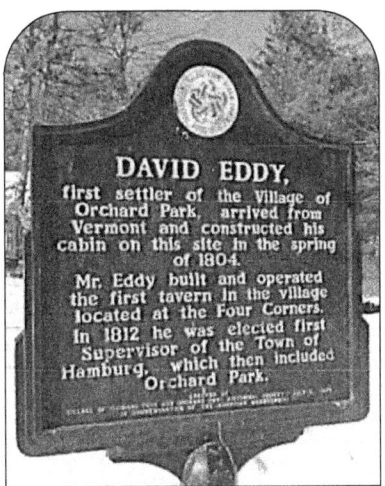

Town of Orchard Park on page 266

Johnson-Jolls House on page 269

Buffum Inn on page 274

Charles E. Burchfield Nature & Art Center on page 287

Village of Williamsville on page 300

Williamsville Meeting House on page 311

Figure 1 This Marker will be found next to all of the Registered Historic Places in this book

Acknowledgement & Dedication

I would like to thank the many people who assisted in providing information for this book. It was a project that began in early 2024 and took over 18 months to complete, so if I overlooked anyone, my apologies, you will be added to future editions or printings of this book.

Rather than having a separate Dedication Page in the book – this book is dedicated to the following people that contributed to the completion of *Historic Places of Buffalo & WNY*:

- Andrea Haxton
- Anya Puccio
- Bob Castellani
- Brian Kellogg
- Brian Perry
- Carla Castellani
- Carrie Stiver
- Catherine Flickinger Schweitzer
- Chas Gillen
- Cynthia Corey-Trowman
- Daniel Regan
- Darrell Porter
- Dave Malecki
- Dave Ploetz
- David Dingman
- David Mott Rote
- Deb Gallagher Barger
- Dennis Reed, Jr.
- Doreen Gallagher Regan
- Ellen Mika Zelasko
- Emily Jarnot
- Gene Thompson
- George Scott
- Howard Roeske
- Ian K. Seppala
- Ida Goeckel
- Jake Schneider
- James (Jimbo) McDonald
- James Williams
- Jim Pace
- Jodi Robinson
- John Albanese
- Jolene Hawkins
- Joseph McGreevy
- Judy Tucker
- Julie Roland
- June Crawford
- Justin Higner
- Karen Eckert
- Kate Stapleton Parzych
- Katie Schneider
- Keith Gregor
- Kristan Anderson
- Larry Castellani
- Lindsey Lauren Visser
- Margorie Murray
- Maria Aurigema
- Marsha Falkowski
- Mary Stang Cooke
- Maureen Gleason
- Michael Cellino
- Mike Buckley
- Mike McDonough
- Mike Reid
- Mike Schriver
- Moxie Gardiner
- Nancy Wise-Reid
- Nicole Ruberto
- Paul Lubiencki
- Pat Rodrigues
- Patra Mangus
- Rachel Ravago
- Rob Neubauer
- Robert Goller
- Ron Nagy
- Sam Bova
- Sara Larkin
- Steve Cichon
- Susan Fenster
- Thomas Hawkins
- Tim Zelasko
- Tom Schobert
- Wallace Smith
- Ward Bray
- William Butler
- William Tojek

Introduction

The first four books that I wrote focused on people from the Western New York (WNY) area. *History of Buffalo Music & Entertainment* provided information on the musicians, entertainers, disc jockeys, music management people and other individuals who contributed to entertainment. As explained in the titles of my next two books *Historic & Influential People from Buffalo & WNY – the 1800s* and *Historic People from Buffalo & WNY – the Early 1900s*, they were about people from the 1800s or 1900s. My fourth book *The Spirit of Buffalo Women* profiled 60 women from WNY that achieved local, regional, national or international acclaim.

These books covered the people but what about the places? The homes and businesses where these individuals lived or worked were included but were not the focal point of the profiles. However, people who purchased books continually explained that they enjoyed the books because they could travel through WNY to find places referenced in them.

While doing research on a project I visited the North Tonawanda Library and spoke to librarian Anya Puccio. When discussing the information I was seeking, she mentioned how people enjoyed looking up places that I wrote about. She then added, there has never been a book written providing information on all the Historic Markers across WNY. That would make an interesting book.

When driving home from the library I thought about Anya's suggestion. Yes, there were books written about Historic Markers but usually just a town highlighting the Historic Markers in their community or a Chamber of Commerce mentioning Historic Markers in the area of the businesses they represented.

The next step was to find out if there were sufficient Historic Markers to write about. The National Register of Historic Places is a U.S. government listing of sites, buildings, structures, districts and objects deemed worthy of preservation for their historical significance or great artistic value. This listing is continually updated as places are added or deleted. There are about 95,000 properties individually listed in the National Register of Historic Places. About 6,000 properties and districts are listed in New York State and of these 264 are further designated as National Historic Landmarks, buildings structures, objects, sites and districts of resources according to a list of criteria of national significance.

In WNY there are a total of 461 places listed in the National Register of Historic Places as of July 2025. The distribution is Buffalo (190), the rest of Erie County (83), Niagara Falls (38), the rest of Niagara County (61), Chautauqua County (52) and Cattaraugus County (37). The National Historic Landmarks in WNY are Adams Power Plant (Niagara Falls), Buffalo & Erie County Historical Society (Buffalo), Buffalo State Hospital – H.H. Richardson Complex (Buffalo), Chautauqua Historic District (Chautauqua Institution), Darwin Martin House (Buffalo), Edward M. Cotter Fireboat (Buffalo), Fort Niagara (Youngstown – Niagara County), Kleinhans Music Hall (Buffalo), Lewis Miller Cottage (Chautauqua), Lewiston Lower Landing (Artpark - Niagara County), Millard Fillmore House (East Aurora – Erie County), Niagara Reservation (Niagara Falls), Prudential-Guaranty Building (Buffalo), Roycroft Campus (East Aurora – Erie County), St. Paul's Cathedral (Buffalo) and USS The Sullivans (Canalside – Buffalo).

Some of the Historic Places did not have sufficient information to compile a full page of information, so they were not included. Other Historic Places have not received designation as official historic places, so they were added to the places included in this book.

A total of 250 historic places were selected and for each one a full page of information (350-400 words) and a photo is provided. The places are organized by town, so you can pick an area and visit each of the historic places included in the book. For each town there is a general history of the city, town or village, that provides general information and references some other historic places about the community.

After the listing of 250 places was tentatively identified and I began writing the profiles, I determined this was too big of a project to do on my own. The average time to research and write a profile was two days, one day for research and one for writing. With 250 places and about 20 towns, at two days a profile, that amounted to about 540 days. Since the project began in the Spring of 2024 and I hoped to get it out in the late summer of 2025, assistance was required to get it completed.

I contacted other authors of local history books or writers that might be interested in working on the book. Everyone was busy with their own projects or felt they did not have the time available to contribute to this project.

Ellen Mika Zelasko has a blog called *Hello Buffalo*, writing about homes and buildings in Buffalo. She also published 28 coffee table books about various buildings, homes and streets, along with contributing photos to a couple of my previous books. After she and her husband retired, they traveled, and are assisting in saving the Infant of Prague Parish, that the Catholic Diocese earmarked for closure. When I asked if she was interested in contributing, Ellen replied she was thinking about writing more again and this would be the perfect opportunity. She agreed to write profiles of some Buffalo buildings and churches.

A musician friend that I have known dating back to the 1970s, John Albanese introduced me to his childhood friend Moxie Gardiner, who just published the book *Virgin Snow* about growing up on the West Side of Buffalo. When we met, I found out that Moxie was her pen name. Since she now lived in Washington DC and was continually traveling around the world (now up to 46 countries and all 50 states), she would not be able to contribute material. However, she loved the project and said her sister would probably be interested. Doreen Gallagher Regan was the perfect fit. She grew up in the printing industry as her family owned Gallagher Printing, The West Side Times and Buffalo Rocket newspapers. Doreen was preparing to retire from her 35-year career as an English teacher and was planning to write a history of the Derby community in Evans. She agreed to cover places on the Lake Erie shoreline and parts of the southern tier.

As with past books, I always try to speak to people involved with the individuals or places being written about. Consequently, I asked other area history writers and members of historical societies or town historians to contribute information. Some wrote a historic place or town profiles. Others assisted in providing the information that made the profiles factual and interesting.

The authors contributed new photos of historic places profiled. Old photos were provided by town historical societies, the properties and located in various historical archives. Area photographers, Dennis Reed, Jr. and Mike Shriver, gave permission to use some of their work and Gene Thompson restored some old photos.

Readers liked *The Spirit of Buffalo Women* book cover, so the talents of graphic artist Paul Marko were again enlisted. He came up with the concept of putting the book name in the standard NYS Historic Marker sign and superimposing it over a photo of the South Grand Island Bridges. It connotates the bridging of the historic areas of WNY together in the book.

With the team in place, I had to sell the idea to my editor. Mike Buckley approached me several years ago with some questions about my music book and an offer to edit future books. We both attended JFK High School in Cheektowaga and Mike remembered me as the only full-time musician while we were still in school. He graduated three years after me. Mike was also a musician and his sons were members of the metalcore band Every Time I Die. That band was inducted into the Buffalo Music Hall of Fame, toured worldwide for 24 years and released 10 studio albums, plus other recordings. In addition to the music connection, Mike was a professor of Computer Science/Engineering at UB and facilitated some classes that my son Bryan attended while getting his Computer Science degree at the university.

Mike did not understand why the profiles had to be slightly less than 400 words, feeling they should be as long as they needed to be. I explained that format was necessary for layout of the book, so each profile was one page with a photo. Also had to explain that when writing articles for magazines you are often given a word count for the article. Had to overcome his college professor mentality with the commercial requirements of a book. Mike eventually relented.

While we were working on this book, a listing of places where we could not obtain sufficient information for a 400-word profile was compiled as they were identified. We also did not include that many places from the older area towns like Hamburg, Lockport or Lancaster. There was also not that much information from the more rural areas, especially in Cattaraugus and Chautauqua Counties, including towns like Jamestown, Olean and Ellicottville. When talking to historical societies they mentioned other historic places just beyond the 4 main counties of WNY, including the city of Batavia.

After this book is released, I will start identifying other historic places in the rural and adjacent four counties of Orleans, Genesee, Wyoming and Allegany. Hopefully that book will be completed in two years.

Before that book is completed, editor Mike Buckley has mandated that Profiles Volume III: Historic & Influential People from Buffalo & WNY – the Late 1900s must be completed and I must continue researching and writing the "non-fiction" Science Fiction book *X-Terrestrial Ancestors* that my wife Marsha and I have been working on for the past year.

Until then, I hope you enjoy *Historic Places of Buffalo & WNY* and look forward to seeing you at one of the presentations I give across WNY, at a book signing or local author event.

VILLAGE OF AKRON/ TOWN OF NEWSTEAD PROFILES

This section includes profiles of the Town of **Newstead** and historic places in the nearby Village of **Akron**

Town of Newstead

Newstead was one of the first areas settled in the Holland Land Company area of WNY and was considered part of the town of Batavia from 1802 until 1804. It extended west to New Amsterdam, referred to as Buffalo by the settlers. The area was part of Clarence until 1823 when it was established as the town of Erie, a name that was changed to Newstead in 1831.

The first section of town settled was near the current intersection of Route 5 and Route 93. Peter Vandeventer built a tavern on Route 5, midway between Batavia and Buffalo, where on March 1, 1803 the first town meeting of the Holland Land Purchase was held. Vandeventer was elected the first supervisor, receiving 74 votes, compared to 70 for Jonathan Bemis of Batavia, from the population of Willink that consisted of approximately 144 families.

Most settlements were along Buffalo Road, with people purchasing one to two hundred acres of land for as little as $5.00 down. Homes were log cabins, not frame houses, and a 16 square foot structure, with a floor and one window being considered the normal residence. Settlers raised cattle, hogs and sheep, and grew corn, wheat, potatoes and vegetables. When Timothy S. Hopkins and Otis Ingalls (who lived at the Asa Ransom Tavern in Clarence Hollow) raised the first wheat crop in 1800, it had to be transported to Chippewa in Canada for milling, a four-day journey by ox cart. Archibald Clark opened a store at the corner of Cummings Road and Main (Buffalo) Road. This was not only the first store in Newstead but the first store built in Erie County outside of the village of Buffalo. A post office was established in Clark's store and in 1807 Charles Knight organized a Methodist Church in his house, the first church in Erie County.

Figure 2 Historic Marker Ely Parker in Akron

In 1826, the Treaty of Buffalo was negotiated by the Odgen Company, who bought the pre-emption rights of the Holland Land Company to the Indian Reservations. Bitterly opposed by Red Jacket, the chiefs sold a considerable portion of the Buffalo Creek and Cattaraugus Reservations, including 33,409 acres off the south side of the Tonawanda Reservation. 7,000 acres of this land was in Newstead and only 2,000 acres remained part of the reservation. Civil War General and Seneca Nation attorney Ely S. Parker was born on the Tonawanda Reservation in Akron in 1828.

Hezekiah Cummings purchased part of lot 29 of the reservation, with Nathan L. Barney, James McMullen and Robert Benedict among the landowners in the northern portion of the town. In 1829, Jonathan Russell bought lot 26, where he built a house and opened a store, at the current corner of Clinton and Main Streets. Russell built a schoolhouse at the corner of Church and John Streets, established the Maple Lawn Cemetery opposite the park that bears his name and donated the sites for the Methodist and Baptist churches. This was the beginning of the village of Akron, which before it was given this name in 1836 was referred to as The Corporation.

Jonathan Delano discovered a stratum of hydraulic limestone or water limestone cropping out on the banks of Murder Creek. This formed a high-quality cement that was used for construction by the Canal Commissioners of NYS. James Montgomery purchased Delano's lease and created a company that supplied the cement for the Erie Canal Locks at Lockport and other large projects. Montgomery also found a rich stratum of gypsum that was used for fertilizer, plaster of Paris, a retarder in Portland cement and later plaster board. Enos Newmann became Montgomery's partner, with Enos' brothers Leroy and E.J. Newman joining the company. They added a three-story flour mill to the cement business. Hezekiah Cummings and his sons also expanded the gypsum business by creating Akron Cement Works.

Figure 3 Newman Flouring and Cement Works in Akron New York PD

Perry's Ice Cream was founded by H. Morton Perry in the village in 1918. The Akron Button Company moved into the former Akron Plaster Board Company at 8 Indianola Avenue circa 1910. During WWII the Buffalo Arms plant made 20mm cannons in a plant on Clarence Center Road which later housed a subsidiary of Houdaille Industries. The village includes the Rich-Twinn-Octagon House, the only 8-sided home built in Erie County during the 19th century.

Figure 4 Perrys Ice Cream photo courtesy Brian Perry

The Emergency Work Relief Bureau began work on Akron Falls Park in 1933, with 90 men working 30 hours a week for fifty cents an hour. It was the first Erie County project to receive Presidential approval outside of the city of Buffalo during the Depression. The Work Progress Administration (WPA) became involved in 1935, and in total over $100,000 was committed to create the park, half-moon shaped dam and artificial lake. In 1947, the park became the possession of Erie County.

On June 23, 2013, the first Park Golf Course in the U.S. was opened as Destroyer Park Golf in Akron by wrestler Dick "The Destroyer" Beyer, who was introduced to the game while wrestling in Japan. The game is a cross between golf and croquet, played with a single club, on a 9-hole course that cannot exceed 500 meters. It is played at over 1,300 courses in Japan and has spread to eight countries.

From July 15 to 25, 2019, the classic storefronts on Akron's Main Street from Buffalo Street to Church Street became the movie set for John Krasinski's production *A Quiet Place Part II*. Part of the movie *Marshall* was filmed in Akron in 2016, and the Hallmark holiday movie *Newport Christmas* filmed scenes in 2025 at the Russell Park Pavilion on Clinton Street.

Figure 5 Historic Marker Russell Park

Perry's Ice Cream
1 Ice Cream Plaza, Akron

Figure 6 Perry's Ice Cream 1 Pearl Street Akron photo courtesy Perry's Ice Cream

H. Morton Perry was employed as a broom maker in Lockport when he became gravely ill following the influenza epidemic of 1918. His doctor suggested he seek employment that would bring him outside, where he could receive plenty of fresh air and sunshine. Following his doctor's advice, H. Morton returned to the village of Akron, where he was born in 1888, and purchased a dairy delivery route from Albert Schalge. He named the business Perry's Dairy and began delivering milk by horse-drawn carriage.

Morton continued producing wholesale milk and providing home delivery until 1932, when another twist of fate occurred. Morton's sister-in-law worked in the cafeteria at Akron Central School, and asked him if he could make ice cream for the students' school lunches.

Using a recipe handed down by his mother, Morton made a few small batches with his son Marlo at their 1 Pearl Street home. They slow-cooked the ingredients on their kitchen stove and churned the ice cream in a 2-gallon hand-cranked machine before delivering it the next morning to the school. It was such a hit, they were soon making it in bulk to meet the growing demand from the school, along with nearby stores and restaurants.

Morton and Marlo bought a Buffalo-based ice cream company in 1940 to expand their capabilities, but their production remained at the corner of Pearl and Franklin Street in Akron. Perry's Ice Cream was officially incorporated in 1947. Morton believed in using only the highest quality ingredients and was known for saying "make sure you put in enough of the good stuff!" The company used local farm fresh milk, cream and sugar to make the creamiest ice cream possible "one batch at a time."

In 1982, Perry's moved into a new plant at the end of Ice Cream Plaza in Akron. The computerized plant was designed by third generation family member Thomas C. Perry. To assist in the manufacturing process, the plant dug 60-foot-deep wells to access 50-degree water flowing in abandoned gypsum mines below the plant, and they drew energy from a natural gas well dug on the property.

Perry's completed an $18 million project adding an additional 20,000 square feet of manufacturing space in 2024. The 4th generation family-owned company has remained in the family for over one hundred years and has become a multi-million-dollar industry, employing over 370 people.

by Doreen Gallagher Regan & Rick Falkowski

RICH-TWINN OCTAGON HOUSE
145 Main Street, Akron

Figure 7 Rich Twinn House photo credit Rick Falkowski

The Rich-Twinn Octagon House was constructed for merchant, politician and Indian agent Charles Rich circa 1850. It was built by James C. Twinn, the grandfather of Clark Twinn who later owned the house and it was the only octagonal home in Erie County during that period.

Octagonal homes date back to the Tower of Winds, built by the Romans in 300 BC. They were popular in Holland during the 17th and 18th centuries, with the Dutch bringing the design to the Hudson Valley when they settled in that area. The design was used in churches, schools, businesses and homes, along with toll houses that the Dutch constructed in Pennsylvania.

In 1848 Orson Squire Fowler published a book about octagonal design, explaining that with the eight sides it included more natural lighting and ventilation than a rectangular home, resulting in a healthier living space.

Built in the Greek Revival architectural style, each side of the octagon is sixteen feet two inches long. A one-story porch encircles the house. It includes 15 rooms with 29 large windows, 10 closets and a large central hall with an open staircase and balcony. The ground floor colonial hearth kitchen has a large brick oven, with a rope pully dumb waiter delivering the food to the formal dining room. The cupula has windows in each direction, providing stunning vistas of the countryside.

Rich built the home on several acres of wooded land purchased from original Akron landowner Jonathan Russell in 1850. He sold the home in 1871 to Charles A. Clark, of Jebb Cement Works and the Akron Foundry - important industries in early Akron. Uriah Cummings rented the home from 1879 to 1882, and his son Homer Cummings became U.S. Attorney General under President Franklin D. Roosevelt and served as Democratic Party National Chairman. William Gillings and his wife Sadie lived in the home for 56 years until his death in 1938. Clark Twinn, Assistant U.S. Attorney for the territory of Alaska and grandson of the original home builder purchased the home in 1940, when the house was finally wired for electricity. Twinn was of great assistance in promoting the history of Newstead and the Rich-Twinn House.

The home became the property of the Newstead Historical Society in 1981, was restored in 1995, completely furnished with period pieces and is open to the public for tours.

VILLAGE OF ANGOLA

HAMLET OF DERBY

TOWN OF EVANS PROFILES

This section includes profiles of the Town of **Evans** and historic places in the Village of **Angola,** and the Hamlet of **Derby.**

Town of Evans

The Town of Evans is situated in the southwestern portion of Erie County and is bordered by Eden to the east, Hamburg to the north, Brant to the south, and Lake Erie to the west.

In the late 1700's, Evans was a wilderness inhabited by Native Americans, mainly the Erie Indians, who used Lake Erie (named for them) as a trade route. By the early 1800's, it became a popular stop for westward-bound travelers as well as new landowners buying property from the Holland Land Company. In 1804, Joel Harvey became the first settler in the area, establishing a home near the mouth of Eighteen Mile Creek. He put an addition on his home and opened the Frontier House in 1806, the area's first hotel and tavern.

Figure 8 First Church of Evans PD

Although many visitors stopped here, the settlement didn't develop until 1809 when Aaron Salisbury became the first permanent resident on record. More newcomers followed and built log homes along the lake shore. James Ayer and his large family arrived in 1811, and William Cash with his twelve children set up an expansive farm by the lake in 1812. Many of these early newcomers became prominent figures in the civic affairs of this burgeoning community. During the War of 1812, soldiers on

Figure 9 Historic Marker Aaron Salisbury War of 1812 Evans

British ships patrolling the coast of Lake Erie often came to shore to pilfer goods from the settlers along the lake. Aaron Salisbury gained notoriety for fighting off a British raiding party at Eighteen Mile Creek, and was promoted to lieutenant in the 48th NY Infantry.

Luckily, the war ended rather quickly and prosperity returned to the region. The first sawmill was constructed in 1815 by William Wright and Henry Tuttle, who then built a gristmill the following year. George Sweetland became the resident doctor in 1821 and served the community for the next 60 years.

Figure 10 Bank of Angola early Business District PD

As the settlement grew, the New York State Legislature passed an act creating the Town of Evans, which was previously part of Eden, in March of 1821. The town was named in honor of David E. Evans, a clerk for the Holland Land Company, and nephew of the company's most prominent agent, Joseph Ellicott. David Evan's management of the company's affairs earned him immense popularity among the pioneers as well as his employer. In 1827, he became the resident agent for the Holland Land Company, overseeing the sale of approximately half of all the company's land in Western New York, and generating more revenue than any of his predecessors.

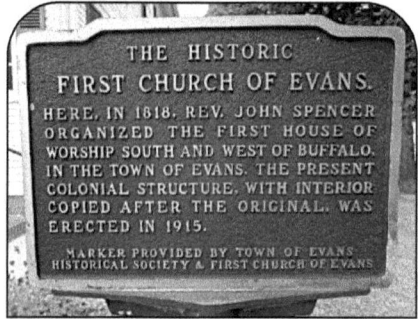

Figure 11 Historic Marker First Church of Evans

As the constant influx of settlers came into the area, the demand for housing increased, which led to the construction of numerous hotels. Initially, the hub of activity was Evans Center, where the first town hall, mills, and stores were located (at the corner of what is now Route 5 and Bennett Road). Other settlements developed, including North Evans, Pontiac, East Evans (Jerusalem Corners), and Derby. Brant was annexed in 1839, and later on, communities like Lake Erie Beach and Highland emerged. When the railroad arrived in 1852, business shifted to Evans Station, near the train depot. This area was later renamed Angola in reference to the Angola post office, which earned this title from the local Quakers who were supporting missionaries in Angola, Africa at the time. The original Town Hall was moved to Angola and it became the Angola Hotel. Other hotels followed, reflecting the town's growth and new industries. The Village of Angola was officially incorporated in 1873, as the railroad continued to spur local business and manufacturing, including the notable Emblem Bicycle Company.

The town's lakeside location also contributed to its early growth, especially at the turn of the 20th Century. Wealthy Buffalonians such as Darwin D. Martin, Spencer Kellogg, Henry Wendt, Jr., George Pierce, and John D. Larkin, Jr. built extravagant summer homes in Evans. The Town continues to be one of the most popular summer destinations in Erie County, with several beautiful beaches and waterfront locales to attract visitors from all over Western New York and beyond.

by Doreen Gallagher Regan

CRADLE BEACH CAMP
8038 Old Lake Shore Road, Angola

Cradle Beach began in 1888 as a summer camp for children needing to escape Buffalo's overcrowded and unsanitary inner city. It was founded by the Fresh Air Mission, an organization started by the Universalist Church and eventually governed by a nondenominational board of wealthy Buffalo citizens. The Charity Organization Society selected the children to attend, and initially brought them out by horse and buggy. Of all the charities supported by Buffalonians at the time, Cradle Beach had the most popular appeal. Donation campaigns urged people to drop pennies into "cradle banks" in local stores.

Cradle Beach Camp was designed to provide a safe and nurturing environment for underprivileged youth, where they could spend time in the countryside getting plenty of sunshine and fresh air along the shores of Lake Erie. The Fresh Air Mission also founded a hospital in Athol Springs near Hamburg for infants with cholera, a disease caused by poor sanitation. In the last quarter of the 19th century, cholera became a significant health crisis, along with several other deadly childhood illnesses throughout America. The Fresh Air Mission believed outdoor activities, nature, and companionship nourished one's physical and emotional well-being.

By the turn of the century, Cradle Beach was hosting nearly a thousand disadvantaged inner-city children every summer. Over the years, the camp's mission evolved, serving children with a variety of challenges associated with poverty, illness, neglect, and abuse. In 1946, after previously focusing solely on impoverished children, the summer program began to take in kids with special needs through the financial backing of the Buffalo Rotary Club. Fifty years later, the decision was made to move the camp down the road to a new location with 66 acres on the lake, where it could be expanded and improved, making it more accessible to children with disabilities.

Figure 12 Cradle Beach vintage postcard

Today, Cradle Beach Camp continues to offer a transformative experience for thousands of children each year with the support of many significant donors. Through a variety of activities, the camp cultivates life skills, builds self-esteem, and fosters positive relationships. From sports to arts and crafts and nature exploration, there is something for everyone. The camp's dedicated staff and volunteers provide a safe, supportive, and fun environment where their guests can thrive. It is now a year-round facility that provides offseason admissions as well, including specialized programming for caregivers.

by Doreen Gallagher Regan

EMBLEM BICYCLE FACTORY
LaSalle Street, Angola

Figure 13 Emblem Bicycle Factory
photo Company Archives PD

During the late 1800's, bicycling became an extremely popular pastime throughout America. It was an easy and inexpensive means of transportation prior to the introduction of motorcycles and automobiles.

The Emblem Cycling Company, founded by William Schack and William Heil, became a lucrative business as a result of this newfound popularity and was one of the most successful industries in the area. Their business had its humble beginnings around 1903, when Schack and Heil began assembling bikes inside a barn in Lake View. A year later, the two men rented a building in the heart of Angola to expand their production of Emblem bicycles. Soon, they were creating single-cylinder motorized bikes.

By 1908, the rapid growth of their industry led them to construct a three-story concrete-block manufacturing facility strategically located next to the New York Central railroad line. A baseball diamond was installed behind the factory for community use, with a large outdoor racetrack surrounding the baseball field so their bicycles and motorcycles could be test-piloted through races.

Emblem became Angola's largest employer, with 300 workers producing 150 bicycles and 25 motorcycles a week. Schack preferred to hire local farm boys because of their outstanding work ethic. He taught the most adept employees every aspect of the business, offering leadership positions and incentives such as stock interests. The company became internationally renowned for its excellent quality and superior workmanship. As motorcycles gained popularity, Emblem produced best sellers such as the light-weight single speed motorcycle "Little Giant" and the "Big Twin" motorcycle with its innovative V-twin engine.

Around 1913, when their competitor Pierce Cycle Company went bankrupt, they acquired the business and took over production of Pierce bicycles, which allowed Emblem to continue prospering into the 1920's. They even survived the stock market crash of 1929, but as the Great Depression loomed and the demand for automobiles grew, bike sales began to plummet. There was a short boost around 1936, but then poor management decisions and the loss of a major sales contract with Sears and Roebuck eventually led them to go out of business by the early 1940's.

The century-old factory has been vacant ever since. A fire in 2023 destroyed the interior, but its giant shell still remains by the railroad tracks, a faded reminder of its significant history.

by Doreen Gallagher Regan

White City – Conner's Poultry Farm
Grandview Bay, Angola

In the early 1900's, Angola was home to the largest poultry farm in the world. William J. Conners Poultry Farm was nicknamed the "White City" because of the thousands of white chickens and ducks that blanketed the landscape. It covered 360 acres stretching one mile along the shoreline of Lake Erie, from what is now Lake Street to Herr Road.

Figure 14 White City - Ducks at Conners Poultry Farm early 1900s postcard courtesy Evans Historical Society Donna Nagel

In 1825, Orange Dibble, a southerner, bought nearly 400 acres of lakefront property from the Holland Land Company. It was around this time that the Erie Canal and railroads were being built, bringing newcomers to Evans, a previously remote area mostly inhabited by fishermen and farmers. One main route, Old Lake Shore Road, ran along the lake westbound from Buffalo, cutting directly through Dibble's land. Dibble owned the property until 1891.

It changed hands over the next few years until W.J. Conners, owner of the *Buffalo Courier* newspaper, purchased it in 1903. At first, Conners considered using the land to create an amusement park, similar to Coney Island in New York City. Instead, he opted to establish a poultry farm. The property quickly expanded to have over 250 structures on it including numerous barns, steam houses, incubator cellars, outdoor brooders, and colony houses. It was soon recognized as the biggest and best poultry farm in the world, known for its superior sanitary conditions and the excellent health of the nearly 150,000 ducks and chickens under its care. While the free-range chickens wandered the grounds, the ducks took to bathing in Lake Erie.

In 1906 a public transport system called the Buffalo and Lake Erie Traction Company allowed for further development as interurban streetcars brought people right through Evans from the city. Conners' business continued to thrive, winning the International Cup for Utility Poultry and Eggs in 1910. But after 18 years in business Conners sold the farm, and all of the buildings were either torn down or burned.

Shortly afterwards, William Stevenson discovered the prime lakefront acreage while out sailing. His son, Bill Stevenson, Jr. established the Evans Land Corporation which purchased the property and developed it into a summer cottage community known as Grandview Bay in 1922. Notable spots such as Mickey Rats, Connors Hot Dog Stand, Evans Town Park and Grandview Bay golf course all exist on the land where the poultry farm once stood.

by Doreen Gallagher Regan

GRAYCLIFF
6472 Old Lake Shore Road, Derby

Figure 15 Graycliff: A Lakefront Masterpiece by Frank Lloyd Wright photo credit Matthew Digati

High on a bluff overlooking Lake Erie sits a majestic estate known as Graycliff. Constructed between 1926 and 1931, it is an architectural masterpiece designed by Frank Lloyd Wright. Commissioned specifically for Isabelle R. Martin, wife of wealthy industrialist Darwin D. Martin, it was built 20 years after Wright designed the Darwin D. Martin House on Jewett Parkway.

Graycliff is one of the most stunning summer residences of Wright's career, masterfully designed in his "Organic style". Isabelle R. Martin's deteriorating eyesight inspired Wright to create a home filled with open air and sunlight. The 5,800 square-foot house integrates indoor and outdoor areas, with natural elements and horizontal lines. Spectacular views of Lake Erie, Canada and downtown Buffalo can be seen beyond its generous windows.

A second home of matching design, called the Foster House, also sits on the property. Originally built as a garage with an upstairs apartment, the structure was altered and expanded to accommodate their daughter, Dorothy Foster, and her family. A third Wright-designed structure, a heat hut, was erected with similar exterior components to the other two buildings.

The landscaping throughout the estate's 8.5 acres was also the ingenuity of Wright himself. It included such elements as a pond, fountain, tennis court and esplanade, along with sunken gardens and stone walls. In 1929, to further enhance the elegant grounds, Ellen Biddle Shipman, one of the most renowned American female landscape architects of the day, was hired to supplement Wright's outdoor design. She added colorful flower beds and picking gardens.

The deaths of Darwin and Isabelle Martin ultimately led to the property being sold to a group of Hungarian priests, the Piarist Fathers, who turned it into a boarding school in the early 1950s. The priests made several modifications to the estate, but the three original Wright buildings remained. When the number of priests dwindled and their school closed, the Piarists could no longer afford the upkeep and listed the property for sale in 1996.

Rumors of possible demolition emerged, and a group of concerned individuals established the Graycliff Conservancy to protect the estate. They purchased the property in 1999, with a mortgage guaranteed by the Baird Foundation. With the support of New York State, Erie County, Empire State Development, the Margaret Wendt Foundation, the Baird Foundation, and the East Hill (Greatbatch) Foundation, millions of dollars in extensive restorations have been completed, and have resulted in Graycliff becoming a historic house museum, with over 10,000 annual visitors.

by Doreen Gallagher Regan

LOCHEVAN- THE KELLOGG SUMMER ESTATE
7200 Lake Shore Road, Derby

Behind a long stone wall stretching down Lake Shore Road, sits a sprawling estate once owned by prominent Buffalo businessman Spencer Kellogg and his family. Kellogg gained significant wealth when his company, Spencer Kellogg & Sons Inc. became the largest manufacturer of linseed oil in the U.S. during the early 1900's.

Figure 16 Lochevan Kellogg Estate
photo credit Doreen Gallagher Regan

Spencer Kellogg originally spent his summers at Idlewood, a private community in Lake View, until he discovered the prime location to create a Scottish style estate and self-sufficient farm along the shoreline of Lake Erie. He purchased over 150 acres in 1891 and named it Lochevan, from the words "loch," Scottish for lake, and "evan," in reference to the Town of Evans. A magnificent 16-bedroom mansion was built on the property, perfectly designed for grand social gatherings. As the years passed, more summer homes were added to the estate as Kellogg's children married and had families of their own.

One of the most outstanding features of the property was the exquisite English style gardens designed by Spencer's wife Jane Morris Kellogg, which were so extraordinary they've been documented in the archives of the Smithsonian Institution. The estate included a gatehouse, boathouse, greenhouse, horse stables, tea houses, tennis courts, and polo fields. There was a pumping station that supplied water from the lake to every building on the compound, and a gas well to supply the homes with heat.

Throughout the summer, Spencer Kellogg and his sons enjoyed commuting to Buffalo on a luxurious steam yacht called Elgrudor, named after his four daughters: Elizabeth, Gertrude, Ruth, and Doris. During World War I, he donated the yacht to the U.S. Navy. Upon Spencer's death in 1922, the estate went into a trust shared by his descendants. His son Howard and Howard's wife Cyrena lived there year-round, and were avid horse enthusiasts who bred, trained, and competed with their thoroughbred hunters. They owned the prestigious Eclipse Stables and were members of the Lake Shore Hunt Club.

The Kellogg family owned the entire compound until the late 1960's when the property was subdivided. A non-profit organization known as The Claddagh Commission purchased the main house and transformed it into a care facility for individuals with developmental disabilities. Since then, most of the other homes have been sold as well, with only a few Kellogg family members still residing on the historic estate.

by Doreen Gallagher Regan

Sturgeon Point Marina

618 Sturgeon Point Road, Derby

Figure 17 The Willows George Pierce Estate

Sturgeon Point Marina was once the summer estate of George N. Pierce and his family. Pierce was a successful industrialist who started the George N. Pierce Company in 1878, which later became known as the Pierce Arrow Motor Company. The business initially produced bird cages, ice boxes and washing machines before transitioning to bicycles. By the turn of the century, the company was producing motorcycles and the iconic Pierce-Arrow automobiles.

George and his wife Louisa had 9 children. In the late 1800's, with his increasing wealth, he and his family began spending their summers in the exclusive private community of Idlewood in Lake View. When one of the Idlewood members, Spencer Kellogg, purchased a large parcel of lakefront land a short distance down the road in Derby, George Pierce bought the adjoining 260 acres at Wahakah Beach and named his property "The Willows". In 1894, he built a rustic Adirondack style summer lodge for his family near the beachfront, with a two-story porch where they could spend the hot summer days taking advantage of the Lake Erie breezes. George took a great interest in farming, and his property was renowned for its exquisite apple orchards.

The Pierce family enjoyed their summer estate for several years, until George passed away in 1910 at the age of 64. His son Percy and his family lived there for a while, but it changed hands over the years. Most of the acreage was divided up and sold off as individual lots, and in 1925 a marina, jetty and breakwater were constructed along the waterfront. The Pierce summer home became a private inn and tavern called The Sturgeon Point Lodge. It was owned by various proprietors until it was acquired by the town of Evans and used as a storage facility during the 1970s. The lodge was completely destroyed by fire in 1982 and torn down, the same year the town took over the marina and started upgrading the breakwater and docks.

Over the decades, Sturgeon Point Marina has had many transformations and upgrades, but is still a beautiful waterfront location owned by the town of Evans. It is open to the public with many amenities available throughout the summer season.

by Doreen Gallagher Regan

SUNCLIFF MANOR - ST. COLUMBAN CENTER
6892 Lake Shore Road, Derby

Figure 18 Suncliff on the Lake photo credit Daniel Regan

Suncliff is a historic mansion, on the shores of Lake Erie. The original structure, named Suncliff Manor, was completed in 1914 as an opulent summer home for Hans Schmidt and his wife Helen, who was the only daughter of prominent businessman Jacob Frederick Schoellkopf. Hans, a German immigrant, began working at the Schoellkopf & Co. tannery in 1882. He eventually became president of the company and married Schoellkopf's daughter in 1893.

Hans and Helen decided to build a stunning three-story Georgian Neoclassical mansion on 15 acres of gorgeous lakefront land as a reflection of their wealth and status, and a refuge from the bustling city. The family entertained guests and hosted lavish parties in the massive structure, fondly known as "The Big House" for over three decades. The interior, adorned with exquisite architectural details, contained 10 rooms on the first floor, 9 bedrooms with adjoining bathrooms on the second and 6 more bedrooms on the third. Outside, luscious gardens surrounded the property, and a tree-lined promenade connected the home to breathtaking views of the lake and beyond.

A natural gas well, still active to this day, was discovered by Helen during the home's construction. Natural gas had been discovered in surrounding areas, so the Schmidts hoped to tap into this resource to power their new estate. After refusing to heed the advice of experts, Helen insisted on a location near the garage. She reportedly plunged her umbrella into the ground and told them to drill in that spot. They complied and hit a gas well so abundant it blew for days, roaring loud enough to attract onlookers from miles around.

After World War II, many wealthy families could no longer afford their extravagant lifestyles. Suncliff Manor was eventually put up for sale, and the Columban Laymen's League, a Catholic association, purchased it in 1947. It became the St. Columban Center, a retreat and conference facility that hosted thousands of visitors for nearly 70 years. A 10,000-square-foot annex was added in 1959 with 46 small bedrooms. The complex was eventually sold to private owners in 2017 who renamed it Suncliff-on-the-Lake-in honor of its history. It is now open to the public as a boutique inn and restaurant. While many changes have occurred over time, the original mansion remains intact, with its grand sophistication and timeless charm.

by Doreen Gallagher Regan

WENDT BEACH PARK
7676 Lake Shore Road, Derby

*Figure 19 Wendt Beach Mansion in 1960s
photo credit Doreen Gallagher Regan*

Wendt Beach Park is a 164-acre public park in Derby, NY bordering Lake Erie. Originally referred to as "The Ridgewood," the land was the summer estate of Henry Wendt, Jr., third-generation owner of the distinguished Buffalo Forge Company. Mr. Wendt was among Buffalo's wealthy elite, an industrialist whose company manufactured blacksmith equipment and various types of machinery. Buffalo Forge gained worldwide notoriety when engineer Willis H. Carrier invented the world's first modern air conditioning system in 1902, contributing to the company's remarkable success.

Like many other prominent Buffalonians, the Wendt family purchased the large parcel of beachfront property sometime around the turn of the 19th century, to enjoy the cool lake breezes during the summer months. The property soon included a 6,000-square-foot mansion, horse stables, a log cabin, a caretakers' cottage, a garage with chauffeur's quarters and a pump house. During its glory days, it was the venue for the annual Derby Horse Show.

The mansion, a Colonial Revival architectural style home, had gorgeous hardwood floors, a spiral staircase, and beautiful bay windows overlooking the lake. The Wendt family enjoyed several decades on the property until shortly after Henry Wendt, Jr.'s death in 1966. The estate was deeded to Erie County and became Wendt Beach Park two years later, offering public access to the beach, lawns, and historic structures.

Despite its initial use as a senior activity center, the mansion fell victim to years of neglect, and was boarded up in 2010. Vandals broke windows, stole copper pipes, and damaged the interior. A lack of county investment left the future of the mansion uncertain, with proposals for demolition looming. However, a glimmer of hope emerged in 2021 with the allocation of $6 million from federal funds. This investment aimed to revitalize Wendt Beach Park, including repairs and upgrades for the historic mansion. In December 2024 it was announced that work had begun on the exterior. Repairs were planned to accommodate occupancy by the summer of 2026.

Currently, Wendt Beach Park offers a wide variety of recreational opportunities. Visitors can enjoy picnicking, hiking, biking, playing soccer, or simply walking the beach and taking in the scenic views of Lake Erie. It remains open to the public, free of charge all year long.

by Doreen Gallagher Regan

CITY OF BUFFALO PROFILES

This section includes profiles of the city of **Buffalo** and several of its historic places.

City of Buffalo

At the western end of the Niagara River, the area that became the city of Buffalo is in a strategic location and subsequently grew into the largest city in the Western New York area. The Haudenosaunee (people of the longhouse) or Iroquois 6 Nations resided across most of upstate and central New York, with the Seneca being the western tribe of the federation. They conquered the Wenro (1643), Neutrals (1650) and Erie (1653), building a village in the late 1600s at Buffalo Creek.

Figure 20 1798 Drawing of Buffalo Peninsula near current location of Times Beach photo Picture Book of Earlier Buffalo

The first European settlement in WNY was a trading post established by Chabert Joncaire in 1758 at the current location of the General Mills plant. When the French lost the French & Indian War, the English obtained possession of the WNY area. If you look at a map of New York State during the time of the American Revolution, the state only extended from the Hudson River west to the Finger Lakes. WNY was the wilderness west of that point.

Lieutenant William Johnson was the Indian Agent for the British stationed at Fort Niagara. He and his half-brother Captain Powell lived with the Seneca during the winter of 1780-1. Cornelius Winney built a trading post; other early residents were Black Joe Hodge, a former slave who was captured by the Seneca, and Martin Middaugh, with his son-in-law Ezekiel Lane, who initially resided in Lewiston. They built their cabins north of Little Buffalo Creek on a bluff about 20 feet above Buffalo Creek, near what is now Washington and Exchange Streets. Johnson was considered the first land owner, as he remained in Buffalo after the British left Fort Niagara, married a Seneca woman and was given the land near the mouth of Buffalo Creek by the Seneca for his contributions in assisting them. All the other residents were squatters.

Joseph Ellicott surveyed the WNY area for the Holland Land Company, later serving as land agent. He wanted to name the area New Amsterdam and laid out the streets with Dutch names. The residents objected and the name of Buffalo prevailed. It is not certain where the name was derived but the village was named after Buffalo Creek. It is possible a Seneca with a name that translated as Buffalo lived along the creek and it was given his name. No one is certain.

Captain Samuel Pratt built the first store on the raised bank or terrace, near the current intersection of Main and Exchange Streets (later the location of the Mansion House). Dr. Cyrenius Chapin opened the first doctor's office on Swan Street between Pearl and Main Streets. Louis LeCouteux opened the first drug store across from Pratt's store on Exchange and Main Street. The village extended down Main Street to Chippewa Street, but all was burned by the British during the War of 1812. Only the home of Margaret St. John at 460 Main Street was left standing, along with the jail and blacksmith shop.

One of the first homes rebuilt after the War of 1812 was the Coit House at Swan and Pearl Streets. The city was quickly rebuilt, with most of the buildings made of brick. It was important to create a harbor at Buffalo Creek so Buffalo could obtain the distinction of the western terminus of the Erie Canal. Judge Samuel Wilkeson formed the Buffalo Harbor Company in 1819 with Ebenezer Johnson, Ebenezer Walden, Charles Townsend, George Coit and Oliver Forward. They moved the mouth of the river 1,000 feet south by building two piers extending 1,000 feet into Lake Erie and took action to remove the sandbar that annually blocked the mouth of the river.

Figure 21 Eagle Tavern, Main & Court Streets 1825
Picture Book of Earlier Buffalo

General Peter Buell Porter led the Black Rock contingent to obtain the Erie Canal western terminus rights. Black Rock had a natural harbor on the Niagara River but strong currents made it difficult to navigate to the mouth of the Niagara River. The Samuel Wilkeson team won the western terminus battle. That is why the city is called Buffalo and not Black Rock, which was later absorbed into the city.

The city of Buffalo was incorporated in 1832 and the boundaries were North Street and Porter Avenue to the north, Jefferson Street to the east, the Niagara River to the west and Buffalo Creek to the south. Land south of the creek was the Seneca Buffalo Creek Reservation. The farm of Louis Allen and lands of Judge Ebenezer Johnson were at the northern border. Just past that were lots owned by William Hodge and Abner Bryant. It was not until 1853 that Buffalo extended north to Kenmore Avenue.

Erastus Granger was appointed Superintendent of Indian Affairs and Collector of Taxes for Buffalo, later also the Postmaster, by President Thomas Jefferson in 1804. He purchased land for his offices in the village but in 1810 purchased 700 acres, 2 ½ miles from the village on Main Street. That land was called Flint Hill and it extended to Scajaquada Creek. The land north of Flint Hill was owned by Daniel Chapin and Washington Russell. These properties became Forest Lawn Cemetery and Delaware Park.

Chapin's Willow Lawn property was purchased by Elam Jewett, who established the Parkside neighborhood next to Delaware Park. Lewis Bennett built the Central Park neighborhood; but the largest Buffalo property owner was the Rumsey family, who possessed 23 of the 42 square miles that constituted the city of Buffalo.

800 WEST FERRY
800 West Ferry Street, Buffalo

Figure 22 800 West Ferry
photo credit Ellen Mika Zelasko

800 West Ferry was built in 1929 by Darwin R. Martin, son of Darwin D. Martin (of the famous Frank Lloyd Wright designed Darwin Martin House). Darwin D. grew up poor, went to work at 13 years old for The Larkin Soap Company, and eventually created an impeccable reputation as a good, trustworthy man.

Darwin R. on the other hand, was a Yale graduate and went into business buying and selling real estate. Unlike his father, he was not known for his benevolence. He borrowed money from banks, investors, friends and family members. He rarely made good on those loans. There is evidence of a family rift between Darwin R. and his sister, Dorothy and her husband, James Forsythe Foster. Dorothy's family suffered more than they probably should have during the Depression because of investments made with Darwin R.

Darwin D. also loaned money to Darwin R. against his better judgement. 800 West Ferry was one of those investments. It is documented that he didn't approve of the plan for 800. Yet, he invested. And so did others.

In 1929, Darwin R. built a luxurious eleven story building on the grounds of the former William Hengerer and William Gratwick, Jr. mansion. It was constructed the same year as the comparable Campanile and Park Lane Luxury Apartments, and came to be known as a building full of mansions. Designed by Bley and Lyman Architects, the first floor had 4 apartments, the next eight floors held 16 two story luxury apartments, and the top two floors held the penthouse used by Darwin R. and his second wife, Laura. The style of the building itself has been described as Art Deco, modern-Tudor and Neo-Gothic, a very 'eclectic' mix. The gargoyles on the upper part of the building feature Darwin R.'s face. Each apartment was decorated according to the tenants wishes, choosing from early American, English, Italian, or French designs.

When the stock market crashed, finding tenants for 800 West Ferry became next to impossible. During the ensuing Depression, the apartments were broken into smaller units in an effort to make them more affordable.

In 1940, the building was emptied, and the two-story apartments and the penthouse were divided into multiple units. The first floor remained as built.

In 1980, 800 West Ferry was converted to 58 individually owned, very well-appointed condominiums. It remains one of WNY's most prestigious addresses.

by Ellen Mika Zelasko

A&P Warehouse
545 Swan Street, Buffalo

The engineering and construction firm of John W. Cowper built this classic "Daylight Factory" style building for the Keystone Warehouse Company in 1917. It is the last and only remaining of eight warehouses built for Keystone between 1903 and 1917 in the Hydraulic Neighborhood of Buffalo. The 250,000, eight story warehouse takes up the entire block bound by Hamburg Street, Jefferson Avenue, Swan Street and Myrtle Avenue.

Figure 23 Ap Lofts at Larkinville photo aploftsatlarkinville.com

The Great Atlantic & Pacific Tea Company (A&P) opened its Buffalo Division in 1918 and occupied a portion of the warehouse. As A&P became the primary occupant of the building, single story wings were added along Jefferson toward Swan and Myrtle so rail freight cars could be directly unloaded off the tracks into the warehouse.

Originally known as Gilman & Company, the company was started by George Gilman in 1858 in Manhattan, who diversified his business interests after inheriting his father's tannery business. The company began as a wholesaler and became a retail business, the Great American Tea Company, in 1863. It also started a mail order tea business, and when the transcontinental railroad was completed in 1869 created the name Great Atlantic & Pacific Tea Company. In 1871 the company began offering premiums (lithographs, china and glassware) with the purchase of tea or coffee by mail or at its stores.

George Huntington Hartford joined the company and by 1871 was responsible for expanding the retail operations outside of the New York City area. Due to increased tariffs on tea and coffee, in 1880 the stores diversified and started also selling sugar. They continued adding other A&P branded products to create the first grocery chain by the turn of the century. In the 1930s the company originated the Supermarket store concept.

From 1915 to 1975, A&P was the largest grocery retailer in the U.S. The company grew to 15,000 grocery stores and 40,000 employees, being the largest retailer of any kind in the country until 1965. In addition to warehousing, the Buffalo location was the divisional headquarters for the company. It serviced 370 stores and had almost 1,000 employees.

The A&P Warehouse closed in 1975 when the company closed all their supermarkets in the Buffalo Division. The warehouse later housed the Mesmer Refrigeration Company. Architects Carmina Wood Morris, worked with developers to remodel the building into 147 apartments as the AP Lofts at Larkinville.

ADAM MICKIEWICZ LIBRARY & DRAMATIC CENTER
612 Fillmore Avenue, Buffalo

Figure 24 Adam Mickiewicz Library Dramatic Circle photo credit Patra Mangus

Several Polish American clubs existed along Fillmore Avenue on the Polish East Side of Buffalo. The only one still standing is the Adam Mickiewicz Library & Dramatic Center. It was formed in the apartment of Joseph Slisz, an employee of the newspaper, *Polaka w Ameryce*. He met with influential Poles to start an organization that would appeal to the Polish Youth. The club was formed on October 13, 1895 and initially met in the St. Stanislaus Parish house.

In 1902 the club purchased 612 Fillmore, where they could promote and preserve Polish literature, history, theater, music and culture by offering theatrical performances, educational lectures and a library. The building was expanded to two stories in 1914 with the addition of a bar, larger theater space and clubrooms.

During Prohibition the club operated as a speakeasy with live jazz and drinks for Polish residents of the east side, who were joined by politicians and the police for the libations. Many of the founding members passed on during the Depression and early WWII, but they were replaced by immigrants fleeing Europe after the war and communism during the Cold War. Second and third generation Polish Americans began joining the club to explore their Polish heritage.

The Dramatic Circle was organized in 1895 and began producing amateur productions of Polish plays. The upstairs library contains over 4,000 volumes of plays and over 400 handwritten scripts of plays. It features over 12,000 books about Poland and eastern Europe, with about 955 of the books written in the Polish language.

It is a private club that holds Polish events including a St. John's Eve Party, a reading of the May 3rd Constitution, and one of the largest Dyngus Day parties after the Broadway Fillmore Dyngus Day Parade. The bar offers one of the largest selections of Polish beers in the U.S. They also feature a selection of Polish vodka, liquors and Krupnik, a traditional Polish honey liquor.

Torn Space Theater produces plays at the building, and with the assistance of grants is converting the adjacent former gas station into additional space for indoor and outdoor theater and musical events.

Referred to as "Mickeys" in the neighborhood, The Adam Mickiewicz Library and Dramatics Circle is the oldest surviving Polish Library in Buffalo and oldest Polish American organization in WNY. Polish is the language of choice at the club, spoken by members and novices alike.

Adult Learning Center

389 Virginia Street, Buffalo

Figure 25 Adult Learning Center

The Adult Learning Center, located at the intersection of Virginia Street and Elmwood Avenue, is Buffalo's oldest public school building still actively functioning as an educational facility. Built in 1888 and designed by prominent Buffalo architect H.H. Little, the school is a beautiful example of the Romanesque Revival style, with Medina sandstone accentuating the brick exterior, a gabled roof, and arched entranceways above recessed double doors.

The land on which the building sits was donated to the city in 1839 by Louis Le Couteulx, a French businessman and philanthropist who played a significant role in the early development of Buffalo. At the time, this section of the city was considered rather remote. Le Couteulx donated land to the Catholic Diocese to build the Church of Immaculate Conception, and Le Couteulx St. Mary's Benevolent Society for the Deaf (renamed St. Mary's School for the Deaf).

Also nearby on Edward Street was the Orphan Asylum, an organization that housed Buffalo's homeless children. Its residents were in need of a school building, so Le Couteulx' provided the land on Virginia St. for a small wooden schoolhouse to be built. As the area's population grew, the school was expanded several times until it was replaced with the current structure in 1888.

Over the years, the building has accommodated a variety of educational programs. For a long while it held classes for students from Central High and Hutchinson High Schools. In 1926, it became an annex to Public School No. 36, located at Day's Park and College Street. From 1946 to 1949 it was used as the Veteran's High School, for soldiers returning from war who needed to resume their high school education. After that program was discontinued, the school sat vacant for seven years, deteriorating from vandalism and damaged by fire. It was renovated in 1955 to reopen as a temporary location for School No. 36, and two years later it became a remedial reading center.

In the mid 1970's, the school became The Adult Learning Center No. 46, and the building was designated part of the Allentown Historic District in March of 1978. It remains to this day as headquarters to Buffalo Public Schools Adult Education Division, running a variety of programs such as GED preparation, English Language Learning, and Career and Technical Education.

by Doreen Gallagher Regan

Albright Knox Art Gallery
1285 Elmwood Avenue, Buffalo

Figure 26 Albright Knox Art Gallery photo credit Rick Falkowski

The Buffalo Fine Arts Academy was founded by the Young Men's Association in 1862. It is the sixth oldest public art institution in the U.S. Artwork of The Academy was displayed as part of the Buffalo Public Library in the Richmond Hotel and 1887 Central Library.

In 1900 philanthropist John Albright donated funds to begin construction of an art gallery. The building was designed by Buffalo architect E.B. Green; the Elmwood Avenue location at the Frederick Law Olmsted designed Delaware Park was selected. It was intended that the building would be the Fine Arts Pavilion for the Pan-American Exposition in 1901. However, it was not completed as what would have been the second permanent building of the Pan-Am - construction delays pushed back the grand opening until May 31, 1905.

John Albright was a Rensselaer Polytechnic Institute (RPI) graduate who earned his fortune as a railroad agent, shipping coal to the west and importing grain from the mid-west. He started the Ontario Power Company in Ontario (it became Niagara Mohawk and National Grid); purchased Buffalo Bolt with Edmund Hayes; invested in Scranton's Lackawanna Iron & Steel Company (Bethlehem Steel) and the Goodyear's Buffalo & Susquehanna Iron Company (Hanna Furnace Company and National Steel Company); and built the Union Ship Canal.

The Knox family established an Art Library for the Albright Art School in 1934 in Clifton Hall, the original Buffalo Society of Natural Sciences building on Elmwood Avenue. Starting in 1939, Seymour Knox II was influenced by A. Conger Goodyear to provide funding for modern art in the Room of Contemporary Art. Knox and other donors expanded the modern art collection, resulting in an expansion of the gallery and it being renamed the Albright-Knox Art gallery in 1962, funded by $1.4 million dollars from the Seymour H. Knox Foundation.

The Art Gallery became internationally known for its abstract art collection and exhibitions. The collection of postwar American and European Art, Abstract Expressionism, Op Art and Contemporary Art required expansion of the gallery.

In 2016 Buffalo native, investment firm founder and art collector Jeffery Gundlach donated $42.5 million towards the $125 million campaign goal. The facility was renamed the Albright-Knox-Gundlach Art Museum or AKG Art Museum. After several years of construction and a two-year closing of the art gallery, the grand opening of the new AKG Art Museum took place in June 2023.

AM&A'S – JN ADAM'S DEPARTMENT STORES
377 Main Street, Buffalo

Robert Borthwick Adam and his brother James N. Adam were born in 1833 and 1843 in Peebles on the River Tweed in Scotland, about 20 miles from Edinburgh. Both brothers apprenticed at dry goods stores in Scotland's capital city.

In 1857 Robert emigrated to the U.S. and settled in Boston, Massachusetts. He partnered with Alexander Whiting and Herbert A. Meldrum, moving to Buffalo in 1867 to open Adam, Meldrum and Whiting at 308-310 Main Street, (later moving to 396 Main Street). Whiting was replaced by William Anderson in 1876, creating Adam, Meldrum & Anderson - AM&A's. In 1886 they purchased a Westinghouse generator, becoming one of the first stores to use electric lights in the U.S. When J.L. Hudson vacated their store at 410 Main Street, AM&A's expanded to include that location.

Figure 27 AM&A's 377 Main St. Still JN Adams Store PD

Motivated by his brother's success, J.N. Adam moved to New Haven, Connecticut, partnering with William H. Hotchkiss. At his brother's suggestion J.N. Adam relocated to Buffalo in 1881 and opened a dry goods store in the White Building at 298 Main Street. Desiring larger facilities, J.N. moved to the corner of Main and Eagle, acquiring 383 – 393 Main Street and eventually adding adjoining properties.

J.N. Adam turned his attention to politics, was elected to the City Council in 1895 and served as mayor of Buffalo from 1906 to 1909. He purchased 293 acres in Perrysburg, New York to establish the J.N. Adam Memorial Hospital to serve tuberculosis patients in 1909.

Beginning in the 1940s, AM&A's on the west side of Main Street and J.N. Adam on the east side, were known for their elaborate Victorian Christmas window displays. In 1948 AM&A's was the first downtown Buffalo store to expand to the suburbs, opening an outlet in the University Plaza, eventually expanding to other major plazas and malls. In 1960 AM&A's moved across Main Street, into the former J.N. Adam's property.

AM&A's was owned by the Adam's family until it was sold to Bon-Ton in 1994. After Bon-Ton filed bankruptcy, all WNY area stores closed in 2018.

The original AM&A's on the west side of Main Street was demolished in 1964 and replaced by the Main Place Mall. The former J.N. Adam store and final AM&A's downtown location was closed in 1996; subsequent owners and legal matters continue to delay its conversion to office space and apartments.

American Radiator Company / Institute for Thermal Research
1807 Elmwood Avenue, Buffalo

Figure 28 American Radiator Company 9-1-1915 photo American Radiator Company PD

The American Radiator Company factory complex on Elmwood Avenue near Hertel consists of three sections: Equipment Plant, Malleable Foundry and Institute of Thermal Research. It was adjacent to the New York Central Belt Line Railway.

In 1881, the Pierce Steam Heating Company was formed by John B. Pierce and Joseph Bond to manufacture steel boilers and cast-iron radiators. The American Radiator Company was formed in 1892 by the merger of Pierce Steam Heating Company, Michigan Radiator & Iron Manufacturing Company and Detroit Radiator. In the late 1800s the company expanded into the European Market, opening a branch in London and manufacturing plants in Europe.

Construction of the Equipment Plant began in 1891 and, as was common at early industrial facilities, additions were added piecemeal on an as needed basis. Remodeling took place in 1906, 1910 and 1924, with separate sections for pattern shops, machine shops, testing rooms and assembly department. Buffalo architect E.B. Green designed these additions.

By the turn of the century the company was one of the largest outfitters of radiators in the U.S, and it was reported that Buffalo manufactured more heating apparatus than any other city in the world. In 1910 Schmidt, Garden & Martin from Chicago designed the Institute of Thermal Research in an architectural style referred to as "Gardenesque," a combination of Classical design elements with Prairie style minimalist detailing. This building contained administrative offices, a lecture hall and laboratories filled with thermometers, humidistats, flue-draft gauges, water meters, fuel consumption recorders and other instruments to measure the performance of radiators and boilers. The company claimed it was the only facility in America devoted to the problems of better warmth.

Their Malleable Foundry was built in 1915 and included 81,000 square feet of space, with the purpose of not sacrificing quality for quantity.

In 1929, Standard Sanitary Manufacturing Company, founded in 1875, merged with American Radiator Company to form American Radiator – Standard Sanitary Company. They purchased Fox Furnace in 1937, and the company name was changed to American Standard in 1948. The factory and institute were shuttered in 1959 with manufacturing transferred to other cities.

The Thermal Institute Building was converted by Rocco Termini to The ARCO Lofts, 38 one- and two-bedroom apartments in 2015. It is part of the Pierce Arrow District of development in the Elmwood Avenue section of North Buffalo.

ANCHOR BAR
1047 Main Street, Buffalo

The Anchor Bar was first opened by Frank and Teressa Bellissimo in 1935 in downtown Buffalo near the Buffalo Harbor. Since it was in the area where Buffalo Memorial Auditorium was being built, they relocated to 1047 Main Street in 1940 in the former Haefner's Restaurant, which was built in 1900.

Figure 29 Anchor Bar photo credit Rick Falkowski

This location at Main and High Street became a popular Italian Restaurant and featured live jazz groups. Of the many early jazz clubs on the East Side and in downtown Buffalo, the Anchor Bar is the only one that remains open in the same location with the same name, and continues to have music.

On the evening of March 4, 1964 Buffalo Wings were born at The Anchor Bar. Stories about the actual detailed evolution of wings vary depending upon the source, but the fact remains that the first wings (as we know them today) were served by Teressa to a group of her son's friends. Dominic was tending bar and a group of his friends said they were starving. The restaurant had sold out of food for the night but Teressa took some chicken wings she was saving for broth, added hot sauce, fried them up with butter and placed them under the broiler. With celery sticks and blue cheese dip, it was a hit and added to the menu.

After chicken wings were introduced, the club continued to feature jazz groups during the 1960s, 70s and 80s. Jimmy Gomes & the Jazz Example, Carroll McLaughlin & Magnitude and Corona were often featured, and jazz legends Al Tinney and Dodo Greene were headliners on a regular basis.

Chicken Wings became the food associated with sports bars, and during the 1970s many WNY bars featured 10 cent wing nights. During the 1980s wings were spread to the rest of the country by chains like TGIFridays and Pizza Hut. When the Buffalo Bills appeared in four straight Super Bowls in the early 1990s, football fans saw the Bills Mafia eating wings at tailgate parties and Buffalo bars. Wings became associated with football; the main Super Bowl Party entree is pizza and wings.

Wing Fest was inaugurated in 2002 at Dunn Tire Park. The festival is now held at The Buffalo Bills' Highmark Stadium and they sell over 20 tons of wings annually at the event. The Anchor Bar is now franchised across the country, and chicken wings are nationally called Buffalo Wings.

In Buffalo, they're just wings.

ANNA KATHARINE GREEN HOUSE
156 Park Street, Buffalo

*Figure 30 Anna Katharine Green House
photo credit Rick Falkowski*

When Anna Katharine Green was three years old her mother died. Her father, attorney James Wilson Green, married Grace Hollister from Buffalo and the family moved to Buffalo where Anna was educated in Buffalo schools.

After graduating in 1866 from Ripley College in Vermont, Anna pursued a career as a poet. Drawing off the knowledge of legal and police matters that she gathered from observing her father's legal career, Green wrote The Leavenworth Case. Published in 1878, it became a best seller and is considered the first American detective novel. During her 45-year career she published 35 novels, 23 short stories and a volume of poetry.

Green is acknowledged as the mother of detective fiction. She created archetypes like: the elderly spinster detective, young female detective, detective cohort, tightly constructed plot with unique turn of events, step by step revelation of the story line, unexpected climaxes and many plot devices still used in the whodunit genre. The Leavenworth Case was so highly regarded that it was part of the Yale Law School curriculum pertaining to trusting circumstantial evidence.

She influenced Sir Arthur Conan Doyle (Sherlock Holmes), Agatha Christie, and former Buffalo detective Lissa Marie Redmond, who has published seven mystery books. In fact, when Doyle visited the U.S. in 1894, he made a trip to Buffalo so he could meet with Green.

Anna married actor Charles Rohlfs in 1884. The family moved from Vermont to Buffalo in 1887 when Rohlfs, who had several stove patents, obtained a position with stove manufacturers Sherman S. Jewett & Company. They lived at 26 Highland until Rohlfs designed and built their Craftsman style home at 156 Park Street in 1912. It was in this house that Katharine continued to write and Rohlfs had his workshop.

Rohlfs began making furniture in the Mission style and modernist designs. He was a competitive contemporary of Gustav Stickley in the Arts & Crafts Movement. They both exhibited at the Pan-American Exposition. Rohlfs' furniture was well received worldwide; he was made a Fellow of the Royal Society of Arts in London and was commissioned to provide a set of chairs for Buckingham Palace.

Katharine and Charles had three children and remained active in Buffalo society and business until their deaths - Katharine in 1935 and Charles in 1936. They are buried in the Rohlfs' family plot in Forest Lawn Cemetery.

Asbury Delaware Avenue Methodist Church
339 Delaware Avenue, Buffalo

Construction of the Delaware Avenue Methodist Episcopal Church began in 1874, designed by Buffalo architect John H. Selkirk, who also designed the Tift House and Buffalo Illuminating Gas Light Company. The Gothic Revival style design was constructed of Medina sandstone with Connecticut stone trim, a roof of Vermont slate and asymmetrical front towers. The interior was finished in rosewood, with a wraparound gallery and old-fashioned side galleries. Stained-glass windows were created by the Buffalo firm of Booth and Reister. It was built at a cost of $130,000.

In 1917 the church merged with Asbury Methodist Church, located at Delaware and Chippewa since 1872. Originally part of the Niagara Methodist Church, they became known as the Pearl Street Methodist Church, organized in 1847, with their first church at Pearl and Chippewa Streets. After the merger, the name was changed to the Asbury Delaware Avenue Methodist Church.

Figure 31 Asbury Delaware Avenue Methodist Church
photo credit Rick Falkowski

When more people moved away from the city center, the church closed in 1969. This ended the downtown presence of a Methodist Church in Buffalo, which dated back to the opening of the Niagara Methodist Church at Schimmelpenninck (now Niagara) and Tuscarora (now Franklin) in 1818.

In 1929, George A. Deon (known as the human fly) was hired to clean the belfry and bells of the church. Deon, who cleaned the Statue of Liberty and Eifel Tower, determined that the reason the bells did not function since the death of President McKinley in 1901 was because of the accumulation of eight tons of pigeon droppings.

The building remained an active church until the 1980s but after years of neglect it was slated for demolition in 1995. There was a public outcry about possibly losing this architectural gem. Musician Ani DiFranco and her manager Scot Fisher purchased the building in 2000 and with the creativity of Flynn Battaglia Architects and Architectural Resources began the lengthy refurbishment.

Transforming the 19th century Gothic Revival Church into a 21st century multi-purpose venue took over 10 years and cost more than $10 million of private and public funds. Originally referred to as "The Church" and now called "Babeville" it features the 1,200 capacity Asbury Hall with 45-foot ceilings, state of the art sound and balcony seating for concerts and events. It also contains the Hallwalls Contemporary Arts Center, The Ninth Ward small capacity listening room, and the offices of Righteous Babe Records.

Belt Line Railroad

10 Starin Avenue and Stations Circling Buffalo

Coming into the Amherst/Starin Station

Figure 32 Belt Line Railroad Central Park Station PD

The New York Central Belt Line is a 15-mile rail route circling the city of Buffalo. It was built in 1883, with some sections dating back to 1836, and included 19 commuter stations that carried passengers from 1883 until the end of WWI. A trip cost a nickel and service consisted of about 26 trains per day.

Prior to the advent of rail service, the most efficient way of transporting freight was by canals and lake shipping. Subsequently, most factories were built near the waterfront or along canals. The opening of the Belt Line resulted in businesses being built along the tracks. Factories like George Urban Flour Mills were built on the East Side, Ford Motor Company in the Central Park area, the Pierce Arrow Company and many other industrial plants in Black Rock. It also served the already established Hydraulics District of South Buffalo.

In addition to changing the industrial landscape, the Belt Line helped build residential communities. Neighborhoods of working man's cottages, two family flats with three bedrooms, one bath upper and lower apartments, were built in Black Rock, on the East Side and Kensington-Grider. The upper middle class suburban atmosphere Parkside and Central Park neighborhoods were created. They were served by the only remaining station at 10 Starin Avenue, which was a Boy Scout clubhouse before being converted to a private home.

The Belt Line even changed the appearance of the city, with rail crossings on all major streets, later converted to bridges over these roads.

The central station of the Belt Line was the New York Central stop at Exchange Street. The 19 stops were about a mile apart. Every portion of Buffalo: East Side, West Side, North Buffalo, South Buffalo, Riverside/Black Rock and Downtown was within walking distance of a station.

During the Pan-American Exposition the Delaware-Linden stop was added for visitors. Afterwards, it accommodated residents of the North Buffalo neighborhood that was built upon the Expo footprint. That station also enabled the formation of Kenmore, the first suburb in WNY, created a mile north of that Delaware Avenue location.

The Belt Line still operates as a freight line, the Buffalo Central Terminal is being restored, and Citizens for Regional Transit is investigating present day uses for this railway that changed the industrial and residential complexion of the city of Buffalo.

Blocher Mausoleum
Forest Lawn Cemetery, Buffalo

Considered the most extravagant monument in Forest Lawn Cemetery, the Blocher mausoleum attracted so many visitors that a separate path was created for access. In the early 20th century, it was considered the most popular monument at a private cemetery in the U.S.

John Blocher owned a successful shoe and boot factory, manufacturing boots for the U.S. Army during the Civil War. His son Nelson fell in love with Katherine Margaret Sullivan, a maid they hired at their 168 Delaware Avenue mansion. Nelson's parents did not agree with the relationship between their upper-class son and a lowly member of their domestic staff. To separate the couple, they sent Nelson to Europe on business for the factory. When Nelson returned from Europe Katherine was no longer employed by his parents. According to his parents, she left without notice, leaving no forwarding address. But many people believed the Blocher's fired her, with instructions to disappear and never return. Regardless, Nelson was heartbroken and relentlessly searched for his lost love. He died three years later of a broken heart.

Figure 33 Blocher Mausoleum photo credit Rick Falkowski

John and his wife Elizabeth were devastated by their son's premature death and either out of remorse or sorrow they decided to build an elaborate monument in memory of their son. They approached McDonnell & Son Granite Company who operated a funerary art and monument company in Buffalo. Motivated by either love or guilt, Blocher could not find anyone to create a mausoleum to his satisfaction, so he designed the monument himself. He created a structure that consisted of twenty slabs of granite cut at the McDonnell quarry in Qunicy Massachusetts. The roof of the mausoleum was cut from a 90-ton slab of granite, whittled down to the 29-ton shape of a bell. Five pilasters support the bell. With four one-inch-thick glass panes manufactured in Paris separating them, providing an excellent view of the interior.

Paul Roche of Rhode Island initially sculptured the interior, but John Blocher was so dissatisfied with his work that he destroyed it with an axe. He then hired Frank Torrey in Carrara, Italy to create the sculpture. It consists of life size marble statues of Nelson Blocher lying on a couch with his parents standing over him. Above Nelson is an angel that has a striking resemblance to the maid Katherine Sullivan.

The total cost of the mausoleum completed in 1888 was $100,000, equivalent to almost $3 million today.

Brisbane Building
403 Main Street, Buffalo

*Figure 34 Brisbane Building
photo early 1900s postcard of Lafayette Square*

The Brisbane Building was built in Lafayette Square at the corner of Main and Clinton Streets in 1895. It replaced the Arcade Building, a similar commercial building at the location that burned down in December 1893.

The Arcade was the largest office building in the city and was built in the early 1850s by Albert and George Brisbane. It housed Shea's Music Hall (Michael Shea's first entertainment establishment), Robinson's Musee Theatre, T.C. Tanke Jewelers and other businesses.

Milton E. Beebe & Son were the architects of the Brisbane Building. The firm designed many notable churches, commercial buildings and mansions in the late 19th century. The building covers a half city block with 180 feet of frontage on Main Street and Washington Street, along with 200 feet on Clinton. Note the original Clinton Street entrance in the photo. Building materials included over 2,000 tons of iron and steel, about three million bricks and over 40,000 square feet of glass, terra cotta and marble. Upon construction, the fireproof structure was the largest mercantile and office building in the city of Buffalo.

Originally named the Mooney and Brisbane Building, James Mooney was reportedly one of the financiers of the Fenian Raid into Canada which climaxed at the June 1866 Battle of Ridgeway. In 1906 James Brisbane assumed complete ownership of the complex.

The Brisbane Building was designed to accommodate retail establishments on the first floor, offices on floors 3 through 7. The second floor was set up as a "Bon Marche" with two immense skylights over a central court that served 16 small stores.

In 1908 three of the largest stores of their business line were on the ground floor of the building. Kleinhans Men's Clothing Store occupied the basement, entire second floor and half of the first floor. Other first floor tenants were Faxon, Williams & Faxon, the prominent grocers at that time and S.H. Knox five and ten cent store, the predecessor of Woolworth's.

Charles Stanley Hunt, the 1911 founder of Hunt Real estate, had an office in the building for 47 years. In 1985 the building was purchased by his son C. Stuart Hunt. Currently operated by Peter and Stephen Hunt, the appearance and mechanics of the building have been updated. Peter Hunt occupies the same second floor office that Edward Kleinhans maintained in the building during the early 20th century.

Broadway Arsenal, Armory, Auditorium & Barn
201 Broadway, Buffalo

When the Broadway Arsenal was constructed in 1858, Broadway was still known as Batavia Road. Designed by Calvin N. Otis in the Gothic Revival style and built with local Onondaga limestone, the turreted structure looked like a castle. It was the home of the 65th and 74th Regiments of the New York National Guard. The 74th moved to the Virginia Street Armory in 1868. A drill shed and administration building were added in front of the original armory in 1884. The 65th occupied the building until moving to the Masten Avenue Armory in 1907.

Figure 35 Broadway Auditorium postcard from 1914 PD

The city of Buffalo took possession of the property and in 1912, under the direction of contractor William F. Felton, added a lighted marquee, bleacher seating and a stage for orchestras. Robert J. Reidpath designed a new steel truss roof with clerestory windows for lighting and ventilation. It was renamed The Broadway Auditorium in 1913.

It was used for various activities, with surfaces constructed and dismantled for events, including curved tracks for bicycle racing, bowling lanes for national bowling tournaments, an ice surface for hockey games and basketball courts for professional and college games.

Indoor lacrosse league games in the early 1930s featured Harry Smith, who changed his name to Jay Silverheels and played Tonto in the Lone Ranger television series from 1949 to 1957.

Friday nights featured boxing matches, including bouts by Joe Lewis, Jack Dempsey and Jimmy Slattery. Political speeches were given by Teddy Roosevelt, Woodrow Wilson, Howard Taft and others.

Concerts were performed by various artists of all musical styles including Cab Calloway and Ella Fitzgerald.

The building was remodeled into a convention hall in 1936, and at the start of WWII it was used as emergency quarters for the U.S. Army. However, in 1940 it was replaced by Memorial Auditorium as the city's primary sports and special events venue.

In 1948 the remains of the original 1858 Arsenal building at the rear of the complex were damaged in a fire and were demolished so the city's Department of Public Works snowplows, garbage trucks and street cleaning equipment could enter through the rear of the building. Additions were added and it was renamed The Broadway Barn.

The oldest continuously occupied civic building in Buffalo is still being used for the storage of Buffalo DPW vehicles. Located in the Michigan Street African American Heritage Corridor, it is planned to become a sports complex with affordable housing.

Broadway Market
999 Broadway, Buffalo

Figure 36 Broadway Market postcard late 1800s PD

The latter half of the 19th century saw a large influx of Eastern European immigrants in Buffalo. Settling on the East Side made good sense to them, as it was natural for them to want to live where people spoke their language, knew the same customs and ate the same food. To find the familiar in their new surroundings, residents sought a way to provide these familiar items to preserve their Eastern European heritage.

In 1888, a group of immigrants started the Broadway Market on a parcel of land donated by the city. Located at 999 Broadway, the Market offered business opportunities as well as providing all types of European staples and treats, such as local produce, baked goods, meats, cheeses, and various other sundry items. It grew to become one of the busiest business districts in Buffalo.

The Market also became a place where residents met to hear news of family and friends in the 'old country' and to keep up with how their neighbors were faring here in Buffalo and beyond. The Market quickly became a lifeline for new Buffalonians. These immigrants understood the importance of keeping a connection to the old, while adapting to their new way of life here in America.

The Broadway Market served all their needs, both materially and socially.

The Market itself has been through many changes over the years. The first Market building burned down and was replaced by a much larger structure. The current building was built in 1956 with over 90,000 square feet of retail space and two levels of free parking above holding just over 1,000 cars. This building was renovated in the mid-1980s, updating lighting and heat. The building was recently given a face lift to improve curb appeal.

Despite the physical changes, the basic plan has always been to provide an incubator for immigrant and locally owned businesses, focusing on fresh and international foods, providing for the ever-changing needs and demographics of the community. Future plans include the same, while continuing to keep the design of the building updated. And while the city still owns it, it is currently being run by a non-profit organization who has taken on the future needs of the Market.

During the Easter season the market is filled with shoppers getting butter lambs, pussy willows and other traditional Easter staples. That needs to again be the everyday norm at the market.

by Ellen Mika Zelasko

BUFFALO & ERIE COUNTY BOTANICAL GARDENS
2655 South Park Avenue, Buffalo

The Botanical Gardens was created by the vision and efforts of David F. Day, Frederick Law Olmsted, John F. Coswell, Frederick A. Lord and William A. Burnham.

During the 1860s, attorney and judge David F. Day was instrumental in including botanical collections in Buffalo, and when he became parks commissioner, he championed a South Buffalo conservancy project. After creating Central Park in NYC, Frederick Law Olmsted was selected to design the parks system for the city of Buffalo. He created The Park (Delaware Park), The Parade (Humboldt Park, Martin Luther King Park) and Front Park, all connected by parkways and stately circles in 1868. As Buffalo expanded, he was commissioned to create Cazenovia Park and South Park from 156 acres of farmland during 1894 to 1900 in South Buffalo.

Figure 37 Botanical Gardens photo credit Marsha Falkowski

Olmsted's design of South Park included a conservancy and formal gardens. UB Botany Professor John F. Cowell was appointed the first director of the botanical gardens in 1894. He gathered plants, trees and flowers from around the world for the conservancy's collections. Cowell guided the gardens until 1915, adding six greenhouses in 1907.

Frederick Lord began building greenhouses in Buffalo in 1849. With his son-in-law he formed Lord & Burnham Company. It became the premier glasshouse manufacturer in the U.S. The company moved to Irvington, New York to be closer to the private estates along the Hudson River and in NYC. They built conservatories across the country, including the Biltmore estate in North Carolina. Lord & Burham returned to their hometown to build The Botanical Gardens in South Park, modeled after glass conservancies in London. Upon opening in 1900, the conservatory was the third largest greenhouse in the U.S. and ninth largest in the world.

In 1929 the city considered demolishing the conservatory, but federal funds became available in 1930 that allowed Lord & Burnham Company to renovate the building, rebuilding it to withstand the harsh Buffalo winters. The building was damaged during the Blizzard of 1977 but the Buffalo and Erie County Botanical Gardens Society, a 501c3 corporation, was formed to revive it to its fullest potential.

The Conservatory was recently rebuilt and in 2023 announced an additional 25,000 square foot expansion plan. Currently Botanical Gardens employees and over 250 volunteers maintain the exhibits that are annually visited by over 140,000 people.

BUFFALO & ERIE COUNTY PUBLIC LIBRARY
1 Lafayette Square, Buffalo

Figure 38 Original 1887 Library being demolished in front of New Library constructed in 1963

The Buffalo Library dates back to the forming of the Young Men's Association (YMA) in 1836. That year 400 men formed the YMA to establish a membership/subscription library, with an annual membership of $2.00.

The first library was located at 175 Main Street; it moved to South Division Street, to the American Block on Main Street, St. James Hall and Richmond Hotel. One of the main functions of the YMA was the presentation of lectures by prominent speakers.

In 1847 the YMA formed the Buffalo Historical Society, Fine Arts Academy and Society of Natural Science. These organizations were included in the Buffalo Library until they became The Buffalo History Museum, Albright Art Gallery and Buffalo Science Museum.

The YMA wanted a fireproof building so it moved into the former Court House while the new library was built in front of it. In 1887, the Buffalo Public Central Library opened, designed by Cyrus Eidlitz and selected over an H.H. Richardson submission. Charlotte Watson, widow of philanthropist S.V.R. Watson who forested establishing the library, was given the honor of turning over the first shovel of dirt at the groundbreaking.

The separate Grosvenor Library, a non-circulating reference library, was formed in 1871 with a $40,000 donation from the estate of Seth Grosvenor. It opened in a room above Buffalo Savings Bank before building a library at Franklin and Edward Streets in 1891. The Grosvenor was considered to have the most complete Music Collection, Genealogy Department and Rare Books Collection of all area libraries. In 1942 it expanded to include a reading room in the adjacent Cyclorama Building.

In 1947, the Erie County Library was formed to provide bookmobile service to the suburban towns of Erie County. In 1954 the Buffalo Library and Grosvenor Library were combined as the Buffalo and Erie County Public Library.

Construction began in 1961 on a modern marble, granite and glass library building designed by James William Kideney & Associates. When the back section was completed, books were transferred and the original 1887 library was demolished. Upon completion of the front section, the Grosvenor Library moved into the building and the $10 million New Library was dedicated on October 17, 1964.

During the 1960s and early 1970s The Buffalo and Erie County Library added 24 branches in the suburbs, expanding to 52 branches. 16 branches were closed in 2005 and they now maintain 37 locations.

Buffalo Athletic Club
69 Delaware Avenue, Buffalo

The Buffalo Athletic Club was formed by members of the Ellicott Club, a dinner club that had quarters on the tenth floor of the Ellicott Square Building. Consisting of business and professional men, they wanted to expand to include health facilities. One thousand members each pledged $1,000 toward the project.

In 1922 they decided to build a new facility that would be named the Buffalo Athletic Club (BAC). They selected land on Niagara Square, which was still predominantly residential property. This displaced mansions at 3 and 11 Niagara Square, along with homes along Eagle Street.

Figure 39 Buffalo Athletic Club - 69 Delaware Avenue photo credit Rick Falkowski

E.B. Green & Son designed a 12 story Colonial Revival style home for the club on Niagara Square. The building contained 156 sleeping rooms for bachelor members and visiting guests, a main dining room, ladies dining room, stone tiled grill and a floor of private dining rooms. Features of the club included a 75-foot-long pool (the largest in the city), a gymnasium, sun lamp room, Turkish baths, three squash courts, eight bowling lanes and a billiard room. Across Niagara Square the Buffalo Statler Hotel also opened in 1923, but construction of City Hall would not begin until 1929.

Gold Wynn Delaware BAC purchased 69 Delaware Avenue for $5 million in January 2017. Owned by brothers Jeffrey and Leslie Wynn from Toronto, they have restored the building back to its original splendor. They consulted the Buffalo History Museum to obtain information about the club and old photos of the building, to recreate the circa 1923 appearance. Being Art Deco enthusiasts, the Wynn's restored existing elements and had the lobby transformed into an art deco wonderland. Murals depict Buffalo's history, display cases are filled with BAC memorabilia, a deco concierge station was restored, staircases were highlighted and the entrance was recreated to showcase the E.B. Green & Company design. They retained the original shoeshine station and reopened a classic barbershop that offers an old fashion haircut and a hot shave.

The building has been renamed the Athletic Club Building. Remaining true to the building's heritage, L.A. Fitness continues to operate a flagship gym. Deco Lounge is open in the area that was formerly Shayleens and more recently Askers Fresh Market & Café.

The 69 Delaware Avenue location remains a prestigious Buffalo address, housing the offices of many well-respected businesses and law firms.

Buffalo Central Terminal
495 Paderewski Drive, Buffalo

Figure 40 Buffalo Central Terminal photo credit Patra Mangus

At one time downtown Buffalo was crisscrossed by fourteen railroad lines that were served by five separate terminals, causing a lot of congestion. The building of this 17-story Art Deco masterpiece consolidated all passenger traffic in a single location, a little over two miles away from the downtown business district. New York Central Terminal was built by the architectural firm of Fellhemier & Wagner, specialists in railroad architecture and responsible for many successful designs throughout North America. Construction began in 1927, with a total cost of $14 million.

It opened in 1929 to handle over 220 trains and 10,000 passengers per day, as well as 1,500 New York Central employees. It included shops, restaurants, soda fountain, Western Union telegraph office, Railway Express Agency office and an underground parking garage. Although the building had the misfortune of opening a few months before the Great Depression, it was an extremely busy place during its first decades of operation; especially during WW ll. Soldiers saying goodbye to their girlfriends would often purchase diamond engagement rings from the jewelry shop in the building, to seal their love before departing. There was also a large stuffed buffalo on display and they would pinch off a piece of fur to save in their pocket as a reminder of home. Central Terminal also played an important role during the Great Migration, when African Americans fled the oppression of the Post Civil War South, to build new lives in the North.

Eventually rail travel declined and New York Central Terminal was put up for sale, but there was no demand for such a large building. Most of the building was "mothballed" and only a smaller station remained open. In 1968 the Terminal complex was absorbed into Penn Central Railroad. Service by Penn Central continued until 1971 when Amtrak took over the operation. The final passenger train departed Central Terminal in October 1979 and Amtrak built the Buffalo-Depew station at 55 Dick Road to replace it.

The terminal remained vacant for years, often vandalized and having artifacts sold off by owners whose plans to rehabilitate the building never materialized. A citizen group trying to protect the building formalized into a not-for-profit Central Terminal Restoration Corp. (CTRC) in 1997. The building is now undergoing a multi-million-dollar renovation, and the green space now called the "great lawn' is used for community events, including music and Shakespeare in the Park.

by Patra Mangus

BUFFALO CITY HALL
65 Niagara Square, Buffalo

Buffalo's previous City Hall was in the current Erie County Hall on Delaware Avenue, built in 1876 on the country's centennial. By 1928, the city's population had quadrupled and new office space for the growing city management was needed. The site on Niagara Square in the former location of city founder Samuel Wilkeson's mansion was selected. Work began on the new City Hall in 1929 and was completed in 1931 for $6.85 million, which made it the most expensive city hall in the country at that time.

Reflecting then-current architectural trends in NYC and San Francisco, the building design by Buffalo architects Dietel, Wade & Jones is considered an Art Deco showcase and masterpiece. The Art Deco ornamentation blends with Iroquois Indian motifs throughout to honor the city's heritage of native American lands and eventual industrialization.

Figure 41 Buffalo City Hall photo credit Rick Falkowski

The building has 32 floors plus an observation deck serviced by 13 elevators, contains 1520 windows (which cleverly swing open inside to eliminate outside window washers), 43 tons of copper electrical wiring and 143 functioning clocks. The exterior is illuminated nightly by 369 floodlights, modernized in 2006 to LEDs. 26 of the floors have office space in daily use. The top floor observation deck is open to the public and offers a panoramic view of the city and the Lake Erie waterfront. The building is cooled by venting prevailing winds off the lake in a non-electrical system.

Visitors to the main floor can view six colorful, oversized murals tied to the time of the building's design and paying tribute to commerce, society, and industry. They are titled: *Frontiers Unfettered by Any Frowning Fortress, Talents Diversified Find Vent in Myriad Form, Construction, Education, Protection,* and *Charity*. The four main corridors on the ground floor each contain a statue and collectively represent Virtue, Service, Diligence, and Fidelity. There are Art Deco sculptured reliefs throughout, Art Deco friezes on the building's outside, and even the window frames, lighting fixtures, paneling and woodwork, floor tiles, and original hardware of this massive building showcase this important early 20th century design style.

Movie producers have taken to using the offices and main assembly chamber as background for period pieces, and Buffalo's City Hall has recently been showcased in Bradley Cooper's *Nightmare Alley* (2021) and Alejandro Monteverde's *Cabrini* (2024).

by Mike Buckley

BUFFALO CLUB
388 Delaware Avenue, Buffalo

Figure 42 Buffalo Club photo credit Rick Falkowski

The Buffalo Club is the only club if its kind to have had two U.S. Presidents as members, Millard Fillmore and Grover Cleveland.

The club was founded on January 2, 1867, with former President Millard Fillmore as its first president. However, William Dorsheimer chaired the committee of 93 founding members that incorporated the Buffalo Club.

Its first location was the Movius House at the northwest corner of Delaware Avenue and Cary Street. The club remained at this location for three years while the Movius family was on an extended European vacation.

In 1870 the Buffalo Club moved to the Ganson House at the northwest corner of Delaware Avenue and Chippewa St. It remained at this location for 17 years.

The Buffalo Club moved into its first permanent home and present location at 388 Delaware Avenue when it occupied the S.V.R. Watson House. This home was built in 1835 by Philander Hodge. That home was expanded by S.V.R. Watson, an investor in real estate, Manufacturers & Traders Bank, Erie Savings Bank, International Railway Company, Watson Grain Elevator; and one of the original members of the Buffalo Club. After his death in 1880, the widow of Samuel Fletcher Pratt lived in the home until the Buffalo Club took possession of the property in 1887.

After William McKinley was shot at the Pan-American Exposition on September 6, 1901, the White House Administration and Cabinet Members used the Buffalo Club as the temporary center of the U.S. government. Several Cabinet members lived at the Club, the director's room became the quasi-cabinet room, and a direct telegraph line was connected to the White House.

Club presidents have included William Fargo, James P. White, Franklin Sidway, Jewett M. Richmond, Wilson Shannan Bissell, Dexter P. Rumsey, Ansley Wilcox, John Milburn, Edmund Hayes, John G. Scatchard, Charles W. Goodyear, Frank H. Goodyear, Roswell Park, Frank B. Baird, James H. McNulty and Thomas Lockwood.

The Buffalo Club was one of the most elite private clubs of the late 19th and early 20th century. Members dined with their upper-class colleagues, lobbied for employment, made contacts for promotions, established friendships to obtain alliances and befriended influential members that could assist them in reaching the top of their profession.

The club continued to expand and remodel over the years. It remains one of the most prestigious private clubs and one of the vestiges of Old Buffalo.

BUFFALO ELECTRIC VEHICLE COMPANY
1219 Main Street, Buffalo

The Buffalo Electric Carriage Company produced the Buffalo Electric automobile from 1900 to 1906 from its factory at 226 West Utica Street. Frank Babcock was a manager of Buffalo Electric Carriage Company at its inception and in 1906 purchased the company, changing the name to Babcock Electric Carriage. In 1912 he consolidated his Babcock Electric Carriage Company with Buffalo Automobile Station Company, Van Wagoner Electric Vehicle Company and Clark Motor Company to form the Buffalo Electric Vehicle Company. A 1909 sales brochure for Babcock Electric was written and designed by the Roycroft's Elbert Hubbard.

Figure 43 Buffalo Electric Vehicle Company
photo credit Rick Falkowski

1219 Main Street was built by Alfred A. Berrick and Edward J. Meyer, with its first tenant being the Denniston Company, a manufacturer of automobile bodies. They had auto showrooms on the ground floor and manufacturing on the upper floors. When Buffalo Electric moved into the building they expanded the showrooms, manufactured pleasure automobiles on the upper floors and continued making commercial electric vehicles at their West Utica Street garage.

Electric and gasoline powered competed for market share, with gasoline cars preferred by men for their speed and portability. Women preferred electric cars because they were quieter, cleaner and easier to start, but they were heavy, slow, unable to climb hills, needed recharging after 20-50 miles and were more expensive. A 1913 two-seater Buffalo Electric was priced at $2,600 while a comparable Ford Model T sold for $525. When the electric starter was introduced in 1913 and even Thomas Edison could not produce a more powerful battery, the gasoline fueled car prevailed.

After Buffalo Electric went out of business in 1916, 1219 Main Street was occupied by Eastern Truckford Company, with manufacturing on the upper floors and showroom on the first floor. Automotive manufacturing departed the building in the 1930s and the upper floors were used by publishing, printing and book binding companies until 2002. The lower floor continued to be used as showrooms by auto dealers until the 1950s, when it afterwards housed music stores, broadcasting facilities and a vocational training center. The one-story addition was originally utilized as auto showrooms and later became a post office, social services offices and a medical clinic.

The building was owned by the Berrick family until the early 1950s. It is now managed by Belmont Housing as Artspace Buffalo Lofts, with 60 live/work apartments that provide rental preference to people involved in the arts.

BUFFALO GAS LIGHT COMPANY
249 West Genesee Street, Buffalo

Figure 44 Buffalo Gas Light Company in 1920s photo Forgotten Buffalo PD

When construction started in 1848, the Buffalo Gas Light Company's lakefront plot had access to rail and canal transportation, allowing coal to be unloaded directly at their facilities. Beginning in 1848, the company began illuminating the streets of Buffalo, replacing ineffective oil lamps.

Also known as the Illuminating Gas Company, the major investor was E.G. Spaulding and his brother-in-law Samuel F. Pratt was the first president. Construction to expand the company began in 1859 with the addition of a coal shed, several large processing buildings, two iron gasometers and a retort house with a stone façade.

John H. Selkirk, considered Buffalo's first architect, designed the Romanesque 250-foot façade of the building. Constructed of ashlar stone, it featured rounded arches, octagonal turrets and corbel tabling along the crest of the wings.

To service their customers, illuminating gas was created by coking coal in a horizontal furnace. The coal gas given off was collected in gasometers, large cylinders that stored the gas, which was piped to the streetlamps. In the 1890s the company also began producing Pintsch gas, a highly compressed, high candle power illuminating gas, that was piped through iron main lines to nearby railroad yards that used it to illuminate their passenger cars.

Three other local gas companies were organized during the 1870s and in 1899 the four firms combined to form the Buffalo Gas Company. In 1917 the company was acquired by the Iroquois Gas Corporation and began distributing natural gas. This company evolved into National Fuel Gas and the complex was used for storage and employee parking until the mid-1990s.

In 2000, despite being listed on the National Register of Historic Places, the entire complex was demolished, except for the ornate stone front. The location of the plant that utilized the 19th century coal to gas process was declared one of downtown Buffalo's largest brownfields, as the coal gasification process resulted in the land filled with petroleum-based contaminants. It cost Blue Cross/Blue Shield $10.5 million dollars to remediate the site.

Blue Cross/Blue Shield, affiliated with HealthNow, utilizing the original stone façade, built an attached six story and eight story building, connected by an atrium. The company now branded as Highmark Blue Cross Blue Shield of WNY, relocated to Seneca One Tower in 2024, it is leasing 249 West Genesee as Genesee Towers and Ingram Micro is moving over 1,000 employees from Williamsville to the building in late 2025.

BUFFALO HISTORY MUSEUM
One Museum Court, Buffalo

The only building remaining from the Pan American Exposition is the New York State Building, which was dedicated as the Buffalo Historical Society on August 6, 1901. It was designed by Buffalo architect, George Cary.

On February 22, 1836, the Young Men's Association was established in Buffalo for the improvement in literature and science of its members. Reverend William Shelton was the first president of the Association, with founders including former U.S. President Millard Fillmore, his law partner Nathan Hall, Samuel Pratt, Elbridge Spaulding, Jewett Richmond and other prominent Buffalo citizens.

Figure 45 Buffalo History Museum back entrance photo credit Rick Falkowski

The Young Men's Association gave rise to the Buffalo Historical Society, the Fine Arts Academy and the Society of Natural Sciences, now respectively the Buffalo History Museum, Albright-Knox-Gundlach (AKG) Art Museum and Buffalo Museum of Science. In 1886 the Young Men's Association became the Buffalo Library.

The Historical Society was founded by the Young Men's Association in 1862 and was originally located in the Richmond Hotel, which was destroyed by a fire in 1887. It was relocated to the Cyrus Eidlitz Library in Lafayette Square, before moving to its permanent home. From 1879 to 1947 the Society hosted lectures and published scholarly publications on the people, events and history of WNY.

The Museum's research library has over 80,000 items in the collections, including the papers of Millard Fillmore, Peter Buell Porter, Mary Burnett Talbert, the Larkin Company, the Marvis B. Pierce Seneca Indian Collection, the Pan-American Collection, Charles Rand Penney historical collections, War of 1812 maps and documents, Crystal Beach ephemera, along with 200,000 photographs, 100,000 artifacts, 20,000 books, 50,000 plans, maps, posters, pamphlets, etc., documenting the people, places, architecture, organizations, businesses and events of the Niagara Frontier region.

Displays and exhibits include, The Victorian Street of Shops, Icons: The Makers and Moments of Buffalo Sports, Neighbors: The People of Erie County, a Pioneers Gallery, Native American Gallery, re-creation of Tim Russert's Office, Buffalo Business Hall of Fame and rotating displays.

In 1960 the Buffalo Historical Society changed its name to the Buffalo and Erie County Historical Society. On the 150th anniversary of the society, in 2012, the building was renamed the Buffalo History Museum.

The Buffalo History Museum offers regular talks by authors and historians in its 200-seat auditorium and annually presents the Red Jacket Awards for achievements in Buffalo History.

BUFFALO MAIN LIGHTHOUSE
Buffalo Harbor, Buffalo

Figure 46 Steamship passing Lighthouse when entering Port of Buffalo in 1900 photo National Archives

The village of Buffalo was declared a port of entry in 1805 and the New York legislature approved a proposal to purchase land and build a lighthouse in 1811. Congress allocated funding for two lighthouses on the Great Lakes in 1817, with the Buffalo and Erie, Pennsylvania edifices opening the following year. The lighthouses were approved together but Erie claims their lighthouse opened a day before the one in Buffalo.

Oliver Forward, collector of the port of Buffalo, paid $351.50 for land near the mouth of Buffalo Creek in 1817. The sloping conical tower was built in 221 days, and a stone breakwater was erected into Lake Erie to enlarge and protect Buffalo's harbor.

When the Erie Canal opened in 1825, boat traffic into Buffalo Harbor between 1826 and 1833 quadrupled. Due to all the smoke generated in the bustling village, you could hardly see the lighthouse. The Treasury Department allocated funding to build a new pier, lighthouse and ice breaker.

The new octagonal tower was constructed of hewn limestone blocks at the end of a pier 1,000 feet east of the original lighthouse. Completed in 1833, the twenty foot diameter base tapered to a diameter of twelve feet in the lantern room. Fifteen oil lamps set in parabolic reflectors were used as the tower's light source. A new chandelier system increased the intensity of the light and in 1852 Buffalo was one of twenty lake houses to receive a third-order Fresnel lens and a fog bell. When the lens was installed in 1856 the tower's height was raised to 68 feet by the addition of a course of stone casement windows and a cylindrical metal service room between the top of the old tower and the two-story lantern room. Kerosene oil vapor lamps replaced the lard oil lamps in 1886 and in 1902 the Lighthouse Board voted to change the light from a fixed glow to white flashes, to stand out from the electrified city lights of the Buffalo skyline.

In the 1950s the Army Corps of Engineers planned to demolish the Buffalo Main Lighthouse as part of a river widening project, but it was saved by public outcry and restored in 1962. Owned by the U.S. Coast Guard but maintained by the Buffalo Lighthouse Association, a 1,400-foot walkway with historical signage leads to the historic 1833 lighthouse, Buffalo's oldest building still standing on its original foundation.

BUFFALO METER COMPANY – BETHUNE LOFTS

2917 Main Street, Buffalo

Designed by Lockwood, Green & Company, who were also the architects of the Pierce Arrow Factory on Elmwood Avenue and Larkin Exchange building on Seneca Street, the Buffalo Meter Company building is acclaimed as an intact example of a daylight factory.

George Barcley Bassett, a Plymouth, Massachusetts descendant, moved to Buffalo

Figure 47 Buffalo Meter Company 1920s PD

with his brother Edward and started Bassett Brothers, a company that developed 53 waterworks in WNY. He established Buffalo Meter Company after inventing a simpler and more practical water meter that was used by over 2,500 communities across the U.S. In addition, the company expanded to make other types of liquid meters, and the primary manufacturer of fuel-oil meters for navel and commercial ships. They provided meters for over 600 U.S. Navy vessels during WWI and WWII. During the first half of the twentieth century the company was one of the most prominent makers of liquid meters.

After starting the company in 1892 in a third-floor loft at 363 Washington Street, the company moved to 290 Terrace Street in 1903 and built their factory on a nine-acre site at 2917 Main Street. The company offices and shipping were on the first floor, the machine shop and assembly were on the second floor, another machine shop and tool room were on the third floor and their brass foundry occupied the fourth floor. When use as a multi-level manufacturing facility became outdated, Buffalo Meter Company moved out in 1969.

In 1971 the building was purchased by the University of Buffalo to house the Department of Art, the Architecture Department and a portion of the University's Continuing Education Department. It was renamed the Louise Blanchard Bethune Hall, after Louise Blanchard Bethune the first woman architect and first woman fellow of the American Institute of Architects. The building was featured as an early 1900s industrial building in the Robert Redford movie The Natural that was filmed in Buffalo in 1983.

The University vacated the building in 1994 and it was auctioned by the State of New York in 2005. Ciminelli Real Estate led a partnership that converted the building to an 87-unit complex of one- and two-bedroom apartments that retained the historic ambiance of the property. Bethune Lofts is in the process of being converted to condominiums and the building is adjacent on Main Street to Bennett High School and All High Stadium.

BUFFALO MILK COMPANY
885 Niagara Street, Buffalo

Figure 48 Buffalo Milk Company Home of the Queen City Dairy 1911 PD

Buffalo Milk Company was incorporated on July 1, 1902 as a depot for the delivery of pasteurized and refrigerated milk throughout the city. It opened in 1903 and transitioned to the name of the Queen City Dairy in 1909, distributing pasteurized milk until 1914.

The three-story Renaissance Revival style brick building with arched windows was designed by Buffalo architect Sidney Hawks Woodruff, known for his design of commercial and factory buildings, along with massive factory complexes. Other buildings he designed include Buffalo Savings Bank, Hewitt Rubber Company, E.R. Thomas Motor Company and L.M. Ericsson Telephone Manufacturing Company. Woodruff relocated to Hollywood where he was a principal developer of Hollywood Hills and one of the investors responsible for the iconic Hollywood billboard.

A U.S. Department of Agriculture commission was created by President Theodore Roosevelt under the Food & Drug Law of 1906 to examine the claims that pasteurization destroyed milk quality. The commission determined that pasteurization not only killed bacteria and prevented sickness, but it also saved lives. The Buffalo Milk Company highlighted its cleanliness, pasteurization and sanitation process as a major point in selling its product and contribution to combating infant mortality.

The Buffalo Milk Company Building was an example of an early twentieth century milk pasteurization facility and milk depot constructed within consolidated works, with the attached Neoclassical administration building shielding the manufacturing facilities. Milk was delivered to the Milk Tank Wing where it was immediately pasteurized and transferred to the two-story boiler room for heating to kill any bacteria. After processing the milk, cream, butter and cheese products were moved to the refrigeration room before being loaded on to horse carts for delivery to customers.

After customers were provided with access to pick up their milk and groceries at stores rather than being delivered, the Queen City Dairy building was converted into Maguire's Real Ice Cream. That company utilized the state-of-the-art facilities and advertised the sterilization and sanitation process adhered to in making their gourmet ice cream and deserts. Other occupants of the building included General Specialty Company, Buffalo Bon Bon Company, a printing shop, metal shop and mattress manufacturing company.

In 2018, the building at Niagara and Massachusetts, near the Peace Bridge, was converted to the Niagara Gateway Apartments by HHL Architects for the Regan Development Company.

Buffalo Seminary
205 Bidwell Parkway, Buffalo

Founded as Buffalo Female Academy in 1851 on Johnson Park, Buffalo Seminary is the first and only non-sectarian private high school for girls in Western New York. An independent day and boarding school, it is among the oldest schools for girls in the U.S.

Figure 49 Buffalo Seminary Bidwell Parkway facade Buffalo Express 1906 drawing by Architect

The original location of the school was in the former home (Evergreen Cottage) of Dr. Ebenezer Johnson, the first mayor of Buffalo. Buffalo pioneer and teacher Jabez Goodell donated land and funding to the school, resulting in the building of classroom space in Goodell Hall. Additional initial trustees included prominent buffalo businessmen Samuel F. Pratt, Aaron Rumsey, Noah H. Gardener, George W. Tifft and others.

On the 25th anniversary of the school, alumnae led by Charlotte Mulligan formed the Graduates Club and purchased a building across from the school on Johnson Park, the first clubhouse owned by women in the U.S. In 1889 the school changed its name to Buffalo Seminary and the Graduates Club purchased a new clubhouse and social center on Delaware Avenue in 1894. Named, the Twentieth Century Club, it was the first club run by women, for women, in the U.S.

In 1900 the school vacated the Johnson Park estate and instruction moved to the third floor of the Twentieth Century Club and nearby Heathcote School. A search commenced for a permanent school location and in 1906 The Graduates Club purchased property on Bidwell Parkway at Potomac Avenue. This was in a prime residential area convenient to the Elmwood Avenue streetcar line and adjacent to Buffalo's Parkways, but sufficiently far away from the noise and dust of the city. Funding was provided by the Graduates Club asking for donations from alumnae and the sale of the Evergreen Cottage and Goodell Hall on the former Johnson Park campus.

Architect George F. Newton designed a three-story T-shaped Gothic Revival and Collegiate Gothic style building for the triangular plot of land. Additions were made to the 1909 building in the late 1920s and in 1953 the Larkin House estate at 65 Lincoln Parkway was donated by Mary Frances Larkin Kellog (class of 1927) for the headmaster residence and athletic fields.

The bestselling 1999 novel City of Light was written by Lauren Belfer, a 1971 graduate of the school. This historical fiction is set in Buffalo during 1901 and features the exploits of the headmistress at a prestigious school for girls, based on Buffalo Seminary.

Buffalo State College
1300 Elmwood Avenue, Buffalo

Figure 50 Buffalo State College Original 1931 Campus buffalostate.edu

On September 13, 1871 the State Normal School and College at Buffalo opened at the corner of Jersey and 13th Street, for the purpose of training teachers for the growing Buffalo public school student population. The school was built on land purchased from the estate of Jesse Ketchum and the first class consisted of 86 students (75 women and 11 men), with 15 faculty members.

By 1901 enrollment increased to 828 students and in 1914 a new Colonial Revival/Georgian Revival building replaced the original school. Dr. Harry W. Rockwell became principal of the State Normal School in 1919 and Catherine Reed was named dean of women in 1926, a position she held until 1954.

The school was renamed New York State College for Teachers at Buffalo in 1928 and it was again determined that the enrollment was too high for the building. The state and city initiated a land swap. New York State gave Buffalo the Normal School building in exchange for 20 acres and $1.5 million to build a campus on Elmwood Avenue, north of Buffalo State Psychiatric Hospital.

In 1931 the former State Normal School became Grover Cleveland High School and the new Buffalo State Teachers College opened in a new five building campus. The flagship building was Rockwell Hall, named after Harry W, Rockwell, president of the college from 1919 to 1951. Rockwell Hall (patterned after Philadelphia's Independence Hall) was originally called the Main Building, containing the college library, cafeteria, administrative offices, faculty offices and auditorium. The other original buildings were Ketchum Hall (vocational building), Bacon Hall (School of Practice), Donald Savage Building (Gymnasium) and Campus House (residence of President Rockwell). The cornerstone was laid by Edward Butler, Jr., using the same trowel his father used when laying the 1914 State Normal School cornerstone.

The college became part of the State University of New York (SUNY) when it was created in 1948 and that year the first dorm Pioneer Hall opened. The Butler Library opened in 1950, the school was designated a liberal arts college in 1960, the Charles Burchfield Center opened in Rockwell Hall in 1966, WBNY radio station began broadcasting in 1982, the Performing Arts Center opened in Rockwell Hall in 1987, the Burchfield Penney Art Center opened in its new $33 million building in 2008 and the school was designated a university in 2023.

Buffalo Veterans' Administration Hospital
3495 Bailey Avenue, Buffalo

The Veterans Hospital in Buffalo provides health care for military veterans, trains future health care providers and conducts important medical research.

Built in 1949, the 1.1 million square foot 14-story building is a limestone panel structure with aluminum framed windows. It was built across

Figure 51 Buffalo VA Hospital old postcard PD

from the University of Buffalo at the intersection of Bailey Avenue, Winspear and Lebrun Road. Land for the building was purchased from the city of Buffalo, who sold the VA a portion of Grover Cleveland Golf Course in the late 1940s, resulting in the reduction of the grounds at the public golf course and the redesign of the course to 5,600 yards.

The VA Hospital provides primary and specialty healthcare for veterans, offering medical, surgical, mental health and long-term care through a range of inpatient and outpatient programs. It is the main referral center for cardiac surgery, cardiology and comprehensive cancer care for veterans in Central and Western New York and Northern Pennsylvania.

For medical training the VA Hospital is affiliated with SUNY Buffalo Medical School and 77 other university and professional schools. Students, interns, residents and fellows receive training in audiology, dentistry, dietetics, health care administration, medicine, nursing, nurse anesthesia, occupational and physical therapy, pharmacy and psychology.

Regarding the hospital's function as a medical research facility, its long history includes the efforts of Dr. William Chardack, Dr. Andrew Gage and engineer Wilson Greatbatch in developing the implantable cardiac pacemaker. The facility features a 40,000 square foot research building.

In March 2024 it was announced by the VA that a new $1 billion hospital will eventually be built near the downtown Buffalo Niagara Medical Campus. These changes will not take place immediately and current upgrades to the present facility are necessary. The operating rooms are undersized; hallways are narrow and the building lacks central air conditioning. It has been determined that $260.9 million in repairs are required. In addition, it costs $14 million annually for operations and maintenance of the existing building.

While awaiting the new building, over $64 million of projects are taking place at the current hospital. Until the funds are allocated and a place for the new building is determined, the 2,000 patients a day that visit the hospital and 2,250 employees will continue working at the Bailey Avenue facility.

Buffalo Water Intake
Buffalo Harbor, Buffalo

Figure 52 Colonel Ward Pumping Station vintage postcard PD

Off the Lake Erie shore in Buffalo Harbor there is a red roofed round brick building. It looks small, but it is three stories high. Many have speculated about the utility of the building. It is in fact very important as this building is the water intake for supplying water to the city of Buffalo.

In the 19th century, raw sewage went directly into the Buffalo River, which was released into Lake Erie and the Niagara River. Outbreaks of Cholera were traced to water contaminated with human waste, so a water intake was constructed in the Niagara River near the current location of the Peace Bridge. That intake is what appears to be an old barge stuck in the water. However, Buffalo Health Commissioner Dr. Ernest Wende discovered that intake was responsible for spreading typhoid.

Buffalo Commissioner of Public Works Colonel Francis G. Ward concluded clean water could be obtained in the Emerald Channel, a section of Lake Erie just upstream from the Niagara River. There the water has sparkling clarity that on still days shines a distinctive green.

In 1907 construction began on the water intake building, which included a mile long tunnel burrowed under the lakebed to the Colonel Ward Pumping Station. Eight workers were killed during construction due to a collapse of the tunnel near the pumping station. Construction was completed in 1913 and until 1924 two employees were required to work there 24 hours a day, before the chlorinator was automated.

125 million gallons a day rushes into the water intake and falls 60 feet to the 12-foot diameter mile long tunnel. Clorine is added in the conduit to control invasive zebra and quagga mussels. A screen house at the Colonel Ward Pumping Station removes sticks and other larger debris. Poly aluminum chloride (PACl) is added as a coagulant to cause debris in the water to bind together as floc. After flocculation and sedimentation, filtration and additional chlorination provides clean water to be pumped to city residents.

Figure 53 Water Intake PD

The water intake sources for Erie County are the Sturgeon Point Treatment Plant for Southern Erie County and Van de Water Treatment Plant on the Niagara River in the Town of Tonawanda for Northern Erie County.

BUFFALO ZOOLOGICAL GARDENS
300 Parkside Avenue, Buffalo

In 1870, Buffalo furrier Jacob Bergtold donated a pair of deer to the city and they were kept in an enclosure in the meadow area of Frederick Law Olmsted's Delaware Park. Five years later, the Buffalo Zoo was established in that area.

Figure 54 Buffalo Zoo photo credit Marsha Falkowski

A building was erected in 1875 and over the next fifteen years animal donations to the zoo included a pair of Buffalo, eight elk and a herd of sheep. The sheep assisted park staff by keeping the grass low in the meadow. In the 1890s the animals' building was expanded, and the bear pits were dug. With these additions, many animals were donated and people began visiting the grounds. Frank J. Thompson was appointed the first curator in 1895.

In 1900 Frank Goodyear offered the city one million dollars to build a new zoo closer to the Art Gallery, near the current location of Shakespeare in the Park. The city refused the offer but accepted Goodyear's donation of an elephant called Little Frank. He grew into Big Frank and an elephant house opened in 1912.

The Zoological Society was incorporated in 1931 and Marlin Perkins was hired as curator in 1938. That year the Works Progress Administration began a modernization project at The Zoo, upgrading many buildings and building a new Main Animal Building. Perkins' animal collection was considered one of the finest in the country. The Reptile House opened in 1941.

In the 1950s the city of Buffalo added a train ride and opened concession stands to produce revenue. The zoo closed for five months in October 1958 for repairs and renovations. A children's zoo was added. The Giraffe House and Animal Hospital opened in 1967.

In 1973 the operation of the zoo was transferred to the Zoological Society and funding was finally provided by both the city of Buffalo and Erie County. An admission charge was implemented to generate revenue for repairs.

Expansion of the Buffalo Zoo included the Gorilla Habitat 1981, Children's Resource Center 1984, Lion & Tiger Habitat 1988, Parkside Entrance 1992, Rainforest Falls 2008, Heritage Farms 2010, Artic Edge 2015 and New Reptile House 2019, named after Donna Fernandes President of the Zoo 2000-2017.

The Zoo now features special exhibits like Zoomagination. It is the second largest tourist destination in WNY and is the third oldest zoo in the U.S.

C.W. Miller Livery Stable
73 West Huron Street, Buffalo

Figure 55 CW Miller Livery Stable before/after photos credit photo restoration by Gene Thompson

Charles Wright Miller's father Jacob S. Miller established the second transit line in Buffalo in 1847, with an omnibus line of four vehicles that ran from the Central Warf to Cold Springs. Jacob died in 1855 and at age 18 Charles took over the business. When he sold it in 1860 to the first streetcar company, he was hired as a manager at a salary of $50.00 a month.

In 1864 Miller purchased a livery stable and with seven horses and buggies created a coach and baggage express to service passengers that arrived in town. Miller then created the first service in the U.S. where a traveler could be picked up at their home or hotel, transported to the train station and have their baggage processed to their destination.

He then organized the livery service for the Niagara Falls hospitality business, started a moving van service, created hearse transportation for funeral directors and built an elegant carriage service so the residents of the Delaware Avenue mansions did not have to retain a horse and driver in their own carriage house. To service clients, in 1879 Miller's Livery was the first business in Buffalo to have a telephone.

In 1892 Miller purchased property at 73 West Huron St. and Buffalo architect Williams Lansing designed what was called "A Palace for Horses" and claimed it to be the finest stable in the U.S.

The six story Romanesque Revival styled brick structure had a Medina limestone façade, pilasters and round arches. A blacksmith shop and horse shoeing shops were in the basement, along with a modern power plant of steam boilers, engines, pumps and electrical generators. A hydraulic system powered three elevators: heavy duty, freight and passenger. The first-floor housed offices and drivers' quarters. On the second and third floors were 300 stalls, with long ramps allowing the horses to walk up to their quarters. The wooden floors were suspended from steel trusses in the attic. A 10,000-gallon water tank on the roof supplied water for washing and watering the horses.

When automobiles replaced horses, in the 1920s the business was converted to a parking garage, the Huron Street Garage and later the Hertz Garage. It was later an auto storage facility but became vacant in 2000. The building was leased to the Buffalo School System and in 2020 opened as the Buffalo School of Culinary Arts & Hospitality Management.

CALUMET BUILDING
46-58 West Chippewa Street, Buffalo

The Calumet Building was built for Robert Keating Root in 1906 at West Chippewa and Franklin Streets, signifying the shift of Chippewa from a residential to commercial district. It was designed by architects Esenwein & Johnson in the Art Nouveau style, known for its ornate decoration using depictions of nature, typically leaves and flowers. The word 'Calumet' is an American-French word meaning 'highly ornamented ceremonial pipe of the American Indians'.

Figure 56 Calumet Building
photo credit Ellen Mika Zelasko

Space was leased to various businesses throughout the years, including The Kay-Bee Adsign Company which was a front for the Klu Klux Klan (KKK). The Klan arrived in 1921 and openly advocated for white supremacy and actively discriminated (often violently) against African Americans, Jews, Catholics and immigrants in general.

Despite opposition from prominent African Americans, the Catholic Diocese, leading rabbis, and the Buffalo press, the Klan boasted 800 members at their first public meeting in October of 1922 and grew to near 4000! While operating out of the Calumet Building, the KKK was infiltrated by Buffalo police detective Edward Obertean, who reported directly to Buffalo Mayor Schwab. In July 1924, the offices of the Klan were ransacked and burglarized, their membership list was obtained and recovered by Buffalo Police who publicly displayed it at their headquarters.

Buffalonians flocked to see who among them were Klan members. After death threats to Mayor Schwab and his family members, plus the fatal shooting of Detective Obertean, the KKK was run out of town by 1925.

During the 1960s Chippewa become a red-light district where prostitution, topless bars and drug use were the norm. The Calumet building was empty for several years. In 1988, author and Buffalo historian Mark Goldman purchased the building and opened The Calumet Arts Cafe showcasing live jazz music and a restaurant, along with The Third Room and La Luna Latin dance club, featuring different entertainment styles. Actor/writer/musician Joey Giambra and The Irish Classical Theater even presented plays at the Calumet. Other investors followed suit. Chippewa became a popular entertainment district, with Goldman's lead sparking this revitalization.

In 2009 the Calumet Building was purchased by a partnership of attorneys Kenney Shelton Liptak Nowak LLP and Angelo Natale of Natale Builders. An elevator and ramp were built at the 233 Franklins Street entrance to the building, making the upper floors handicapped accessible, for the 75-employee law firm on the upper floors. Baccus Wine Bar is currently fronting the Chippewa entrance.

by Ellen Mika Zelasko

Campanile Apartments
925 Delaware Avenue, Buffalo

Figure 57 Campanile Apartments photo credit Ellen Mika Zelasko

The Campanile Apartments were built in 1929. The building was one of three luxury apartments built in Buffalo just before the Depression, the other two were The Park Lane and 800 West Ferry. The West Ferry apartments were built by Darwin R. Martin, son of Darwin D. Martin, an executive with the Larkin Soap Company.

The Campanile Apartments were designed by architect B. Frank Kelly, a Canadian architect who came to Buffalo in 1921 and set up his firm in the Ellicott Square Building. Their location of the Campanile at the northeast corner of Delaware Avenue and Bryant Street afforded occupants an address on Delaware Avenue, much sought after by the movers and shakers in Buffalo and is within walking distance to the mansions on "Millionaire's Row".

There was a trend in Buffalo around this time for children of some of those millionaires to rebel against their parents' traditional way of living. Most of the millionaires were self-made men. They worked hard and were well established by the time they built homes along Delaware Avenue. But many of their children grew up with money, and some were not used to working like their fathers. They preferred apartment living, without all the responsibility that came with the massive estates of their parents.

The Campanile fit the bill. It is a massive, C-shaped, Italian Renaissance Revival style building with a courtyard in the rear. Built with red brick, terra cotta and limestone, it could be described as exquisite. The red tiled roofs are striking. Although it appears there might be a hundred apartments inside, there are just 38 extremely large apartments. The average size is 2000 square feet. Many of them cover two floors. Some have terraces. Two of them span from one side of the building to the other, including two 'towers' in one apartment. One has 3 floors, with 8 bedrooms and 8 ½ baths.

The building is and always was a co-op, which is unusual in Buffalo. This means the residents own shares in the building. The number of shares depends on the size of the apartment owned. The owners employ a full-time staff for the building, including maintenance, doormen, concierge, laundry service, etc. The staff physically open doors for residents and visitors.

The Campanile is an elegant, very private place to live and is certainly like no other in Buffalo.

by Ellen Mika Zelasko

CANALSIDE
44 Prime Street, Buffalo

Canalside, previously known as the Erie Canal Harbor, was built in 1825 as the terminus of the Erie Canal. At that time, Buffalo was a bustling village, located near a Seneca Indian village on Buffalo Creek (now Buffalo River). When the Erie Canal was being built, Buffalo lobbied for and won the rights to the Canal western terminus.

Figure 58 Canalside Boardwalk with Naval Park and Apartments
photo credit Ellen Mika Zelasko

The opening of the Erie Canal catapulted Buffalo into a fast-growing metropolis. The canal served as a much easier way to move goods and people from east to west and west to east. This opened trade routes and put Buffalo on the map as a major port town. People travelled on specially made canal boats, giving them a much quicker and easier way to head west. Seeing opportunities here, some of those people stayed to chase their dreams. There were fortunes to be made. Others continued through the Great Lakes to points further west. Buffalo thrived.

As might be expected, the harbor developed into a crime ridden area. Freighter crewmen were paid when they reached Buffalo, and they spent their money freely in bars, brothels and third-rate music halls that sprang up in the district, which Buffalonians gladly provided. At one time, Buffalo's Erie Canal Harbor was viewed as one of the most dangerous places in the country.

Despite this, business along the waterfront thrived. Shipping became a main industry. Railroads, automobiles and aeronautics followed, along with all the small, locally owned businesses that supported these giants.

After the turn of the 20th century, the neighborhood changed somewhat. Gone were most of the bars and brothels. Neighborhoods sprang up with the building of tenement housing.

With the opening of the St. Lawrence Seaway in 1959, Buffalo was no longer as needed as a port. The ships travelled through the Seaway to the Great Lakes and beyond. Buffalo fell on hard times. Commercial slips were filled in, no longer necessary. Businesses closed and moved out of the city. The waterfront suffered.

In the 1990s, the city began to explore developing the harbor into a historical 'canal side' attraction. By 2005, funding was secured, and work began. It opened to the public in 2008. Development has continued since, adding attractions, always including Buffalo history, while simultaneously looking forward to Buffalo's future. The 'Erie Canal Harbor' is once again a bustling, relevant area of the city.

by Ellen Mika Zelasko

CANISIUS COLLEGE
2001 Main Street, Buffalo

Figure 59 Old Main at Canisius College photo camisius.edu

St. Michaels Church was formed in 1851 when the Alsatians separated from St. Louis Church. Bishop Timon donated the Squire Estates on Washington Street to the congregation led by Jesuit priest Rev. Lucas Caveng. The parish dedicated a new church in 1868 and German Jesuits arrived to minister at the parish.

At the request of Bishop Timon, in 1870 Canisius College was founded by a group of German Jesuits at 222 and 434 Ellicott Street. Canisius is named for St. Peter Canisius, a renowned Dutch educator and one of the original members of the Society of Jesus. Timon wanted a school for the German immigrants in this area of Buffalo.

The Jesuits had close ties to St. Michaels Church at 651 Washington Street and after two years they moved to a building adjacent to the church. Their curriculum was the Germanic Progynasium, a six-year course of study that made students eligible for admission to professional schools of law, medicine and divinity. Courses were to be taught in Latin but most of the students had little background in Latin. The faculty spoke German and the students spoke English, learned on the streets and at Catholic elementary schools.

In 1897 the school was authorized to award a Regents Diploma for the first four years of study and it was decided to separate Canisius High School from Canisius College. Both schools were occupying the four-story building next to the church. A retreat site at Main Street and Jefferson Avenue, purchased from the Sisters of St. Joseph in 1874, was selected as the new college location. A building committee was formed and raised over $100,000 in 32 days to fund the building of the Old Main, which opened for classes in January 1913 and still serves the campus. The second building completed was the Hornan-O'Donnell Science Building in 1937.

Later buildings included Christ the King Chapel, designed by Duane Lyman and opened in 1951. The former Sears Roebuck store at Main and Jefferson became the Science Hall, the 11 story Churchill Academic Tower designed by Leroy H. Welch opened in 1971, Montante Cultural Center opened in the former 1926 St. Vincent de Paul Church and the Koessler Athletic Center opened in 1968 at 1839 Main Street.

Designated Canisius University in 2023, it now offers bachelor's degrees in over 100 majors, minors or special programs and master's degrees in 35 master's and certificate programs.

Canisius High School - Rand Mansion
1180 Delaware Ave, Buffalo

The Rand home was built between 1918 and 1923, for George Rand, Sr. The architects were Franklyn J. and William A. Kidd, who also designed the Rand Building downtown. It was designed in both the Tudor Revival and Jacobean Revival styles.

George F. Rand, Sr., was born in North Tonawanda in 1867, and began his banking career when he was 16. He married at 21 to Vina S. Fisher. They had four children, Evelyn, George Jr., Gretchen and Calvin.

Figure 60 Canisius High School Rand Mansion photo credit Ellen Mika Zelasko

When he was 21, George Sr. was elected president of the First National Bank of Tonawanda. Rand moved to Buffalo in 1901 when he became the president of Columbia National Bank of Buffalo. He was made president of the Marine National Bank of Buffalo only a few years later. Rand is largely credited with giving New York State its first consolidated banking system by merging several banking institutions into the Marine Trust Company, which eventually became the Marine Midland Corporation.

Sadly George Rand, Sr. passed away in a plane crash in 1919, before the home was completed. His wife, Vina had passed earlier that year. George Jr. Finished the home and in 1921 moved in with his siblings.

In 1925 the house was sold to the Freemasons, who converted it into the Buffalo Consistory. They added a Neoclassical style auditorium, with ten columns supporting the elaborate ceiling molding. The balcony was the largest continuous, free-standing balcony in America. In front of the stage, there is a mural of the earth surrounded by Tiffany-stained glass representing the sun and its' rays. Beyond that is another painting depicting stars and the Milky Way. The effect is stunning.

After the Depression, the Masons were unable to pay their taxes, and the city took possession of the property. It was used for various purposes until 1944 when Canisius High School, an independent college prep school established in 1870 by the Jesuit order, purchased it. It has been home to Canisius High ever since.

In 1976, Gregg Allman, who was living in Buffalo for a short time rehabbing a drug addiction, performed a secret, daytime, acoustic concert in the auditorium for the student body. One of the students had written to Gregg asking him to come play at the school. Admiring the students' moxy, Greg obliged. His wife Cher was in attendance at the concert.

by Ellen Mika Zelasko

Coit House
412 Virginia Street, Buffalo

Figure 61 Coit House photo credit Ellen Mika Zelasko

The Coit House is the oldest residential home in the city of Buffalo. It originally stood at the southeast corner of Swan and Pearl Streets. Built in 1815, after all but one of Buffalo's homes was burned in the War of 1812, it's a great example of Buffalo's 'pioneer-era' residences, and was typical of the homes built by wealthier Buffalonians at the time. It is of the Federal style and boasts all hand-hewn woodwork.

George Coit, the original owner, expanded the house at least twice, adding a third floor, and extending the home lengthwise. Remarkably, the home remains largely intact as he left it.

George Coit is originally from Norwich, Connecticut. He and his lifelong associate Charles Townsend came to Buffalo in 1811, where they immediately rose to the forefront of the community, largely because they arrived with 20 tons of provisions. In 1812 they bought a piece of property on Swan Street, between Main and Pearl Streets. They opened a drug store in an existing building on the site. It would be the first of many joint business ventures the two undertook. They lost the store when the village was burned during the War of 1812. Luckily, they had managed to escape with some of their goods the day before the fire and returned to rebuild.

George Coit and Charles Townsend worked with Oliver Forward and Samuel Wilkeson to build the Buffalo Harbor, eventually winning the battle for the terminus of the Erie Canal for Buffalo. This resulted in increased shipping, in which Coit and Townsend immediately invested. Shipping helped establish the grain processing, lumber and iron industries. With the subsequent addition of railroad transportation, facilitating industry expanding into motor vehicle, aerospace and all the smaller supporting businesses, Buffalo was catapulted to one of the largest and most prosperous cities in the country. Without Coit's pioneering efforts at Buffalo Harbor, none of that would have happened.

When Buffalo's industrial core moved from the canal to Swan Street, most prominent families gravitated north of the city center. George Coit stayed at the corner of Swan and Pearl Streets in, when considering his wealth, was a somewhat humble home. He passed away in 1865 and is buried in Forest Lawn Cemetery.

In 1867 the home was moved to its present resting place on Virginia Street. It is now the home of Fika Midwifery at The Coit House Birth Center.

by Ellen Mika Zelasko

COLORED MUSICIANS CLUB
145 Broadway, Buffalo

In the early 1900s, musicians were required to be a member of the musician's union to perform at theaters, nightclubs and hotels in downtown Buffalo. However, there was a problem. Black musicians were not allowed to join the white musician's union.

In 1917, Local #533 of the American Federation of Musicians was formed for black musicians. The Buffalo local was the eighth Black Musicians Union formed in the U.S. One of the organizers was Raymond Jackson, who rose to a national position with the union and assisted in organizing Black Musicians Unions across the country.

Figure 62 Colored Musicians Club construction in progress photo credit Rick Falkowski

There were stringent qualifications to become a new member of the union. Prospective members had to audition before a panel of musicians, sight read music and transpose songs to other keys. If you could not read music, you could not become a member. The Buffalo union had the reputation of high-quality musicianship. Members were recruited to join national touring bands.

The Black Musicians Union offices were on the first floor of 145 Broadway at the corner of Michigan Avenue. After performing at downtown establishments, musicians would gather at the second-floor clubhouse to pay their union dues, unwind, discuss performances, have something to eat and engage in jam sessions that lasted into the night. Crowds packed the club for the jam sessions and friendships were formed between national stars and local musicians.

When Local #533 merged with the Local #43, the White Musicians Union, to form Local #92 in 1969 the white union thought they would move their offices to 145 Broadway. However, the building was owned by the Colored Musicians Club, not Local #533. It continued as a private club for musicians that were interested in jazz. Black and white musicians interacted based upon their love of music and it was one of the first integrated clubs in WNY.

The Colored Musicians Club is the longest continuously operating African American Musicians club in the U.S. The first floor was converted into a museum in 2018, with displays and exhibits preserving the history of jazz in Buffalo. The second floor continues to host big band rehearsals, and the club hosts the Queen City Jazz Festival every summer.

The club is part of the Michigan Street African American Heritage Corridor, has received funding to renovate/expand the building and continues its mission of promoting the history of jazz in Buffalo.

CONNECTICUT STREET ARMORY
184 Connecticut Street, Buffalo

Figure 63 Connecticut Street Armory shortly after construction PD

Built for the 74th Regiment in 1899, the Connecticut Street Armory was the largest armory in the U.S. when it was constructed.

The 74th Regiment of the National Guard was formed in 1854 and initially shared its headquarters with the older 65th Regiment at the Broadway Arsenal, 201 Broadway. In 1868 it moved into an armory at Virginia and Elmwood Avenue. That burned down in 1884 and was replaced by a new Virginia Street Armory designed by Louise Blanchard Bethune (later remodeled into the Elmwood Music Hall). By 1894 the 74th expanded to over 500 officers and men, requiring a larger drill hall.

In 1894 the Old Prospect Hill Reservoir, which at that time was the primary source for drinking water in Buffalo, moved to Jefferson Avenue between Best and Dodge Streets, later the location of War Memorial Stadium. The 74th Regiment acquired rights to the former reservoir at Niagara and Connecticut Streets. Its property extended along Niagara to Vermont Street, where a skirmish was fought against the invading British during the War of 1812.

The castle like armory was designed by Isaac G. Perry and Captain Williams Lansing. Lansing was also the commanding officer of Company F, 74th Regiment New York National Guard and was appointed Superintendent of Construction by the State Armory Board. After Buffalo State Hospital, the Armory is the most expressive use of native Medina sandstone of any building in Buffalo. A Richardsonian Romanesque style structure, it incorporates towers, turrets, crenelated roof lines, tall slit windows and other fortress features. It is entered through a recessed Syrian archway formed by large wedge-shaped stones called voussoirs. The interior possesses carved oak staircases, newels, doors, crown molding, fireplaces and wainscoting.

It opened during the Spanish American War and also hosted the Third Sangerfest held in conjunction with the Pan American Exposition in 1901. The festival featured 105 choirs, from 40 societies with 2,000 singers, before an audience of 10,000 people. In addition, the 74th Regimental Band was one of Buffalo's most prolific brass bands, with performances ranging from President Lincoln's funeral procession in 1865 to concerts at Crystal Beach in the early 1900s.

The back portion of the armory was destroyed by a fire and rebuilt in 1982. It is still utilized by the National Guard, remains the second largest armory in New York State and one of the largest in the country.

CORNELL MANSION
484 Delaware Avenue, Buffalo

Samuel G. Cornell moved to Buffalo in 1852 and established his Cornell White Lead Company in the current location of the Midway Rowhouses, on Delaware Avenue between Virginia and Allen Steets. His son S. Douglas Cornell built a home across the street from the complex in 1894.

This home was designed by architect Edward Austin Kent, designer of many Buffalo buildings including the Unitarian Church on Elmwood. Kent was the only Buffalo resident to die on the Titanic. The mansion is a four-story French Renaissance Revival style, built of light-colored limestone, with a tower, circular porch with gothic pillars, large bay window and an interior of cherry woodwork.

Figure 64 Cornell Mansion photo credit Rick Falkowski

In addition to being an executive in the Cornell Lead Company, S. Douglas Cornell was a Colonel in the National Guard, a successful Colorado gold miner and an 1860 graduate of Hobart College, where he excelled in oratory and dramatics. Cornell had Kent design a fully equipped theater in the attic, on the fourth floor of the mansion, complete with a stage, foot-curtain, scenery and seating. The Buffalo Amateurs, who included members of prominent families living on Delaware Avenues Millionaires Row, produced four plays a year in this home theater.

The Cornell family's love of theater resulted in S. Douglas Cornell's son, Dr. Peter C. Cornell, leaving the medical profession to manage the Star Theater and Tech Theater where he developed a relationship as an investor in the business of his assistant John Oishei, founder of Trico. Granddaughter Katherine Cornell was too young to participate in the plays but was influenced by her experience watching the productions and as an actress became known as the First Lady of American theater.

After the death of his wife in the early 1900s, Cornell rented 484 Delaware to Frances Bass Wolcott, who entertained celebrities and royalty at the mansion, later writing the novel Heritage of Years chronologizing the society of her youth. It was then purchased by Albert Jay Wright, considered the dean of Buffalo stockbrokers and the only Buffalo member of the New York Stock Exchange.

The mansion was converted into a rooming house in the 1930s, a nightclub during the 1940s, Green Door Antique Shop in the 1950s, Zeigler Medical Supplies in the 1960s and 70s and a photography studio in the 1980s.

Attorney Thomas J. Eoannou purchased the property in 1994, extensively restoring it into offices.

CURTISS AIRCRAFT – CONSOLIDATED, BELL, M WILE
2050 Elmwood Avenue, Buffalo

Figure 65 Consolidated Aircraft 2050 Elmwood Avenue 9/9/1927 PD

Curtiss Aircraft began building airplanes in Buffalo at the former Thomas Automobile Manufacturing Company at 1200 Niagara Street in 1915. Demand for their Curtiss JN-4 during WWI resulted in a move to a new plant on Churchill Street which was quickly outgrown, necessitating the building of a new factory at 2050 Elmwood Avenue in 1917.

When this 31-acre facility was built it was the largest airplane manufacturing plant in the world. Curtiss built over 10,000 aircraft at the factory during WWI, an average of 100 planes a day. In addition to the Jennies, other airplanes built at the factory included the NC-4 Flying Boat (the first aircraft to cross the Atlantic Ocean), Eagle Transport (the first tri-engine commercial passenger aircraft) and the A-1 Triad (a hydroaeroplane converted to the first plane to launch from an aircraft carrier).

In 1924 Consolidated Aircraft moved into the plant and manufactured the Catalina PBY and the Commodore, the largest seaplane at that time. Larry Bell moved to Buffalo in 1928 to work for Major Ruben H. Fleet, becoming president of the Consolidated Canadian subsidiary Fleet Aircraft in Fort Erie and general manager of the Consolidated Aircraft operation in Buffalo.

When Consolidated decided to relocate to San Diego in 1935, Larry Bell and other former Consolidated employees formed Bell Aircraft and moved into the 2050 Elmwood Avenue facility. Bell Aircraft began by making wings for the Consolidated flying boats, and as a subcontractor for other Consolidated products. The company developed the YFM-1 Aircuda at the Elmwood Avenue plant and received a large contract for the P-39 Airacobra. They exceeded the space available at 2025 Elmwood and built their new factory on Niagara Falls Boulevard next to the Niagara Falls Airport, continuing manufacturing through WWII at both plants.

After Bell Aircraft vacated the factory, it became the home of M. Wile Clothing Company Warehouse and Outlet. The Terminal Warehouse Corporation leased portions of the property to various businesses. Over the years the building housed sports facilities, restaurants, stores and the Super Saver Cinema 8.

The property is now owned by Benchmark Development, and there is a Home Depot and other businesses on the site of the Curtiss Factory. The remainder of the historic aircraft plant was considered a safety hazard and demolished in 2018.

CURTISS BUILDING – CURTISS HOTEL
210 Franklin Street, Buffalo

Built in 1912 and 1913, the Harlow C. Curtiss Building is a six-story glazed terra cotta steel framed Chicago style commercial and office building at the corner of Franklin and Huron Streets. The former C.W. Millery Livery Stable is adjacent to the building on Huron Street, while the Continental Restaurant/Nightclub was next to it on Franklin Street.

The building was financed by attorney Harlow C. Curtis, who graduated from Central High School in Buffalo and Trinity College in Hartford, Connecticut. After receiving his bachelor's degree in 1881 he read law with Cleveland & Bissell, where Grover Cleveland was the senior partner. In 1884 he opened his own office and practiced law for over 40 years, along with owning apartment buildings on Delaware Avenue, North Street and Allen Street. He married Ethel Mann in 1896, the daughter of Dr. Matthew Mann, the attending physician to President McKinley after he was shot at the Pan-American Exposition. Curtiss owned homes at 479 Delaware, 864 Delaware and 100 Lincoln Parkway.

Figure 66 Curtiss Hotel photo credit Rick Falkowski

Architect Paul Mann, Curtiss' brother-in-law, designed the Curtiss Building which was built by Theodor and Karl Metz of Buffalo's Metz Brothers Construction Company. Among the first tenants were Kittinger Furniture (nationally known handcrafted furniture manufacturers), lawyers, stationers and paramedical companies. In 1920 the building was sold to William Morgan; it became known as the Eisele Building in 1921, after it was purchased by the jewelry company King & Eisele. The building was purchased by the Hoelscher Building Company in 1945, with Hoelscher's selling office equipment at the building until the early 1990s.

In 2002 the property was purchased by Mark Croce, with the intent of building a destination 5-star hotel. Each of the 68 rooms had a budget of over $285,000 per room, to provide the best room amenities in the WNY market. The two high speed elevators (almost double normal speed) cost about $650,000. The 200+ seat Chez Ami Supper Club, named after the historic Delaware Avenue restaurant, features a revolving bar that completes two revolutions per hour. An indoor/outdoor "urban hot spring" is open year-round with 102-degree water. A rooftop level patio lounge cost over $1 million and features views of the urban skyline from weather protected enclosures.

Opening in 2017, the Curtiss Hotel is operated by Mark Croce's widow, Jessica Croce, and continues to offer a luxury hotel and dining experience in downtown Buffalo.

Cyclorama Building – Grosvenor Library
369 Franklin Street, Buffalo

Figure 67 Cyclorama Building in 1890 photo Library of Congress

The Cyclorama Building was designed by architects Cyrus K. Porter & Sons in 1888. A two story, 26,000 square foot, sixteen-sided brick structure, it is only one of four existing historical cyclorama buildings in the U.S. and 30 in the world.

During the 1880s, prior to the invention of motion pictures, the cyclorama provided the opportunity to visualize historic places or events and get the experience of actually being there. The Buffalo Cyclorama Company commissioned a French painter to make a 400 foot long and 50-foot-wide canvas of Niagara Falls. The painting was sent to Paris and London to promote the grandeur of the falls to Europeans. It was such a success that the company decided to build a cyclorama building in Buffalo and bring this style of exhibit to American soil.

The building in Buffalo was hastily constructed in three months and opened on September 6, 1888. It had no windows or interior walls, with only skylights and lanterns used to illuminate the panoramic painting. A guide described the painting as patrons circled around the building, giving them the sensation of actually being inside the artwork. An open stairway stood in the center of the building to observe the painting at other levels, providing the impression of being in the center of the action.

Premiering in 1888, View of Jerusalem on the Day of the Crucifixion of Christ drew over a thousand visitors a day for two years to the presentation. That was followed by another successful two-year display of The Battle of Gettysburg. Cycloramas soon lost their popularity and in 1907 the building was acquired by the city of Buffalo and used as a roller rink, livery and taxi garage.

The building fell into disrepair and was condemned in 1937. It was taken over by the Depression Era Public Works Administration. Large windows were added to the exterior and a second floor was constructed inside. On February 15, 1942 the adjacent Grosvenor Library opened the Cyclorama Building as a reading room and lecture hall for the research library. When the Grosvenor merged with other Buffalo libraries, the Cyclorama closed in 1963 and remained vacant for 25 years.

In 1985 Frank Ciminelli Construction purchased the building for $110,000 and after two years of preserving and refurbishing the building, opened it as an office complex. In 2012 Lumsden McCormick moved into and continues to occupy the building.

D'Youville College
320 Porter Avenue, Buffalo

In 1851 Bishop Timon invited the Oblates of Mary Immaculate to help meet the needs of Buffalo's Catholic population. They opened Holy Angels Church and shortly afterwards, the Oblates invited the Grey Nuns of the Cross from Ottawa to serve alongside them in Buffalo.

The Grey Nuns founded Holy Angels School in 1857, and incorporated the institution with the Secretary of State in 1865 under the name The Holy Angels Infirmary Academy and Industrial School for Benevolent Charitable and Scientific Purposes. The first official school building was the Koessler Administration Building which opened in 1872. That building was expanded three times, adding the east and west wings in the late 1800s and the Prospect Wing in 1907.

Figure 68 Koessler Administration Building at Holy Angels School 1887

In 1908, encouraged by Bishop Colton to expand Holy Angels Academy and provide access to additional students, the Grey Nuns chartered a college and changed the name to D'Youville College. It was named after their patroness Saint Marie-Marguerite d'Youville, who established the order in 1837. The Sisters committed themselves to fighting for the rights of the most marginalized of society in Canada, and starting in the 1840s became a major provider of health care and social services throughout Quebec, Western and Northern Canada and the northern U.S.

D'Youville was the first women's college in WNY and conferred degrees to three students in 1912. The school emphasized the teaching professions, and intellectual interests guided students toward extra-curricular activities focusing on dance, music, drama, language and political debate. Enrollment grew from 37 in 1912 to 400 by the 1940s. As the country entered WWII, D'Youville expanded its educational focus to include nursing programs, becoming the first college to offer baccalaureate degree programs in nursing for women in WNY.

The Oblates renovated a former poorhouse into a seminary school, adjacent to Holy Angels Church. To accommodate the large number of students they constructed a building at Porter and West in 1906. In addition to the Oblates mission, the building also housed the recital hall for D'Youville's music and drama departments. That building is now part of D'Youville College and contains the acclaimed Kavinoky Theater.

In 1971, D'Youville became a co-ed institution and is the top ranked private healthcare educator in WNY. With over 2,500 students, they offer degrees in over 15 different healthcare programs. D'Youville became a university in 2022 and now offers doctorate programs in Clinical Psychology, Chiropractic, Nursing, Pharmacy, Physical Therapy and Education.

Darwin Martin House
123 Jewett Parkway, Buffalo

Figure 69 Darwin Martin House
photo credit Mike Shriver buffalophotoblog.com

The Darwin Martin House is one of the best examples of Frank Lloyd Wright's Prairie School era and is considered an architectural gem.

Wright designed a home for Darwin Martin's brother William in Oak Park Illinois, where Wright opened his first office. Darwin was impressed with the design and invited Wright to visit Buffalo in 1903. Wright designed a home for Darwin's sister who married Larkin Company executive George F. Barton at 118 Summit Avenue.

In 1904 Wright began work on the Darwin Martin House and was awarded the contract to design the Larkin Company Administrative Office at 680 Seneca Street. The building was considered the most modern office complex in the world and was a pivotal commission during Wright's early career. Homes of Walter V. Davidson and William R. Heath, two other Larkin Company executives, were also designed and still exist in Buffalo.

The Jewett Parkway complex is the largest and most highly developed Prairie House on the east coast. In addition to the two main residences for Martin and his brother-in-law George Barton, the property includes a long pergola with a conservatory, a carriage house-stable and gardener's cottage. It has almost 400 art glass windows, with all the furnishings and creative design elements conceived by Wright.

The residence and landscape include 7,000 bulbs, 2,000 perennials and hundreds of shrubs and trees, incorporated in the half-circle floricycle that Wright created to provide flowers during the eight-month Buffalo growing season.

After the Martin family abandoned the property in 1937, it was neglected and partially demolished. Architect Sebastian J. Tauriello purchased the home in 1954 and made efforts to save it until it was purchased by UB as the president's residence in 1967. The contributions of the *Buffalo News*, M&T Bank and Rich Products were augmented by the formation of the Martin House Restoration Corp. Stanford and Judith Lipsey funded the Gardener's Cottage and the Eleanor and Wilson Greatbatch Pavilion opened as a visitors' center in 2009.

Other Wright properties in the Buffalo area include Darwin Martin's summer home Graycliff in Derby, the Frank Lloyd Wright Gas Station in the Pierce Arrow Museum on Seneca Street, Fontana Boathouse at the West Side Rowing Club and Blue-Sky Mausoleum in Forest Lawn Cemetery. These Frank Lloyd Wright properties assist in making WNY one of the biggest architectural tourist destinations in the U.S.

Delaware Midway Rowhouses
Delaware Avenue between Virginia & Allen, Buffalo

In the 1890s, Buffalo's elite built grand estates along Delaware Avenue, later dubbed Millionaire's Row. We've lost some of them, but thankfully quite a few still exist.

Figure 70 Midway Rowhouses photo credit Ellen Mika Zelasko

Most had extensive real estate surrounding them. The mansions along the west side of Delaware had yards that extended all the way to Richmond Avenue. (This was, of course, before Elmwood Avenue existed.) These estates had extensive terraces, beautiful flower gardens, vegetable gardens, orchards, creeks, ponds and more. Management of the grounds was a full-time job. The owners of these incredible estates hired people to manage and maintain their properties, but in the end, the owners had to make all the decisions related to the upkeep.

Rowhouses are a popular style of building in many east coast cities. Single-family units are set in a property line, sharing common walls and their roofline. The building of these remarkably upscale rowhouses on Delaware between Virginia and Allen Streets turned out to be an incredible idea. These homes allowed wealthy socialites to enjoy life in a mansion, but without all the property to maintain. It gave them easy access to their socialite friends, genteel living and that coveted Delaware Avenue address. One of these homes would be perfect for a single man, a single woman, or maybe the widow of a wealthy businessman - anyone who simply wasn't interested in all the work of a grand estate.

These homes were all built in the 1890s, on the site of the former Cornell Lead Works, and were designed by some of the best architects our city had to offer: Green & Wicks, Marling & Johnson and George Cary to name a few. The architects showed amazing talent by working within the constrictions of the other designs to create a cohesive, beautiful row of some of Buffalo's best homes.

On the south end of the block, there was originally a home where there is now a parking lot. It was torn down in the late 1980s after a small fire. Due to preservation efforts, we've come to appreciate the architectural treasures that grace our streets, and steps are now taken to preserve them.

The Delaware Midway Rowhouses boasted, and still boast, some big Buffalo names, such as Bryant B. Glenny (son of William H. Glenny), Katharine Pratt Horton, Buffalo Attorney Harlow Curtiss, Dr. Bernard Bartow (Founder of Children's Hospital), and Michael Meade, CEO of Sullivan's Brewing Company.

by Ellen Mika Zelasko

DL&W Terminal & Train Sheds
29 South Park Avenue, Buffalo

Figure 71 DL&W Train Shed 1919 postcard

During Buffalo's reign as a railroad transportation center, there were three major downtown rail terminals. New York Central's terminal was moved to the Buffalo Central Terminal on the east side, Lehigh Valley's terminal gave way to the General Donovan State Office Building and I-190 but the DL&W outlasted its competitors.

The terminal was built in 1917 for the Erie Railroad. It was designed by architect Kenneth M. Murchison and sits at the foot of Main Street at the Buffalo River between Michigan Avenue and the present-day Erie Basin Marina. It served rail passenger and freight service as well as lake ships that could dock alongside the building to discharge passengers.

Its three-story passenger concourse and offices provided waiting rooms on the first and second floors of the terminal, complete with ticket offices, a women's parlor, smoking room, shops, newsstands, parcel booths and restaurants. The mezzanine had rooms for railroad employees and waiting rooms for immigrants. On the third floor were administrative offices.

Due to declining passenger traffic, the terminal closed in 1962, remaining vacant and looted by vandals and scavengers for the following two decades. All the windows were broken and every fixture was stolen. In 1979, the property was sold by the city of Buffalo and Conrail, to the Niagara Frontier Transportation Authority (NFTA) for $190,000.

The NFTA demolished the DL&W terminal and signal tower powerhouse, retaining just the train sheds that were designed by Lincoln Bush. These two-story modular train sheds were constructed of cast iron, steel and concrete, with the roof consisting of skylights and slots for the escape of fumes. The DL&W train sheds in Buffalo were considered the oldest in existence. They are now used by the NFTA for maintenance and storage of rail vehicles for their Light Rail Rapid Transfer (LRRT) system that opened in 1984.

The NFTA selected Savarino Companies as its partner in redeveloping the upper levels of the historic train shed structure. Savarino retained the international public places consultant Project for Public Spaces to revitalize it into a mixed-use public and private hub for Arts, Culture and Entertainment, with food and beverage options that are currently being developed. The DL&W Railroad Station Museum will be part of this complex and it will have access to the Riverwalk, Canalside and KeyBank Center.

Dun Building
110 Pearl Street, Buffalo

The Dun Building is a city of Buffalo Landmark and is located within the Joseph Ellicott Historic District. It was designed by E.B. Green and William Wicks for the Union Central Life Insurance Company, who never built it. The plans were acquired and set into motion by R.G. Dun & Company, a credit check service.

R.G. Dun & Company later became Dun & Bradstreet, which still operates globally.

It was built on the site of Buffalo's first schoolhouse, which was burned in the war of 1812.

At 10 stories the Dun Building was the tallest building in the city when completed, in keeping with the building trends of the late 19th century, as cities were becoming more and more crowded. Building up seemed to be the only way to go. This status lasted only a short time because the Guaranty Building, at 13 stories, was completed within a year after completion of the Dun Building.

Figure 72 Dunn Building PD

It is, however, considered Buffalo's first high-rise building. But it's not a skyscraper in the true sense of the word. By 1890 most architects knew that steel frame construction was the wave of the future, but were unsure how to use it, and didn't quite trust its strength. These architects were pioneers of a sort, testing the newest technology on the newest type of buildings.

When Green & Wicks set out to build the Dun Building, they started with a steel frame design, with load bearing masonry walls ensuring the strength that the tall, oddly shaped building needed. They built it in three distinct 'layers.' Some refer to it as a 'wedding cake' design. The first two floors were built first, the third through seventh floor followed, and the three uppermost floors came last.

It is Neoclassical in style, but it has both Greek and Roman influences, as evidenced by the large arched windows and the highly decorative round windows. It is an odd shape as well, referred to as a flatiron.

There is a restaurant space in the basement which has independent entrances, along with approaches from inside the building. It was one of the early buildings serviced by underground utilities, located under the sidewalk along Swan Street.

The Dun Building was purchased in 2013 by 110 Pearl LLC, an affiliate of Priam Enterprises.

by Ellen Mika Zelasko

E & B Holmes Machinery Company Building

55 Chicago Street, Buffalo

Figure 73 E.& B. Holmes Building in 1876 PD

The E. & B. Holmes Manufacturing Company was one of the leading barrel makers in the country and it transformed into one of the leading woodworking machine manufacturers. Located in the Old First Ward, the company property at 55-59 Chicago Street dates back to 1852.

It consists of three buildings. The Mill Building was built in the 1870s, replacing the original building from the 1850s that was destroyed in a boiler explosion and devastating fire. The Forge Building dates back to a one-story structure from 1864 and was expanded to three stories by Colson-Hudson in 1910-1912. The Pattern Building was designed by Lansing, Bley and Lyman in 1913. All the buildings were architecturally linked during the construction of the Pattern Building, but parts of the buildings were lost due to deterioration during a collapse in 2007.

The company was formed by brothers Edward and Britain Holmes as a lumber yard and planning mill in Lancaster in 1840 and they evolved into barrel making and other products when they moved to the Buffalo waterfront. Edward Britain Holmes, the son of Edward, replaced his father and uncle as owner upon their deaths in 1906. He married Maude Gordon in 1911, with Maude taking over the business when her husband died in 1934.

Maude Gordon Holmes became one of the few manufacturing executives in the country and when the demand for wood barrels declined, she reallocated the expertise of the company into manufacturing a variety of woodworking and specialty machinery. She sold the company to employees Fred Henry and Martin Elskamp in 1950 and it was purchased by company treasurer Andrew S. Krafchak in 1971. When the company downsized and relocated in 2002 it was the oldest company operating in the same location under the same name in Buffalo.

In addition to running the company, Maude was the founder of the Garden Center Institute of Buffalo, that worked on many horticulture beautification projects in WNY, including the Mirror Lake Japanese gardens in Delaware Park.

The property was purchased by Newark Niagara LLC, headed by architect Clinton Brown in 2005 and sold to Ellicott Development in 2018. The former Pattern Building of the cooperage complex remains, but most of the other buildings had to be demolished and replaced by new construction. It now houses a mixed use of the Cooperage Apartments, businesses and Resurgence Brewing Company.

E.M. HAGER & SONS COMPANY
141 Elm Street, Buffalo

Figure 74 EM Hager & Sons - Planing Mill
photo credit Rick Falkowski

After serving in the Civil War, Edward M. Hager started a construction company on Mortimer Street in 1868, building factories, grain elevators, schools, churches and private residences. In 1883 he formed the partnership of Clark, Hager and Feist – Planing Mill which moved into Feist's Mill at 141 Elm Street, a three-story building that was constructed in 1878.

Ralph Clark retired in 1887 and Hager purchased the company from John Feist in 1894. Edward's sons George J. and August C. joined the business and in 1902 E.M. Hager and Sons Company was formed. August retained management of the company until his death in 1954. During the 1800s the company operated six days a week, ten hours a day and used 100 rail cars of lumber a year, delivered by horse cart to their factory.

The company was one of the prime construction contractors for the 1901 Pan-American Exposition, opening an on-site woodworking plant to fill the tremendous demand. In addition, they were the contractors for the mayor's office in City Hall (the only woodwork in the building), Twentieth Century Club, UB Medical School on High Street, Statler Hilton, St. Paul's Cathedral, Canisius College and many of the elaborate mansions built in Buffalo.

Demand for the company's services was so great that a two-story addition was added to the original building in 1880, a three-story wing in 1920 and they occupied 75% of the city block bounded by Elm, Clinton, Michigan and William. The first floor of the complex housed the planing mill and lumber storage, while the second and third floor were used for manufacturing - the carving, glueing and painting of the woodwork.

As steel and concrete replaced wood framing, the company focused on interior furnishings, transitioning to making store fixtures, tavern bars, school and bank equipment. Eventually the company concentrated on millwork, producing fine wood carved interiors for many of Buffalo's stately mansions and office buildings.

When the company ceased operations in the early 1980s the building was converted to the Spaghetti Warehouse in 1988. Additional restaurants/nightclubs including Your Father's Mustache, Sweetwater's and SensationZ operated at 141 Elm Street, with SensationZ closing in 2004.

Several developers proposed plans to convert the building into apartments and in 2013 construction was commenced by TM Montante Development for an $8 million renovation to The Planing Mill, a mixed-use property with first floor commercial spaces and 22 loft apartments.

Edward M. Cotter Fireboat & Icebreaker

155 Ohio Street, Buffalo

Figure 75 The Edward M Cotter
photo credit Ellen Mika Zelasko

The Edward M. Cotter was built in 1900, and was christened the William S. Grattan, named for the first paid fire commissioner in Buffalo. Thus, Engine 20 in the city of Buffalo was born. She is the oldest active fireboat in the world, is 118 feet long, and originally had two steam engines and coal burning boilers. Her prow (or front of the hull) is 1-1/2-inch-thick steel, making her perfect for ice breaking. Keeping the ice broken up is integral to fighting fires along Buffalo's extensive waterfront.

In July of 1928, while fighting an oil barge fire in the Buffalo River, the Grattan caught fire and was severely damaged. The firefighters on board were forced to abandon ship and swim to shore. The boat's chief engineer was killed, and seven crew members were injured.

The boat sat for eighteen months until she was rebuilt at the Buffalo Dry Dock Company in 1930. It was at this time her boilers were converted from coal to oil, foam fire retardant firefighting capabilities were added, and her engines were rebuilt.

In 1952, the boat was sent to Sturgeon Bay, Wisconsin for some modernization. Her steam engines were replaced with two diesel engines, twin props replaced the single propeller, and the firefighting platform was outfitted with hydraulics. It was now capable of pumping 15,000 gallons of water per minute!

The Grattan was returned to Buffalo in 1953, and was given a new name, the Firefighter. In 1954 she was renamed again and became the Edward M. Cotter, named for a Buffalo firefighter who was a very popular leader of the local firefighter's union and had recently passed away.

In the spring of 2019, the Edward M. Cotter was sent to Toronto for two months, to receive much needed repairs to her hull and the installation of two new propellers. These repairs were paid for with grants received through the Cotter Conservancy.

The Cotter was named a National Historic Landmark in 1996. This opened the Cotter to much needed funds to maintain the aging boat. The Fireboat E.M. Cotter Conservancy, a non-profit organization, was formed in January 2016 to raise money so that the Cotter will be in the waters of Buffalo for a long time into the future.

by Ellen Mika Zelasko

Ellicott Square Building
295 Main Street, Buffalo

When the Ellicott Square Building was constructed in 1896, it was the largest office building in the world. Designed by Chicago architect Daniel H. Burnham, it was referred to as an office block, occupying the entire space between Main, South Division, Washington and Swan Streets in downtown Buffalo. It only took one year to complete construction, at a cost of $3.5 million.

*Figure 76 Ellicott Square Building Late 1890s
photo restoration by Gene Thompson*

The Italian Renaissance style ten story 447,000 square foot building included 60 offices and 40 stores, with an expansive central court, highlighted by a glass roof and two grand staircases to an iron railed mezzanine. The lobby featured mosaic and rare marble tiles with a floor mural symbolizing the strength of business organization in the U.S. After opening, the building housed over 4,000 employees and was visited daily by up to 50,000 people.

The exterior consists of granite, iron and terracotta, with pearl-grey brick and terra cotta trimmings, crowned by a massive cornice. The effect replicates the grandeur of the palaces of Rome and Florence Italy.

When Joseph Ellicott laid out the village of Buffalo in 1797, he selected the area where the Ellicott Square Building stands for his personal residence and estate. His heirs and their successors retained title to the property that was referred to as Ellicott Square for 100 years. The property was purchased and the building erected by the Ellicott Square Company, comprised of several prominent Buffalo businessmen, with John N. Scatcherd as president from 1894 to 1906.

Scatcherd leased the basement restaurant to then unknown hotelier Ellsworth Statler in 1896. The top floor originally housed the Ellicott Club, a businessmen's club that held the "Electric Buffalo's" Banquet on January 12, 1897. At this event 400 of Buffalo's elite, engineers and investors celebrated Tesla's transmission of AC power from Niagara Falls to Buffalo, with Tesla giving a speech on the concept of "wireless technology."

A section of the basement was the location of the Mark Brother's Edisonia Hall and Vitascope Theater, the first space built specifically as a motion picture theater in the U.S. The lobby has been utilized for many large political rallies, and it was used for the hotel scenes in the 1984 movie The Natural.

Since its construction the building has continually undergone extensive improvements that have preserved the original architecture but added modern enhancements for energy efficiency, convenience and safety.

F.N. Burt Company Factory

500 Seneca Street, Buffalo

Figure 77 F.N. Burt Company 500 Seneca St. PD

The F.N. Burt Company originated in 1886 when Frederick N. Burt opened a printing shop at 440 Main Street, where they printed labels for boxes. It was more profitable to make their own boxes, so beginning in 1896 the company utilized a Brightwood machine to manufacture folding boxes and soap boxes for the Larkin Company.

After moving to several larger facilities, in 1901 the company began construction at the corner of Seneca and Hamburg Streets, closer to the shipping depots on Exchange Street. The first 500 Seneca Street structure was a five-story timber framed building designed by Niederpruem, Gibbs & Schaaf. They added two wings in 1903, built additions in 1910 and 1916, with their largest expansion in 1926 when Plumer and Mann designed their reinforced concrete building. Eventually they occupied over 400,000 square feet in six buildings, all still standing.

In 1901, F.N. Burt developed a technique to produce small oval and circle boxes, which became their most successful product. The company was purchased by Moore Corporation Limited of Canada in 1909, who provided additional capital to build more machines. They started making cigarette boxes, manufacturing over 200 million a year or 98% of the total produced world-wide. In 1917 F.N. Burt received an order from the California Perfume Company, which became Avon and F.N. Burt was their major supplier of packaging. The firm became the world's largest manufacturer of small set up boxes, producing up to four million boxes a day for the cosmetic, pharmaceutical and other industries.

Mary Cass served as General Manager and Vice President of F.N. Burt for 24 years, being one of the highest paid and most successful female manufacturing executives in the country. The company also manufactured folding carton boxes in their 100,000 square foot plant at Main and Bryant Streets and occupied factory C at 1502 Niagara Street, now the Cresendo Lofts.

F.N. Burt moved out of 500 Seneca Street in 1959, relocating to 2345 Walden Avenue in Cheektowaga. The Seneca Street building became the home to New Era Cap Company, who continued manufacturing at the plant until 2004. Savarino Companies purchased the building in 2010 for $200,000 and invested $35 million to create Five Hundred Seneca. a 380,000 square foot mixed use facility that includes Class A office space for numerous companies, 97 market rate apartments, a Fitness center, wine purveyor, canine daycare, hair salon, massage therapy salon and restaurants.

Forest Lawn Cemetery
1990 Main Street, Buffalo

Figure 78 Forest Lawn Cemetery photo credit Marsha Falkowski

The rural cemetery movement began in 1804 with the establishment of Pere-Lachaise Cemetery, located on an estate that balanced nature with art, overlooking the city of Paris, France. In the U.S., Mount Auburn, built in Cambridge, Massachusetts, adopted the same concept in 1831, encouraging people to walk the grounds, admire the funerary art and commune with nature.

Attorney Charles C. Clarke recognized the need for a cemetery of substantial size to serve the booming population growth of the city of Buffalo. In 1849, he purchased 80 acres of land at $150.00 per acre from the estate of Erastus Granger. It was located two- and one-half miles from the center of Buffalo on Delaware Avenue and north of Scajaquada Creek. This location fit the rural cemetery model of Pere Lachaise and Mount Auburn with its rolling hills and charming valleys, spring fed lakes and a meandering creek. Clarke designed wide roadways that intertwined with the landscape, providing interesting vistas and parking space for horse drawn carriages. He thinned out trees and planted others in the meadows to shade the graves, putting lawn under the forest and forest on the lawns, creating Forest Lawn Cemetery, proclaimed by the Buffalo Commercial Advertiser as "one of the most-lovely resting places for the dead in the country."

The first burial took place in 1850 with Reverend William Shelton, rector of St. Paul's Cathedral, officiating at the funeral of John Lay, Jr. Since that first internment, many famous Buffalo residents have been buried on the grounds, including former President Millard Fillmore, Seneca Chief Red Jacket and most of the founding Fathers and Mothers of the city.

The Margaret Wendt Archive and Resource Center has been built on the grounds. Forest Lawn also features trolley tours and costumed actors representing some of the luminaries buried in the cemetery. The Frank Lloyd Wright Blue Sky Mausoleum, that was commissioned by Darwin D. Martin in 1918, was erected at Forest Lawn in 2004.

Forest Lawn comprises 269 acres of incomparable beauty for its permanent population of over 165,000. It continues to serve both the dead and living, with over 100 varieties of more than 3,500 trees, over 240 kinds of birds, and paths for walkers to admire this outdoor sculpture museum, while paying respect to those buried in the landscape provided by nature.

FOSDICK-MASTEN PARK HIGH SCHOOL– CITY HONORS
186 East North Street, Buffalo

Figure 79 Original Masten Park High School 1905 postcard

In anticipation of the 1832 cholera epidemic, the city of Buffalo purchased five acres of land from William Hodge in a remote area away from the city center. Bordered by Best to East North Street and Michigan to Cemetery Street, it was named Potter's Field, where poor, indigent and those without religious affiliation could be buried. The cemetery fell into disuse and in 1886 the graves were moved to Forest Lawn Cemetery.

Cemetery Street was renamed Masten Avenue in honor of Buffalo mayor Joseph Masten and in 1887 the former cemetery grounds became Masten Park, part of Frederick Law Olmsted's city plan. The city decided to build a second high school, in addition to Central High School, and constructed Masten Park High School within the park in 1897.

In 1912, a fire engulfed the high school, with principal Frank Sheldon "Fearless" Fosdick repeatedly going back into the building to ensure all 1,100 students and faculty made it out safely. The principal was the only one seriously injured during the fire.

A new Masten Park High School, designed by architects Esenwein & Johnson, opened in 1914. The school is a 3 ½ story H-shaped brick building sheathed in white glazed terra cotta tile. Fosdick served as principal until 1926 and after his death in 1927 the school was renamed Fosdick Masten Park High School.

In 1953, Buffalo school district moved the Girls Vocational Program into the building, making it an all-girls school and renaming it Fosdick-Masten Vocational High School. The curriculum offered classes in business, foods, clothing, beauty culture and practical nursing. Enrollment in the program waned and in 1979 the school closed. It was scheduled for demolition to provide additional space for the Pilgrim Village housing development that was constructed in the former park next to the school in 1977. Designation as an Erie County Landmark helped save the building.

The City Honors gifted and talented program was established at Bennett High School in 1975. It moved to the P.S. 17 at Main and Delevan, across from Canisius College, adding grades 5-8 and becoming a court mandated magnet school. In 1980 City Honors School relocated to Fosdick-Maston, serving grades 5 to 8 and 9 to 12. A $40 million construction project was completed in 2010, renovating the school building and re-establishing the athletic field.

City Honors is annually recognized as one of the highest achieving schools in the country.

Foster Mansion
50 Tudor Place, Buffalo

Orin Foster lived at 891 Delaware Avenue and in 1927 had a new home built on Tudor Place, a street created on the former John Albright estate property between Cleveland Avenue and West Ferry Street.

The mansion at 50 Tudor Place was designed by architect Paul F. Mann, who created other Buffalo buildings including the Curtiss Hotel and Trico Plant #1, along with several other significant upscale Buffalo mansions. Mann received his degree in architecture from Massachusetts Institute of Technology (MIT), the first American school to have an architectural curriculum that emulated that of the Ecole des Beaux-Arts in Paris.

Figure 80 50 Tudor Place photo credit Ellen Mika Zelasko

50 Tudor Place is an 8,695 square foot Traditional style, 6 bedroom, 5 ½ bath traditional home with a 3 ½-car garage and 2-bedroom carriage house on a double lot. Orin Foster moved into the home with his wife Emily and daughter Helen. When Orin passed away in 1928 at the age of 88, his wife remained at the home until her death in 1937, with their daughter continuing to make it her residence. Helen's sister Edna Foster Smith lived across the street at 33 Tudor Place in a 9,307 square foot, 5-bedroom, 4-bathroom mansion.

Patrick and Kimberly Francabandiero purchased 50 Tudor Place in 2012 and extensively refurbished all aspects of the interior, exterior and grounds before listing it for sale. They even traveled to France to purchase period specific chandeliers, sconces and furniture. It was listed in May 2024 for $4.25 million and sold in March 2025 for $3.5 million, the most expensive home sale since 120 Lincoln Parkway sold for $1.96 million in 2021.

Marketing the sale of a premier property of this caliber goes well beyond just listing and showing. Listing agents Kristan Anderson and Tracy Heneghan of Gurney Becker & Bourne created a hard cover book about the property, detailing renovations and featuring numerous photos. They held an event for neighbors, interested buyers and individuals who might know people that would be interested in the property. There was local and out of town interest with the buyers Kyle and Kaylin Roche, moving back to Buffalo from Miami.

The sale is a reflection of the strength and affordability of Buffalo's high-end luxury real estate. Even with the $3.5 million sale price, the home would have had a two to five times higher cost in other major metro areas in the U.S.

Foster Mansion – DeRose Foods
981 Delaware Avenue, Buffalo

Figure 81 Foster Mansion
photo credit Mike Shriver buffalophotoblog.com

Orin Elliott Foster built this Arts and Crafts style mansion at 981 Delaware Avenue in 1905.

Born in Colden, NY on May 17, 1840, Foster moved to Canada with his family when he was just six months old. During his youth Orin worked on the family farm in Whitby, Ontario and at 28 he took a $400 per year job as salesman for a Toronto drug firm. Orin traveled all over eastern Canada for eight years making sales from a horse-drawn wagon. In 1876 he formed a partnership with Thomas Milburn, creating Foster-Milburn, a patent medicine manufacturer and distribution company.

Relocating back to Buffalo, the Foster-Milburn Company opened an office and factory at 1280 Main Street. Their first successful product was Dr. Thomas' Eclectic Oil, a pain relief remedy and general cure all. It was based upon a formula they purchased from S.N. Thomas in 1876. The company produced an almanac, pocket memorandum book and trading cards to promote their products. They also made Burdock Blood Bitters and Dr. Fowler's Extract of Wild Strawberry, but their most successful product was Doan's Kidney Pills, still being sold today.

In 1905 architect Frank Henry Chappelle designed an 8,200-square-foot grey and white marble Mediterranean Revival or Spanish Colonial Revival style home at 981 Delaware Avenue. The house features a rough-textured stone exterior and front porch with arched openings, stone columns and railing. The second floor has arched windows, topped with voussoirs, beneath a low-pitched hip roof with Craftsman style rafters and dormers on all four sides. Behind the house stands a simpler carriage house, built in a complimentary style, with a hipped roof and wall dormers.

Foster contributed $400,000 in 1921 to the University of Buffalo to fund Foster Hall, the Hall of Chemistry and the first building constructed on the Main Street Campus. The building is currently a classroom and research facility for the UB School of Dental Medicine.

Foster moved to 50 Tudor Place in 1927 and the Delaware Avenue house was eventually turned into offices. 981 Delaware was later owned by DeRose Food Brokers, who gifted the building to Canisius High School in 2006. It was purchased by Dr. Leonard Kaplin for $1.5 million in 2023 to house his preventive medicine and wellness center – OWM Integrative Wellness. OWM refurbished the mansion and now offers their Functional Medicine, holistic alternative medicine therapies at the property.

Francis Fronczak House
806 Fillmore Avenue, Buffalo

Francis Fronczak was born in Buffalo in 1874 and grew up in a home built by his father at 508 Fillmore Avenue. Fronczak's parents moved to the Broadway Fillmore neighborhood so their only son could attend St. Stanislaus school run by Father John Pitass.

Fronczak was the first Polish American to graduate from Canisius College (BA 1894 and MA 1895) and the UB Medical School, later obtained a Law Degree from UB. He served in the NY Legislature, was the first Health Commissioner of Buffalo, founded the Erie County Health Department, wrote about Polish American issues for Buffalo newspapers, published 27 books on medicine, worked on war relief in Poland after WWI and WWII, served on the United Nations Polish Relief Committee and worked with Polish leaders, Ignacy Jan Paderewski and Roman Dmowski.

Figure 82 Francis Fronczak House photo credit Patra Mangus

The home at 806 Fillmore Avenue was built in 1897 for Dr Irving Potter, who was President of the Erie County Health Commission. He sold the house to Dr. Fronczak in 1907.

In 1941, Polish American architect Joseph Fronczak designed an expansion of the house, with a brick addition on the front of the building. Dr Fronczak entertained dignitaries and often dined there with notable people including Paderewski, General Jozef Haller and Nobel Prize laureate Wladyslaw Stanislaw Reymont.

After his death in 1955 the building became the office of his daughter Dr. Eugenia Fronczak Bukowski, whose husband Dr. Edward Bukowski succeeded Fronczak as Commissioner of Public Health. In the 1970's it was sold to Rev. Alexis Zaryk who converted it to SS Vladimir & Olga Ukrainian Orthodox Church.

Ron Fleming, founder and publisher of Fine Prine News purchased the house but after his death in 2010, the property was abandoned and fell into disrepair. Due to unpaid taxes, in 2013 the city of Buffalo ordered demolition of the property

After spending $11,000 in legal fees, the property was purchased by the Broadway Fillmore Neighborhood Housing Services. By March 2017 almost $150,000 had been spent to stabilize and seal the building, with at least another $300,000 being required to restore the building. The community hopes to obtain a historic marker at the home and renovate it into a museum or library in Dr Fronczak's honor.

by Patra Mangus

GARRET CLUB
91 Cleveland Avenue, Buffalo

Figure 83 Garret Club photo credit Rick Falkowski

The Garret Club was formalized at a meeting in 1902 at the home of Margaret Scatcherd, the driving force behind the club. It was visualized as a congenial place for young women to socialize in a less rigid setting than the more dignified Twentieth Century Club, corresponding to the initial Saturn Club and Buffalo Club relationship.

Original furnishings of the club were donated by members from their attics, inspiring the name "garret", a top-floor or attic room traditionally inhabited by an artist. Another reason for the name was that it expressed the informality which was to characterize the club.

They initially rented an apartment at 18 Ashland Avenue, moved to 205 Bryant Street and in 1916 purchased a lot at 91 Cleveland Avenue. Architect Robert North was hired to design a frame building at the cost of $18,000.

Club membership outgrew the original facilities and in 1928 E.B. Green, Jr. was given the commission to design a new clubhouse. The club's signature room is called "The Garret", fashioned to resemble an attic with lofty ceilings and beautiful wood paneling, floors and beams. Other rooms include the Dining Room, Living Room, Founders Room, Loggia and Red Room. The outdoor Garden Courtyard features lush landscaping within the privacy of a stucco wall.

When the newly expanded clubhouse opened in December 1929, it featured the production of plays, ensemble recitals and performances by well-known classical musicians. The high point of the club's entertainment was an annual original, liberal and often edgy production titled "The Show." Actress Katherine Cornell was an active member and she often appeared in this play. The clubhouse was placed on the National Register in 2007.

In addition, the club's programs today continue the tradition of featuring seminars, workshops, lecture dinners and morning talks on a variety of topics ranging from health and wellness, arts and literature, to history, current events and fashion, plus an investment club, croquet, and trips around WNY.

The Garret Club was formed to promote the well-being and advancement of women. This included the struggle for gender equality in all occupations and areas of modern life. Subsequently, the club played an important role in the suffrage movement and ideals of Mary Garrett Hay. Newsletters, rosters and activities of the club from 1902 -1988 are chronicled in The Garret Club: History and Manual in the Grosvenor Room of the Buffalo and Erie County Public Library.

GENERAL ELECTRIC TOWER
535 Washington Street, Buffalo

Buffalo obtained the moniker of the Electric City due to the distribution of electricity from Niagara Falls to the Pan American Exposition in 1901. However, the electrification of Buffalo began twenty years earlier.

In 1882 a company was formed for the distribution of electricity to streetlights through a Brush arc dynamo. The first demonstration was across Buffalo Creek in what was known as The Island. A franchise was granted by the Buffalo Common Council to the Brush Electric Light Company. Their distribution originated in the First Ward and the company provided street lighting to the South Buffalo area. The Brush was successful in building a power station to provide alternating current (AC) to AM&As store, the first commercial installation of alternating current based electrical power in the U.S.

Figure 84 Electric Tower in 1927 photo Company Archives

The Thompson-Houston Electric Light Company was formed in 1886 to provide service to the West Side. However, progress of the two companies was not satisfactory and in 1892 they merged to form the Buffalo General Electric Company with Daniel O'Day president, George J. Urban, Jr. vice-president and Charles Huntley general manager.

These companies used steam plants to generate electricity. In Niagara Falls Jacob Schoellkopf's Niagara Falls Hydraulic Power Company harnessed the falls to produce direct current (DC) electricity, but it could not be transmitted over a mile. The Niagara Falls Power Company and Cataract Construction Company joined forces under Edward Dean Adams to build a plant to transmit electricity by alternating current. On November 16, 1896, Nicola Tesla flipped the switch to deliver electricity to Buffalo.

The Electric Tower was designed by architect James A. Johnson of Esenwein & Johnson, who drew inspiration for the design from the Tower of Light at the 1901 Pan-Am. Originally the home of The Buffalo General Electric Company, it has 14 stories following a Beaux-Arts Classical architectural style. The building was expanded in 1924 and 1926, under the direction of architect E.B. Green. In the 1930s the white terra-cotta structure was renovated with Art Deco style elements. It was home to various local power companies, becoming the Niagara Mohawk Power Corporation in 1950. In addition, the building was a showroom for appliances, exhibiting the modern conveniences that use electricity.

In 2007 Iskalo Development Company invested $28.4 million dollars to update the building and restore previous design elements. It is currently an office building and centerpiece for the annual New Year Eve fireworks in Roosevelt Square.

Goodyear Mansion
888 Delaware Avenue, Buffalo

Figure 85 Goodyear Mansion photo credit Ellen Mika Zelasko

Charles Goodyear came to Buffalo to study law in 1868. He practiced at a few different firms including one started by Grover Cleveland (Cleveland, Bissel & Sicard) who was a close friend. Goodyear had an excellent reputation and served as Assistant District Attorney, and later as District Attorney.

He eventually went into the lumber business with his brother Frank. The two owned extensive timberland in Pennsylvania and Louisiana, and they started a railroad company - the Buffalo and Susquehanna Iron Company. They pioneered the use of railroads to move lumber.

These two businesses earned the Goodyears immense wealth. It was during this time of great prosperity that Charles Goodyear and his wife Ella Portia Conger decided to build a home suitable for a family of such affluence.

The home is an exquisite example of the French Renaissance style. It was designed by Buffalo architects Green & Wicks (E.B. Green was the principle). It has a mansard roof, dormers with semi-circular pediments and keystones above the windows and above those are porthole dormers. Tuscan columns surround the now reopened front portico.

Inside there were 11 bedrooms, each with a marble fireplace, and adjoining bathrooms. On the first floor was the main hall, a dining room, a breakfast room, a library, and a loggia which opened to the terrace and garden out back.

The Goodyears were close friends of Grover and Frances Cleveland, and during World War I, Ella Goodyear hosted King Albert of Belgium, Queen Elisabeth of Bavaria, and their son, Prince Leopold.

The Goodyears enjoyed this home together from its completion in 1903 until 1911 when Charles passed away.

Ella lived in the home until her death in September of 1940. Shortly after, the Blue Cross Corporation purchased the home. In 1950, the Catholic Diocese of Buffalo purchased it to be used as the all-girl Bishop McMahon High School. Since the school closed in 1988, the building changed hands several times. It was purchased by Women and Children's Hospital and the Robert B. Adam Educational Center and then Oracle Charter School.

888 Delaware LLC (Priam Enterprises) acquired the property in October of 2019. They have painstakingly restored the home as close to its original detail as possible, including reopening the front portico, while transforming the entire building into apartments.

by Ellen Mika Zelasko

GREAT LAKES & PARAMOUNT THEATERS, NEMMER FURNITURE AND THE CITY CENTRE CONDOS
600 Main Street, Buffalo

This building at 600 Main Street near West Chippewa has had three lives.

In 1927 it was built as Fox's Great Lakes Theater, designed by architect Leon H. Lampert with interior design by Gustave Brandt. It had two entrances, 612 Main Street and 9 West Chippewa. When it opened the theater featured movies, along with vaudeville on stage. Only four years after it opened, in 1931 ownership was transferred to Sheas Theaters, who operated all the major theaters in the theater district and the most theaters in Buffalo.

Figure 86 Buffalo Theatre District 1963 postcard

The name of the movie house was changed to The Paramount Theatre in 1949. It was not Buffalo's most grand theater but The Paramount was still quite elaborate and seated about 3,000 people. Up until the early 1960s the theater district was extremely vibrant, packed with theaters, restaurants and nightclubs.

After the Paramount closed on February 20, 1965 the auditorium was demolished a couple weeks later on March 2, 1965. The front section and lobby were retained, with the former auditorium space converted to a parking lot.

Nemmer Furniture began selling upholstered items manufactured at their Genesee Street factory in 1924. They moved into the building on Main Street in 1957, after the upper floors were formerly home to Select Furniture. Nemmers eventually occupied all nine floors of the building as showroom and warehouse space. By the time Nemmer's closed in the early 1970s, most of the theater district was vacant, property owners stopped improving their properties and the theaters were either closed or converted to showing low budget or X-rated films. In 1975 all that remained in the building was Smiley's Adult Books, Films and Magazines, akin to the red-light district on West Chippewa Street.

The Nemmer building remained vacant until the late 1980s when the City Centre Condo project was announced. Five additional stories were to be added to the building that was to be refaced in glass and transformed to a mixed used commercial and condominium project. Work started in 1991 but halted when the development filed for bankruptcy. It was finally completed in 1996 and was the first successful downtown Buffalo condominium project.

This building has served multiple purposes over the past century and once again sparkles as one of the gems of downtown Buffalo.

GUARANTY BUILDING - PRUDENTIAL BUILDING
140 Pearl Street, Buffalo

*Figure 87 Guaranty Prudential Building
photo credit Ellen Mika Zelasko*

Hascal Taylor commissioned the architectural firm of Dankmar Adler and Louis Sullivan to build the Guaranty Building. They designed a skyscraper with a steel frame construction, wrapped in fireproof, decorative terra cotta. Taylor passed away before construction began. When completed, it was the tallest building and the first skyscraper in Buffalo.

In 1898 the Guaranty Construction Company defaulted on their loan. The Prudential Insurance Company refinanced the mortgage. The building was renamed The Prudential Building. Both names still appear on the building.

With the invention of the elevator in the 1850's and the crowding of urban areas, architects were looking for ways to build higher. Adler and Sullivan were pioneers in steel frame construction and led the way in designing skyscrapers in the 1890's. The Guaranty Building is a perfect example of their genius.

Adler was the engineer who made the building work, while Sullivan had the artistic vision. Sullivan designed each piece of terra cotta on the outside of the building and its tree of life motif, emphasizing the verticality of the building. Inside, he designed the bronze elevator cages, the art nouveau lobby skylight, the mosaic tile design on the walls, right down to the brass door handles.

The Guaranty Building is one of Sullivan's best works, surviving the demolition frenzy the country embarked upon in the 1960's, 70's and 80's. Luckily, it was saved from the wrecking ball by preservationist Jack Randall, with the help of Senator Daniel Patrick Moynihan in the late 1970's after it suffered damage on several floors due to a fire.

It was renovated and reopened for tenants in 1982-83.

In 2002, Buffalo's oldest law firm, Hodgson Russ, bought the building and renamed it the Guaranty Building. They began an extensive restoration that included foundation work, and the creation of a mini museum on the first floor showing the history of the building complete

*Figure 88 Terra Cotta Design of
Guaranty Building
photo credit Ellen Mika Zelasko*

with a model of the original building, a video highlighting its history, and the terra cotta molds used by the local company Boston Valley Terra Cotta to restore worn or damaged exterior tiles.

by Ellen Mika Zelasko

 # HOLY ANGELS CHURCH
348 Porter Avenue, Buffalo

The Oblates of Mary Immaculate began in 1816 when French priest Eugene DeMazenod formed a group of evangelizing priests to revive the Catholic faith that had been widely forsaken during the French Revolution of 1789. The Oblates became a religious congregation in 1826 and DeMazenod was named Bishop of Marseilles.

After organizing the Diocese of Buffalo, Bishop Timon realized the need to train priests. He visited DeMazenod in Marseilles and invited the Oblates to open a seminary. Initially, the Oblates were not satisfied with the circumstances in Buffalo in 1850 and departed to St. Peter's church in Montreal.

In 1851 Reverend Edward Chevalier of the Oblates visited Bishop Timon while traveling through Buffalo. They signed an agreement to establish a seminary and chapel for the poor in a converted barn, next to St. Joseph's Cathedral rectory on Franklin Street. Classes began in September 1851 with 28 students.

Figure 89 Holy Angels Church photo credit Ellen Mika Zelasko

A year later Chevalier purchased 18 acres near the outskirts of Buffalo on Prospect Hill. It contained a county poorhouse that was converted into a college and dormitory, and an insane asylum that became their chapel. The Oblates administered to the spiritual needs of the predominantly Irish population of the shantytown on the current site of LaSalle Park.

Construction began on a permanent house of worship in 1856 and on May 10, 1859 Bishop Timon dedicated the incomplete Holy Angels Church, with its distinctive French Romanesque twin spires and shortened nave. The present appearance of the church was not finished until 1874. The interior was renovated in 1898 adding four marble side alters, marble mosaic flooring in the sanctuary, hand carved Stations of the Cross made in Switzerland and two Tiffany windows flanking the main alter.

To accommodate seminary education, in 1891 the Oblates instructed aspirants in a building adjacent to Holy Angels Church in a high school division called Holy Angels Collegiate Institute. That was transferred to Newburgh New York in 1947 but the Oblates administered Bishop Fallon HS on Main Street in Buffalo from 1950 to 1975 and St John Neuman H.S. in Williamsville from 1961 to 1979.

Holy Angels Church was sold to D'Youville College in 1999 and its school building is the Montante Family Library. The Oblates of Mary Immaculate now minister at Our Lady of Hope and Holy Cross in Buffalo. Father Eugene DeMazenod was declared a Saint by Pope John Paul II in 1995.

HOTEL LAFAYETTE
391 Washington Street, Buffalo

Figure 90 Hotel Lafayette
photo credit Ellen Mika Zelasko

The Hotel Lafayette was intended to open for the Pan American Exposition in 1901, but due to financial difficulties it was not completed in time and opened in 1904. It was built for Walter B. Duffy, a Rochester capitalist. The well-respected Buffalo architectural firm of Bethune, Bethune & Fuchs was engaged to design it, with Louise Blanchard Bethune taking the lead on this project and credited with the design. Bethune was the first professional woman architect in the country.

Jenny Louise Blanchard was born in 1856 in Waterloo, NY, less than four miles away from Seneca Falls, the birthplace of the Women's Suffrage Movement, which began shortly before her birth. Her parents were both educators and the family moved to Buffalo when Louise was a child. She graduated from Buffalo Public High School in 1874.

Shortly after, she accepted an apprenticeship with the Buffalo architectural firm of Richard Waite and F.W. Caulkins. In 1881 she started her own firm with Robert Bethune, a former colleague from Waite's company. The two were married later that year, forming Bethune & Bethune. William Fuchs became a partner in 1891.

In 1888, Louise was honored with being the first female member of the American Institute of Architects, and one year later was named the first woman Fellow of the AIA. She was inducted into the National Women's Hall of Fame in 2006.

The Hotel Lafayette is considered one of her best works. The French Renaissance building was a showcase both inside and out. With its interior of marble and mahogany, 225 guest rooms, hot and cold running water in every bathroom, and telephones in all the rooms, it was indeed grand for its day. The New York Times said of the hotel when it opened, "one of the most perfectly appointed and magnificent hotels in the country".

Fifty years after its opening, the Hotel Lafayette was still being run by the Duffy family, but eventually, the out-of-town ownership allowed the hotel to decline and fall into disrepair. Some parts of it were left vacant for years. However, during this time the Lafayette Tap Room blues nightclub operated in the building.

The hotel changed hands in 2011, and it underwent a 45-million-dollar renovation by developer Rocco Termini. It reopened in 2012 and now has 92 apartments in addition to 57 hotel rooms, restaurants, banquet facilities, a working brewery, and retail space.

by Ellen Mika Zelasko

HOTEL LENOX

140 North Street, Buffalo

The Hotel Lenox was built in 1896 as the Lenox Apartment House, consisting of 24 apartments. It was transformed in 1901 to the 48-room residential hotel to house many of the officials and guests from the Pan American Exposition.

An 8-story building on North Street near Delaware Avenue, it was designed by the architectural firm of Fred Henry Loverin and Frederick A. Whelan. In addition to the Lenox, the firm designed the Berkeley, LaSalle, Valois, Algonquin and Hudson apartment houses. The grounds of the Lenox were part of Holland Land Company lot #52 which Ebenezer Walden purchased in 1809 for $232.50. In 1830 Lewis F. Allen purchased five acres of that lot to create the North Street Cemetery.

Figure 91 Lenox Hotel early 1900s original entrance PD

Early advertising for the hotel, which pictured horse drawn carriages, promoted that the hotel operated its own rapid electric motor carriages exclusively for its patrons through the Buffalo business district and to all depots and wharves for principal trains and steamers. Rooms were available at $1.50 per day and up. It was billed as Buffalo's most luxurious hotel.

In 1898 the Fitzgerald family moved to Buffalo, when their son, future author F. Scott Fitzgerald was 1 ½ years old. They lived in the Lenox Apartments from 1898 to 1901. At that time, the Root House was next to the Lenox at the corner of Delaware and North, now Walgreen's Drug Store. Across the street was the Metcalfe House (demolished in 1980) and the still existing Williams/Butler Mansion. The Fitzgerald's later moved around the corner to 29 Irving Place.

The Lenox was a fashionable place to live and is walking distance to the mansions of Delaware Avenue. Some early 20th century units were large enough to include servants' quarters. Many affluent individuals stayed at The Lenox upon moving to the city, lived there if they did not desire to own a residence or made it their home during a temporary tenure in Buffalo.

It was remodeled in the 1940s to increase the number of rooms to 150. Currently the Lenox Hotel and Suites offers hotel rooms, some hotel rooms with kitchen facilities, along with apartments available for short term or long-term rentals. A full-service restaurant is in the building, free parking is available and the building is walking distance to Allentown area restaurants and stores.

Hotel Lenox remains the longest continuously run hotel in the city of Buffalo.

Japanese Gardens of Buffalo
One Museum Court, Buffalo

Figure 92 Japanese Gardens in Delaware Park photo courtesy Buffalo Olmsted Parks Conservatory

The Japanese Gardens are located behind the Buffalo History Museum in the Olmsted Conservancy's Delaware Park.

In December 1962, Buffalo joined the United States Sister City International initiative and was connected as the sister city with Kanazawa, Japan. The idea of the Gardens was conceived in 1970; construction started in 1971 and was completed in 1974. The six-acre site includes over 1,000 plantings, nearly 20 globe-type lights and three islands connected to the mainland by bridges.

In 1983, renovations were begun by clearing overgrown vegetation on the upper banks, repairing the bridges, replanting the islands, creating a seating area on the main island and new plantings of trees and shrubs along the shore and paths. Later, during the 1980s, the main path along Mirror Lake was reconstructed as part of a pathway development throughout Delaware Park.

Beginning in 1994, American landscape architects worked with Japanese Garden designers, and American contractors worked together with a Japanese Garden crew. Over a couple years they restored the islands with Japanese pines and maples, pruned by the Japanese experts. A natural stone stairway was installed using stones brought over from Japan and several stone lanterns, with a Shinto gate were imported for the Garden from Japan. Cherry blossom trees were also planted.

In 1996, the Gardens were rededicated and expanded to an oasis between the foothills of the Buffalo History Museum and Mirror Lake, in the heart of Frederick Law Olmsted's lush green park plan. It is designed in the style of a Japanese Strolling Garden so that when a visitor moves through the garden, they experience different views and experiences. It is recommended to visit the gardens in each season as the appearance changes throughout the year.

The 40 flowering cherry trees resulted in the creation of the Buffalo Cherry Blossem Festival in 2014, to build awareness of Japanese culture. It is held in late April when the cherry blossoms and azaleas are anticipated to bloom. Special events during the festival include: the Tea Celebration, International Costume Show, pink boat rides on Mirror Lake, a parade, Shibuki Taiko Drum Performances, Odori no Kai Dance Group, bonsai, origami, Japanese language lessons and crafts. It is a celebration of the sister city affiliation with Kanazawa, Japan.

The Friends of the Japanese Garden of Buffalo also offer walking tours of the Japanese Garden.

KLEINHANS MUSIC HALL
3 Symphony Circle, Buffalo

Edward Kleinhans was one of the founders of the Kleinhans men's clothing store located in the Brisbane Building. He married Mary Seaton, an accomplished pianist and singer. They moved to Buffalo in 1901. The two were great music lovers and attended concerts and recitals often.

At that time, Buffalo didn't have a dedicated music hall. Most concerts were held in smaller buildings built for other purposes and facilities such as the Broadway Auditorium, which was large, but was built in 1858 and served as an Armory from the Civil War until 1907. In 1910, the building was renovated into an auditorium. It was used for everything from boxing matches and circuses to conventions and concerts.

Figure 93 Kleinhans Music Hall photo credit Ellen Mika Zelasko

The Elmwood Music Hall (designed by Louise Blanchard Bethune, a Buffalo architect credited with being the first woman architect in the country) on Virginia Street at Elmwood Avenue was also used for concerts, but it too was built as an armory. The problem with both buildings was that people could often hear traffic and trolley cars outside during performances.

Buffalo needed a dedicated music hall.

Having no children, when they passed away three months apart in 1934, the Kleinhans left their entire estate ($710,000) to the city to erect a proper music hall to be used for the enjoyment of the people of Buffalo. Public Works Administration, a Depression era government organization, funded the balance of the cost ($600,000).

Kleinhans Music Hall was completed in 1940. It was designed by the father and son architectural team of Eliel and Eero Saarinen, along with architects F.J. and W.A. Kidd, in the International style. No expense was spared on this building, and its unique design is lauded worldwide for its acoustic perfection.

From above, the building of Kleinhans Music Hall resembles the body of a stringed instrument, it is most often compared to a violin or a cello. There are three music rooms inside, the Main Auditorium, Livingston Hall (which was named in memory of Edward's mother, Mary Livingston) and the Mary Seaton Room (named for Edward's wife, Mary Seaton Kleinhans).

The Buffalo Philharmonic Orchestra, under the direction of Franco Autori, played the first concert at the newly opened Kleinhans Music Hall on October 12, 1940, and it has been the orchestra's home ever since.

Kleinhans Music Hall was designated as a National Historic Landmark in 1989.

Knox Mansion
800 Delaware Avenue, Buffalo

Figure 94 Knox Mansion photo credit Rick Falkowski

The original owner of 806 Delaware (renumbered 800 Delaware) was George Howard, who worked with Aaron Rumsey in establishing his Buffalo tannery business in 1838. Howard partnered with Myron Bush to form a successful leather business. George Rumsey Howard sold the home to the Knox family in 1915.

Seymour Knox and his cousin started Woolworth & Knox 5 and 10 Cent Store, opening their first Buffalo store in 1888. He bought out his cousin's interest in the Buffalo store and formed S.H. Knox & Co. Knox married Grace Millard in 1890 and they lived at 414 Porter Avenue and 467 Linwood Avenue before building a mansion in 1903 at 1035 Delaware Avenue. Knox merged his stores with his cousin to form the F.W. Woolworth Company in 1911. Seymour purchased the Howard home, next to the Clement Mansion at 786 Delaware, with the intention of razing it to build a larger home. Unfortunately, Seymour Knox died before they could begin construction.

Grace Knox commissioned C.P.H. Gilbert, who deigned Woolworth's Winfield Hall, to build a 27,965 square foot Beaux Arts style 25-room mansion at a 1917 cost of $600,000 (over $16 million current value). The rotunda was constructed with six different types of marble and featured stained glass windows with a peacock design by Tiffany. Mrs. Knox moved into the home with her children and played a prominent role in Buffalo society. She donated $500,000 in 1916 to establish the University of Buffalo Liberal Arts Department, formed the Junior League of Buffalo at the mansion in 1919 and began the Knox family support of the Albright Art Museum. Future donations by Seymour II resulted in it being renamed the Albright Knox Art Gallery.

The Knox family remained at 806 Delaware until 1969 when they sold it to The Montefiore Club, a private Jewish members club. They added a 20,000 square foot athletic center. An attempt by IBM to demolish the home to build a modern complex was halted and in 1978 it was sold to Computer Task Group, an IT company formed by Randolph A. Marks and C. David Baer of Buffalo.

In 2021 the house was purchased by Ross Cellino of the Cellino Law firm. The mansion was refurbished to its original grandeur and it was the 2021 Junior League Decorators' Show House. Free weekend tours are now offered of one of Buffalo's most elaborate and celebrated homes.

 # LAFAYETTE HIGH SCHOOL
370 Lafayette Avenue, Buffalo

Lafayette High School is the oldest public high school in Buffalo that remains in its original building and been in continuous use as an educational institution.

The first public high school in Buffalo was Central High School that opened in 1848 on the third floor of School #7 on South Division Street. In 1851 the city purchased the former Burt Mansion on Franklin and Court Streets, which was expanded in 1869 and 1889 into a large, impressive building. It was the only high school in Buffalo until Masten Park School opened in 1897. Central High School relocated to Hutchinson Central High School in 1914 and the original Masten Park School burned down, rebuilt as Fosdick-Masten Park High School.

Figure 95 Lafayette High School early 1900s postcard

A location at Lafayette and Baynes Avenue was selected by city of Buffalo officials and 32 designs were submitted for consideration. The building committee chose a design by the Buffalo architectural firm of Esenwein and Johnson. Construction by Mosier and Summers began in 1901 and the French Renaissance Revival building with a steeply pitched hipped pavilion roof and French doors opened in 1903. Estimated construction costs were $250,000 but actual costs were $400,000.

The school is an E-shaped brick building with the outer wings each three stories high and containing the classrooms. A two-story center section contains the auditorium. The signature feature of the school is the central ornamental 120-foot-high tower, with a mansard roof. It was built in an Upper West Side residential neighborhood, comprised of two-story late 19th century homes. In 1921, a rear addition was constructed that houses the gymnasium, swimming pool and cafeteria.

By 2010, Lafayette High School was one of the lowest achieving schools in the state and had one of the lowest graduation rates in Buffalo, with only half its students getting a diploma. For the 2011 school year it was restructured as Lafayette International High School. In conjunction with International School 45, the schools formed an international school campus with School 45 serving pre-kindergarten through 6th grade and the high school housing grades 7 to 12.

In 2016, the school became part of the International Network for Public Schools, a not-for-profit organization that supports schools designed for English Language Learners. 95% of the students are economically disadvantaged and the school has a 91% minority enrollment. It is an integral part of the Buffalo school system, serving the growing immigrant population of the city.

LAFAYETTE SQUARE
Main at Court Street, Buffalo

Figure 96 LaFayette Square 1907 with German Insurance Co. and original Lafayette Theater historic postcard PD

Lafayette Square was part of the original plan of the village of Buffalo when it was laid out by Joseph Ellicott of the Holland Land Company in 1804.

After the War of 1812, the county courthouse was built on the eastern section of the square that was first called Court House Park. Buffalo was the county seat of the original Niagara County and after 1821 the country seat of the land separated from it to create Erie Country. A jail was built behind the court house in 1833. Hangings took place on the jail grounds and when Grover Cleveland was sheriff of Erie County he presided over the execution of two murderers. He was the only president to serve as an executioner.

General Lafayette spoke at Court House Park in 1825 and in 1873 the park was renamed Lafayette Square to commemorate his visit and speech. On August 9 and 10, 1848, over 20,000 people met at Court House Park for the political convention of the Free-Soil Party. They nominated former U.S. President Martin Van Buren for president. Their platform was No Slavery would be allowed in the land acquired from Mexico during the Mexican American War. The Free-Soil Party merged into the Republican Party when it was formed in 1854. President Abraham Lincoln also gave a speech at the square.

The Eagle Tavern, Buffalo's main stagecoach stop, was across Main Street from Court House Park, and The Theater, where the first plays were presented in Buffalo in 1821, was next the square. In 1887 the Buffalo Public Library was built on the location of the courthouse. Buffalo Mayor Grover Cleveland laid the cornerstone for the Soldiers & Sailors Civil War Monument in 1882, and dedicated it in 1884 when he was NYS governor. After the monument began leaning, it was rebuilt by Buffalo's McDonnell & Sons in 1889. When Broadway was extended to Main Street, changing Lafayette Square to a circle, the cannons around the monument were moved to Colonial Circle and the War of 1812 memorial in Delaware Park. There were public bathrooms under Lafayette Square but the entrances were removed in the 1950s.

Other buildings around Lafayette Square included The Arcade, Brisbane Building, Buffalo Savings Bank, Lafayette Hotel, Lafayette Theatre, Liberty Building, Main Court Building, 10 Lafayette Square, Rand Building, Tishman Building, and German Insurance Company. Lafayette Square was also the home of the popular Thursday at the Square Concerts.

LINDE AIR PRODUCTS FACTORY
155 Chandler Street, Buffalo

Located five miles from downtown Buffalo, the historic Chandler Street buildings are east of Military Road and across the street from the former New York Central Railroad's Belt Line. Chandler Street was a small, local industrial corridor and a number of other early-twentieth century industrial buildings remain on both sides of the street along with empty lots where similar buildings once stood.

Figure 97 Linde Air Products Chandler Street Factory National Register of Historic Places Submission 2017

Listed on the National Register of Historic Places, the former Linde Air Products plant at 155 Chandler Street is located in the Grant-Amherst neighborhood, which developed following the 1883 completion of the New York Central Railroad Belt Line that looped the city of Buffalo. The Belt Line opened new portions of Buffalo to industry, particularly in the city's sparsely settled northwest quadrant.

The Grant-Amherst neighborhood, bordered to the north and west by the Belt Line's tracks, was one of the major beneficiaries of the industrial growth that developed at several points along the railroad. These areas of development encouraged immigrants, primarily from Eastern Europe, to settle in neighborhoods like Grant-Amherst and work in the factories. Chandler Street became one of the Grant-Amherst neighborhood's most significant industrial streets.

In 1906, German industrialist Carl Von Linde decided to expand his oxygen extraction company overseas, specifically targeting America, where there was no competition. Along with Cecil Lightfoot, in 1907, he opened the Linde Air Products Factory. His first plant in America was located at 155 Chandler Street in Black Rock. The original two-story section was built in 1907 of solid masonry construction with double-hung wood windows, brick piers, and pitched roofs. A second building was added in 1910. Architects included James B. McCreary and Esenwein & Johnson.

The building housed the first oxygen extraction facility in America and was later dubbed "the birthplace of the oxygen industry in the United States." It also served as the primary research facility for the Linde Air Products Company from 1923 until 1942.

During World War II, the Chandler Plant was one of two Linde/Union Carbide sites included in the Manhattan Project. This location was involved in the development and production of a particle barrier for the Oak Ridge Gaseous Diffusion Plant.

After Linde vacated the factory in 1948, it was leased by Bell Aircraft from 1951-1957. The building is included in the Rocco Termini - Signature Development Chandler Street renovation into apartments, offices and restaurants.

by Paul Lubienecki, PhD., Black Rock Historical Society

MARGARET WENDT HOUSE
570 Richmond Avenue, Buffalo

Figure 98 Wendt Family Home 570 Richmond courtesy Wendt Foundation

William Franz Wendt married Mary Gies Wendt in 1882, a year before he became the sole owner of Buffalo Forge, the largest forge company in the U.S. Their daughter Margaret was born in 1885, when the family was living in a small brick house at 19 Irving Place. In 1895, Williams built a home at 570 Richmond Avenue, between Breckenridge and Auburn Streets and a block from Colonial Circle.

The Colonial Revival style570 Richmond Avenue 5,270 square foot home had 6 bedrooms, 4 ½ bathrooms, with a carriage house in the rear. The brick residence featured ornamental spandril panels, palmette flanked by cornucopia panels, swan's neck pediments, guilloche trims, scroll modillion supporting the cornice, fluted pilasters, ionic columns, leaded glass bow windows with engaged copper roof, oriel bay windows and lattice windows in dormers with flared roofs.

In addition to this city home, due to the Wendt family's love of animals, they owned the Wendt Farm in Lockport. William Wendt died in 1923 at the Richmond Avenue home and left the home, farm and his assets to his wife Mary and daughter Margaret. After the death of her mother in 1940, Margaret sold the Lockport farm to William Kenan of Randleigh Farms and purchased beachfront property in a colony of affluent summer homes in Thunder Bay Ontario.

Margaret never married and dedicated her life to anonymously supporting charitable and public service causes in WNY. In 1957 Margaret was assisted by her pastor Reverend Dr. Ralph W. Loew of Holy Trinity

Lutheran Church to establish the Margaret Wendt Foundation, of which Rev. Loew was one of the foundation's three trustees.

The Margaret Wendt Foundation is one of the largest private foundations in WNY, funding the arts, community development, education, social services, religious organizations, youth agencies, human resources and energy & the environment. It has provided grants to numerous organizations and projects including the Margaret L. Wendt Archive & Resource Center at Forest Lawn Cemetery, Burchfield Penney Art Center, Darwin Martin House, Graycliff Visitors Center, Roycroft Inn, Lutheran Home, BPO, Freedom Crossing Monument, Letchworth State Park, Boys & Girls Club, Buffalo Therapeutic Riding Center and many more.

In 1959 Margaret suffered a stroke, remaining in a coma for 13 years. She died in her home at 570 Richmond in 1972, leaving the bulk of her $14,557,348 estate to her foundation, which continues to benefit the WNY community.

Market Arcade
617 Main Street, Buffalo

The was built in 1892 and was designed by the architectural firm of Green & Wicks, arguably Buffalo's most prolific architectural firm. The Arcade is three floors of shops and offices connected by a long narrow atrium, which is covered with frosted glass, giving the interior protection from the elements, while providing soft, even light that helps to create the comfortable vibe within.

*Figure 99 Market Arcade Interior
photo credit Ellen Mika Zelasko*

The Arcade spans from Main to Washington Streets and both facades are identical. Built for G.B. Marshall, it is modeled after the Burlington Arcade in London, which was designed to connect to its surrounding neighborhood. In that way it maintains close ties with the street life around it. Having two identical entrances, both on busy streets, Buffalo's Market Arcade followed suit.

On the Main Street side there were and are numerous businesses, offices and apartments, and on the Washington Street Side there used to be the Chippewa Market (well-known in the early 1900's as the largest market west of the Hudson River), when the Arcade was built. The many people passing through one entrance to get to the other had to be attractive to the small businesses renting space in the building. It meant a lot of foot traffic.

The Chippewa Market property was sold by the city in 1965 to be used as a parking lot for the Buffalo Savings Bank (Goldome).

A young Common Council member, Jimmy Griffin, opposed the sale of the market to the bank and was quoted in the Buffalo Evening News on February 24, 1965, saying, "I can't see where we're going to get any real value out of a bank parking lot." Griffin went on to become mayor of Buffalo, serving 16 years.

With the sale to the bank foot traffic decreased, and tenants began to leave the Market Arcade. Buffalo was declining by then as well. In the 1970's the building was shuttered. The sale of the Washington Market contributed to the loss of at least two Buffalo institutions.

The city acquired the Arcade in a bankruptcy hearing, and by the mid 80's a restoration was underway. It was completed in 1995. Use of the Arcade slowly increased. In 2013 the city put the building up for sale. It was purchased by Sinatra & Co. Realty in 2014 for $1.4 million. It remains open as retail and office space, and as a venue for weddings and events.

by Ellen Mika Zelasko

Mayfair Lane
North Street, Buffalo

*Figure 100 Mayfair Court
photo credit Marsha Falkowski*

Mayfair Lane is located off North Street and was built between 1926 and 1929. It was designed by E.B. Greens, Sr. and Jr.

Green Sr. graduated with a bachelor's degree in architecture from Cornell University in 1878, one of the first architectural degree programs in the country. Before then, architecture was seen as more of a trade than a profession.

In 1881 he partnered with William S. Wicks and the firm of Green and Wicks moved to Buffalo, NY. Over the next 36 years, they left an indelible mark on Buffalo. Wicks retired in 1917, Green worked with his son until 1933 and with Robert Maxwell James, Rufus W. Meadows and Lewis E. Howard until his death in 1950.

Green Sr. was so sought after in Buffalo that it is rumored that when John J. Albright's home, designed by Green, burned to the ground, Albright encountered Green on the property watching the fire. He immediately said to him, "Well, Green, have you brought the plans for the new home?"

In the end, Green designed and built over 370 buildings during his career, 200 of which were in Buffalo. Roughly 160 of them are still standing today.

Mayfair Lane is set up to resemble an English lane, complete with Tudor style architecture. It was innovative for its day, in that it was done condominium style, or townhouse-like, with a parking garage for each home at the street level off North Street. There is a stairway on North Street leading up to the sandstone tiled lane itself. Twenty Tudor townhouses face each other with the lane in between resembling a very charming English garden.

The whole lot is just 100 feet wide by 300 feet long. The homes are spacious, well-appointed and comfortable.

At the end of the lane sits a castle, complete with drawbridge and cannons. It is a 5 bedroom, 3 ½ bath, 4,043 square foot architectural masterpiece that sits on an 8,786 square foot lot. The castle is opulent and quirky simultaneously. This is where E.B. Green, Jr. lived until his early death in 1933.

The castle was purchased in 2017 by developer Noel Sutton, known for his dedication to the art of preservation. He has transformed the historic castle into a high-end short-term rental, promising guests a private fairytale getaway.

The elder E.B. Green lived out his last few years at number 19 Mayfair Lane.

by Ellen Mika Zelasko

McDonnell & Sons – Granite Works
858 Main Street, Buffalo

Patrick McDonnell began his career as a stonecutter at a granite quarry and opened a granite business in Quincy, Massachusetts in 1837. His company became one of the leading granite firms in Quincy and later the entire country. After his death, Patrick's sons John and Thomas decided to expand into the retail side of the business.

In 1884 John selected Buffalo as their business location. His choice was based upon Buffalo being the eighth largest city in the U.S. and having the most millionaires per capita. The city was also chosen due to its railway connections providing transportation of monuments to locations across the country.

Figure 101 McDonnell & Sons Co. photo enhanced by Gene Thompson

He purchased 858 Main Street, between Virginia and Allen Streets, as the location of his offices, showroom, sculpturers studio and workshop. Shortly after relocating to Buffalo, McDonnell was hired to design an elaborate monument by John and Elizabeth Blocher for their son John. This life-sized marble carving of John Blocher and his parents, with an angel in the crypt's interior, enclosed in imported plate glass, was completed in 1887 and erected at Forest Lawn. It is considered one of the most popular monuments at a private cemetery in the U.S.

The 85-foot-tall Soldiers & Sailors Monument in Lafayette Square was built by a different contractor in 1884 and within a few years was crumbling and leaning to one side. McDonnell & Sons was contracted to rebuild the monument, which is still standing tall 140 year later.

In addition to their headquarters at 858 Main Street, the company purchased the former Limestone Hill Granite Company at 914 Ridge Road as their Southtown's branch near Holy Cross Cemetery in Lackawanna. They continued operations of their original plants and quarry in Quincy, Massachusetts and purchased state of the art facilities in Barre, Vermont. In 1922 the company claimed to be the largest granite firm, by sales volume, in the country.

At Forest Lawn Cemetery the company has designed and built monuments for many of the prominent families in Buffalo. They have also completed monuments for municipalities, politicians, military and notable individuals across the country.

Their building at 858 Main Street was purchased by First Amherst Development and with the assistance of the Buffalo Preservation Board, it was converted into the first mixed use redevelopment in Downtown Buffalo and is considered the gold standard for reuse and historical preservation in WNY.

Mentholatum Company
1360 Niagara Street, Buffalo

Figure 102 Mentholatum Company - mid-1900s
photo Company Archives

The roots of the Mentholatum Company date back to 1889 when Albert Alexander Hyde formed the Yucca Company in Wichita, Kansas. The company sold soaps, toiletries and shaving creams. Their products used essential oils and supplements extracted from non-native plants, including the Yucca plant. Another prominent essential oil was menthol, extracted from peppermint plants in Hokkaido. Japan.

To create a product more profitable than soaps and shaving creams, Hyde decided to concentrate on a cough syrup called Vest Pocket Cough Specific, containing a blend of camphor and menthol. In 1894 the company introduced a salve created by Hyde to relieve muscle aches and congestion. It contained menthol and camphor, mixed with petrolatum, a jelly that adhered to the skin and created direct contact between the oils and pores. It was named Mentholatum and was so successful that the company discontinued their other products and changed its name to The Mentholatum Company.

Due to its advantageous location and access to efficient transportation systems, Buffalo was chosen as the primary manufacturing plant for making Mentholatum. In 1903 they opened a plant on South Division Street and eleven years later opened a second plant in Fort Erie, to service the Canadian Market. Business was so successful that in 1919 the company built an 80,000 square foot factory at 1360 Niagara Street, between Lafayette and West Delevan Avenue.

The four-story Daylight Factory building was designed by Buffalo architect George Townsend, featuring large windows set between steel reinforced concrete piers. The wide-open floor plan was broken only by several rows of concrete columns. After their corporate headquarters moved to Buffalo in 1945, additional expansions were completed in 1947 and 1966.

In 1997 the Hyde family-owned company was sold to Rohto Pharmaceutical, a small family drugstore in Osaka, Japan that expanded into a pioneer in over-the-counter medicines and healthcare products. Mentholatum moved their operations to Orchard Park and the building was sold to the Garrett Leather Company. They occupied the complex until 2016, when they relocated to Cheektowaga.

Ciminilli Real estate Company purchased 1360 Niagara Street from Garrett Leather and began converting the property to mixed commercial use and apartments. The Mentholatum Apartments features 49 apartments, commercial space on the first floor, basement parking and a view of the Niagara River.

The Mentholatum Company is still headquartered in Orchard Park and their products are distributed in over 110 countries worldwide.

# MICHIGAN AVENUE BAPTIST CHURCH
511 Michigan Avenue, Buffalo

A group of African American men, led by Elisha Tucker, formed the Second Baptist Society of Buffalo in 1836. Land was purchased east of downtown on Michigan Street in 1845 by a group of trustees, under the direction of Reverend John Sharpe. Funding was supplied by Peyton Harris, a former enslaved person who became a successful Buffalo businessman. Reverend Samuel Davis, a mason by trade, led the congregation and is credited with building the church and with Harris, purchasing the materials. The church opened in 1849, when the African American population of Buffalo was about 350.

*Figure 103 Michigan Avenue Baptist Church
photo credit Petra Mangus*

The church became the center of activity for Buffalo's growing Black community and is often referenced as a last stop on the Underground Railroad. Although there is no documented proof, it is often mentioned that escaped slaves were hidden in the basement of the church before being ferried across the Niagara River into Canada under the cover of darkness. Prior to the Civil War, members of the church were associated with abolitionist meetings of African Americans in and most of the church members listed birthplaces that identified them as most likely being enslaved people. Black abolitionists Frederick Douglass, William Wells Brown, Henry Highland Garnet, Martin Delany and others made frequent appearances in Buffalo. Wells was a Buffalo resident.

In 1891, Oberlin College graduate and future civil rights leader Mary Burnett married William Talbert of Buffalo. Talbert was the maternal grandson of Peyton Harris and son of Robert Talbert, a successful California Gold Rush prospector and owner of a Buffalo real estate company. The Talbert home was next to the Michigan Street Baptist Church.

Reverend Jesse Edward Nash became pastor of the Michigan Street Baptist Church in 1892, a position he held for the next 61 years. Nash and Mary Burnett Talbert worked together in making the church the center for the social justice movement and civil rights activities of the Black community. W.E.B. DuBois worked with the church to properly represent African Americans at the 1901 Pan American Exposition. Booker T. Washington spoke at the church in 1910 and Adam Clayton Powell, Sr. was a frequent guest minister. Nash and Talbert were founding members of the Buffalo NAACP, Talbert formed the Phyllis Wheatly Club and Nash brought the Urban League to Buffalo.

A national historic site, The Michigan Avenue Baptist Church is a centerpiece of the Michigan Street African American Heritage Corridor.

Monroe Building – Record Theatre
1786 Main Street, Buffalo

Figure 104 O'Neill Motor Company later became Record Theatre photo enhanced by Gene Thompson

The Monroe Building was designed by architect George Morton Wolfe in 1920. Wolfe specialized in industrial and shopping centers and also designed the Circle Theatre at 444 Connecticut Street, Parkside Candy Company at 3208 Main Street, the Henkel Building at 1358 Main Street and the Amherst Theatre at 3500 Main Street.

Building owner Charles Monroe was an agent for Marmon & Velie Motor Companies and operated his automobile dealership in the building. When he filed for bankruptcy in 1931, the Ford Motor Company purchased the structure and remodeled it into their new model of a full-service dealership. This concept featured factory trained mechanics and parts for every model of Ford vehicles on the market, emphasizing service and repairs to make cars last longer for cash strapped Americans during the Depression.

In 1936 Ford sold the business to the Birk & Bailey automobile dealership. The building housed a variety of other automobile dealers, including O'Neill Motor Corp., through the early 1970s.

Lenny Silver began working in a Rochester record store after serving as a radio operator in the U.S. Navy during WWII. He moved to Buffalo in 1954 to work for a Buffalo company in the promotion and distribution of records. He successfully promoted artists including Andy Williams, Bobby Vinton and the Everly Brothers. In 1964 he opened his own company to promote and distribute records nationally, expanding it into the fourth largest record distribution company in the U.S.

In 1976 he opened the first location of Record Theatre in the former Monroe Building with an address of 1800 Main Street. It became the largest record store in the world, ringing up sales of $80,000 per day. The store concept was successful, and Record Theatre expanded to 37 locations. Transcontinental Records, (the parent company of Record Theatre, the distribution company and record company) employed 350 people with annual sales of $50 million.

Lenny Silver died at the age of 90 in 2017. The Record Theatre chain had been reduced to two locations 1800 Main Street and the University Plaza location at 3500 Main Street. On August 27, 2017, the original Record Theater at 1800 Main Street closed its doors.

After being vacant for several years, the metal siding that covered the original façade was removed and the $8.4 million rehabilitation of The Monroe Buildings into a mixed development of 17 apartments and 11,400 feet of commercial/retail space has been completed.

Nash House Museum
36 Nash Street, Buffalo

Reverend Jesse Edward Nash arrived in Buffalo on June 26, 1892 and began a ministry as pastor of the Michigan Avenue Baptist Church for the next 61 years. He remained a bachelor until 1925 when he married Frances Jackson Nash, the sister of Raymond E. Jackson, one of the founders of the Colored Musicians Club. They purchased a home at 36 Potter Street, directly behind his church.

As pastor of the Michigan Avenue Baptist Church, Nash invited black leaders with whom he had made acquaintance. Booker T. Washington, W.E.B. DeBois, Adam Clayton Powell, Sr. and other luminaries spoke at the Michigan Avenue Baptist Church, other locations in Buffalo and were houseguests at his home.

Figure 105 Jesse Nash House photo credit Rick Falkowski

Nash also worked closely with Mary Burnett Talbert who lived on Michigan Avenue two houses away from his church. For the Pan-American Exposition, with W.E.B. DeBois, Talbert and Nash coordinated the African American involvement and exhibits at the Pan-Am that featured advancements made by Blacks in the arts, education, business, medicine, science and more. Talbert and Nash were the instrumental founding members of the Buffalo NAACP and Nash was responsible for bringing the Urban League to Buffalo. He was also secretary of the Ministers Alliance of Buffalo, member of the Council of Social Agencies, chaplain at Meyer Memorial Hospital (now ECMC), treasurer of the WNY Baptist Alliance and the most widely known and respected African American in Buffalo.

Upon his retirement in 1953, Potter Street was renamed Nash Street in honor of his service to the Michigan Avenue Church and city of Buffalo. He died in 1957 and his widow remained at their home until her passing in 1987. Their son Jesse Nash, Jr., retired Canisius College Professor (1965-1998), musician and community leader, then rented the first floor of the home to Bishop William Henderson, who became pastor of the Michigan Avenue Church. Neither Mrs. Nash nor Bishop Henderson disturbed Reverend Nash's second floor office. When it was toured by the Michigan Street Preservation group in 1999, they entered a time capsule of a pre-WWII African American home complete with Nash's typewriter, desk, victrola, furnishings, books and papers.

His papers were preserved by the African American Studies Department at UB. The home is now open for tours as the Nash House Museum and is part of the Michigan Street African American Heritage Corridor.

NIAGARA SQUARE
Downtown Buffalo

Figure 106 Niagara Square Buffalo in 1920s PD

In 1804 Niagara Square was the central public square of the village of New Amsterdam, renamed the village of Buffalo. Prior to becoming the land agent for the Holland Land Company, Joseph Ellicott assisted his brother Andrew in surveying Washington DC. His design of Buffalo was influenced by Pierre L'Enfant's radial plan for the U.S. capital.

Four major streets converge at Niagara Square, resulting in eight arterials radiating like spokes from the city center. The streets were originally named after Indian tribes and the principals of the Holland Land Company: Delaware Street, Busti Avenue, Cazenovia Avenue and Schimmelpennick Avenue. The street names were changed to Delaware Avenue, Genesee Street, Court Street and Niagara Street.

On June 17, 1825, the Thayer Brothers were hung at gallows in Niagara Square, erected near the current location of the front entrance to City Hall. The population of the village was only about 2,000 but between 20,000 to 30,000 came to witness their execution.

After Buffalo was incorporated as a city in 1832, the square became a prime residential area. Several mansions were built, with some constructed in 1836. Starting at the western portion of the square was the Wilkerson Mansion, blocking the western extension of Court Street. Clockwise was the Balcom/Chandler House, Henry H. Sizer House, John Hollister Mansion (purchased by Millard Fillmore), Burt House, Stephen G. Austin House and Herman B. Potter House.

These properties became the first gas station in downtown (followed by City Hall in 1930), Niagara Square Baptist Church/Peoples Church (now the Robert H, Jackson Courthouse), Spencer Kellog Company, Hotel Fillmore/Castle Inn (Statler Hotel built in 1923), Central High School (replaced by William J. Mahoney State Office Building), Federal Court Building/Buffalo Police & Fire Headquarters, Buffalo Athletic House and Women's Union/Townsend Hall (City Court Building in 1974).

A Civil War Memorial arch, designed by architect H.H. Richardson and approved by Frederick Law Olmsted's plan for the city, would have arched over Delaware Avenue. It was proposed by Maria Love and the Ladies Monument Association in 1874, but due to a lack of funds it was never built.

In the center of the square is the McKinley Monument, erected in 1907 to commemorate the assassination of President William McKinley at the Pan American Exposition in 1901.

NIETZSCHES, MULLIGANS BRICK BAR, THE OLD PINK
Allen Street, Buffalo

For decades the western end of Allen Street, before it turns into Wadsworth Street, was the home of several iconic bars. Nietzsche's is still with us but The Old Pink and Mulligans Brick Bar burned down in mid-2024 and early 2025.

Nietzsche's at 248 Allen Street was The Jamestown Grill from the 1930s through the 1982 and was known for featuring burlesque floor shows. Joe Rubino purchased the building and in 1982 it became Nietzsche's. The club presented all styles of music but catered to original bands and hosted on the rise regional groups like Phish, Tragically Hip, the Goo Goo Dolls, 10,000 Maniacs and others before they became nationally touring acts. Michael Meldrum hosted a Monday open mic at Nietzsche's for decades and assisted Ani DiFranco in getting her start.

Figure 107 Mulligans Brick Bar photo credit Steve Cichon

The long narrow room had a small performance area in the front bar and a stage at the back of the 248 capacity, 3,500 square foot building. Old style balconies lined both sides of the back room and the bathrooms left a lasting memory.

In 2024, Rubino sold the building and business to new owners that included musicians John Weber and Sam Marabella (a former owner of Broadway Joe's). They refurbished the interior, rebuilt the balconies, updated the mechanics, added in-house sound, lighting and refreshed bathrooms. But it still retained the dive bar ambiance. Best of all, they upgraded the upstairs green room for touring bands and will continue the Nietzsche's legacy of offering an eclectic experience, showcasing cutting edge musicians.

The rejuvenation of Nietzsche's is welcome news for the Allentown area due to the tragic loss of the Old Pink and Mulligan's Brick Bar.

The building that housed The Pink at 223 Allen Street was built in 1863, became Jimmie Oats Grill in 1942, Birdies 19th Hole, Mark Supples opened the Pink Flamingo in 1983, sold it to the Brinkworth family and it was considered WNY's premier dive bar.

Mulligans at 229 Allen dated back to 1897, was a speakeasy during Prohibition and Benjamin Mulligan got a proper liquor license in 1934. During the 1930s and 40s it featured floor shows and country western bands in the 1950s and 60s. In 1970 Michael Mulligan, Kevin Kell and Ben Kell renamed it Mulligan's Brick Bar, becoming Allentown's premier party bar.

Many memories went up in flames with those two bars but Nietzsche's will continue to shine.

North Park Theatre
1428 Hertel Avenue, Buffalo

Figure 108 North Park Theater early photo PD

Michael Shea believed a movie theater should capture the imaginations of filmgoers when they enter the building, lifting people out of their daily routine to watch their dreams come true on the silver screen. When the North Park Theatre opened on November 21, 1920, Shea felt he had accomplished his goal.

The North Park Theatre's Neoclassical foyer and auditorium were designed by Buffalo architect Henry Spann, and Pan American Exposition artist Raphael Beck painted the murals. Beck's vividly colored murals depict stylized scenes inspired by classical mythology. Five murals adorn the ceiling's dome and the sixth crowns the theater's proscenium. The two-story foyer had three Art Nouveau stained-glass windows above the front entrance, leaded glass windows above the doors, gouged dentil molding, fluted plaster pilaster, friezes and wainscoting. The exterior was cast concrete with swag and cartouche frieze, with terra cotta roof tiles. Seating in the auditorium was originally 1,222.

In 1941 Flexlume Signs installed the Art Deco marquee signage above the front entrance. Flexlume is a Buffalo based company founded by the Wiley brothers in 1904. By the 1920s they were the largest sign manufacturer in the world.

After being operated by Shea's Theaters and owned by Paramount, the North Park changed to Loew's in 1948, Dipson in 1963 and independent ownership. To reduce heating costs, a drop ceiling was installed in the lobby covering the ornamental molding, three balconets and hanging chandeliers. Remodeling in 1958 lowered the seating capacity to 800 seats.

In 2014 Thomas Eoanneau and Mike Christiano purchased the North Park and began a multi-million-dollar remodeling project. Swiatek Studios, who completed the remodeling of Shea's Buffalo downtown, was hired to seal and repaint the crumbling ceiling, repaint and restore all the decorative plaster work and remove layers of grime and tobacco stains from the ceiling paintings and walls, along with installing Art Deco lighting fixtures and wall sconces. They removed the dropped ceiling in the lobby to expose the grandeur of the ceiling, again highlighting the original stained-glass windows. Flexlume Signs found the original 1940 blueprints to return the marquee to its original appearance.

When Buffalo's Vincent Gallo released the locally filmed movie Buffalo '66 in 1998 the premiere was held at the North Park Theatre. Other Buffalo filmed movies staged their premiers at the theater and it hosts portions of the Buffalo International Film Festival. Michael Shea's dream remains a reality.

OLD COUNTY HALL
92 Franklin Street, Buffalo

Erie County Hall was built on the site of Franklin Square Cemetery, which was one of Buffalo's first burial grounds. The cemetery operated from 1804-1836, and primarily held the War of 1812 dead. The property was purchased by the city in 1851, and the graves were moved to Forest Lawn Cemetery a year later.

Completed in 1876, the building was a joint effort of the city of Buffalo and Erie County to house government offices. A Rochester architect, Andrew Jackson Warner, designed the building. It is generally described as High Victorian Romanesque or Norman Romanesque. The style is evidenced in the use of rounded arches in the windows and entrances, and in the use of piers instead of columns.

Figure 109 Old County Hall photo credit Ellen Mika Zelasko

The center of the building is dominated by the 270-foot-tall clock tower. The clock itself was backlit by reflected gas light. Quite a sight in 1876! Resting on the tower are four 16-foot-tall stylized female figures, each carved from 30-ton blocks of granite. Each one is slightly different, representing Agriculture, Mechanical Arts, Justice and Commerce. They were sculpted by Giovanni F. Sala.

The two sides of the County Building are mirror images, save for the imposing tower. In 1965 a four-story addition was added to the Delaware Avenue side of the building with a hallway that joins the two.

In 1882 Grover Cleveland became the mayor of Buffalo. He had his office in the building, before moving on to become Governor of New York State and eventually the President of the United States.

In 1891 a tunnel was built connecting the Erie County Jail on Delaware Avenue to County Hall, providing safe and simple prisoner passage to the courts. The tunnel is still in use today.

President William McKinley lay in state in the building after being tragically assassinated at the Pan American Exposition in Buffalo in 1901. McKinley's assassin, Leon Czolgosz, was tried and sentenced to death in this building.

In 1932 both the city and the county offices had outgrown the building, and the city of Buffalo offices moved into their new and current home on Niagara Square.

The Old County Hall Building is an official Buffalo Landmark and was added to the National Register of Historic Places in 1976.

Today, it houses Erie County Courts and Records.

by Ellen Mika Zelasko

Oscar Meyer Motor Corp – Coles Restaurant
1104 Elmwood Avenue, Buffalo

Figure 110 Cole's Restaurant in 1934 PD

The building at 1104 Elmwood Avenue near Forest has been known as the location of Coles Restaurant for decades but it began as an auto showroom.

In 1904 the Automobile Association of America (AAA) inaugurated what became the Glidden Tour, an endurance race in which all the early automobile manufacturers participated. Industrialist Charles J. Glidden was an auto enthusiast that took part in the race and became a naming sponsor. In 1906 the race passed through Buffalo and ironically the winning car in the first five Glidden Tours was the Buffalo made Pierce Arrow.

Behind 1104 Elmwood the first structure in Buffalo to be used solely as a garage business was erected. Charles J. Glidden gave them permission to name it the Glidden Garage and in return whenever Glidden stayed at a downtown Buffalo hotel, he stored his car at the garage on Elmwood near Forest.

By 1909 larger quarters were required for the business and it was doubled in size to 8,000 square feet. Further expansion took place in 1917, adding a two-story structure on Forest Avenue to house offices, accessories and a paint shop. A Chevrolet showroom was created in the front portion of 1104 Elmwood Avenue in 1921 and the business was renamed the Oscar Meyer Motor Corp.

The first cars serviced were noisy gas chariots with side cranks, acetylene lamps, steering wheels on the right side and a maze of straps holding together the top and bottom windshields. In addition to being a high-volume Chevy dealership, the showroom featured an assortment of used vehicles of all models, including Pierce Arrows that were manufactured a couple miles down Elmwood Avenue.

When Prohibition ended in 1934, the building was turned into a restaurant. The 28-foot mahogany bar at Coles has served patrons for nine decades.

In 1973 Korean War veteran and Buffalo firefighter Davie Shatzel, Sr. purchased the bar. It had already been a popular tavern for 40 years and his father Elmer Shatzel owned three different bars in Lackawanna, the first near the Bethlehem Steel Plant, followed by locations on Ridge Road and Electric Avenue.

The Cole's tradition continues in this three-story watering hole that is like walking back in tavern history time, has served the Elmwood strip for ninety years and three generations of the Shatzel family have provided food and spirits for the past fifty years.

Packard Motor Car Showroom
1325 Main Street, Buffalo

The Packard Motor Car Company Showroom and Service Building at Main and Riley Streets was designed in 1926 by Albert Kahn, one of America's foremost Industrial architects. In Buffalo Kahn also designed the Pierce-Arrow factory on Elmwood and Ford Moter Company plant on Main Street.

A three-story Neoclassical style, 68,000 square foot reinforced concrete frame building featured a showroom on the first floor, with sales offices on the second floor and substantial auto storage on the third floor. The front third of the building was dedicated to the showroom and decorated befitting a luxury atmosphere for expensive automobiles. It had oak paneled walls, leaded glass windows and doors, and a double stairway with decorative wrought iron railings.

*Figure 111 Packard Building
photo enhanced by Gene Thompson*

Along the Northeast side of the building, a sweeping ramp allowed cars that entered on Riley Street to reach the second and third floors. The upper floors and back two thirds of the building housed a service and preparation area for the Packards that arrived in Buffalo by freighter from Detroit. This was a Packard Distribution Center, with the cars being forwarded to dealerships across the Northeastern U.S.

Ralph E. Brown was the president of the dealership that moved into the building in 1927, from their previous site at 300 Delaware Avenue. Brown was previously a representative for Winton Automobile. When the Buffalo Showroom opened in the 1920s, Packard produced more automobiles annually than any other American luxury car manufacturer and was equally respected in Europe for its quality. Packard also had a South Buffalo dealership at 680 Seneca Street and a service center at 202 West Utica. Brown ran the dealership until 1931.

The Ostendorf family became associated with the company in 1933, when George Ostendorf, who was with Syracuse based Franklin Automobile Company since 1907, joined the business. They purchased the building from Packard in 1948 and operated it until Packard ceased production in 1958.

In 1960 the building became the home of Brenner Music, with pianos being sold where Packards had been displayed. It was later D'Amico Discount House, a furniture store, Manpower Training Center and in 1970 the home of the CETA job training program. For a number of years, it was a carpet cleaning company and in 1992 was sold to Schmidt's Garage.

The Packard Building was purchased by Regan Development and has been converted into the Packard VA Clinic and 40 apartments.

Palace Burlesk, Studio Arena, Shea's 710 Theatre

710 Main Street, Buffalo

Figure 112 710 Main Street Palace Theater under construction

Dewey Michaels opened the Palace Burlesk Theater in Buffalo's Shelton Square in 1925. Its location was on Main Street where the M&T Bank Tower now stands, across Division Street from the Ellicott Square Building. A 1940s matchbook cover proclaimed it "clever comics and pretty girls at the Moulin Rouge of Buffalo."

Considered a burlesque house, the shows at the Palace were largely Vaudeville, the American rendition of British music hall entertainment. Shows featured singers, jugglers, magicians, baggy-pants comedians, chorus lines, skits, live bands and of course headlining solo burlesque dancers with their fans, veils, feathers and other props. Any nudity was brief, more perceived than actually existent, titillation rather than skin. Compared to the X-rated film house and even modern television, the shows were quite innocent.

The 720-seat theater was often filled to capacity for their shows that ran from noon to midnight. Construction of the Church Street extension project resulted in the theater closing on April 6, 1967 at a sold-out red-carpet gala.

Michaels invested his $375,000 settlement and built a new Palace Theatre at 710 Main Street at West Tupper, designed by architect Theodore A. Biggie. It opened to a sold-out crowd of 700 patrons on December 28, 1967. However, the popularity of burlesque waned, with audiences gravitating to the Canadian Ballet and exotic dance clubs. When it closed ten years later, only 24 people were in attendance for the final night. Micheals lost 100% of his original investment.

Studio Arena moved to 710 Main Street from the former Town Casino, across the street, at 684 Main Street. Many prominent actors performed at Studio Arena early during their careers and the theater staged prominent plays and world premieres.

In 2011, the building at 710 Main Street was acquired by Shea's Buffalo to host touring shows and local productions. Currently named Shea's 710 Theatre, under the tutelage of Shea's Buffalo, a $5 million renovation project transformed the exterior and interior of the building, adding a two-story lounge and cabaret that opened to a seasonal outdoor patio.

Shea's President, former U.S. Representative Brian Higgins, announced that MusicalFare Theatre signed a 20-year agreement to relocate to Shea's 710 Theatre from its former Daemen University home. The relocation of MusicalFare will result in an additional 100 shows at the complex, making it an almost year-round venue and providing more activity in the theater district.

Parade / Humboldt / Martin Luther King, Jr. Park
Olmsted Park System, Buffalo

The Parade was designed by Frederick Law Olmsted and Calvert Vaux as part of their original design for the Buffalo Municipal Parks system in 1868. It was designed so you could travel on tree-lined parkways, with large medians, between the parks without ever leaving the park-like atmosphere.

Figure 113 Martin Luther King Park Parade Pavilion Picture Book of Earlier Buffalo photo restored by Gene Thompson

That design was inspired by the parklands, boulevards and squares of Paris, France. The Parks included The Park (now Delaware), The Front, The Parade, Riverside and South Park. The Parkways were Bidwell, Chapin, Humboldt, Lincoln, South Side (now McKinley), Porter, Red Jacket and The Avenue (now Richmond). And the circles consisted of Agassiz, Bidwell (now Colonial), Ferry, Chapin Place (now Gates), Woodside (now McClellan), McKinley, Soldiers and The Circle (now Symphony).

When The Parade was designed Olmsted's original intent was a place where soldiers could practice marching. At the entrance was the Parade House, designed by Calvert Vaux. From the long verandas of the building, spectators would watch activities on the parade field. The large ornate wooden structure featured a restaurant and meeting rooms, was considered the primary place in the Buffalo Parks system for festive socializing. The large German population living near the park enjoyed the restaurant and dancing on an outdoor wooden floor, to an orchestra performing overhead on the balcony. The Parade House was considered one of the most lavish and fanciful structures to grace an American municipal park.

In 1895 the park was redesigned with a 500-foot diameter wading pool replacing the marching grounds and renamed Humboldt Park in 1896. Changes in addition to the new pool included The Shelter House added in 1903, Greenhouse in 1909, Casino in 1925 and Museum of Science Building in 1929.

When the park system project was completed, Olmsted proclaimed… "Buffalo to be the best designed city in the United States, if not the world."

During the 1960s the connection between Delaware Park and Humboldt Park was lost when the Kensington Expressway was constructed. In 1978 The Buffalo Friends of Olmsted Parks was formed to advocate for Olmsted's Park system. The Conservancy became the first not-for-profit organization to manage a public parks system in the country when it entered into a partnership with the city of Buffalo in 2004.

In 1977 the park was renamed Martin Luther King, Jr. Park and it is the home of Juneteenth and other activities on the East Side of Buffalo.

PARKSIDE CANDY
3208 Main Street, Buffalo

Figure 114 Parkside Candy Main & Oakwood watercolor by Dr. V. Roger Lalli

In 1927 George Kaiser and his wife decided to expand the modest candy store they opened in 1919 at Main and Oakwood, near Sisters Hospital. Due to the success of their homemade candies, they needed more space to keep up the demand for their sweets.

Architect Morton Wolf created a classic designed early 20th century ice cream store, soda shop interior with solid walnut candy cases, table and soda fountain. Built in 1927 by George W. Butler Company, the facility had to be expanded by the same contracting company in 1938 to double their production capabilities. The oval interior of the store and dining area retains that nostalgic look, complete with some original light fixtures and booths.

When the movie The Natural, starring Robert Redford and Glenn Close, was filmed in Buffalo during 1983 two scenes took place inside Parkside Candy to recapture the appearance and spirit of the 1930s. Other Buffalo locations like the Ellicott Square Building, Central Terminal, War Memorial Stadium, All High Stadium and Buffalo Psychiatric Center were also utilized to retain that pre-WWII look. Some Parkside Candy employees were cast as extras, working in the store during production.

The business was purchased in 1981 by Philip Buffamonte from the estate of George Kaiser. He further expanded the business by making their signature sponge candy, old-fashioned lollipops and taffy available wholesale throughout the Northeast, including the resort areas of Lake George, Cape Cod and the Jersey Shore. During the Christmas, Valentine's Day and easter holidays, the Parkside factory gears up for production of candies for the corresponding season. In addition, all the Parkside products are available online at parksidecandy.com or at the other six locations the store has opened across WNY.

In 2017 the interior and exterior of the 3208 Main Street store at Main and Winspear Streets was refurbished, updating but retaining its classic appearance. After over 40 years of running the business Buffamonte announced in early 2025 that he is planning to retire. He maintains any sale is contingent upon the stipulation that the new owners retain the current use of the store and factory so future generations can continue enjoying the traditional treats that have been offered by Parkside Candy for over a century.

Peace Bridge
1 Peace Bridge Plaza, Buffalo

The building of a bridge connecting the U.S. and Canada at Buffalo was first discussed in 1853. Due to the swift currents of the Niagara River between Buffalo and Fort Erie, the costs involved and the fact that federal laws would have to be passed by both countries, the bridge did not progress beyond discussions.

Figure 115 Peace Bridge photo credit Ellen Mika Zelasko

In the 1890s Alonzo Mather again proposed a bridge between Buffalo and Fort Erie. He purchased land on the Canadian side and on the U.S. side next to Fort Porter. Since the U.S. government did not approve the project, the bridge was not built but the land Mather purchased in Fort Erie was named Mather's Park in his honor.

The International Railroad Bridge of Buffalo opened in 1873 but it was built only for rail traffic. When the 100th anniversary of the War of 1812 took place, serious discussions renewed but WWI delayed any action. In 1919, businessmen in Fort Erie and Buffalo were successful in getting approval by an International Joint Commission to build the bridge. A private company would finance the bridge through bond sales and it would become the property of NYS and Canada when collected tolls retired the debt.

In 1925 the Buffalo and Fort Erie Bridge company was incorporated with Frank B. Baird of the Buffalo Chamber of Commerce as president and Canadian politician William M. German as vice-president. Construction began with the contractors being R.B. Porter of St. Catherines and Turner Construction of Buffalo. The length of the bridge is 5,800 feet, consisting of 3,500 feet of steel work. In addition, the bridge includes 9,000 tons of structural steel and 800 tons of reinforcing steel. Chief engineer of the project was Edward Lupfer, who later designed the Rainbow Bridge in Niagara Falls.

The grand opening ceremony on August 7, 1927, was attended by international dignitaries. To commemorate over 100 years of peace between the USA and Canada, it was named the Peace Bridge. When the bridge reverted to government ownership in 1934, the Buffalo & Fort Erie Public Bridge Authority was formed, with Frank B. Baird the first commissioner. He is considered the "Father of the Peace Bridge."

Until 1992 the Peace Bridge was the busiest U.S./Canada border crossing and in 1993 an $88 million renovation was announced. Plans to build a new bridge have been held up in litigation since 1997 and continue to be delayed.

Pierce Arrow Factory
1695 Elmwood Avenue, Buffalo

Figure 116 Pierce Arrow Factory 1921 brochure PD

In 1865, George Pierce moved to Buffalo and worked for Heinz, Pierce & Munschauer, a company that manufactured bird cages, ice boxes, washing machines and bathtubs. He bought out his partners in 1878 and started concentrating on making bicycles. By 1895 George N. Pierce & Company was just producing bicycles and the company introduced the Cushion Frame which incorporated springing in the rear shock device and evolved into spring forks. The Pierce bicycle was considered one of the best bicycles manufactured in the U.S.

At the 1901 Pan-American Exposition Pierce introduced the single cylinder, two-seater Motorette, followed by the two-cylinder Arrow in 1903 and upscale four-cylinder Great Arrow in 1904. The bicycles and automobiles were manufactured at their 6-22 Hanover Street at Prime Street plant. George Pierce sold his rights to the Pierce Motor Company in 1907 and in 1908 the Pierce-Arrow Motor Company was formed, with George Birge as president.

Pierce continued manufacturing bicycles and began making motorcycles at the Hanover Street plant. In 1906 Albert Kahn designed the Pierce-Arrow factory at 1695 Elmwood Avenue at Great Arrow in North Buffalo for the expanded automobile manufacturing. The company successfully manufactured two-to-five-ton trucks, selling over 14,000 to the French and British governments by the end of WWI, but discontinued that line to concentrate on luxury cars.

The Elmwood plant was one of the first to fully utilize the Daylight Factory Industrial architectural style, which dominated early 20th Century Factory design. It was designed to make maximum use of natural light with a zig-zag roof structure. The building was made almost entirely of reinforced concrete, required hundreds of thousands of square feet of glass and encompassed over one million square feet. The complex was built in the area where the midway existed during the Pan-Am Exposition, in 1916 employed over 3,000 workers and the administration building was designed by Buffalo architect George Cary.

Studebaker purchased the company in 1928 and Pierce-Arrow sales peaked at 8,500 cars in 1929. The Stock Market crash and following Depression reduced the number of wealthy individuals that could afford to purchase cars that sold for over $10,000. Studebaker went into receivership in 1932 and a group of Buffalo businessmen led by George Rand, Jr. attempted to keep the company afloat, but Pierce-Arrow filed for bankruptcy in 1938.

The historic building has been converted into the Pierce-Arrow Lofts, consisting of 1-, 2- and 3-bedroom apartments with modern amenities.

PIERCE ARROW SHOWROOMS – VERNOR BUILDING
752-8 Main Street and 2421 Main Street, Buffalo

The Pierce-Arrow Company was started by George Pierce in Buffalo as a manufacturer that eventually specialized in bicycles. They were considered one of the best bicycles made in the U.S. and all the police patrolling the Pan-American Exposition in 1901 rode Pierce Bicycles.

At the Pan-Am, George Pierce unveiled his single cylinder, two-seater Motorette. It was the talk of the fair and a great introduction for Pierce Automobile. In 1903 Pierce produced the two-cylinder Arrow and the Great Arrow the following year. George's son Percy Pierce entered the Great Arrow in the 1904 American Automobile Association race to the St. Louis World's Fair and was voted the winner of the race. Charles Glidden created the Glidden Tour endurance race which the Pierce Arrow won the first five years. This established the car as a quality reliable vehicle and the company concentrated on producing luxury automobiles. When President George Taft ordered two Pierce-Arrows as the official automobile of the White House, the car became a status symbol owned by Hollywood stars, business tycoons and members of royalty.

Figure 117 Pierce Arrow Showroom PD Detroit Public Library photo restored by Gene Thompson

In 1903 S.H. Woodruff is credited with designing the building at 752 Main Street (next to the Teck Theatre) which was billed as the largest automobile salesroom in the world. This building in the theater district remained the showroom for Pierce vehicles until they moved to their Art Deco dealership at Main and Jewett in 1928. After they moved, 752 Main Street was sold to the James Vernor Company and converted into the bottling plant and retail outlet for Vernor's Ginger Ale. After Vernor sold the building in 1951 it declined and was demolished in 2007. It is now an undeveloped grassy lot at the corner of Main and Edward.

Figure 118 2421 Main Street watercolor by Dr. V. Roger Lalli

The Pierce showroom at 2421 Main Street was a Cadillac dealership from 1936 to 1998, operated by Maxson, Tinney, and Braun Cadillac. It was purchased by Buffalo Savings Bank and is now a Key Bank branch.

The Pierce-Arrow name continues in Buffalo as the Pierce-Arrow Museum created by Jim Sandoro at 263 Michigan Avenue. While the former factory at 1695 Elmwood Avenue has been converted to apartments.

Rand Building
14 Lafayette Square, Buffalo

Figure 119 Rand Building
photo credit Ellen Mika Zelasko

The Rand Building was built in 1929, the last skyscraper completed in Buffalo before the stock market crashed. It was designed by Franklyn & William Kidd, along with James W. Kideney & Associates. The building was supposedly the inspiration behind the Empire State Building! It is a very conservative example of the Art Deco style of architecture.

Located on the northeast side of Lafayette Square, the spot it sits on used to be a lumber yard when Buffalo was first incorporated as a city in 1832. It was later the site of several churches, and at least two theaters (The Lafayette Theater & The Olympic Theater). There was also a private residence on the corner of Washington and Lafayette, which was later torn down and a German Restaurant called the Park Hof was built on the site. This corner building would become the Lafayette National Bank and was eventually purchased by the Marine Trust Company, who later purchased the Olympic Theater as well.

The Marine Trust Company built the Rand Building. It was named for George F. Rand, Sr., who was born in Niagara County in 1867, and began his banking career when he was 16 as an assistant cashier at the State Bank of North Tonawanda.

In 1888, George Sr. was elected president of the First National Bank of Tonawanda. He moved to Buffalo in 1901 when he became the president of the Columbia National Bank of Buffalo. He was made president of the Marine National Bank of Buffalo only a few years later. Rand is largely credited with giving New York State its first consolidated banking system by merging several banking institutions into the Marine Trust Company, which eventually would become the Marine Midland Corporation, now HSBC.

Sadly George Rand, Sr. passed away in a plane crash overseas in 1919, at the age of only 52. His son George Jr. followed him as President of Marine Trust in 1926. He was present and participated in the laying of the cornerstone of the Rand Building in 1929.

Buffalo radio stations WGR and WKBW moved into the building when it opened and remained tenants until the late 1950's. The 'GR' in WGR stands for George Rand. Now, the stations in the Townsquare Media cluster reside there, among many other tenants.

The Rand Building is presently owned by Priam Enterprises, LLC.

by Ellen Mika Zelasko

RICHARDSON OLMSTED CAMPUS – BUFFALO STATE HOSPITAL
444 Forest Avenue, Buffalo

In 1869 a new mental institution was approved by the New York State Legislature for the WNY area. Buffalo was selected as the site for the complex due to its population, location with access to transportation, medical college and atmosphere, with Frederick Law Olmsted just completing the Buffalo Parks System including nearby Delaware Park.

Figure 120 Richardson Olmsted Campus photo credit Marsha Falkowski

Olmsted was selected to design the 203-acre asylum campus and was asked to recommend an architect. He suggested Henry Hobson Richardson, who created a plan that conformed with the Kirkbride Plan of Treatment. This treatment encouraged creating a calm, airy environment, believing a peaceful atmosphere would help treat mental ailments.

Construction began in 1872 and the institution was named the Buffalo State Asylum for the Insane. The first patients were admitted in 1880, after the completion of the two administrative towers and the five connected western wing buildings. Construction of the main buildings would continue for the next twenty years, with the construction of the five connected eastern wing buildings beginning in 1889 and completed in 1896. Richardson died in 1886, but Green & Wicks and W.W. Carlin designed the other structures inspired by the Richardsonian Romanesque architectural style.

With the change in the nature of mental illness treatment evolving from the Kirkbride Plan of moral management to a cottage style approach, numerous small cottages and buildings were constructed on the campus from 1900 through WWII. In 1918 the slate shingles of the towers were covered in copper, providing the distinctive appearance of the complex.

The 203-acre campus featured the design of landscape architect Frederick Law Olmsted and landscape engineer Calvert Vaus. The northern 100 acres were dedicated to farmland, with patients working the land as part of their therapy. After production decreased and food was delivered, the northern half of the campus was sold to establish Buffalo State College in 1927.

Parking lots covered the landscaping in front of the Tower Buildings and tennis courts were built behind them. Patient population peaked at 2,766 in the 1950s but by 1974 patients were moved to the adjacent Strozzi Building.

In 1986 the site was designated a National Historic Landmark, in 2006 the Richardson Center Corp. was formed, in 2013 Olmsted's greenspace was reclaimed and in 2017 Hotel Henry and event space opened in the center three buildings. The property has been acclaimed as one of the largest preservation projects in the U.S.

RICHMOND – LOCKWOOD HOUSE
844 Delaware Avenue, Buffalo

Figure 121 Richmond Lockwood Mansion photo credit Mike Shriver buffalophotoblog.com

Levi Allen built several houses on Delaware Avenue, living at Delaware and Summer Street before selling it to Aaron Rumsey in 1860 and living at 844 Delaware before selling it to Jewett Richmond in 1873. Richmond was the owner of the Richmond Grain Elevator and president of Marine Bank, Erie County Savings Bank, the Buffalo & Jamestown Railroad, Buffalo Southwestern Railroad and the Buffalo Gas Light Company. He was also a member of the Buffalo Board of Trade, Merchants Exchange and City Council, along with serving on the Young Men's Association and Charity Organization of Buffalo.

When Richmond owned the property, the lawns, gardens and orchards extended to Rogers Road, which was renamed Richmond Avenue in his honor. The estate had sufficient land for cows to graze and multiple stables for their horses. The original home was destroyed by a fire in 1887 and rebuilt.

In 1881 Richmond turned down the nomination for mayor of Buffalo, suggesting the position be offered to Grover Cleveland. That was the first office of significance held by Cleveland, culminating with his election to the U.S. Presidency.

Thomas Lockwood purchased the home, with it being remodeled by architects Esenwein & Johnson in 1918. During Lockwood's ownership of the home, the library became the largest room in the mansion. The library and study were filled with autographed photos of his favorite authors, while the shelves included first editions and rare books. In 1935 Lockwood donated $400,000 to the University of Buffalo to build Lockwood Memorial Library designed by architect E.B. Green. Lockwood also donated his book collection to the university. When the college expanded to Amherst, the main university library retained the Lockwood name and was relocated to the North Campus.

In 1950 the Lockwood family sold 844 Delaware to The Catholic Diocese of Buffalo. The mansion was converted to the Mother of Mary Retreat House and in 1952, it became an annex to Bishop McMahon High School, located in the former Goodyear Mansion at 888 Delaware Avenue. The diocese renamed the building the Preparatory Seminary of Boys in 1969.

During the 1970s, IBM proposed purchasing the home and adjoining properties at 824 and 830 Delaware. Their intention was to demolish the houses to build a new office building. The homes were saved and 844 Delaware Avenue is now the headquarters for Child & Family Services.

ROBERT T. COLES HOUSE & STUDIO
321 Humboldt Parkway, Buffalo

Robert T. Coles opened the first African-American owned architecture firm in NYS and built a signature home/office at 321 Humboldt Parkway.

After graduating from Technical High School in Buffalo, Coles received a BA and Bachelor of Architecture from the University of Minnesota. He earned his Master of Architecture degree in 1955 from MIT, with his thesis titled "Community Facilities in a Redevelopment Area – A Study and Proposal for the Ellicott District in Buffalo, NY."

Figure 122 Robert T. Coles House
photo courtesy National Trust for Historic Preservation Jalen Wright

While studying at MIT, Coles entered a design competition, and he was awarded a stipend to study architecture in Europe. From October 1955 to May 1956, he traveled to ten European countries and was exposed to historic and contemporary European architecture, witnessing how the rebuilding after WWII allowed people to comfortably live, work and navigate urban spaces.

Returning from Europe, Coles remained in the Boston/Cambridge area and joined a firm that designed and manufactured Tech built modular homes, considered the Mid-Century Modern style. The homes were designed to fit their surroundings, coinciding with Coles' vision of creating affordable, livable, functional urban residential and public buildings.

In 1960, Coles received a call that would result in his return to Buffalo. The director of the Buffalo Urban League submitted Coles' master's thesis to the Ellicott District Urban Renewal and Development Agency and the firm that received the commission to build the Ellicott District Recreation Center (renamed the JFK Recreation Center). This development was included in his master's thesis and the architectural firm hired Coles to consult on the project.

Coles opened his own firm in 1963 and designed the William-Emslie YMCA, which replaced the historic Michigan Avenue YMCA. He also designed Alumni Arena at UB Amherst Campus, Apollo Theatre conversion to the city of Buffalo Telecommunications Center, Utica Street Subway Station, The Frank Merriweather, Jr. Library and many other properties.

Coles revised the design of a home he planned to build in Cambridge and for his Buffalo home office. The home incorporated the modern features, prefabricated components of the Tech built homes. Being located on Humboldt Parkway, which was being transitioned from a Frederick Law Olmsted parkway to a multi-lane expressway, the front of the home faced the tranquil rear court, and the street side was the windowless rear of his home studio. The unique design of this 1961 home resulted in it being placed on the National Register of Historic Places in 2011.

ROSWELL PARK COMPREHENSIVE CANCER CENTER
665 Elm Street, Buffalo

*Figure 123 Roswell Park entrance
photo credit Rick Falkowski*

Doctor Roswell Park moved to Buffalo in 1883 to accept the position of Chairman and Professor of Surgery at the UB Medical Center. He established himself as a leader in the WNY social and medical community.

In 1898 Roswell Park and *Buffalo News* publisher Edward Butler, Sr. obtained a $10,000 grant from the New York State Legislature to fund cancer research. This established the New York State Pathological Laboratory of the University of Buffalo, in three rooms at the U.B. Medical School on High Street. It was the first laboratory in the world to focus exclusively on cancer research and the first cancer research lab financed by the government.

Lumber baron William Gratwick suffered from colon cancer and was treated by Dr. Park. After his death his wife Martha Gratwick donated $25,000 in 1901 to fund cancer treatment and the research facilities at High and Elm Streets were renamed the Gratwick Research Center. When the center became the State Institute for the Study of Malignant Disease, chemist/physicist George H.A. Clowers pioneered new methods of chemotherapy research for the treatment of cancer. The Gratwick family later donated funds for the purchase of land to further expand Roswell Park facilities and the Gratwick Family Endowment continues to contribute to the institution.

In 1913 the first hospital for cancer treatment called Cary Pavilion opened at High and Oak Streets. It housed 25 inpatient beds and an outpatient clinic. The New York Times called it "the most modern of hospitals." When Roswell Park died in 1914, his institution served as the model for 12 research centers in the U.S. and 8 internationally.

Equally renowned for its treatment and research facilities, doctors Carl and Gerty Cori conducted their 1947 Nobel Prize in Physiology or Medicine at Roswell Park and in 1938 Dr. Morton Levin began researching the effect of smoking that led to his 1950 "Cancer and Tobacco Smoking" in the Journal of the American Medical Association. In 1972 the National Cancer Institute named Roswell Park among the nation's first three comprehensive cancer centers.

The hospital was named the Roswell Park Memorial Institute in 1946 and Roswell Park Cancer Institute in 1992. After the 11 story Scott Bieler Center opened in 2016, the name was changed to the Roswell Park Comprehensive Cancer Center, occupying 15 buildings, almost two million square feet, in the Buffalo Niagara Medical Campus.

SATURN CLUB
977 Delaware Avenue, Buffalo

The Saturn Club was formed in 1885 by a group of thirteen members of second or third generation affluent Buffalo families. Mostly college graduates in the 20s or 30s, the group was led by Carlton Sprague, William F. Kip and Francis Almy. This younger generation wanted their own club, separate from the Buffalo Club which they considered their fathers' or grandfathers' club.

Figure 124 Saturn Club
photo credit Ellen Mika Zelasko

Since the club met on Saturday (Saturn's Day) they named it The Saturn Club. Members considered calling their annual meeting Saturnalia until they discovered that meant an orgy. Original membership was limited to 31 members that paid a $100.00 annual fee. Within a year the authorized number of members was increased to 100.

Their first meetings were held in Carlton Sprague's grandfather's house that was temporarily available.

In 1886 they moved to the back of an apartment building at 640 Main Street, followed by a move to 331 Delaware and in 1889 a move to 393 Delaware Avenue. The 150 members incorporated the Saturn Club in 1890 and purchased a lot at 417 Delaware Avenue at Edward Street where they built a three-story clubhouse. That location was sold to the Montefiore Club, which became the center for Jewish social activity in Buffalo. The Montefiore Club was destroyed by a fire in December 1969 and that club moved to the former Knox Mansion at 800 Delaware Avenue.

The final and current home of the Saturn Club is 977 Delaware at the corner of West Utica. A Tudor Revival style building was designed by Duane Lyman. The October 21, 1922 grand opening of the building was an elaborate ceremony, with the members in full academic regalia proceeding down Delaware Avenue from the old clubhouse at Edward Street to the new building at West Utica.

The differentiation of the Buffalo Club as the elderly or middle-aged club and the Saturn Club as the young men's club only remained for about a decade. Over time many Buffalo residents became members of both clubs.

In 2003 the Saturn Club added two international singles squash courts and renovated the former squash courts into a state-of-the-art fitness center. The club remains true to its origins and considers itself a social club, that offers recreation, fine dining, fitness programs, member friendly banquet facilities and meeting rooms with high tech support.

SCHENCK HOUSE
Grover Cleveland Golf Course, Buffalo

*Figure 125 Schenck House
photo courtesy Erie County Parks, Recreation & Forestry*

The Schenck family emigrated to the U.S. from Germany in 1709 to flee religious persecution for being Anabaptist Mennonites. They first settled in Pennyslvania and in 1821 relocated to Buffalo in two covered wagons, purchasing land at $15 per acre at the Buffalo and Town of Amherst border. Their farm included six buildings on 180 acres of land.

Michael Schenck and his son Samuel built a Continental Pennsylvania German House from locally quarried limestone in the three rooms over three rooms style. It included a central fireplace and cooking on a 10-plate stove and pipe. Completed in 1822, the house is one of the oldest existing homes in the city of Buffalo. A front porch and two-story back addition were added in the late 1800s.

Three generations of the Schenck family farmed the land and practiced Polyculture and environmentally friendly techniques. They employed crop rotation, letting lands lay fallow to regenerate, producing multiple food products and the use of cow manure for fertilizer. In the German tradition, they grew hay to feed their animals during the winter and sheltered them in large barns (the English continued to leave their animals outdoors).

In 1898 the Schenck property was sold to the Country Club of Buffalo. The club retained the buildings and added tennis courts, a polo field, large clubhouse and a golf course that was built upon most of the farm's original 180 acres. The course was designed by two of the most famous golf architects of the early 20th century, Walter J. Travers in 1902 and redesigned by Donald Ross in 1920. The 1912 U.S. Open was held at this golf course.

The Country Club sold the grounds to the city of Buffalo in 1927 and in the 1970s an agreement was negotiated with Erie County to maintain the golf course, with Buffalo retaining ownership of the property. It was renamed Grover Cleveland Golf Course when purchased by Buffalo and it is the only public golf facility in North America designed by the acclaimed golf course designers Travers and Ross.

*Figure 126 Schenck House Restored
photo courtesy Erie County Dept. of Parks, Recreation & Forestry*

In 2022 the Erie County Legislature invested RENEW Plan and American Rescue Plan funds to restore the Schenck House. That project was completed in 2025, with this profile showing the before and after photos.

SENECA INDIAN CEMETERY
Buffum Street, Buffalo

The Seneca Indian Cemetery was established on the Seneca Creek Reservation, on what is now on Buffum Street off Seneca Street in South Buffalo. Seneca Nation Christians built the Indian Church next to the cemetery on Indian Church Road and a mission school was built across Buffum Street from the cemetery.

Figure 127 Seneca Indian Cemetery photo credit Mike Buckley

Prominent members of the Seneca Nation that were buried in the cemetery, include Red Jacket, Mary Jemison, Young King, Destroy Town, Captain Pollard, Tall Peter, Little Billy and many warriors. They were buried on an elevated area near the center of the cemetery, in graves all uniformly facing the sun.

Red Jacket defended the traditional ways and religion of the Seneca and vehemently opposed the sale of Seneca lands. Before his death he said he wanted to be buried with his people and white man not be allowed to bury him. In accordance with his wife's wishes, he was buried in the Indian Cemetery in 1830.

Mary Jemison lived most of her life on Seneca land near the Genesee River. She moved to the Buffalo Creek Reservation in 1831 and died there at the age of 90 in 1833. She was buried near Red Jacket in the Indian Cemetery.

The Treaty of 1842 eliminated the Buffalo Seneca Creek Reservation and the cemetery grounds were encroached upon by white burials and settlement. By 1851 there were discussions about removing the remains of Red Jacket, Mary Jemison and other Native Americans from the cemetery.

Red Jacket was removed from his burial site and in 1879 the Buffalo Historical Society obtained his remains, storing them in a pine coffin at a vault in Western Savings Bank. Mary Jemison was reburied in March 1874 by William Pryor Letchworth on the Council Grounds near Glen Iris, which became Letchworth State Park. A seven-foot bronze statue, on a marble monument, was erected in 1910.

During a solemn ceremony in 1884, Red Jacket was buried at Forest Lawn Cemetery with the other prominent Seneca that were moved from the Seneca Cemetery. In 1891 a bronze statue of Red Jacket was placed upon the granite base near the Delaware Avenue entrance to Forest Lawn Cemetery.

In 1909 John D. Larkin purchased the Seneca Indian Cemetery so the sacred land would not be developed. It was donated to the city of Buffalo as Seneca Indian Park in 1912. An inscribed granite boulder identifies the site.

SHEA'S BUFFALO THEATRE
646 Main Street, Buffalo

Figure 128 Shea's Theatre Grand Opening 1926 photo sheas.org

The construction of Shea's Buffalo Theater was the pinnacle of theater empresario Michael Shea's legacy. His career began with the opening of Shea Music Hall in the Arcade Building at 10 Clinton Street in 1892 and reached its zenith with this $2 million theatrical palace.

To design the theater, which had the original moniker of Wonder Theatre, in 1926 Shea selected C.W. and George Rapp, who were considered the leading architects of early twentieth century movie palaces, designing over 400 theaters. Their three most memorable creations were considered the Paramount in New York City, Oriental in Chicago and Shea's in Buffalo. The general contractor was John Gill & Sons of Buffalo, interior decorations by William Hengerer of Buffalo and the Louis Tiffany Company (only one of four theaters with the interior designed by Tiffany), furnishings by Chicago's Marshall Field Company, immense Czechoslovakian crystal chandeliers, massive bronze doors, marble staircases, pillars and walls, rich carpeting, mirrors of paneled glass, a seven story high theater dome and the mighty Wurlitzer organ, created by Rudolf Wurlitzer Co. of North Tonawanda, with pipes ranging from the size of a straw to 32 feet in length.

The theater originally seated over 4,000 people and everyone could afford the price of admission. There were no reserved seats and little cultural pretension. The emphasis was on the dazzling trappings and popular live and film programs. All the popular entertainers performed at Shea's Buffalo.

Most of the movie palaces in urban downtown centers of the U.S. were demolished or had their interiors renovated to simplify maintenance. The Buffalo theater was spared this fate but by 1974 it fell into foreclosure for nonpayment of taxes. The non-profit group Friends of the Buffalo Theater made arrangements to take over the building.

Since the grand reopening on its 50th anniversary in 1976, restoration of Shea's Buffalo Theatre has continued. Over $40 million has been spent expanding the stage and backstage area to accommodate Broadway productions, restoring the exterior, repainting the ceiling to its original glamor, recarpeting the floors, replacing the seating, replicating the 65-foot Shea's Buffalo sign and upgrading the mechanics of the building.

The theater now presents special events and traveling Broadway plays to sold out audiences. It is the jewel of the Buffalo Theatre District and remains one of the best-preserved big city movie theaters from this vintage period, retaining an overwhelming amount of its original décor.

Shea's Seneca
2178 Seneca Street, Buffalo

*Figure 129 Shea's Seneca 2019
photo credit Katie Schneider Photography*

Movie entrepreneur Michael Shea felt every neighborhood should have a first-rate theater so the residents of that area could experience the magic of motion pictures, in opulent caverns of glamor and fantasy, where they could escape daily urban life. His largest three neighborhood theaters were the North Park, Kensington and Seneca, with the Seneca being the largest, seating over 2,500 patrons.

It was designed by Buffalo architect William T. Spann and opened on January 11, 1930. The façade of the building was impressive with its pilasters and crowning pediment, ornamented with terra cotta swags, rosettes, scrolls and medallions. The two-story colored marble lobby, with ornamental plaster, had arched windows, like downtown's Shea's Buffalo.

The theater closed in 1961 but in 1965 the South Buffalo Businessmen's Association under the leadership of Harry Lotz reopened the theater with seating reduced to 1,332. Side seating was removed to create a dancing area for local bands that performed on stage on weekends, in conjunction with the movies. Eventually all the seating was removed and on September 27, 1968 the psychedelic rock club Psycus opened. It was one of the largest concert clubs in WNY and featured national recording acts like The Buckinghams, Country Joe & the Fish, Bob Seger and top local bands. A liquid bubble light show, equivalent to that at the Fillmore Ballroom acid rock scene in San Francisco, filled the auditorium and a black light Alice in Wonderland theme accented the lobby. It was short lived – the auditorium was torn down in 1970.

A 100,000 square foot storefront area lined Seneca Street in front of the auditorium, including stores like Woolworths, Grants, Endicott Johnson Shoes, along with other retail and service businesses. An entrance to the left of the building led upstairs to a bowling alley, later converted to the Skyroom Banquet Facility. That area became nightclubs called Rooftops, The Salty Dog and Country Club Skyroom, where concerts by groups like Inxs, Stevie Ray Vaughan, REM and others performed to capacity crowds of over 1,000 people.

The nightclub closed, the retail area became mostly warehouse space and in 2009 AmeriCorps moved their training, service and volunteer programs into the building. In 2019 Schneider Development Services refurbished the property into a mixed-use complex including 23 apartments, banquet/theater space, restaurants and retail stores. In 2024 Schneider also renovated a former bank, across the street at 2221 Seneca Street, into a premier concert club/restaurant called The Caz.

St. Joseph's Cathedral
50 Franklin Street, Buffalo

Figure 130 St. Joseph Cathedral photo credit Ellen Mika Zelasko

The Catholic Diocese of Buffalo was established in 1847, and John Timon was sent to become Buffalo's first bishop. Timon was the son of Irish immigrants and was proud of his Irish heritage.

When he arrived in Buffalo there were just three Catholic churches, St. Louis which was the first Catholic congregation in Buffalo, St. Patrick's and St. Mary's. St. Louis was the largest of the three and seemed to be the best equipped to become the seat of the diocese. But the German population there did not take kindly to an Irish Bishop. In fact, they treated him so poorly that Timon spent most of his time at St. Patrick's, where the mostly Irish congregation welcomed him with open arms.

Timon decided to build a cathedral. While in Rome to report on the newly formed diocese of Buffalo to Pope Pius IX, Timon fundraised for the cathedral and secured thousands of dollars while there, $2000 from the pope himself.

While he was away, some property came available for a very good price, and his assistant purchased it. It was on Niagara Street at Swan. When Timon returned home, he approved the purchase.

Timon hired Patrick Keely, an Irish architect, to design the cathedral. Construction began in 1851, and the church was dedicated in 1855. It was named for St. Joseph. A good amount of labor was completed by the Irish immigrants. What they lacked in money, they made up for with skill and a willingness to work. Fundraising continued throughout the project, and at times work slowed due to lack of funds.

The church is a Gothic design, built with limestone brought in on the Erie Canal from Lockport, NY. There are French influences such as the rose window above the main entrance, and the triple gabled doors on Niagara Street. The stained-glass windows behind the altar were added in the early 1860's.

Timon invited the Jesuits to Buffalo. They built St. Michael's Church, founded Canisius College, and Canisius High School. He also brought the Sisters of Charity to Buffalo, who opened Buffalo's first hospital and are still here today.

Bishop John Timon passed away in 1867 at the age of 70. He is buried in a crypt in the cathedral. St. Joseph's remains the seat of the Buffalo Catholic Diocese.

by Ellen Mika Zelasko

St. Louis Church
35 Edward Street, Buffalo

Buffalo was originally part of the Archdiocese of New York and by the 1820s a number of Catholics had settled in the village. Reverend Stephen Badin, a missionary from Kentucky, spent six weeks in Buffalo and said mass at the home of Louis LeCouteulx. Father Badin recommended that a Catholic congregation be formed and in 1829 LeCouteulx donated land at the corner of Main and Edward Streets for a church, cemetery, school and priest's rectory.

Bishop Dubois of New York City visited Buffalo, celebrated mass at the courthouse and appointed the Reverend John Nicholas Mertz as the first pastor of Buffalo. Since a church had not yet been built on the donated land, Mertz rented a temporary church building on Pearl Street behind the Eagle Tavern. In 1832 the Lamb of God Church, a wooden structure, opened at Main and Edward Streets. The church was renamed St. Louis parish and in 1843 a brick church was constructed.

Figure 131 St. Louis Church late 1800s PD

In 1836 Reverend John Neumann was assigned to assist Father Mertz at the church. Neumann was later canonized as the first male saint from the U.S. In 1847 Reverend John Timon was named the first Bishop of the Catholic Diocese of Buffalo, with St. Louis being the Mother Church of the Diocese. St. Louis was built by French, German and Irish Catholics but controversy over the language of the sermon developed. The Irish built St. Patrick's at Broadway and Ellicott and the French built St. Peters at Broadway and Washington, with St. Louis becoming a German Catholic church. Bishop Timon had disputes with the trustees of St. Louis Church and moved the bishop's church to St. Patrick's. He subsequently built St. Josephs Cathedral at 50 Franklin Street, as the home church of the Diocese of Buffalo.

The first parochial school in WNY was built behind in the 1830s and was replaced in 1850 by a larger building. In 1885 a fire at the Music Hall, located on Main Street across Edward Street from St. Louis spread to the church. The current gothic St. Louis Church was consecrated with a mass on the Feast of Saint Louis on August 25, 1889. That church remains on the site of the first Catholic Church built in Buffalo.

St. Paul's Episcopal Cathedral
139 Pearl Street, Buffalo

Figure 132 St Paul's Episcopal Church photo credit Rick Falkowski

St. Paul's Episcopal Church incorporated in 1817. Reverend William Shelton came to St. Paul's in 1829. He remained rector until 1881 and died in 1883. Shelton kept St. Paul's focused on its mission of helping the poor among us. He was so popular that people referred to the area around the church as Shelton Square and after his death, in 1897 the city named it Shelton Square.

President Millard Fillmore was a member of St. Paul's, and was laid in state in the church before being buried out of it when he passed away in 1874. It was Shelton who gave the sermon at his funeral. Shelton also conducted the first graveside service at Forest Lawn Cemetery on July 10, 1850.

By 1849 in Buffalo, the waterfront was booming with commerce and St. Paul's was burgeoning with congregants. They needed a larger church to accommodate their growing numbers. Shelton presided over the building of the permanent church we know today. Well known architect Richard Upjohn was engaged to design it.

Built of red Medina sandstone on a triangular piece of property, it is English Gothic in style, evidenced by its pointed arches, lancet windows, and asymmetrical design. The new church was consecrated in 1851.

In 1888 there was a gas explosion in the basement of the church. The roof and the entire inside of the building were destroyed by fire. But the sandstone walls stood strong.

The congregation decided to rebuild. Richard Upjohn, having passed in 1878, was not an option for the redesign. Robert Gibson was engaged, who was well known for his English Gothic church designs. For the most part, he worked off Upjohn's design. He did change a few things. The roof was changed to include the hammer-beam ceiling, and the clerestory windows. Gibson also added transept-like extensions on the sides. The whole effect of the changes gives the appearance of a tall, wide-open space.

Off to the left as you face the altar, is a Tiffany-stained glass window depicting 'Christ on His Way to Emmaus'. To the right of the altar there is a painting by Jan Pollack, 'The Adoration of the Magi' that dates to the 15th century. It's been said that this is one of the most valuable works of art in the city.

In 2017, the congregation of St. Paul's celebrated its bicentennial year as an incorporated church.

by Ellen Mika Zelasko

St. Stanislaus Roman Catholic Church
123 Townsend Street, Buffalo

The story of St. Stanislaus is heavily interwoven with the story of Buffalo's early Polish immigrants.

The latter half of the 19th century saw a large influx of European immigrants in Buffalo. One of them, Joseph Bork, owned a large tract of land on the East Side. He noted that many Polish immigrants came to Buffalo but only stopped on their way further west. He felt that if there were a Polish church here in the city, they would stay. So, Bork donated a prime piece of land to the Diocese to be used for a Polish Church and school. It was located at the corner of Peckham and Townsend Streets.

The Diocese brought in Polish immigrant Fr. John Pitass to be the first pastor of the new congregation. In 1873 a wooden church was built and dedicated. The school opened a year later. In 1881 the Felician Sisters were brought from Poland to teach at the school. Between 1881 and 1882, the parish doubled in size.

Figure 133 St. Stanislaus Church photo credit Patra Mangus

St. Stanislaus Church quickly became the center of Polish American life in Buffalo, because Joseph Bork was right. The Poles were now staying, in great numbers. He constructed housing for the newly arrived Poles. Upon learning that most of the immigrants arriving were sending money back to their families in Poland so they could join them here, Bork began to build two story homes. This enabled families to buy a home, rent out half of it, and when family arrived from Poland, they already had a place for them to live.

In 1883, construction began on a new, larger church. Most of the building was finished by 1886. A four-story school was built in 1890. By 1908 the steeples and the bells were added.

At one point the church counted among its congregation 20,000 Buffalonians.

The Social Hall was built in 1960. Between the years 2003 and 2009, extensive renovations were undertaken to both the interior and exterior of the entire church complex.

Dwindling enrollment in the school caused its closure in 2008, after 127 years. The Felician sisters staffed it until the end.

St. Stanislaus Church is now also a diocesan shrine to all Polish Martyrs as well as a Polish Cultural Center.

by Ellen Mika Zelasko

STATLER HOTEL
Washington and Swan Streets, Buffalo

*Figure 134 Statler Towers
photo credit Rick Falkowski*

When the 19 story Hotel Statler was built in 1923, it was the tallest building in New York State outside of New York City. It replaced the original Buffalo Statler, which was the first permanent hotel constructed by Ellsworth Statler of the Buffalo based Hotel Statler Co. Ellsworth previously built temporary hotels for the 1901 Pam American Exposition in Buffalo and 1904 Louisiana Purchase Exposition in St. Louis.

Ellsworth Statler was born in 1863, the tenth of eleven children in a poor family on a farm near Gettysburg, Pennsylvania. Statler grew up in Bridgeport, Ohio, across the river from Wheeling, West Virginia. Ellsworth quit school in second grade to help support the family and before he was twenty years old became a successful businessman in the Wheeling hospitality industry.

In 1896 Statler moved to Buffalo where he opened a restaurant in the Ellicott Square Building. He remained a Buffalo resident, living in his hotels until building a mansion at 154 Soldiers Place.

When the 1,100 room Hotel Statler opened, the original 300 room Buffalo Statler, which opened in 1907 at Washington and Swan Streets, changed its name to Hotel Buffalo. To ensure the Statler was the leading hotel of Buffalo, Ellsworth purchased and closed the Iroquois Hotel so its manager Elmore C. Green, the leading society figure in WNY, could become the general manager of the new Statler. Elsworth Statler then built the Erlanger Theatre across Delaware Avenue from the hotel to entertain guests with theatrical plays and concerts.

Hotel Statler was built on the site of the former home of President Millard Fillmore on Niagara Square. Prior to the Pan Am, it was combined with the adjoining Hawley Mansion to form the prestigious Castle Inn.

When Statler died in 1928, his company operated hotels in Buffalo, Cleveland, Detroit, St. Louis, NYC and Boston, later adding properties in Washington DC, Dallas, Pittsburgh, Hartford and Los Angeles. He left 1/6 of his estate to start the Statler Foundation, which remains headquartered in Buffalo and donates to assist hospitality education at Cornell, ECC, Niagara and other colleges.

Statler was named the "Hotel Man of the Half Century" in 1950 and when the Statler Hotel chain was acquired by Conrad Hilton in 1954 for $110 million, it was the largest transaction in the history of the hotel industry. The Statler Buffalo is now owned and being refurbished by Douglas Jemel.

SWANNIE HOUSE
170 Ohio Street, Buffalo

At the corner of Ohio and Michigan Streets a rooming house was opened in the first ward by either Polish immigrant James Swanerski or the Swanney family from Scotland. One legend claims the Swanerski family changed their name to Swannie to be accepted in the Irish neighborhood, while another states the Swanneys changed their name to Swannie. Regardless, if Polish or Scottish, the owners became named Swannie.

Figure 135 Swannie House during early 1900s photo contributed by family PD

The tavern dates back to 1886, making the Swannie House the second oldest continuously operating tavern in Buffalo. On the second-floor, rooms were rented to ship captains and officers, while the third-floor rooms were rented to seamen of lower ranks.

With factories like General Mills and the many grain elevators nearby, the tavern became a popular stop for workers after their shifts, including third shift workers who stopped in for a cold one in the morning. It later became popular for lunch with downtown office workers, a hangout for reporters and fans after sporting events at the Aud or Arena, and the Friday fish fries drew people back to the First Ward for dinner and drinks, at neighborhood bar prices.

In 1983 the Swannie House was purchased by South Buffalo natives Timothy and Marlene Wiles. With their family and friends, they worked hard to restore the building, purchasing and installing the flooring from the old Plaza Suite Restaurant (1970s landmark on the top floor of the M&T Bank building). When painting the exterior of the bar, firefighters from the fireboat Cotter docked across Michigan Avenue convinced them to restore the Kentucky Whiskey sign on the side of the building rather than painting over it.

Marlene re-established the kitchen with her chili, wings and burgers, and Tim ran the front of the house, often sitting on his favorite stool at the end of the bar. For over 40 years it was a family business with the Wiles' three children, aunts, uncles, cousins and friends working at the bar. Marlene died in 2013 and Tim's second wife Debbie Wiles-Fetterman worked with him until she passed away in 2023.

With Tim's passing in November 2024 and his children all living out of state, the family will not continue the Swannie House legacy. Former bartender Yvonne McCormick is reopening the former Marinaro's Larkin Tavern at 131 Van Rensselaer to fill the void but the Swannie House future is awaiting the next proprietor.

TEMPLE BETH ZION
805 Delaware Avenue, Buffalo

Figure 136 Temple Beth Zion photo credit Rick Falkowski

In May 2025, Temple Beth Zion celebrated its 175th anniversary.

Temple Beth Zion was instituted in 1850, having had several addresses prior to the current building. As the city and its Jewish population grew, so did Temple Beth Zion. In the late 1880's, construction began on the congregation's first landmark building, which opened at 599 Delaware Avenue. This Byzantine-inspired architectural masterpiece, built from Medina sandstone, featured a striking copper roof and a Tiffany-stained glass window, located on the first electrified block in the world.

Tragically, in October 1961, the first Temple Beth Zion was destroyed by a fire caused by spontaneous combustion. The loss was devastating, with few items surviving. In the aftermath, Jewish philanthropist Nathan Benderson championed the decision to rebuild on Delaware Avenue. Maintaining a landmark presence in Buffalo ensured Jewish representation among the city's prominent religious institutions.

This led to the construction of the current synagogue at 805 Delaware Avenue, designed by an unlikely industrial and commercially renowned architect, Max Abramovitz, and completed in 1968. Abramovitz also completed the smaller, more intimate Sisterhood chapel in 1966 within the synagogue complex. The main modern structured synagogue, with distinctive scalloped walls and the abstract stained-glass artwork by Ben Shahn, marked a new chapter in the temple's history. Shahn also created the free-standing menorah and the large Ten Commandment tablets with mosaic letters that rise from the altar. This Brutalist style building serves as a powerful reminder of the thriving Jewish community at the heart of Buffalo, with its round outstretched perimeter walls lifted upward in pray and praise.

In 1978, Temple Beth Zion opened the first Judaic Museum in Buffalo. In 2023, The Cofeld Judaic Museum was relocated and reimagined and is now an immersive exhibit throughout the hallway.

Recognizing the need for major renovations at this historic site, the Temple embarked on a capital campaign, raising over $3 million. Additions include a new conference room, clergy studies, and a remodeled gift shop. Administrative offices were relocated downtown, with elevator access, to integrate with the second-floor offices of Jewish Family Services. The Fink Auditorium was transformed into a vibrant showcase event space.

Through the efforts of Temple leadership, Temple Beth Zion was named to the National Register of Historic Places in 2018.

by Ida Goeckel

Thomas Motors/Curtis Aeroplane/Rich Products
1200 Niagara Street, Buffalo

Edwin Ross Thomas moved to Buffalo in 1898 and started manufacturing bicycles in the former Globe Bicycle Company at Broadway and Elm Streets. He began producing motor assisted bicycles that were called the Thomas Auto-Bi, considered the first production of motorcycles in the U.S. This necessitated moving to 1455 Niagara Street but when he added a four-wheel model, demand for his products resulted in moving to a larger factory at 1200 Niagara Street.

Figure 137 Thomas Motor Company in 1905 Buffalo of Today PD

Designed by architect Sidney H. Woodruff, the front building was built in 1901 and rear buildings were added from 1905 to 1908. The complex occupied Niagara Street from West Ferry to Breckenridge It is an example of an early twentieth century, urban, brick office and factory building complex. In Figure 72, the 1816 General Peter Buell Porter house, in which Lewis Allen resided for 50 years, can be seen to the right of the complex. It was torn down in 1911 to create additional industrial manufacturing space.

The reinforced concrete rear factory buildings are where the Thomas Flyer that won the 1908 New York to Paris auto race was built. The expensive handmade luxury automobile was in demand due to winning the NY to Paris Race but it could not compete with Henry Ford's low priced Model T and Thomas sold the company in 1912.

In late 1915, due to the demands by European Powers for airplanes at the beginning of WWI, Glen Curtiss moved his Curtiss Aeroplane and Motor Company into the building. The Curtiss JN-4, known as the Curtiss Jennie, was developed in this factory. The 1200 Niagara Street location was outgrown before the end of WWI and Curtis moved to a new plant on Churchill Street and eventually 2050 Elmwood, which at that time was the largest airplane factory in the world.

1200 Niagara Street was acquired by Rich Products and it is part of their massive complex along Niagara Street. The building today houses the BrightPath Rich Family Child Care Center and other Rich Products corporate uses. BrightPath is the only on-site corporate childcare center in WNY for employees and affiliates only. The E.R. Thomas name is still proudly displayed above the front entrance to the building.

Ticor Title Building – Unitarian Church
110 Franklin Street, Buffalo

Figure 138 Ticor (Austin) Building PD photo restored by Gene Thompson

Built in 1833 as the First Unitarian Church, this Greek Revival structure is the oldest standing building in downtown Buffalo. It is also the oldest remaining religious structure in the downtown area and the second oldest house of worship in the city. The oldest is the Black Rock Union Meeting House built in 1827 at Breckenridge and Mason Streets on land donated by General Peter Porter.

The First Congregation of the Village of Buffalo was formed in 1831. They commissioned Benjamin Rathbun to build the church for $6,000 on the lot at Franklin and Eagle Street that they purchased for $2,000. One of the original twelve charter members of the church was Millard Fillmore. It is the only remaining building constructed by Rathbun, the prolific builder of Buffalo properties, who was jailed for a massive forgery scheme in 1836.

In 1836, under the direction of pastor Reverend George Hosmer, a free school was opened for poor children in the basement of the church. It was the first such institution in Buffalo. The building was sold by the church in 1880, when they moved to Delaware Avenue between Huron and Mohawk, before relocating to their current Elmwood and West Ferry location in 1904.

New owner Stephen G. Austin hired architect F.W. Caulkins in 1880 to convert the property to offices, add a third floor and lengthen the Eagle Street side of building. It was the home to the Buffalo Fine Arts Academy, the forerunner to the Buffalo AKG Art Museum, from 1881 to 1886. For a number of years, the building also housed the offices of Green & Wicks, the architectural firm of E.B. Green.

After being renamed the Austin Building in 1886 it was occupied by Buffalo Abstract and Title. That company became Ticor Title and Guarantee Company. During most of the 20th century it was known as the Ticor Building, until the company relocated to 70 Niagara Street in 2000.

In 2001 the building was purchased by Erie County and renamed the Lincoln Building, in honor of President-elect Abraham Lincoln attending services as a guest of former President Millard Fillmore on February 17, 1861, on the way to his first inaugural. The county spent $5.2 million restoring the 20,000 square foot building and converting it into the Erie County Health Department Covid-19 response hub.

TIFFT NATURE PRESERVE
1200 Fuhrmann Boulevard, Buffalo

Situated just five minutes south of downtown Buffalo, Tifft Nature Preserve is a 264-acre wilderness refuge dedicated to environmental conservation and education. The land has undergone a dramatic metamorphosis over the years, from its origins as Native American hunting grounds to a thriving ecosystem amidst an urban landscape.

In 1847 industrialist and developer George Washington Tifft purchased 600 acres of land along Buffalo's outer harbor from Bela D. Coe, Joseph Clary and the Pratt Family. He established a large dairy business known as Tifft Farms. By the early 20th century, now owned by the Lehigh Valley Railroad, it evolved into a bustling industrial hub for shipping coal and iron ore. Unfortunately, its industrial use declined throughout the 1950s and 60s when it became an unofficial dump site. In the early 1970s, the city of Buffalo purchased it for use as a landfill, furthering its environmental decline.

Figure 139 Tifft Nature Preserve photo credit Doreen Gallagher Regan

In 1973 two million cubic yards of city trash was spread across the Tifft property. A few years later, public outcry over the massive garbage dump led to the founding of a not-for-profit group dedicated to rehabilitating the area. In 1982 the not-for-profit merged with the Buffalo Museum of Science, and after years of concerted efforts to restore the land, the nature preserve was born. The name was changed from Tifft Farms to Tifft Nature Preserve to better reflect its purpose as a preserve rather than a farm. Several tons of refuse and hazardous waste were removed. Contaminated soil was remediated, ponds were enlarged, and native plant species were reintroduced.

Tifft's journey from a neglected dumping ground to a cherished nature sanctuary is a remarkable feat of ecological restoration. Today, it is a thriving habitat that serves as a vital stopover for migratory birds, and a haven for diverse wildlife residing in its ponds, marshes and woodlands, including white-tailed deer, muskrats and beavers. Dedicated volunteers work tirelessly to continue improving the land, as visitors enjoy the lush greenspace along five miles of numerous nature trails and boardwalks. The preserve has become a popular destination for a variety of outdoor activities during all four seasons, while an indoor education center provides amenities such as information sessions, displays, event space and restrooms. Fishing is allowed in the ponds. There is a public parking lot at the entrance, and the trails are open year-round from dawn to dusk.

by Doreen Gallagher Regan

Times Beach
11 Fuhrmann Boulevard, Buffalo

Figure 140 Times Beach Wilkinson Pointe before development PD

In 1931, the *Buffalo Times* newspaper proposed a free bathing beach in the area from the south pier extension, which houses the Buffalo Lighthouse and U.S. Coast Guard Base, to where the South Michigan Street Bridge crossed the Ship Canal. This campaign by the Buffalo Times is how the area got its name.

The Times Beach area was formed in 1819 when Samuel Wilkeson, with other city founders, formed the Buffalo Harbor Company. They built the south pier extension to stop sand from accumulating at the mouth of the Buffalo River. After the pier was extended, sand began accumulating along the narrow spit of land across from the Central Warf (now Canalside) between Lake Erie and the Buffalo River. Storm surges or seiches washed over the land and in 1838 a 3,770-foot-long sea wall was built.

After the Civil War, Buffalo Harbor developed into the world's largest grain port. In the area behind the sea wall, squatters moved in and built a shantytown, known as Seawall Beach or Buffalo's Bohemia. It was inhabited primarily by impoverished Irish who made their living in commercial fishing or as grain scoopers. They built shanties that evolved into houses. Taverns were opened and rowing clubs were established.

These squatters, over 1,000 in number, did not own the land and did not pay taxes. After a protracted legal battle, the city began evicting the residents in 1917. However, people still used the beach to wash their cars or unofficially swim. The 1931 Buffalo Times campaign and a bacteriologist's proclamation that the water was free of contamination, resulted in the U.S. government giving permission to use it as a beach, contingent upon water quality. The beach was closed in 1935 due to health hazards caused by industrial and sewer runoff.

Starting in the 1940s, the U.S. Army Corps of Engineers turned the area into a contained disposal area for harbor and Buffalo River dredge. They used it through the mid-1970s but changing values and contamination resulted in abandoning its use as a dumping site. Nature reclaimed the area and by 1978 migratory birds, butterflies and other species moved in to create a wildlife oasis.

Times Beach Nature Preserve was established in 1987 and the 50-acre wildlife habitat has a series of trails, boardwalks, overlooks and observation blinds. It is recognized as one of the most significant natural sites on the Great Lakes.

Town Casino
681 Main Street, Buffalo

The Town Casino, a legendary Buffalo nightlife destination, was founded and operated by Harry Altman and Harry Wallens. From the 1940s through the 1960s, this premier supper club was the heart of the city's entertainment scene, attracting both high society and music lovers with its unmatched ambiance and world-class performances.

Figure 141 Town Casino

Stepping inside the Town Casino was like entering a world of glamour. Guests were greeted by white linen-covered tables, impeccably dressed waiters, hat-check attendants, and cigarette girls circulating among the patrons. The club's big band orchestra played the hottest tunes of the day, setting the perfect backdrop for an evening of fine dining and entertainment. Hosting the festivities was emcee Lenny Paige. WEBR-AM had a booth in the front lobby providing live radio broadcasts and interviews. The club ran an ambitious three shows per night - 7:30, 10:30, and 1:30 AM - each featuring some of the biggest stars in music.

The Town Casino attracted an unparalleled lineup of entertainers, including jazz, blues, and pop icons: Nat King Cole, Lena Horne, Duke Ellington, Miles Davis, Les Paul, Dizzy Gillespie, Sammy Davis, Jr., Joey Bishop, Peter Lawford...and many more.

Beyond the Town Casino, Harry Altman also owned the Glen Casino in Williamsville, originally opened as Glen Barn in 1934. The two venues operated in a seasonal rotation—Town Casino ran from September to May, while Glen Casino took over from May to September—ensuring Buffalo had year-round access to top-tier entertainment.

The final night of entertainment at the Town Casino was New Year's Eve, 1964. Soon after, the venue underwent a dramatic transformation, reopening as the Studio Arena Theatre, a not-for-profit professional regional theater. This new institution remained in the building until 1978, when it relocated to the former Palace Burlesque Theater at 710 Main Street. The former Town Casino space then became home to the University at Buffalo's Theatre and Dance Department, known as the UB Pfeiffer Theatre.

In the early 2000s, the venue saw yet another shift when it was remodeled into a nightclub under the name Sphere Entertainment Complex.

In 2005, Artie Kwitchoff and Donny Kutzbach took over the historic venue, determined to restore its former glory. They rebranded it as the Town Ballroom, bringing back its rich tradition of hosting top-tier musical acts. Today, it stands as one of Buffalo's premier live music venues, continuing its long legacy of entertainment excellence.

by Ellen Mika Zelasko & Susan Fenster

Tri-Main Center
2495 Main Street, Buffalo

Figure 142 Ford Motor Company at 2495 Main St. PD

The Tri-Main Center was designed in 1915 by architect Albert Kahn as Henry Ford's manufacturing plant in Buffalo. Over 600,000 of the 15 million Ford Model T's produced by Ford Motor Company were built in this plant by 1927. With the Belt Line Railroad behind the building, the Model T cars could be shipped by railroad throughout the Northeast or to the waterfront for transport by lake freighters.

In 1931 Ford sold the building and transferred its production facilities to the Fuhrman Boulevard plant in Woodlawn. The building was leased to various companies including Hercules Motors, who made diesel engines for the Navy. Bell Aircraft leased space on the upper floor in the building and under utmost secrecy built the first jet powered airplane. Employees working on the project were not allowed to tell their families or other employees about the nature of the project. To camouflage the building, small structures were built on the roof, so it looked like a residential neighborhood from the air.

The Bell P-59B Airacomet was shipped out of the building in the middle of the night. In the event German spies were observing the shipment, a fake propeller was attached to the jet, which was powered by two General Electric J-31 jet engines. The plane was transported by train to California where test flights took place at Edwards Air Force Base.

After WWII, the building was purchased by John Oishei's Trico Products, the world's largest manufacturer of windshield wipers. It was known as Trico Plant #2 and they expanded the building to 650,000 square feet. It was during this time that Trico was the largest employer in the city of Buffalo.

In the mid-1980s, Trico moved their manufacturing facilities to Mexico and 2495 Main was sold to Tri-Main Development, headed by Elgin Wolfe and Wayne Purdon. In the early 1990s they repurposed the former Trico Building into space for a variety of businesses. Over 100 diverse organizations, from architects, engineering and data processing companies to marketing agencies, artists, not-for-profit organizations and schools fill the six floors of the building.

Tri-Main center offers high ceilings and plenty of natural light for work or office space that can be configured to the specifications of the tenant. Abundant parking is available behind the building and the location is conveniently located on Main Street near the Kensington Expressway.

TRICO PLANT #1
628 Ellicott Street, Buffalo

John Oishei reached an agreement with engineer John W. Jepson to manufacture and market his Rain Rubber, a squeegee inserted between the upper and lower portion of the automobile windshield that the driver manually pushed from side to side. Oishei formed a partnership in 1917 that began making the windshield wiper at 2665 Main Street.

After WWI, Oishei bought out Jepson and incorporated as Trico Products Corp. In 1920 the company moved into the former Christian Weyand Brewery cold storage building at 624 Ellicott Street, built in 1890. Additional buildings were added with architects Harold E. Plummer and Paul F. Mann designing an early 20th century Daylight Factory style building characterized by reinforced concrete piers, large gridded windows stretching between vertical piers and red brick spandrels alternating between the windows.

Figure 143 Trico Apartments photo credit Rick Falkowski

Architects Burton and Ellicott followed their lead and the complex grew to ten combined buildings, seven stories high and encompassing 500,000 plus square feet, along two blocks of Ellicott and Washington Streets from Burton to Goodell Street. Employment at all the Trico factories peaked at almost 5,000 workers, making it the largest employer in the city.

Starting in the 1980s, Trico began moving production to Texas and Mexico. The building was vacated in 1999 and it was purchased by the Buffalo Niagara Medical Campus and University at Buffalo in 2007, with the title transferred to the Buffalo Brownfield Restoration Corp., a quasi-public agency. Krog Group purchased the property in 2016 and began work on reuse plans including residential, hotel and commercial space. Covid delayed construction and when work restarted it became primarily a residential project with no hotel and limited commercial space. Architectural Resources was the architect for redevelopment and interior space was designed by Antunovich Associated.

The initial 138 apartments became available in August 2024 and the remaining 104 in February 2025. Entrance is from Ellicott Street and the former icehouse of the Weyand Brewing Company was demolished to create a center courtyard. The studio to four-bedroom apartments have 12-to-14-foot ceilings, open layouts, large operable windows, motorized roller shades, stainless steel appliances, quartz countertops, wood style plank flooring, central air, full-size laundry machines and smart home features. Amenities include a fitness center, community room, rooftop deck with grilling stations, sixth floor dog park, bike storage and heated indoor parking for 240 cars.

The $115 million project bridges the Medical Campus to the Theater District.

Trinity Church
371 Delaware Avenue, Buffalo

Figure 144 Trinity Church photo credit Rick Falkowski

The origins of Trinity Church date back to 1836, when due to overcrowding, St. Paul's Episcopal Church authorized the formation of a new church by interested members. Several congregation members formed Trinity Episcopal Church and in 1839 they bought a small church from the Universalists. A larger church was built in 1842 on a lot they purchased at Washington and Mohawk Streets. In 1846 a third Episcopal church was organized by former members of Trinity Church. The new congregation was named St. John's, and they constructed their church at Swan and Washington Streets.

St. John's purchased land at 371 Delaware Avenue, where in 1871 they built a Chapel and laid the foundation for a church. Upon completion of the construction the congregation was renamed Christ Church. The congregation experienced financial problems, never finished construction of the church and sold the lot where the church was to be built.

When Trinity Church still needed a larger building, members favored relocating to Delaware Avenue. After purchasing land at Delaware and Park Place, they decided in 1884 to merge with Christ Episcopal Church. Under the terms of the merger Christ Church would contribute the Chapel and Trinity Church would purchase the adjoining lot, which included the completed foundation, and complete construction of a new church.

Christ Church Chapel was designed by architect Arthur Gillman in 1869. He also drew plans for the church. After Trinity and Christ Church merged, architect Cyrus K. Porter reworked Gillman's plans and the new church opened in 1886. The original rectory was replaced by a Parish House designed by Cram, Goodhue and Ferguson in 1903 and that firm also remodeled by Chapel in 1913.

Trinity Church includes some of the finest stained glass in America. John LaFarge created five scenes in the apse and the rose window. He also created five other windows in the church, along with five windows by Louis Comfort Tiffany. LaFarge's "Sealing of the Twelve Tribes of Israel" was exhibited at the 1889 Paris Exposition for which the French government awarded LaFarge the insignia of the Legion of Honor, the highest award bestowed on a foreigner

The church is one of few places in the country where the work of stained-glass pioneers, John LaFarge and Louis Comfort Tiffany, are displayed side by side.

TWENTIETH CENTURY CLUB OF BUFFALO
595 Delaware Avenue, Buffalo

The Twentieth Century Club was the first club run by women, for women in the United States. It was started in 1894 by social benefactor, music teacher and music editor of the *Buffalo Courier Express* Charlotte Mulligan as an evolution of the Buffalo Female Academy's Graduate Association. The club's Johnson Park facility became too small, so they purchased the former Delaware Avenue Baptist Church building and contracted the architectural firm of Green & Wicks to add a three-story clubhouse in front of the redesigned area of the existing church.

Figure 145 Twentieth Century Club photo credit Rick Falkowski

After the new club facilities were purchased, it was decided to open it to all women, not just graduates from Buffalo Female Academy, the forerunner of the Buffalo Seminary. This resulted in the name being changed from the Graduates Club to the Twentieth Century Club.

During the late 19th century women were politically disenfranchised and seldom stepped out of their prescribed social roles. A women's club movement gained momentum as cultural organizations to provide middle- and upper-class women with an outlet for their intellectual energies. Rather than being just a club to work towards social goals like women's suffrage, ending child labor and other current controversial questions, Mulligan wanted to advance interests in education, literature and art. By 1906 there were over 5,000 women's clubs and the Twentieth Century Club is the second oldest club in the country, only preceded by the Acorn Club in Philadelphia.

In 1901 during the Pan American Exposition the club opened its doors to many of the city's celebrated visitors. Receptions were held for Vice President and Mrs. Theodore Roosevelt and their daughter Alice; Governor and Mrs. Benjamin Odell; Mr. and Mrs. Booker T. Washington; the Chinese Minister Wu Ting Fang; and the wives of foreign diplomats. The club extended membership to Mrs. Roosevelt and Mrs. McKinley.

Since the inception of the club, musical events and lectures have been held on Wednesdays by international musical artists, noted writers, speakers and personalities. The Wednesday speakers' luncheons continue today with the sponsoring committee still wearing white gloves when greeting club members and the president still entertains the speaker and members of the committee in the private dining room.

The lavish elegance, culture and tradition from the turn of the century continue in the muraled meeting rooms and formal gardens of the Twentieth Century Club.

Ulrich's Tavern
674 Ellicott Street, Buffalo

Figure 146 Dobmeier's Hotel in 1900 photo from Ulrich's Tavern Archives restored by Gene Thompson

Opening in 1868, Ulrich's is the oldest tavern in the city of Buffalo. It remains at the corner of Ellicott and Oak Street in what is now the medical district and was then the distillery district.

The 1869 city directory listed the building under the heading of Grocery-Salon, with the owner a German immigrant named Fredrick Schrerier. This was the German section of Buffalo, and many grocers kept a back-room grog shop. These back-room establishments were respected neighborhood centers where people congregated to hear the latest news and gossip. People would buy their sausage or soap, discuss events over a beer and take home a pail of the local brew.

Beginning in the 1880s, until 1919, a barber shop was also operated in the business by George Fromholtz. The grocery store closed in 1883, and the second floor became a hotel and rooming house for nearby brewery workers. Over the next 25 years Ulrich's was operated by several different people but owned by two breweries, The Christian Weyand Brewery (located in the lot that became the *Courier Express* building) and Ziegele Brewing Company (directly behind Ulrich's at Washington and Virginia Streets). Most taverns during this time were a tied house, meaning it was owned by the brewery and only sold the products of that brewery.

After operating under various names, in 1906 management of the tavern was taken over by Michael Ulrich, a former beer wagon driver for the Rochevot Brewery on Jefferson and a brewery union officer. He bought out the Ziegele Brewery and renamed the business Michael Ulrich's Sample Room. That meant he sold beers from various breweries in Buffalo and beyond.

During Prohibition the downstairs barroom visually became a delicatessen and restaurant, but the hotel was transformed to a speakeasy for the political community called the Hasenpheffer Club. Whiskey and wine were made in the basement and beer smuggled in at night. A lift that is still in the basement of the building delivered the spirits to the second floor and business flourished. It remained a political watering hole before, during and after Prohibition, catering to the Republican Party but Democrats were usually welcome.

Jim Daley from the First Ward and his Bavarian wife Erika purchased Ulrich's in 1954 retaining the German atmosphere but adding an Irish twist. In 2014 Sal Buscaglia became proprietor of Ulrich's and continues to restore and preserve Buffalo's oldest bar.

Union Ship Canal
Outer Harbor Drive, Buffalo

Around the turn of the 20th century, Buffalo was home to many businesses that used iron to make steel and iron/steel products. The increasing demand for raw iron in Buffalo and the Great Lakes region led to the formation of the Buffalo and Susquehanna Iron Company in 1902, which later became the Hanna Furnace Corporation. The Union Ship Canal was an integral part of its operations, built on the collaborative effort of railroad, shipping, banking, and iron smelting businesses.

Figure 147 photo early 1900's courtesy of the Steel Plant Museum of Western New York Facebook page

In 1902, Rogers, Brown, & Company S.M. Clements of the Marine National Bank, and Frank and Charles Goodyear of the Buffalo and Susquehanna Railroad (BSR) formed the Buffalo and Susquehanna Iron Company. The Goodyear family controlled the railroad lines that transported coal from Pennsylvania to Buffalo. They also had interests in Great Lakes shipping, which could bring iron ore from Michigan and Minnesota.

Working with the Pennsylvania Railroad, the BSR began digging the Union Ship Canal, originally called the "Goodyear Slip", in 1903. The canal started at Lake Erie and crossed Fuhrmann Boulevard, which was equipped with a rolling bridge as part of the canal's construction. The canal was extended by 950 feet in 1910, reaching a final length of 2,240 feet and a width of 222 feet, allowing it to accommodate vessels with a draft of up to 23 feet deep.

The Union Ship Canal was essential for docking large cargo ships that delivered iron ore and limestone. Huge freighters, typically carrying between 10,000 to 20,000 tons of bulk minerals, commonly served the Bethlehem Steel plant in Lackawanna, which was just west of Hanna Furnace. Six crane bridges were used to unload iron ore from the freighters, where it could be scooped up and piled into the storage yard. During the summer months, shipments ran around the clock to provide minerals for smelting and building up reserves for winter.

The Union Ship Canal was also used for docking ships that transported pig iron from the Hanna Furnace Plant to automotive plants, steel mills, and foundries across Canada and the U.S. via the Great Lakes. Following the demolition of the Hanna plant and the Pennsylvania Railroad ore dock between 1983 and 1985, the Union Ship Canal stopped being used for bulk cargo shipments. The inland slip is now the centerpiece of the Ship Canal Commons, a 22-acre greenspace open to the public.

by Doreen Gallagher Regan

Unitarian Universalist Church
695 Elmwood Avenue, Buffalo

Figure 148 Unitarian Church early 1900s photo buffalouu.org PD

The Unitarian Universalist Church of Buffalo can trace its roots to the Unitarian Church and the Universalist Church, both organized in 1831.

In 1833 the cornerstone was laid for the First Unitarian Church at Franklin and Eagle Street. It is the only remaining building built by Benjamin Rathbun in Buffalo and former President Millard Fillmore was one of the contributors to its construction. Fillmore was joined by Presidents John Quincy Adams and Abraham Lincoln in his pew at the church.

The Universalist Church of the Messiah was originally located at Washington and Swan, but is best recalled for its twin spired church built at Main and Huron in 1866. That church was demolished for the building of the Kent & Flint Department store, which became the Grant's store that was torn down to building Fountain Square. The church moved to North and Mariner in 1892 before relocating to Lafayette and Hoyt in 1911.

John Albright sold land from his West Ferry Street estate at the corner of Elmwood Avenue to the Unitarian Church at a bargain price. Architect Edward Kent, a son of Kent & Flint store owner Henry Kent and member of the church, designed the English Country Gothic church that opened in 1906. Its design was a return to hand craftmanship and utilization of natural forms and light, incorporating Arts & Crafts influences. A hammerbeam ceiling soars in elegant arches from stone corbels. That Gothic design continues with hand carved dark oak woodwork. Nouveau style stained-glass windows were designed by Harry E. Goodhue and the pipe organ in the choir loft was built by the Hutchings-Votey organ company in 1906, rebuilt by the Delaware Organ Company of Tonawanda in 1960. The walls and floors of the church are built of Indiana limestone.

The Unitarian and Universalist Churches in Buffalo merged into the congregation at the Elmwood Avenue and West Ferry Street church in 1953, preceding the national merger of the two denominations in 1961. Completion of a 2001 construction project made the church handicapped accessible and created the garden entrance to the church Parish Hall, featuring an old-style English perennial garden that has been recognized for its excellence by receipt of the Buffalo in Bloom - City Garden Award.

Over the years the church has served as a center for social action causes, harboring draft resistors during the Vietnam War and more recently promoting LBGTQ causes.

UNIVERSITY OF BUFFALO - SOUTH CAMPUS
3435 Main Street, Buffalo

The University of Buffalo (UB) was started by the Young Men's Association with the opening of the Buffalo Medical College at Washington and Seneca Street in 1846, moving to their first building at Main and Virginia Street in 1849. Millard Fillmore served as the first chancellor from 1847 to 1874. A School of Pharmacy was added in 1886, Law School in 1887 and School of Dentistry in 1892.

Figure 149 UB in 1950s Foster Crosby & Hayes Hall archplan.buffalo.edu

Vice-Chancellor Charles Norton proposed moving to a site next to the Albright Art Museum and Buffalo History Museum or a larger tract of land near where the Piercer Arrow plant was being considered. Attorney and real estate magnate Edward Michael learned that Erie County was looking to move its almshouse out of the city. The 106-acre poor house was purchased for $50,000 in 1909, with the stipulation that the school take possession of the property within ten years or it reverted to county ownership.

In 1913 the American Medical Association decreed that all medical students must complete one year of Arts & Sciences curriculum. The Women's Union offered UB their Niagara Square building as Arts & Sciences college with two stipulations, the university raise $100,000 and it be named Townsend Hall, after long time Women's Union president Harriet Townsend. Grace Millard Knox donated $250,000 to establish the liberal arts school and Townsend Hall became part of UB in 1916.

The ten-year deadline to take possession of the campus at Main and Bailey was approaching and after obtaining a one-year extension due to WWI, Chancellor Norton held the ground-breaking for Foster Hall in 1920. Orin Foster donating $400,000 and the liberal arts program opened in the building in 1922, with Samuel Capen becoming the full-time chancellor of UB. After Erie County opened its Home and Infirmary in 1926, UB purchased the additional property, creating a 178-acre campus. The former county hospital was converted to Hayes Hall by a $389,000 bequest from Edmund Hayes. The architectural firm of E.B. Green & Son was hired to design Norton Hall (from a bequest by Chancellor Norton), Crosby Hall (financed by the William H. Crosby family) and Lockwood Library (from a donation by Thomas and Marian Birge Lockwood).

UB remained a private college until it became part of SUNY in 1962. It has added a North Campus plus buildings in the downtown Medical Campus and is rated among the top 40 public universities in the U.S.

War Memorial Stadium
285 Dodge Street, Buffalo

Figure 150 Civic Stadium historic postcard

In the 1830s the source of drinking water for the city of Buffalo was Jubilee Water Works, located near Delaware and Auburn. The city outgrew this supply system and adopted a reservoir system filled with water from Lake Erie. A reservoir on top of Prospect Hill at Niagara and Connecticut Streets was the primary reservoir. When the Connecticut Street Armory was built at that location, a second Prospect Reservoir was established on Jefferson Avenue.

The main building along Jefferson Avenue between Dodge and Best Streets was the Gerhard Lang Brewery built in 1875. Alvin Dodge, Jr. owned several hundred acres of farmland bounded by Main, East Ferry, Best and Jefferson. In 1880 he subdivided that property into building lots and sold the land across from the brewery to the city of Buffalo. It was upon that land that the new Prospect Reservoir was built in 1893. When the Colonel Ward Pumping Station opened in 1915, as the new source for the Buffalo water supply, the reservoir was decommissioned.

In 1937 a stadium was built on the former reservoir site as a WPA project and named Roesch Memorial Stadium after the mayor of Buffalo, renamed Grover Cleveland Stadium and finally named Civic Stadium in 1938. The 36,500-seat arena was primarily used for college football games. During the 1940s a racetrack was added to the interior perimeter and it hosted midget and stock car races, that became NASCAR events in 1956.

When the Buffalo Bisons moved from Offerman Stadium and the Buffalo Bills received an AFL franchise in 1961, the stadium was renamed War Memorial Stadium. Seating was increased to 46,306 people in 1965. The football Bills drew sellout crowds but the baseball Bisons struggled and moved to Winnipeg in 1970. After the AFL NFL merger the stadium was deemed too small, so the Bills relocated to Rich Stadium in Orchard Park in 1972. The affectionately called "Rockpile" stood vacant until the Buffalo Blazers soccer team began play in 1976, the Buffalo Bisons returned in 1979 and Canisius College held baseball and football games in the stadium. The movie The Natural was filmed there in 1983 but when the Bisons moved to Pilot Field in 1988 and Canisius opened the Demski Sports Complex in 1989, War Memorial Stadium was demolished.

In 1992 the Johnnie B. Wiley Amateur Athletic Sports Pavilion opened at the site, preserving the original War Memorial entrance.

WEED BLOCK BUILDING
284 Main Street, Buffalo

The northwest block of Main Street at Swan was known as 'The Weed Block', named for Weed & Company Hardware, first located at that corner. Cousins George and Thaddeus Weed came to Buffalo in 1818 and opened their hardware store at a time when Buffalo was busy rebuilding after the city was burned in the War of 1812. The company was run by family members for nearly a century.

By 1842, Weed & Company had outgrown their building, and a three-story building was built. In 1857, a new, five story building replaced that. This new building was a mixed-use boarding house with the hardware store on the first floor.

Figure 151 Weed Company Building 1857 PD

Grover Cleveland moved into 'room F' of the Weed Building in 1873. Cleveland never owned a home during the nearly thirty years he lived in Buffalo, living instead in boarding houses. His law firm Cleveland and Bissell (at the time) moved into the same building the following year. Millard Fillmore practiced law out of the Weed Building as well. So, both presidents from Buffalo had offices in the Weed Building.

By 1895, the hardware business had outgrown this building, and it was moved to a storefront in the middle of that same block, a much more spacious showroom. Thus, the name Weed Block.

In 1893 well-known Buffalonians John Albright, George V. Forman, John Satterfield and Franklin Locke, founded the Fidelity Trust Company. The five-story Weed Building was torn down in 1901 to make way for the Fidelity Trust Building, which was completed in 1909.

Architects of the building were Green & Wicks, a very prolific Buffalo architectural firm. The building's clean lines and understated details are in keeping with the banking industry. The first two floors and mezzanine of the building are spectacular with ornate hand painted ceilings, and well-appointed details still in existence. Fidelity Trust Company merged with Manufacturers and Traders Bank, which was founded here in Buffalo in 1856 by Pascal Pratt and Bronson Rumsey.

The two banks formed the Manufacturers and Traders Trust Company, or M & T, which has maintained a strong presence in Buffalo, although no longer in this building.

The Ellicott Development Company acquired the building in 1989, and they have referred to it as Swan Tower ever since. They completely renovated the building including the meticulous restoration of the amazing hand-painted ceilings.

by Ellen Mika Zelasko

WERNER PHOTOGRAPHY BUILDING
101-103 Genesee Street, Buffalo

Figure 152 Werner Photography Building block photo credit Rick Falkowski

Constructed in 1896, the Werner Building was designed by architect Richard A. Waite and built by Nicholas Kenyss for a cost of $10,000. It was constructed in the Genesee Gateway Historic District on the south side of Genesee Street between Ellicott and Oak Street, Buffalo's German business district in the mid to late 1800s.

The Giesser family came from Wurttemberg Germany, with Gabriel Giesser establishing himself in the cutlery business in Buffalo by 1870. He operated his business of making and repairing cutlery, barber and butcher supplies at 99 Genesee Street. In the 1870s he purchased the adjacent properties at 101-103 Genesee Street. When construction was completed, the Giesser family lived at the 99 Genesee Street address and the business moved to the new building, that was in his wife Frederike's name.

The four-story building at 101-103 Genesee was constructed for photographer Albert Werner. Previously, the Caulkin's Building, 85-89 Genesee Street at Ellicott Street was built in 1886 for the photography business by architect F.W. Caulkins. That building also featured a waterfall skylight, that dominated the appearance of the Werner Building. The building got its name from the prominent Werner Photographic Gallery sign painted on the side of the structure but Werner only occupied the studio until 1899. With the Caulkins and Werner Building, the block became known as the photography district.

The natural light from the skylight made the studio perfect for the photography business. After Werner departed, photographers Hanson D. Tufford (1900-1906) and Jacob J. Ginther (1901-1906) moved into the building. Other photographers followed including Dora Barnhard, Chauncey W. Rykert, Hernando O. Slicker, John Garner, Clarence S. Williams and the Foto-Art Studio in 1940.

After 1940 a shoe store, dentist and mattress company moved into 101-103 Genesee Street. In the 1940s Charlie Barker Clothier, operated by H. Seeberg Company at 121 Genesee Street, moved into the building and remained there until the 1980s. The building fell into disrepair and was purchased by Willard A. Genrich, who bought most of the Genesee Gateway buildings. He refurbished the interiors and skylight of the Werner Building but was not successful with the project.

In 2007, Genesee Gateway LLC with assistance from the Margaret L. Wendt Foundation, rehabilitated the buildings along Genesee Street from Ellicott to Oak Street. The Werner Photography sign was repainted, a U.S. Passport Agency opened and Eddie Brady's Bar is the western anchor of the block.

WILCOX MANSION – THEODORE ROOSEVELT INAUGURAL SITE
641 Delaware Avenue, Buffalo

The block bounded by Delaware, Allen, North and Main Streets was part of Holland Land Company lot #52 that Ebenezer Walden purchased in 1809. Known as Walden Hill, in 1838 Walden leased it to the U.S. government who built the Poinsett Barracks, where a garrison was stationed to keep the peace between the U.S. and Canada/England after the Caroline Incident during the 1837 Mackenzie Patriot War.

Figure 153 Wilcox Mansion Circa 1900 PD

Known as the Buffalo Barracks, the fort became the largest U.S. military installation in the early 1840s, housing over 600 men. Many prominent military officers served there, and it was visited by 13 U.S. Presidents, with future Confederate President Jefferson Davis stationed at the fort while serving in the U.S. Army. The U.S. terminated their lease in 1846 after General Bennett Riley's 2nd Regiment was reassigned during the Mexican War and Fort Porter opened on the Niagara River, near the current location of the Peace Bridge.

Joseph Maston purchased the property in 1847 for $3,500. He hired architect Thomas Tilden to remodel the former officers' duplex for the commandant and post surgeon into a single-family home called the Chestnut Lawn. The front entrance was reconfigured to face Delaware Avenue rather than the Parade Grounds, now Franklin Street. In 1863 the home was purchased by Albert Lanning, partner in a law firm with Grover Cleveland.

In 1883 Dexter Rumsey purchased the home as a wedding gift to his daughter Mary Grace after her marriage to attorney Ansley Wilcox. They further remodeled the home and when working on acquiring the Porter family property in Niagara Falls for New York State, Wilcox befriended Theodore Roosevelt. During the Pan-Am, Roosevelt stayed at the Wilcox home and after the assassination of William McKinley, Roosevelt was inaugurated president of the U.S. at the mansion in 1901.

The Wilcox furnishings were auctioned off in 1935 and in 1938 the mansion was converted into a restaurant and banquet facility. The Kathryn Lawrance Tea Room, Dining Room and Senate Bar became a popular destination from 1939 to 1959.

After the restaurant closed, it was almost demolished to make space for a parking lot. Historical groups worked with Representative Thaddeus Dulski to save the mansion. Liberty Bank purchased the property until it could be transferred to the National Park Service. The mansion was restored to its configuration at the time of Roosevelt's Inauguration and in 1971 it opened as a national historic site.

WILLIAM CONNERS MANSION
1140 Delaware Avenue, Buffalo

*Figure 154 Conners Mansion
photo credit Rick Falkowski*

This 12,594 square foot stone mansion was built at the southwest corner of Delaware and West Ferry for Thomas C. Meadows, the general manager of Buffalo Fertilizer Company. Before it was completed in 1908, it was sold to William Conners, Sr.

Conners was the former saloon operator that became the infamous Old First Ward labor boss who controlled freight handling on the Buffalo docks in the late 1800s. He employed over 6,000 men that were hired and paid at Conners' or his associates taverns. Resistance to his hiring practices were led by Catholic Bishop James E. Quigley and Longshoreman's Union, resulting in the 1899 Buffalo dock strike. That labor action virtually shut down the grain elevators and shipping industry in Buffalo, backing up business throughout the Great Lakes.

Prior to the strike, Conners diversified his business holdings to the brewery business by purchasing Mangus Beck Brewing and investing in Roos (later known as Iroquois) Brewery, operating lake steamers, investing in electric railway interests and purchasing extensive land holdings in South Buffalo. He began an interest in operating newspapers in 1895, eventually merging the *Buffalo Express* with the *Buffalo Courier* to form the *Buffalo Courier-Express* in 1926. The first Conners family home was at South Park and Tifft, a property sold to the Sisters of Mercy who established the first home Mercy Hospital on the grounds.

Relocating to 1140 Delaware Avenue in 1908, that home had the first indoor swimming pool in Buffalo located in the basement of the mansion, magnificent living quarters on the first and second floors, with an auditorium on the third floor. William Conners, Sr. purchased a winter home and property in Palm Beach Florida in 1917, to which he devoted most of his interests. He died at 1140 Delaware in 1929 when he returned to Buffalo to review the plans of the *Courier Express* Building at Main and Goodell Streets.

William Conners, Jr. lived at 1140 Delaware until his death in 1951. At that time all the Conners' business interests were dissolved, except for the *Courier-Express*, which remain in the family until 1979. The mansion was sold to various parties, becoming Gilda's Club of Buffalo under the auspices of the Center for Hospice & Palliative Care.

In 2017, the building was purchased by Canisius High School, who converted it to their center for fine and performing arts, located across West Ferry from the high school campus.

WILLIAM DORSHEIMER HOUSE
434-438 Delaware Avenue, Buffalo

The William Dorsheimer House played an important role in the careers of Frederick Law Olmsted and H.H. Richardson in Buffalo.

Dorsheimer met landscape architect Frederick Law Olmstead during the Civil War and invited him to visit Buffalo to discuss designing the Buffalo Parks system. Their first meeting with Olmstead was at the Delaware Avenue home of Sherman Jewett and later the Dorsheimer house.

Figure 155 William Dorsheimer House
1965 photo Library of Congress

H.H. Richardson and Olmsted were both members of an architects' group in NYC and he recommended Richardson to Dorsheimer. In October 1868, H.H. Richardson was given the commission to design a home for William Dorsheimer on property he purchased from the pioneer Buffalo LeCouteulx family. It was the third commission Richardson received after returning three years previously from studying at Ecole des Beaux Arts in Paris.

For the house Richardson created a townhouse design that was popular in the Paris suburbs during the 1850s and 1860s, called the Louis XIII style. The building's simplicity and planarity, with incised decoration recalling rosettes and triglyphs reflect the influence of the French Neo-Grec movement. It has horizontal bands of gray sandstone across the ochre façade and vertical stone courses at the building corners. The windows are framed by vertical bands of sandstone and the dark gray slate mansard roof with large dormers, relieved by a band of red tiles, lends a picturesque quality to the home.

Dorsheimer, Richardson and Olmsted visited Niagara Falls in 1869, which led to Olmsted's involvement with preserving and designing the first State Park in the U.S. at Niagara. Olmsted's work on the Buffalo Park system continued for decades. Due to Dorsheimer's influence, Richardson received the commissions for Buffalo State Hospital and the William Gratwick house. When Dorcheimer was NYS Lt. Governor he hired Richardson and Olmsted, assisted by Leopold Eidlitz, to complete the Albany State Capital Building.

The Dorsheimer House was one of the initial great houses built along Delaware Avenue and became one of Buffalo's principal residences, visited by Millard Fillmore, Grover Cleveland and Samuel Tilden. After Dorsheimer left Buffalo, his home was purchased by Charles W. McCune, who owned the Courier Company, a printing company, and the *Buffalo Courier* newspaper.

George Bleistein succeeded McCure as owner of the Courier Company and 438 Delaware Avenue. He sold the *Buffalo Express* to William J. Conners and became a leading member of Buffalo Society.

The building at 438 Delaware has been converted into an office building.

WILLIAMS-BUTLER MANSION
672 Delaware Avenue, Buffalo

Figure 156 Williams-Butler Mansion photo credit Ellen Mika Zelasko

The Williams-Butler Mansion was built for George L. Williams, a successful banker, and his wife Annie. It was completed in 1899, at a time when Buffalo's elite were moving north of the city in search of a more genteel lifestyle.

The architect was Stanford White, of McKim, Mead and White Architects. White worked with HH Richardson when he designed the Richardson Olmstead Complex on Forest Avenue. He also designed the James F. Metcalfe House located at 125 North Street which, ironically, was demolished in 1980 to provide a parking lot for the Williams-Butler Mansion.

The style of the home is Georgian Revival, built with Roman bricks. It is 16,000 square feet, and the carriage house is 8,000 square feet. Built on a hill, at that time it afforded a view of Lake Erie from the terrace.

Williams was one of the promoters of the Pan American Exposition. President William McKinley was scheduled to have a state dinner, hosted by the Williams family in their home on September 6, 1901. That day McKinley was shot and the dinner was cancelled. Due to bad weather and the assassination, the Exposition lost money. Williams brought the proceeds from the Exposition home and before the expenses were paid distributed money to the original investors, many of whom were his friends. A small scandal ensued.

In 1905, Williams left Buffalo and sold the home to Edward H. Butler, owner of the Buffalo Evening News.

Butler came to Buffalo in 1873 and started The Sunday News. Circulation grew and in 1880 he established the Buffalo Evening News, which became one of the longest running news outlets in the city.

Butler passed away in 1914, and his son, Edward H. Butler, Jr., inherited the house and the paper. Family members lived in the home until 1974, when it was sold to the William C. Baird Foundation, which eventually donated it to Roswell Park Hospital.

In 1979, Delaware North Companies purchased the house and the adjoining Metcalf home. They did extensive renovations before using it as office space. They sold it to Varity Corp in 1990, which used it as their global headquarters until selling it back to Delaware North in 1999. Jeremy M Jacobs, CEO of Delaware North, then donated the property to SUNY Buffalo, and was used as the Jacobs Executive Development Center.

In 2023, the home was acquired by Douglas Jemal (Jemals Williams-Butler LLC).

by Ellen Mika Zelasko

WURLITZER – TENT CITY BUILDING
674 Main Street, Buffalo

674 Main Street was built in 1895 before this portion of Main Street became the Buffalo Theater District, making it one of the oldest structures in this district. It was designed by architect Edward Kent as a five story, Neoclassical commercial design, which has also been described as Beaux Arts Classicism.

It was built as the showroom and factory for the A.E. Perron Company, a manufacturer of carriages, sleighs, harnesses and automobiles. The Poppenberg Motor Car Company purchased the building in 1905 and it was considered the largest automobile dealership between New York City and Chicago. The building was also the showroom for the pianos the company manufactured at their Main and Carlton Street factory. This 1920s photo of the Poppenberg Motor Company was taken before Greyhound Bus Lines moved next door to their building in 1941.

Figure 157 Poppenberg Motor Car 674 Main Street PD

In the early 1930s the building was purchased by the Wurlitzer Company based in North Tonawanda as a showroom for the musical instruments and other products they manufactured. They sold pianos, organs, radios, televisions, records, band instruments, violins, drums and accordions. Over the five floors of the business, they provided sales rooms, practice rooms, studios and repair facilities. The Wurlitzer store was open for over 60 years, closing in 1996.

Washington Surplus purchased the building in 1997 and opened Tent City at this location. Washington Surplus was Buffalo's original Army/Navy store, selling surplus armed forces clothing and equipment after WWII. Charles Kushner, the son of Washington Surplus' founder, intended to retain the Tent City retail location on the first floor and build 12 apartments on the other four floors, but those plans never came to fruition. Kushner started the renovation and received awards from the city for his efforts in restoring the building however Tent City closed in early 2020.

Figure 158 Wurlitzer Store 674 Main Street PD

In 2020 the property was purchased by Drew Blum who restored and renovated the property into four full floor condominiums on the second to fifth floors and commercial spaces on the first floor. Named the Wurlitzer Flats, each of the condos is 3,200 square feet, with the elevator programmed to only allow owners to access their floor of the building. There is a rooftop patio on the second floor and private parking behind the building off Pearl Street.

YMCA Building, Olympic Towers
45 West Mohawk, Buffalo

Figure 159 YMCA Building
Library of Congress 1908 Detroit Publishing Co.

In 1844 the Young Men's Christian Association (YMCA) was started in London as a refuge for young men to escape the hazards of the Industrial Revolution's urban streets. Its core values were caring, honesty, respect and responsibility, applying these Christian principles to build a healthy spirit, mind and body.

The first YMCA in North America was established in Montreal in 1851 and the first in the U.S. was formed in early 1852 in Boston. In June 1852 the second U.S. YMCA opened in Buffalo. Afterwards chapters opened in nearly every major American city. The first YMCA annual convention was held in Buffalo in 1854.

There were several early Buffalo YMCA locations and in 1883 a five-story high Victorian Gothic style building was erected at 305 Pearl Street. By 1900 it was the fourth largest YMCA in the country, but the membership outgrew the building. Land was purchased for $100,000, overlooking the large triangular space created at the juncture of Mohawk and Genesee, between Franklin and Pearl Streets. It displaced a residential area that included the home of three-time Buffalo mayor Philip Becker.

Green & Wick's was awarded the commission, from a competition of ten architectural firms that were requested to submit plans. At a cost of $300,000 they designed a steel framed English-Flemish style structure clad in tan-colored brick, with white sandstone decorated quoins, stringcourses, windows and doorways, and base of gray granite.

The ten-story structure had a two-story portico of Tuscan columns at the Genesee Street main entrance. An Association Spa, adjoining the main lobby, served nonalcoholic beverages. It was the first YMCA to include a spa, a feature that became standard in all YMCA buildings around the country. The tower featured laboratories, a library, auditorium, gymnastic facilities, a tenth-floor restaurant and over 60 rooms for lodgers. It was one of the first YMCA buildings to provide extensive accommodations. The building was topped with arched stone and brick dormers, rising to a steep pitched slate roof. The four-story eastern wing contained a swimming pool, while the four-story western wing was called the Boy's Department.

The Buffalo Convention Center was built in 1976 and Genesee Street was reduced to an alleyway, closing the YMCA Genesee entrance. When the YMCA closed in the early 1980s, the property was converted to office space called The Olympic Towers, with a four-story addition at 300 Pearl Street connected by a glass atrium.

CATTARAUGUS & CHAUTAUQUA COUNTIES PROFILES

This section includes profiles of **Cattaraugus** and **Chautauqua Counties** and several historic places in the Town of **Chautauqua**, the Village of **Fredonia**, the Hamlet of **Irving**, the Hamlet of **Lily Dale**, the Town of **Perrysburg**, and the Town of **Westfield**

Counties of Cattaraugus and Chautauqua

On March 11, 1808 the NYS Assembly formed Cattaraugus, Chautauqua and Niagara Counties from Genesee County, with the stipulation that each county have at least 500 inhabitants.

The name Cattaraugus is derived from the Seneca word that translates as "bad smelling banks." This is in reference to the odor of natural gas leaking from the rock seams. The name Chautauqua comes from a Haudenosaunee word with multiple meanings that include a bag tied in the middle or two moccasins tied together, which describes the shape of Chautauqua Lake.

In 1804 William Peacock was assigned to survey the southern tier area of the land purchased by the Holland Land Company. At the western shore of Chautauqua Lake, a town was formed named Mayville after the maiden name of Elizabeth May, the wife of Paul Busti, senior agent of the Holland Land Company. The first settler was Dr. Alexander Mcintyre, who built a log cabin in 1804 on South Erie Avenue, followed by a tavern built by Captain John Scott in 1807. Mayville was named the county seat for Chautauqua County and William Peacock settled in the town in 1810 as sub agent for the Holland Land Company. The Holland Land Company office was burned by disgruntled settlers in 1834, with only the office vault remaining, still standing across from the County Courthouse.

In 1803 Major John Hoops and his nephew Major Adam Hoops purchased 20,000 acres of land from the Holland Land Company. Adam Hoops had been an aide to General John Sullivan and was named Surveyor of Pennsylvania. He became familiar with the southern New York State area from his work in Pennsylvania. He was also associated with Robert Morris, a financier of the American Revolution who sold his land holdings to the Holland Land Company, and U.S. Treasurer Alexander Hamilton. This allowed him to purchase the Olean area with little capital investment. Olean became the migration point for western settlers traveling to Ohio. They traveled on the Allegheny River from Olean Point to Ohio and the west. In 1818, 3,000 settlers embarked from Olean, with Olean Point being better known than Pittsburgh or Buffalo. The name Olean was derived from "oleum" the Latin word for oil, due to Olean's proximity to where the first oil well was drilled in the U.S.

Figure 160 Olean High School 1935
Olean Historical Society PD

Only a few historic places have been included in this book from the outlying areas of WNY. A second edition of Historic Places of Buffalo & WNY is planned. That book will contain locations overlooked or where sufficient information could not be compiled to include them in the first edition. It will also concentrate on historic places in the smaller towns of southern and central WNY.

ATHENAEUM HOTEL
3 South Lake Drive, Chautauqua

The Athenaeum Hotel is a historic landmark located on the grounds of the Chautauqua Institution. It has been in continuous operation since it was built in 1881 and is one of the last remaining wooden hotels of the Victorian era. The name "Athenaeum" comes from the Greek goddess of wisdom, Athena, to reflect Chautauqua's focus on education, learning, and intellectual pursuits.

The Chautauqua Institution was founded in 1874 by Lewis Miller and John Heyl Vincent as a summer teaching camp for

Figure 161 Athenaeum Hotel Chautauqua Institution

Sunday school instructors. Visitors initially resided in tents or small wooden cottages along the lake. As the institution's curriculum expanded to include music, art, and recreation, Chautauqua's popularity grew and so did the need for better lodging. In turn, Lewis Miller, along with his brother Jacob and Clement Studebaker (of the automobile fame) commissioned architect W.W. Carlin to design the grand hotel. It cost $125,000 and a team of ninety men to build it in ninety days. Miller appointed his son-in-law, Thomas Edison, to wire the structure for electricity, making it one of the first hotels in the world with electric lights. The original hotel had a mansard cupola atop the central tower, but this was removed in 1923. The following year, a 48-room annex was built to accommodate the increasing flow of visitors, bringing the total number of rooms to 160.

The iconic hotel is often referred to as the "Grand Dame of Chautauqua". A magnificent exterior staircase leads up to the 200-foot wrap-around veranda where guests can sit and admire the waterfront view. The lobby features the original front desk, placed under a bellmen's callboard that has spinning arrows pointing to the room numbers. It also has an original manually-operated Otis elevator.

Many high-profile figures have stayed at the Athenaeum over its long history, including several U.S. Presidents - Ulysses S. Grant, Theodore Roosevelt, and Bill Clinton to name a few. Other distinguished guests consisted of Amelia Earhart, Susan B. Anthony, Duke Ellington, Robert F. Kennedy and Sandra Day O'Connor.

In 1982, the hotel underwent a $2 million renovation to fix the roof, upgrade the kitchen and add private baths to each room. The Atheneum Hotel continues to operate during Chautauqua's 9-week summer session, as well as off-season for weddings, conferences and banquets April to October.

by Doreen Gallagher Regan

Chautauqua Institution

1 Ames Avenue, Chautauqua

Figure 162 Docks at the Chautauqua Institution

The Chautauqua Institution sits on 2000 acres along the shores of Chautauqua Lake. It was founded in 1874 by inventor Lewis Miller and Methodist Bishop John Heyl Vincent as a modest summer camp for Sunday school teachers with a nondenominational intent. As the humble tent community transitioned to include cottages, rooming houses, inns and hotels, Chautauqua blossomed into a vibrant summer community. It was soon touted as a center for high-minded pursuits, focusing on self-improvement and civic engagement. Participants attended academic lectures, concerts, social events, and recreational activities throughout the season. In 1878, Vincent began The Chautauqua Literary and Scientific Circle, one of the oldest book clubs in America still in operation today. Its primary purpose was to inspire individuals who could not afford college to acquire intellectual gain through self-study. The Chautauqua Boys and Girls Club was created in 1893 as a children's day camp, and The Chautauqua Children's School was started in 1921 for preschoolers, one of the earlier pioneers of nursery school education.

The ideals of the Chautauqua Institution quickly spread across the United States, greatly impacting the American culture. Thousands of independent Chautauqua assemblies popped up all over the country, reaching audiences of more than 45 million through their education, art and music programs. Lewis Miller's daughter, Mina Miller Edison, wife of inventor Thomas Edison, provided Chautauqua diplomas to students completing the literary classes she offered in Fort Myers, Florida.

Figure 163 Chautauqua Institution Gymnasium

Over the 150 years since its inception, numerous dignitaries have spent time in Chautauqua, including several American presidents and many famous politicians, authors, actors and musicians. In 1973, the Chautauqua Institution was added to the National Register of Historic Places, and to this day continues to thrive as a popular summer destination offering a wide variety of programs. Almost every religious denomination in the U.S. is represented within the Institution. The Chautauqua Literary and Scientific Circle (CLSC) adds several new books to its reading list each year, and many distinguished authors come to the Institution to discuss their publications. During the 9-week summer season, nearly 100,000 people visit Chautauqua annually to take advantage of its programs and events. Most of the original Victorian cottages and rooming houses still line the quaint narrow streets, and many offer accommodations both on and off season.

by Doreen Gallagher Regan

LEWIS MILLER COTTAGE
24 Whitfield Avenue, Chautauqua

Figure 164 Lewis Miller Cottage from the Library of Congress website

The Lewis Miller Cottage is a National Historic Landmark and the oldest house still standing in The Chautauqua Institution. It was the summer home of Lewis Miller, the inventor and philanthropist who co-founded Chautauqua in 1874. The prefabricated Swiss chalet style cottage was constructed and assembled in Akron Ohio, then shipped by steamboat to the corner of Whitfield and Vincent streets on the grounds of Chautauqua in 1875. It was one of the first prefabricated homes in America. Lewis, his wife Valinda, and their eleven children spent many summers there. While the five daughters stayed in the two upstairs bedrooms, their six sons camped out in tents by the front porch. President Ulysses S. Grant visited the cottage soon after it was built and allegedly napped in one of the boys' tents.

The Millers loved nature and the outdoors, and their summer months were filled with activities such as swimming and sailing in Chautauqua Lake, or attending the lectures and classes that the Institution offered. A boarding house was built behind the cottage early on, but it was taken down around 1900 and its stone foundation became the back wall of the cottage's garden.

Mina, the ninth child of Lewis and Valinda, married Thomas Edison in 1886 after he became widowed and left to care for three young children. He was 20 years older than Mina. They had three more children and spent many idyllic summers at the cottage during the 45 years they were married, until his death in 1931. Mina made extensive renovations to the little cottage, especially around the 1920s. Her tiny kitchen revealed her lack of interest in cooking. She preferred to eat at the Athenaeum Hotel, where she had her own private table in the restaurant. Mina adored gardening and birdwatching. She became founder and president of Chautauqua's Bird and Tree Club, and hired famed landscape architect Ellen Biddle Shipman to design the lush gardens surrounding the cottage.

The Miller house remained in the care of the family and their descendants for 130 years, until it was sold to the Chautauqua Foundation in 2015, to ensure its preservation as a historic landmark. It sits across from Miller Park and the Miller Bell Tower, also named in honor of the institution's beloved co-founder.

by Doreen Gallagher Regan

FREDONIA GAS LIGHT & WATER COMPANY
Canadaway Creek at West Main Street, Fredonia

Figure 165 Historic Marker - First Gas Well in Fredonia

The first commercial natural gas well in the U.S. was dug in 1825 (often incorrectly reported as 1821) along the banks of Canadaway Creek, near the West Main Street bridge in the village of Fredonia by William Hart. This natural gas well preceded the drilling of the first oil well in Titusville, Pennsylvania in 1859 the U.S. by 34 years.

Existence of natural gas has been known since ancient times, with the Oracle at Delphi being created in 1,000 BC on Mount Parnassus in ancient Greece where natural gas seeped from the ground into a flame. In the U.S. Native Americans would ignite gases that seeped into and around Lake Erie, exhibiting it to French explorers in 1626.

William A. Hart was a gunsmith who noticed youngsters burning gas that was bubbling on Canadaway Creek. He used his wife's washtub to trap the gas, drilled a hole in the tub and shot his gun in the hole to light the gas. That led him to dig a hole 27 feet into the shale, drilling a 1.5-inch diameter borehole another 43 feet and reaching gas at a depth of only 70 feet.

Hart built a shed over the hole, accumulated the gas in a crude gasometer and created a pipeline made of hollowed out logs, connected together with tar and rags. He sold it to customers at $1.50 per year for each light. His initial customers were a grist mill and four other buildings, including a tavern across West Main Street (current location of the Fire House) that was the stagecoach stop between Cleveland and Buffalo. Other shallow gas wells were drilled through the Chautauqua County shale belt, including the first lighthouse illuminated by gas at Barcelona New York in 1828.

The Fredonia Gas Light and Water Works was incorporated in 1857 and a spring of cold water was located shortly afterwards. In 1878, former Fredonia Academy (now SUNY Fredonia) student, Preston Barmore, drilled a 127 foot deep well a mile north of Hart's original well. With the blast of 8 pounds of gunpowder, he stimulated a substantial shale gas well that was connected by lead pipe to an eight-sided gasometer in the center of Fredonia to provide lighting for the village street lamps and homes.

This started the commercial gas distribution industry and Fredonia Light was the precursor to today's billion-dollar energy corporation, National Fuel.

SUNSET BAY BEACH CLUB
1028 South Shore Road, Irving

The Sunset Bay area has been a popular location for lake cottages and entertainment dating back to the early 20th century. However, its history goes further back than most settlements in WNY.

In 1803, the Dickinson, Cleveland and Howard families moved from Berkshire County in Massachusetts to what is now the town of Hanover and village of Silver Creek. They purchased land from the Holland Land Company, with John E. Howard settling south of Cattaraugus Creek. The other settlers returned to New England but Howard remained and in 1805 he opened a tavern with accommodations. Before and after the War of 1812, Howard's Tavern was one of the most popular stopping places for travelers and immigrants between Buffalo and Erie Pa.

Figure 166 Burghardt Sunset Bay Beach Club in the 1940s
photo courtesy Sam Bova

During the early 1940s the Burghardt family opened an entertainment center on Sunset Bay in the town of Hanover. It had a great sandy beach, snack hall, amusement rides, miniature golf and a beer hall. During the 1950s and 1960s it expanded into an arcade with a multitude of mechanical games for the kids and plenty of draft beer for adults. Cottages filled the area toward the creek and the roads around the cottages always seemed to be covered by sand.

Prior to the New York State Thruway opening in 1961 Silver Creek could be reached by taking Routes 5 & 20 until you arrived at the Seneca Reservation north of Cattaraugus Creek. This was before the smoke shop days, and the reservation shops featured hand carved artifacts and an assortment of Native American merchandise.

In 1972 Mulligan Beach Club purchased the property and created a beachfront club that became one of the prime party destinations in WNY. Mulligans operated until 1984 when it became the Sunset Bay Beach Club, owned by Sam Bova, who also operated Manikin's – the former Three Coins Nightclub. Calico Jack's transitioned into Cabana Sam's and Sunset Bay Beach Club expanded to include music and dancing inside, on the patio and special concerts/events on the five-acre beach. All styles of music are featured, catering to all age groups. It has always been a summer club, open from May until the end of September, when the Annual Boat Buring closes the season.

Kelly Borrello, who managed the properties for 14 years, purchased them from Sam Bova in 2018. She operates them, along with the year round Villagio Italiano, with her husband State Senator George Borrello.

Thomas Indian School
Cattaraugus Reservation, Irving

Figure 167 Thomas Indian School Iroquois Genealogy Society PD

The Thomas Indian School opened in 1855 on the Cattaraugus Indian Reservation by missionaries Asher and Laura Wright, to house orphaned and abandoned children. It had the distinction of being the first Indian orphanage.

Asher and Laura Wright operated a Mission House for the Seneca Indians since 1831 at the Buffalo Creek Reservation on Buffum Street off Seneca Street. When the Seneca were removed from the Buffalo Creek Reservation in 1845, the Wrights moved with them to the Cattaraugus Reservation. Poverty, disease, alcoholism and domestic abuse ran rampant in the Seneca community, necessitating Indian families that were unable to care for their children to surrender them to the boarding schools. On occasion they were forcibly removed from their homes by federal or state authorities.

In 1854 Laura Wright wrote to the Seneca Nation of Indians and received approval to create a boarding school, acquire land on the reservation and expand the mission house to accommodate eight to ten children. Asher Wright secured a charter for an asylum from the state. With the support and generous gift of $100.00 from Philip Thomas, a Quaker businessman and philanthropist, the school was named the Thomas Asylum for Orphan and Destitute Indian Children.

When the Asylum was founded in 1855, it began as a somewhat benevolent institution. The Wright's were teaching in the Seneca language and employing teachers sympathetic to the plight of the Seneca children. However, the Asylum was operated more like a child labor camp, than a school. The boys working as farm laborers and the girls learning domestic chores, with little time dedicated to academic subjects.

Due to financial difficulties, Asher Wright contacted his friend William Letchworth, the founder of Pratt & Letchworth and administrator of the NYS Board of Charities. Through Letchworth's efforts in 1875 the school was transferred to the NYS Board of Charities where the children were placed in custodial care and classified as crippled or defective, being referred to as inmates instead of students. The Asylum experienced high death rates, offered little instruction, children did not understand why they were institutionalized and many just ran away.

In 1905 it was renamed The Thomas School. During its existence, 2,470 children attended the school that became an agent of deculturalization, divesting Indian children of their language, culture, heritage and family. It closed in 1957, surviving longer than most other Indian boarding schools.

Lily Dale Assembly
5 Melrose Park, Lily Dale

The advent of the Spiritualist Movement can be traced to Laona, NY, on Route 60 just north of Cassadaga Lake.

In 1844, Dr. Moran from Vermont, was invited to the village of Laona to demonstrate mesmerism, the manipulation of the universal magnetic fluid or unseen energy flowing around a person, by strokes or passings around a person to redirect their energy flow back into harmony and balance.

Figure 168 Lily Dale Forest Temple photo lilydaleassembly.org PD

Dr. Moran demonstrated the procedure to a group of interested people but left town before physically disabled Jeremiah Carter could be treated. The group applied the procedures to Carter; he became entranced and spoke to spirits who further demonstrated the healing laying of hands. He was cured of his aliments and in 1855 the First Spiritualist Society of Laona was formed to practice healing and mediumship.

Jeremiah Carter was directed by spirit voices to the Willard Alden farm on the east bank of Lake Cassadaga. In 1873, the Spiritualist group began summer picnics and camp meetings in the Leolyn Woods and near the current location of the Leolyn Hotel. When Mr. Alden died, the Spiritualists purchased the 20 acres next to his farm in 1879. That is the founding date of the assembly which took the name of the Cassadaga Lake Free Association, becoming The City of Light in 1903 and Lily Dale Assembly in 1906.

After clearing the land, a dedication was held under a canopy of boughs known as the Bough House. The first speaker was Elizabeth Lowe, a liberal dynamic suffragette speaker. Marion Skidmore was a founding member. Her father William Johnson invited Moran to speak in Laona in 1844. The Marion Skidmore Library and Lily Dale Museum (in the former schoolhouse), contain the world's largest collection of Spiritualist books and memorabilia in America.

For an entrance fee you can attend lectures in the 1883 Auditorium (1,200 seats), 1888 Assembly Hall built or 1890 Octagon Building. Public demonstrations and message services take place at The Stump in Leolyn Woods and 1894 Forest Temple, both are areas of spiritual energy. Healing services take place in Healing Hall. Info is available about The Fox Sisters Cabin, where Spiritualism was inaugurated, that was moved to Lily Dale but burned down.

You can visit Lily Dale for the day or stay at the 1880 Maplewood Hotel, Leolyn Inn just outside the gate or several Guest Houses. Private readings can be scheduled with mediums.

J. N. Adam Memorial Hospital
10317 County Road 58, Perrysburg

Figure 169 J.N. Adams Hospital Artvue postcard PD

The J. N. Adam Memorial Hospital was a historical tuberculosis treatment center in Perrysburg, NY that opened in 1912 and was named in honor of James Noble Adam.

James Noble Adam was the brother of Robert Borthwick Adam, who relocated to Buffalo in 1867 and opened AM&A's Department Store. When a property for another dry goods store became available in Buffalo in 1881, Robert suggested that J.N. move his New Haven, Connecticut store to the city. He operated J.N. Adams store on the east side of Main Street, with Robert's AM&A's across the street. Eventually AM&A's moved into the J.N. Adams location.

After the death of his wife in 1895 J.N. Adams dedicated his life to politics and enhancing the community. He was elected to the City Council in 1895 and served as the 45th mayor of Buffalo from 1906 to 1909.

During the early 1900's, tuberculosis was a major health crisis, so the city of Buffalo was authorized to build a hospital to treat its victims. Medical professionals at the time believed the best cure for tuberculous was natural exposure to sunlight, or "heliotherapy". Adam purchased nearly 300 acres of land in Perrysburg for $20,000 and donated it to the city of Buffalo to build a facility that could accommodate 150 TB patients at a time. Unfortunately, Adam passed away from a stroke shortly before the hospital opened.

The state-of-the-art hospital had large outdoor verandas for sunbathing and its own freshwater reservoir, along with on-site livestock and vegetable gardens to provide fresh meat and produce for the patients. There was also an open-air school for children suffering from tuberculosis, and a cottage on the grounds where non-infected children could stay while their mothers were in the hospital.

By 1960, vaccines and antibiotics were available to treat tuberculosis, so the hospital was no longer needed for this purpose. It was converted into an institutional mental facility as a division of the Gowanda State Hospital, and served as a temporary residence while the children's psychiatric hospital in West Seneca was being built. It was listed on the New York State Register of Historical Places in 1985, but officially closed in 1993 and never reopened. Due to years of vandalism and neglect, the hospital has deteriorated to a point where either demolishing or refurbishing the facility have proven too costly, so it remains abandoned and gated off; its proud history merely a distant memory.

by Doreen Gallagher Regan

Barcelona Lighthouse
8234 E Lake Road (Route 5), Westfield

About an hour's drive south of Buffalo stands Barcelona Lighthouse, the first natural gas lighthouse in the world. Once known as Portland Harbor Light, it was completed in 1829 in the small town of Portland, on the shoreline of Lake Erie.

The harbor area, renamed Barcelona after the town of Westfield, NY was officially established, was an important location for commercial fishing and transportation in and out of the Chautauqua region. It was a popular rest stop for passengers traveling between Erie, PA and Buffalo, NY, and a destination for cargo ships carrying goods to nearby warehouses.

Figure 170 Barcelona Lighthouse 1900
photo courtesy Patterson Library Archives

Because of the harbor's importance as a busy industrial hub, it was designated as an official port of entry by the U.S. Congress in 1827. Local congressman Daniel Garnsey persuaded the government to provide funding for a lighthouse and keeper's cottage, securing $5,000 for the project. The land was purchased for $50 from the Holland Land Company, and Judge Thomas B. Campbell was selected to oversee its construction.

The lighthouse, a 40-foot conical tower with a 22- foot diameter base, is a classic example of early American architecture, constructed of native fieldstone. The light was powered by an innovative system using natural gas supplied from a nearby "burning spring" and transported through wooden pipes. At night, it could be seen across the lake in Canada more than 25 miles away, shining so brightly it appeared as if the entire tower was ablaze.

During its three decades of service, Barcelona Lighthouse played a crucial role in countless rescues and maritime incidents. It endured fluctuating lake levels and fierce gales. However, a devastating storm in 1844 destroyed many of the lakeside warehouses, and the advent of railroads as a means of cheaper alternative to water transportation eventually led to the lighthouse's demise.

Barcelona Lighthouse was deactivated in 1859 and the property went into private ownership. It remained dark for over a century until 1962, when a new gas beacon was installed by Iroquois Gas Co. as a nod to its historic past. It was added to the National Register of Historic Places in 1972 and was eventually acquired by the New York State Office of Parks, Recreation, and Historic Preservation in 2007. While it is no longer utilized for navigational purposes, the lighthouse remains lit and visible to this day, and is open to the public as a reminder of its vital role in maritime history.

by Doreen Gallagher Regan

 # WELCH GRAPE JUICE FACTORY
101 North Portage Street, Westfield

Figure 171 Welch's Grape Juice Company vintage postcard

Welch Factory Building No. 1 in Westfield, NY is a historic landmark that was built in 1897. It played a major role in the growth of the grape juice industry and remains an important remnant of the region's agricultural heritage.

The first unfermented grape juice known to be processed in the United States was introduced by Dr. Thomas Bramwell Welch, a minister and prohibitionist who opposed the use of alcoholic beverages. Dr. Welch, also a successful dentist at the time, lived in Vineland, NJ where concord grapes were prevalent. He, along with the 19th Century Methodist church, embraced the belief that unfermented grape juice should be used in communion instead of alcoholic wine. He was fascinated by Louis Pasteur's theory of pasteurization, so in 1869 he decided to try pasteurizing grape juice. With his wife and 17-year-old son Charles, Dr. Welch gathered Concord grapes from a trellis on his property, cooked the grapes in his kitchen, squeezed the juice through cloth bags, and bottled the fresh grape juice. To preserve it, he stoppered the bottles and boiled them in water to prevent fermentation. The process was a success, and his use of the pasteurization method pioneered the industry of bottled fruit juices throughout America. Dr. Welch persuaded the local churches to adopt this non-alcoholic beverage for communion services, and it was called "Dr. Welch's Unfermented Wine."

In 1890 Dr. Welch and his son Charles founded Welch's Grape Juice Company, and their juice gained widespread popularity when it was introduced at the World's Fair in Chicago. After Dr. Welch retired, Charles transferred the juice operations to Westfield, NY, and in 1897 Welch's Grape Juice Company was incorporated, marking the beginning of its commercial production. Welch Factory Building No.1 was constructed, and 300 tons of grapes were processed into juice during its initial year.

A few years later, the factory had to be expanded significantly to meet increasing demand for grape juice, and Westfield became known as the Grape Juice Capital of the World. Although the original Factory Building No. 1 has long been shuttered, Welch's continues to process around 320,000 tons of grapes each year. It currently operates as a cooperative, owned by about 700 family farmers. Grapes go from the vine to the press within 8 hours of being picked. Chautauqua County is considered the second largest grape-growing region in the United States.

by Doreen Gallagher Regan

TOWN OF CHEEKTOWAGA

VILLAGE OF DEPEW

PROFILES

This section includes profiles of the Town of Cheektowaga and several historic places in **Cheektowaga** and in the Village of **Depew**.

Town of Cheektowaga

The name" Cheektowaga" is derived from the Erie-Seneca word Ji-ik-do-wah-gah or place of the crabapple tree. One of the few Indian villages in WNY was located in central Cheektowaga and was named Falls Village, located along the Indian trail on the north bank of Cayuga Creek. Long houses were built from Bordon Road, near Broadway, along the creek to Union Road.

In 1809 Apollos Hitchcock became the first resident of Cheektowaga when he purchased land on both sides of Batavia Road from the Holland Land Company. He built a log cabin along Cayuga Creek, west of Borden Road, and farmed the lands of the former Indian village. Hitchcock later built a frame home at Broadway and Dick Road, that was razed in the 1920s when the railroad underpass was built. Since Hitchcock had a distillery to convert corn into liquor, Dick/Cayuga Road was also called Whiskey Road, along with being considered Williamsville Road. He later purchased land which he leased to German immigrants, with the promise of purchasing their corn for the distillery.

Elnathan Bennet built a home-tavern on Walden Avenue, east of Harlem Road, in 1816. Several other residents built mills on their property. E. Sheldon Ely built a sawmill on Cayuga Creek in the Bellevue area. There was also a mill on Ellicott Creek near Sugg Road and on Slate Bottom Creek north of French Road.

The land that is now Cheektowaga was part of Clarence and then Amherst. It was in Genesee County, Niagara County and finally Erie County, when that county was formed in 1821. The Town of Cheektowaga was formed on March 22, 1839 from the southern part of Amherst. It extended to the middle of Buffalo Creek Reservation at Cazenovia Creek. The first town meeting was in the Bennett Tavern and Alexander Hitchcock was named the first Supervisor, also succeeding his father Apollos as Indian Agent.

Plank Road (now Genesee Street) and Batavia Road (now Broadway) were the main roads through the town. Both were toll roads, with the toll on Broadway just north of Union, not removed until the early 20th century. The first school was in the home of Roxana Hitchcock, followed by a log school nearby on Williamsville Road. A second school was built at the corner of Maryvale and Cayuga. A third school was in a service building for the cemetery on Harlem Road near Huth Road, which became the Cleveland Hill School System.

Another early resident of Cheektowaga was Joseph Batt, who purchased 138 acres from the Holland Land Company for $859.84 in 1837. This land centered around the current intersection of Union Road and Genesee Street, where Batt built Our Lady of Christians Chapel. The chapel became a pilgrimage site to the Blessed Mother and was associated with the first two saints of the Catholic Church in the U.S. - Father John Neumann and Mother Frances Xavier Cabrini. In 1890 Our Lady of Christians was the largest parish in the diocese of Buffalo and all other churches in Cheektowaga were from this church.

Railroads played an important part in the development of Cheektowaga. There were five railroad stations spread across the town and the Buffalo, Bellevue, Lancaster Electric Railway was built south of Broadway. This helped create the villages of Sloan and Depew in the town, along with the Bellevue section in south Cheektowaga.

Germans moved eastward across the city line along Genesee Street, while Polish moved along Broadway and William to make Cheektowaga a growing suburb.

Entertainment in Cheektowaga included Liberty Park at Union & William, which had amusement park rides and a bingo/dance hall. Bellevue Park, along Cayuga Creek, was a 30-acre park with boating, picnic areas and a dance hall, near the end of the Bellevue Electric Trolly. Gypsies camped along the creek, offering fortune telling and other entertainments. The Bellevue Hotel and Reinstein Woods wildlife sanctuary were part of this park area.

Figure 172 Liberty Park 1949 Cheektowaga Historical Museum

In 1935 what was billed as the "World's most modern Greyhound Track" was built at the cost of $100,000 at the corner of Maryvale and Harlem Roads. It had a seating capacity of 4,000 people and the clubhouse held another thousand. On opening day over 6,000 people were at the track and a special "Jungle Jockey Night" with monkeys riding the greyhounds drew over 12,000 people. Admission was 40 cents general admission, 75 cents for box seats and $1.00 for the clubhouse. The racetrack was closed when the gambling system set up by the track was declared illegal.

Bell Aircraft developed the Bell Model 30 and 47 helicopters in a former automobile garage at Losson and Union Road. In addition to the Buffalo Niagara International Airport, the Becker Airfield was at the intersection of Union and Genesee, now occupied by the Airport Plaza. One of the first shopping centers was the Thruway Plaza, opened in 1952 at Walden and Harlem Roads. The Walden Galleria, the largest shopping mall in WNY, is located near the intersection of Walden and Union Road.

Figure 173 Gardenville Union Garage Union & Losson Bell Helicopter

BUFFALO NIAGARA INTERNATIONAL AIRPORT
4200 Genesee Street, Cheektowaga

Figure 174 Buffalo Airport Art Deco Terminal Built in 1939

Aviation began in Buffalo at the Hotel Lennox in 1900 when the Aero Club of Buffalo was formed by members of the Automobile Club of Buffalo, Buffalo Bicycle Club and Carrier Pigeon Club of Buffalo. In 1909, the Aero Club received its charter as the first U.S. Aero Club Chapter from the Federation Aeronautique Internationale of France, making it the world's second oldest aero club and the oldest in America.

The club president was John Satterfield and members included George Urban, Jr., Dr. Charles Cary and Ralph Sidway. They built their own planes and tested them on the polo grounds of the Buffalo Country Club at Main and Bailey. In 1915 forty members of the Buffalo Aero Club formed the 2nd Aero Company, Signal Corps, New York National Guard which trained at the Curtis Flying Field on Niagara Falls Boulevard and served in WWI.

After the war Sattenfield worked with the Aero Club and Buffalo Chamber of Commerce to establish an airport. In 1925 they purchased 200 acres from the Buffalo Trap & Field Club along Genesee Street and Cayuga Road in Cheektowaga. The airport opened in 1926, making it one of the oldest public airports in the country. It had a small terminal, one hanger and four cinder runways, 3,000 feet long and 100 feet wide.

Passenger and airmail service commenced in December 1927, with service to Cleveland (home of the oldest U.S. municipal airport). In 1939 a new WPA built, Art Deco V-shaped terminal with a large cylindrical tower opened to replace the original terminal. During WWII Curtiss Wright flew planes from their Elmwood terminal to the Buffalo airport and their adjacent manufacturing plant, for transfer to the Army Air Corps. After WWII the Curtiss Plant became Westinghouse and was later demolished to accommodate airport expansion.

A new terminal was completed in 1955 and in 1956 the Niagara Frontier Port Authority (renamed the Niagara Frontier Transportation Authority – NFTA) was established to run the airport. In the 1960s the east terminal was expanded and in 1971 a West Terminal was added. A completely redesigned modern airport opened in 1997, with further expansions annually completed.

There was another Cheektowaga airport named Becker Airfield on Genesee Street at Union Road, extending to Maryvale and Beach Road. It closed in 1943 and it is now the location of the Airport Plaza.

CHAPEL OF OUR LADY HELP OF CHRISTIANS
4125 Union Road, Cheektowaga

Joseph Batt vowed that if he and his family survived the storm encountered by their ship The Marie during an Atlantic crossing in 1837, upon arrival in America he would build a chapel in honor of the Blessed Mother. After settling on 138 acres in southern Amherst, which became part of Cheektowaga in 1839, he began planning the chapel. In 1851 he donated three acres for a chapel, school and graveyard.

Bishop Timon dedicated the church in 1853 as a chapel under the jurisdiction of St. Peter & Paul Church in Williamsville. Inspired by the Alsatian Pilgrimages to the shrine of the Blessed Mother in the village of Marienthal, Alsace, during the Buffalo Cholera epidemic of 1854 pilgrims began visiting the Cheektowaga Chapel. By 1864 pilgrimages visited Maria Hilf – Our Lady of Christians Chapel on a recurrent basis and stories of mysterious cures were circulated. An article in the 1894 *Buffalo Courier Express* referred to the Chapel as the Second Lourdes.

Figure 175 Our Lady Help of Christians Chapel
photo courtesy Cheektowaga Historical Society

Trolley service was extended to The Chapel at the turn of the century and thousands of people visited the shrine in veneration of the Blessed Mother. When trolley service was discontinued in 1950 and the buses only ran to the city line, people would walk over two miles down Genesee Street to Union Road. The largest attendance at the Chapel was V-J Day August 15, 1945 when the line of people extended all the way down Genesee Street to downtown Buffalo.

In 1890 Our Lady Help of Christians was designated a parish that included all of Cheektowaga, making it the largest parish in the diocese of Buffalo. Mother Cabrini, the first U.S. citizen to become a Saint (Cabrini movie filmed in Buffalo in 2021) visited the Chapel in the early 1900s. The first male saint in America was also associated with The Chapel. When the formation of Our Lady Help of Christians was discussed in 1839 at St. Peter & Paul in Williamsville, the pastor was St. John Neuman.

Father Nelson Baker, who was named the Venerable Nelson Baker in 2011 and is on the road to sainthood, led a movement to stop demolition and save the Chapel in its original state, and laid the cornerstone for the Chapel School in 1924. The church was officially proclaimed the oldest place of worship in Cheektowaga in 1964.

George Urban Mansion
280 Pine Ridge Road, Cheektowaga

Figure 176 Res of George Urban, Jr. Pine Hill Town of Cheektowaga Erie County NY PD

George Urban, Jr. expanded his father's flour business from facilities at Genesee & Oak Streets to a new plant on Kehr Street, along the Beltline railway. The Urban Milling Company was the first mill entirely powered by electricity.

Urban was one of the trailblazers in hydroelectric power. He formed the Brush Electric Light Company in 1880, which was Buffalo's first municipal lighting plant and was an officer in the companies that merged to form the Buffalo General Electric Company. In addition, Urban was a land developer with the Bellevue and Depew Land Companies.

Boulevard is named after him. He was also an officer of several banks and a director of many companies including the German Insurance Company and Ellicott Square Company.

In 1875 Urban married Ada. E. Winspear and started expanding the farm at 280 Pine Ridge Road. The Cheektowaga property was originally called Pine Hill Farms and was purchased by the Winspear family in 1841. James Winspear settled on the property in 1842 and it was inherited by Pennock Winspear, Ada's father. Ada was born at Pine Hill Farms and was the winner of the first Jesse Ketchum gold medal presented at Central High School in Buffalo. The Urban and Winspear families owned over 120 acres of Cheektowaga by the early 1860s.

The nine-acre property was a large working farm with a horse racing track and poultry house that annually raised over 800 chicks. With Urban being an avid horticulturist, it included a vineyard with over 29 varieties of grapes and a garden that included over 150 varieties of roses. Urban was a friend of Thomas Edison, so the home was wired for electricity before it became widely available and large pipes were installed below the house because Urban heard indoor plumbing was going to be developed.

Although Urban was a prominent Republican, including serving as chairman of the Erie County Republican Committee, Democratic Grover Cleveland announced his presidential campaign during a picnic at the Urban Mansion in 1883. Urban did not endorse or vote for Cleveland, but they remained good friends.

Generations of the Winspear and Urban families lived at the estate until 1954 and the location of Villa Maria High School and College were on the property. The home is still privately owned, and it is the 2025 Junior League of Buffalo's Decorator's Show House.

Figure 177 George Urban House photo credit Rick Falkowski

REINSTEIN WOODS NATURE PRESERVE
93 Honorine Drive, Cheektowaga

The New York State Department of Environmental Conservation (DEC) assumed ownership of 292 acres of undeveloped land from the estate of Dr. Victor Reinstein in 1986. It was open to the public on a limited basis until 2001, when the DEC expanded its educational programs and developed a volunteer program. The DEC encouraged the volunteers to form a non-profit corporation Friends of Reinstein Nature Preserve Inc. in 2003 to support the education and volunteer programs.

Figure 178 Reinstein Woods - former Reinstein Family Summer Building photo credit Marsha Falkowski

Victor Reinstein was a medical doctor and attorney, but like his mother Dr. Anna Reinstein he purchased large tracts of property in the Bellevue section of Cheektowaga. He became one of the largest landowners in Cheektowaga and accumulated his wealth by renting out low-cost apartments and buying/selling land.

In 1932 Victor purchased 292 acres of forested wetlands and ponds, off Como Park Boulevard. Assisted by his sons Robert and Victor Jr., Reinstein planted 30,000 trees and built 19 ponds, marshes and swamps. He was dedicated to nature conservation and the preservation of old-growth forests, which include Champion Beech tree, the oldest beech tree in NYS. The Reinsteins created over 3 ½ miles of gravel or grass trails traversing the nature parks forests, swamp lands and lily ponds. These paths can be enjoyed by nature lovers of all ages and are handicapped accessible.

The Reinstein Woods Environmental Education Center opened in 2007, with the DEC and Friends of Reinstein Woods offering education programs for school children, teachers, youth from underserved neighborhoods and the general public. Nature walks and walks under the full moon are held to explore and enjoy fireflies, wildflowers, wildlife, bats, frogs and fungi. A wooden boardwalk extends to a lookout point in the lily pond.

Special events are scheduled throughout all seasons. Snowshoeing and cross-country skiing are available during the winter. Entrance to the park and parking in their paved lot is free.

In addition to Reinstein Woods, Victor and his wife Julia Reinstein donated the land for Stiglmeier Park, Nokomis Park and the Julia Reinstein Library on Losson Road. The Anna Reinstein Library on Harlem is named after his mother. Julia Reinstein was appointed Cheektowaga's first historian, was founder of the Cheektowaga Historical Society, Cheektowaga Historical Museum, the History Building on the Erie County Fairgrounds, the Julia Boyer Reinstein Center in front of the Buffalo Historical Society and she helped create 28 historical societies in WNY.

St. Stephen's Evangelical Lutheran Home
3350 Broadway, Cheektowaga

Figure 179 St. Stephens 1898 PD
History of Germans of Buffalo & Erie County

In 1877 St. Stephen's Church purchased 25 acres of land on Broadway, about two miles beyond the Buffalo city limits, and in 1880 erected a three-story home for the aged in what was then called Forks, New York.

Under the leadership of Reverend Friedrich Schelle, the institution accommodated up to 50 residents and provided all the modern improvements. The building initially had a small vestibule front entrance that was expanded to an open porch with a 2nd floor balcony. It featured a cupola, decorative cornices, arched windows, corbelled chimneys, stone sills and a stone basement. Shortly after opening, a two-story rear addition was constructed and the grounds had orchards, a promenade garden, stables and was located outside the city limits, free from the smoke of factories and noise of the city.

In 1950 a campaign was started for a new home, which was built on the site of the former Hoyt Mansion at 1190 Amherst Street, next to Nichols Academy. Known as the United Church Home Society, when that facility opened the Broadway location was sold to Owen Nursing and Convalescent Home, a private nursing home in 1956.

After the nursing home closed it was opened as Keith Gregor's Music Mall in 1979. This was a band rehearsal facility with 30 practice rooms. It included Musicians Hardware Center music store owned by Danny Hairfield, SEE Electronics repair shop run by Jim Saba, The Guitar Gallery where Joe Zon sold his custom-made guitars and Trakworks Recording Studio operated by Vince Cerilli, Danny Hairfield and Dan Roland.

United Church Home Society closed their Amherst Street building in 2003 and currently operates the United Church Manor at 50 North Avenue in West Seneca and is the founder of one of WNY's premier retirement communities, Fox Run of Orchard Park.

The Music Mall was purchased by the Cheektowaga Historical Association/Museum in April 2024, saving one of the oldest commercial buildings in Cheektowaga. It is still operating as a band rehearsal space. Over time the Cheektowaga Historical Association Museum will relocate from their current museum across Broadway into the former nursing home. The building will eventually be converted into a 20,000 square foot museum for the Town of Cheektowaga, featuring space for town history, police, firemen, WNY music, other organizations and historical societies.

WAR OF 1812 CEMETERY
Aero Road, Cheektowaga

The War of 1812 Cemetery is also referred to as the Garrison Cemetery as it was located on the grounds of the General Military Hospital at Williams Mill, New York. It is the burial place of American and British soldiers who died in the military hospital at Williamsville during 1814 and 1815.

After an unsuccessful attempt to invade Canada, in the winter of 1812 General Alexander Smyth retired his army to winter quarters in Williamsville. Cabins were built to house the troops along Garrison Road between Main Street and Ellicott Creek, extending to the southeast.

The cabins were abandoned in April 1813 when the troops rejoined the battles in Canada. The following

Figure 180 From the War of 1812 Cemetery photo credit Rick Falkowski

October the cabins were used as a winter hospital, each room holding six patients. Over 250 sick and wounded troops were transferred from Fort George and Fort Niagara, by way of Lewiston and Fort Schlosser, to the Williamsville hospital. A wounded Colonel Winfield Scott and captured British Commanding General Phineas Riall were treated at the Evans House. After Buffalo was burned by the British in December 1813, residents fled to Williamsville for refuge. Over 5,000 troops were based in Williamsville during the winter of 1813/1814 and the drill grounds were the current location of St. Peter & Paul Church on Main.

Due to overcrowding, in 1814 the farm of Rapheal Cook was leased to construct a wood and brick general hospital. It was located further southeast of Williamsville along Ellicott Creek. After the Battle of Chippewa, a hospital for wounded troops was built at Sandy Town, near Buffalo Creek. Those patients and soldiers from other field hospitals were transferred to the hospital in Williamsville, considered the main treatment facility in WNY.

There was no designated burial ground for the soldiers that died at the hospital. Graves were dug on ground southeast of the hospital on property owned by the Holland Land Company. U.S. soldiers were buried on one side of the grounds and British/Canadian on the other. In total over 200 were interred, with most dying from dysentery or diarrhea, not battle wounds.

In 1898, the War of 1812 Cemetery was deeded to the Buffalo Historical Society, with a cannon dedicated and fenced archway built on the grounds. Various VFW and Veteran's Posts maintained the property and in 1985 it was deeded to the Town of Cheektowaga and Cheektowaga Historical Association.

TOWN OF CLARENCE PROFILES

This section includes profiles on the Town of **Clarence** and many of its historic places.

Town of Clarence

Clarence was occupied for thousands of years by many different Native American peoples. Their fires have long burned out and their villages, longhouses, and wigwams have decayed away, but their stories are not forgotten. Their stone tools, cooking vessels, and material culture can still be found in the ground, throughout the town.

The town was referred to as Ta-Num-No-Ga-O or place of the hickory tree. According to Morgan (1852), hickory was used by the Native Americans for arrow shafts, bows, and snowshoe rims. The bark was made into strips for basket making and also had medicinal properties.

The town's namesake is from the English House of Clarence. It is not known why the town's founding fathers named it after the Duke of Clarence, King George III's third son. Clarence was founded as one of the three (Cambria & Willink) original towns of Niagara County which covered the majority of what is now Niagara and Erie County.

Joseph Ellicott and 150 men braved the wilderness and surveyed the Western New York tract in 1798-1804. In 1799, Asa Ransom took Ellicott's offer to settle on a 150-acre plot, Township 12, Range 6, Lot 12. Asa was born in Connecticut in 1765 during the beginning of the colonial upheaval with Great Britain. Asa was a silversmith and goldsmith and used these skills to befriend the natives who lived in the area. Making trinkets for the local native population was an important skill, as they were highly valued and traded for.

Following Asa Ransom, early settlers came mainly from Massachusetts, Connecticut and Pennsylvania. The first pioneers settled in the Hollow (1799), then Harris Hill (1807) and then Clarence Center (1829), Swormsville (1840's) and Wollcottburg (1870's). The town of Clarence was established one generation after the Revolutionary War and was settled by veterans of the war.

The Town's first meeting was held in Elias Ransom's Tavern on Main Street in present-day Williamsville, on March 11th, 1808. Twenty-two men gathered to discuss issues like roads, wolves and taxes. The first problem discussed was wolves and it was determined the town would pay $5.00 per wolf pelt. Panthers, mountain lions, rattlesnakes and bears also existed in the forests of early Clarence. The land had to be cleared and the wilderness tamed to make it livable for the early pioneers.

The earliest industry was hospitality as taverns were built to house Revolutionary War veterans, adventurers and pioneers heading west. In order to survive the harsh conditions of the early 1800s, land was cleared to farm wheat, grain, and corn, as many settlers found farming to be an essential industry. Joseph Ellicott also tasked the early settlers to erect mills near their taverns. Several saw and grist mills were built along waterways and used throughout the town. Farming remained the prominent industry until the mid-1900s and is still currently important.

The clay of Ransom Creek that was once used to craft the pots and pipes of the natives was industrialized in the mid-1800s to make bricks. The Eshelman family used the quality clay to build their homes and store in Clarence Center. Most of the early brick homes in Clarence were built with local clay which is the remnants of the Tonawanda Lake bed.

The same escarpment that was used as a pathway and resource for making stone tools by the natives was also used to build houses and make gravel for road beds. Mining was another early industry in Clarence. Many gravel pits can be found littering the southern half of the town. The most prominent one is Spaulding Lake, an old gravel pit that hit a natural spring and filled up with water in a day. The Onondaga Escarpment provided hard limestone. Farmers used the limestone to make kilns to cook the limestone down to be used for many different things on the farm. Remnants of a few lime kilns can still be seen throughout the region.

After farming, one of the largest employers in town was the National Gypsum mines (1926-1982) on Roll Road, just West of Clarence Center. The gypsum was determined to be the purest in the eastern United States. Gypsum is a naturally occurring soft mineral that is used for a variety of building materials, mainly for making gypsum board, or today referred to as drywall. The National Gypsum Mine in Clarence Center was one of the largest manufacturers of building materials in the country and advanced different technologies to make the boards. The mine closed in 1982 because most of the gypsum was mined out.

Figure 181 National Gypsum Company on Roll Road in Clarence Center
photo courtesy Clarence Town Historian

With one big industry closing, another filled the void. Wilson Greatbatch started Greatbatch Inc. in 1982 and is located on Wehrle Drive and has been a large employer with over two hundred workers today. Many other small businesses reside in the town as well.

Throughout the town's two hundred-plus years, it has remained a farming community. Much of northern Clarence is still farmed. In more recent years, some of the farmland has been developed with many new houses built. However, Clarence maintains a small-town feel with a rich heritage and interesting history.

by Joseph McGreevy, Clarence Town Historian

Asa Ransom House
10529 and 10897 Main Street, Clarence

After Fort Niagara was transferred from British to American jurisdiction in 1796, silversmith Asa Ransom, his wife Keziah Ransom and their daughter Portia moved west from Geneva. In 1797 they built a log cabin near Main and Terrace and became the first family to settle at the mouth of Buffalo Creek.

In 1799, The Holland Land Company offered lots ten miles apart to any proper man who would build and operate a tavern upon it. Asa Ransom took up Joseph Ellicott's offer and purchased 150 acres at $2.00 per acre. He built a log home and tavern (the first hotel in Erie County outside of Buffalo Creek), located near the corner of Main Street and Ransom Road. An early map showed the Ransom House to be on the west bank of Ransom Creek on Buffalo Road.

Figure 182 Ransom House at 10897 Main Street
photo courtesy Clarence Historical Society

When the town of Willink was carved out of the town of Batavia in 1804, Asa Ransom was named town assessor. The 1807 annual Willink town meeting was moved to Ransom's tavern, with Ransom being elected town supervisor. In 1808, the 33rd session of the New York Legislature was held at the Ransom property.

Research suggests that the original house built by Asa Ransom in 1799 was not torn down, it was moved from Clarence Hollow up the East Hill. After the deaths of Asa and Keziah Ransom, the tavern was purchased by two Masons and moved to property owned by a Masonic Lodge at 10897 Main Street. There is no record of the original Ransom house building after 1837 and no building documented as existing at 10897 Main Street until 1855. The described physical appearance of both buildings was similar and the Town of Clarence designated the 10897 Main Street property as Ransom's Tavern.

The property at 10529 Main Street known as the Asa Ransom House Inn & Restaurant from 1970 to 2002, is about a block away from where the original Ranson Home/Tavern stood at Main & Ranson. Ruins of the grist mill built in 1803 are behind the building and it is believed Asa Ransom, Jr. constructed the brick portion of the building in 1853. The Asa Ransom House was featured in a 1994 PBS show Inn Country USA when owned by Bob and Judy Lenz. It was purchased by Bradley and Cassandra McCallum in 2021 and is now called The Duke of Clarence, boutique hotel and Adelaide's fine dining.

Clarence Town Park Club House
10405 Main Street, Clarence

Figure 183 Clarence Country Club photo courtesy AAA

In 1911 the Automobile Club of Buffalo built a country clubhouse, designed by August Esenwein and James Johnson, architects that designed several prominent Buffalo buildings, including the Temple of Music at the Pan-American Exposition. The clubhouse is of the "Arts and Crafts" style, influenced by the designs of Frank Lloyd Wright, Gustav Stickley and Elbert Hubbard. The grandfather clock at the top of the main staircase was crafted by Buffalo furniture maker Charles Rohlfs.

Land for the Automobile Club was the former William Lusk Farm, which Lusk purchased from Wayne Dodge in 1870 and was part of the property Asa Ransom obtained from the Holland Land Company in 1799. It was a pleasant country destination after an adventurous 20-mile drive from the city of Buffalo by members in their Pierce Arrows or other stylish automobiles. The facilities included a large clubhouse, dining rooms and kitchen on the first floor. The second floor featured smaller dining rooms, salons and overnight accommodations. Dinner was also served outdoors on the east side porch, overlooking a grassy knoll and pond, before the porch was enclosed as part of the clubhouse.

It was available to the 10,000 members of the Automobile Club of Buffalo and all automobile clubs affiliated with the American Automobile Association – AAA. The Auto Club of Buffalo was one of the first auto clubs in the U.S. to manage a members-only country club. It was the only institution of its kind east of St. Paul Minnesota and one of not more than six automobile country clubs in the U.S. The guest register maintained at the clubhouse included the names of motorists from every state in the U.S. and guests from around the world.

The 70 acres of grounds provided for outdoor activities including a trap-shooting range, tennis courts and a spring fed lake for swimming and other aquatic sports. The front garden along Main Street bloomed with thousands of perennials and was named The Urban Gardens after pioneer club member George Urban, Jr., who also stocked the fishing pond with over 10,000 trout.

In 1957 the Town of Clarence purchased the property and renamed it Main Street Park. The clubhouse is now used by local clubs for weekly meetings and organizations for dinners and fund-raising activities.

HISTORICAL SOCIETY OF CLARENCE & GOODRICH-LANDOW CABIN

10465 Main Street, Clarence

The Clarence Historical Museum is located on land that was part of the 144-acre purchase by Asa Ransom in 1803. In the 1840's, Abraham Shope purchased the property and donated it to the Church of Christ. The congregation used local Onondaga Limestone from the ledge to construct their church in 1849. The structure was known as "The Meeting House on the West Hill".

Figure 184 Clarence Museum
photo courtesy Clarence Historical Society

After holding services in the church for 26 years, the congregation built a larger church in the hollow and sold the building to Dr. Jared Parker in 1875. This mid-nineteenth stone Greek Revival building remained a private residence for the next fifty years.

In 1925 the Buffalo Automobile Club bought the property, with the Club superintendent using it as his residence named Club Villa. A fire gutted the residence in 1956 and it was converted to a series of restaurants, included one known as The Meeting House. In 1989, the Eleanor and Wilson Greatbatch Foundation purchased the land and building to be used as a historical museum. It was acquired by the Town of Clarence in 1994, becoming the home of the Historical Society of the Town of Clarence.

Levi Goodrich and his family settled in Clarence in 1815. He built a log cabin on the east side of Goodrich Road, north of Lapp Road in 1825. Goodrich was a land surveyor and laid out several major roads in Clarence, including the one named for him. When the Goodrich family relocated to Michigan in 1836, Gustave Landow incorporated the cabin as part of his farm, where it stood for 165 years.

One of the best surviving Yankee log cabins in Erie County, the cabin was moved to the grounds of the Clarence Historical Museum in 1990. The whitewashed, saddle-notched, round log building was oriented to the compass points of the original site. Mortar between the logs was restored with a mixture of local clay, sand and animal hair and surfaces were whitewashed with natural lime. The restored fireplace and bake oven, is an amazingly intact and rare surviving original feature.

Figure 185 Goodrich Landow Log Cabin
photo courtesy Clarence Historical Society

The Watchman's Flag Shanty that guarded the West Shore Railroad crossing on Main Street in Clarence Hollow has also been moved to the Clarence Museum.

Spaulding Lake
Development in Clarence

Figure 186 Undeveloped Spaulding Lake
photo courtesy Historical Society Town of Clarence

Spaulding Lake off Main Street and Goodrich Road in Clarence is one of the most prestigious communities in WNY, featuring many million-dollar homes around a 40-acre lake. The community boasts exclusive amenities including a clubhouse, tennis courts, private beach and large common areas. A professionally run Homeowners Association includes a recreational committee that publishes a Community Newsletter.

The origins of the property date back to The Carroll Brothers Quarry that opened a gravel pit on the north side of Main Street across from Gunnville Road. Gravel was in great demand by the railroads who used it as ballast along the tracks. Excavation created a deep quarry, with a huge stone crusher and railroad cars on tracks along the quarry base to remove the stone.

It was a dangerous work environment and in 1919 the blasting of explosives opened a vein of water in the limestone, creating a spring that flooded the quarry overnight. Submerged in the water was mining equipment and a small locomotive engine. The quarry workers who lived in an area called Pumpkinville, named because the gravel pit owners gave their employees excess orange paint for their homes, had to seek new employment at other mining and quarry operations in the Clarence/Akron area.

Elbridge Gerry Spaulding, grandson of Buffalo mayor and Congressman Elbridge Gerry Spaulding, settled in Clarence near the lake that filled the former Carroll Brothers Quarry. Spaulding was the founder of Spaulding and Yates, the largest distributor of coal in the WNY area, and his grandfather was the Father of the Greenback Dollar, a silver backed dollar that helped the U.S. finance the Civil War. Spaulding's ownership of the land resulted in the crystal-clear water, limestone quarry being named Spaulding Lake

Contrary to other reports, during the 1960s and early 1970s the current location of Spaulding Lake was not the popular hotspot called Hard Rock Quarry, that had live, local and national rock bands, performing to large crowds of swimming partiers. Hard Rock Quarry was further east on Main Street, just before Cummings Road, in the Kelley Island Lime & Transport Company (later General Crushed Stone) quarry.

In 1982 the Clarence Town Board approved the first phase of residential development around Spaulding Lake. Several of the areas' elite developers began building elaborate homes and the community leads the WNY area in the sale of million-dollar houses.

VILLAGE OF EAST AURORA

TOWN OF AURORA

TOWN OF MARILLA PROFILES

This section includes profiles of the Village of **East Aurora** and several historic places in the Village, and in the Towns of **Aurora** and **Marilla**.

Village of East Aurora

Jabez Warren was hired by Joseph Ellicott to build a 43-mile-long road from near Geneseo to Lake Erie. It was called Big Tree Road, now known as Route 20A and went through East Aurora. Warren liked the area, purchased 1,443 acres from the Holland Land Company at $2.00 per acre and built the first house in the town in 1805 at the corner of Main & Pine Street.

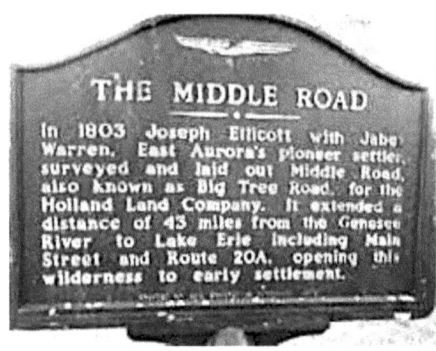

Figure 187 Historic Marker
The Middle Road East Aurora

His son General William Warren opened the first commercial business in town, a tavern on Main Street. Ten people were certified to operate taverns there before the first store was built. In 1806, Mary Eddy opened the first school, on Main near Pine, and in 1815 Robert Persons opened the first mercantile business at the southwest corner of Main and Olean Streets. His brother Charles Parsons opened the Globe Hotel nearby in 1824. Pine Street becomes Olean Street when it crosses Main Street. This was called the Upper Village and is the oldest section of East Aurora.

Calvin Fillmore, Millard Fillmore's uncle, moved to East Aurora in 1816 and purchased Warren's tavern, located next to Spooner & Gundlach's Store. Millard's father Nathaniel Fillmore moved to the village and established the family farm at Olean and Lapham Roads in 1819.

Millard built a home for his wife Abigail on Main Street in 1821 across from the current location of Viddler's 5 & 10. That home was moved to Millard Fillmore Place when the Aurora Theater was built. In 1930 it was relocated to 24 Shearer Street by Irving Price, the founder of Fisher Price Toys. His wife Margaret Evans Price, who designed the first toys for the company, used the home as her design studio. It is the only remaining home that was hand built by a president of the U.S.

The area near the traffic circle, in what is now called the West End, was considered the Lower Village. Major Phineas Stevens built the first saw mill south of Buffalo in this area in 1806. The following year Stevens built a house and grist mill on what is now Hamburg Street. That home built in 1807 is the oldest remaining house in the village and was relocated to 65 Willow Street.

A grist mill was constructed by Humphrey Smith in 1809 in what would become Griffin's Mills, named after Obadiah Griffin who later purchased the mill. Abram Smith also built a mill in West Falls, and in 1820 Lemuel Spooner built a mill on Cazenovia Creek where it crosses Big Tree Road. East Aurora's first blacksmith Ephraim Woodruff arrived in the Lower Village in 1807.

At the time the East Aurora area was settled, it was part of the town of Batavia and in 1805 became a portion of the town of Willink, named after William Wilink who was an investor of the Holland Land Company. When the towns of Holland (Colden), Wales and Aurora were created in 1818, Willink ceased to exist. The area originally part of Genessee County, then became part of Niagara County in 1808 and

Erie County when it was created in 1821. East Aurora was not incorporated as a village until 1874, and the town of Aurora includes East Aurora, Jewettville, Griffins Mills, West Falls and portions of South Wales.

Beginning in the 1860s farmers in East Aurora began making cheese. Each neighborhood had its own cheese factory, but in 1879 Harvey W. Richardson conceived having a central building where cheese could be brought from the various factories to be cured and sold from one location. A large brick building was constructed in the eastern section of East Aurora on Elm Street convenient to the railroads. The company became Richardson, Beebe & Company in 1882. They used 200,000 pounds of milk daily and 30 million pounds annually to produce up to 1,500 tons of cheese a year.

Cicero J. Hamlin, Henry Jewett and J.D. Yeomans opened stock farms in East Aurora where they raised thoroughbred horses, along with quality cattle. Hamlin created Village Farms, which had 800 horse stalls and was considered one of the greatest trotting nurseries in the Western Hemisphere. Hamlin had a racetrack but Jewett Farms on Grover Road

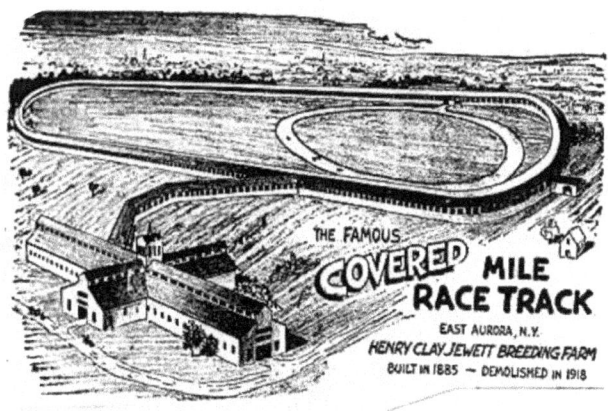

Figure 188 Jewett Farms Covered Mile Horse Racetrack photo Aurora Historian

had the world's only mile long indoor track. Seymour Knox named his property Ideal Stock Farms, training standardbreds, carriage houses and polo horses. The town was the horse racing capital of the world in the late 1800s.

The love of horses was one of the factors that drew Elbert Hubbard to East Aurora. It was only a 25-minute train ride to the Larkin Company Headquarters in Buffalo. After resigning from Larkin, Hubbard created the Roycroft Movement on Main Street in the village.

Fisher Price Toys was formed in the home of Irving Price at 259 Main Street in East Aurora in 1930. Their first factory was at 70 Church Street before they built their factory in 1951 on Girard Avenue. Aerospace company Moog Inc. started in the basement of Bill Moog's East Aurora home in 1951. Their headquarters remains just outside the town on Jamison Road in Elma.

Due to the charm of the village streets, a number of Hallmark Christmas movies have been filmed on Main Street.

FISHER-PRICE TOY COMPANY
636 Girard Avenue, East Aurora

Figure 189 Fisher Price Girard Avenue facility fpclub.org

Fisher-Price, one of the most iconic toy brands in the world, emerged from humble beginnings on a quiet residential street in East Aurora. In 1930, Herman Fisher, who had previously worked for a toy business in Churchville, NY, decided to start his own toy company. He joined forces with Irving Price, a retired Woolworth executive who was the mayor of East Aurora at the time. Price's wife Margaret was a well-known children's book author and illustrator, and Helen Schelle was a toy store owner from Binghamton. The four entrepreneurs created the Fisher-Price Toy Company, initially working out of a small house at 70 Church Street. Driven by the principles of ingenuity, sturdy construction and affordability, the company gained huge success when they showcased their toy line in 1931 at the American International Toy Fair in New York City. Their toys were soon on the shelves of Macy's in New York City and Harrod's in London.

In 1933, the term "preschool toys" emerged after Herman Fisher's mother, a preschool teacher, helped influence the designs for this age group. Two years later Fisher-Price acquired licensing to create toys based on Walt Disney's cartoon characters. During World War II, toy production halted for nearly four years while Fisher-Price switched to manufacturing aircraft parts, medical supply crates, and military ship fenders. By the mid-20th century, Fisher-Price was back to making toys, as the baby boom emerged after the war and plastic was the newest trend, allowing toys to have brighter colors, more contours and better durability.

In 1951, the company moved into its current campus on Girard.

Although Fisher-Price had always enlisted local children to test out their toys, Herman Fisher decided in 1961 to create a room especially made for observing them playing with the company's newest inventions. It was called the Play Laboratory. This was a novel concept in the toy industry at the time, but it paved the way for the extensive research and development facilities that are used today on the Fisher-Price campus.

In 1969 the company was acquired by Quaker Oats and it became a subsidiary of Mattel in 1993. Toys are now manufactured at plants around the world, but the headquarters remains at 636 Girard Street. Fisher Price Toy Town Museum opened in 1987 in front of the headquarters for people to experience the toys that originated in East Aurora, but closed in 2009.

by Doreen Gallagher Regan

GLOBE HOTEL
711 East Main Street, East Aurora

The Globe Hotel is the oldest business in East Aurora that is still in its original location. It was built by Charles P. Persons in 1824 as a stagecoach stop, restaurant, general store and hotel near the corner of Main Street and Olean Road. Person's brother Robert had previously opened a business at the southwest corner of that intersection in 1815.

It was an important stagecoach stop along the dirt roads from the fledgling city of Buffalo to the outlying lumber and agricultural areas. The opening of the Erie Canal brought business to the entire WNY area and traffic increased on the muddy, rutted Main Street of East Aurora.

Figure 190 Globe Hotel 1890
photo courtesy Archives of the Aurora Town Historians Office

Prior to being elected to the presidency of the U.S., both Millard Fillmore and Grover Cleveland, frequented the business. Fillmore had his law office and lived upon the same block on Main Street. Cleveland was often in East Aurora while he was sheriff of Erie County and because he was a landlord that owned land at the corner of Davis Road and Route 20A.

The exterior of the building has not changed much since the Civil War days and the interior still features an 1800s beamed ceiling in the dining room, tin ceiling in the bar and twin fireplaces. Five volumes of hotel guest registers are preserved and on display at the Aurora Town Historians Office, listing the signatures and home addresses of guests from 1890 to 1924. Included are travelers from across the country including performers, politicians and newspaper publishers, and the interior retains the historic charm of that era.

The restaurant continued operation through the late 1800s and was later purchased by Victor H. Balthasar, who managed it since 1920 and operated it until 1975. During the 1960s the restaurant was known for its saloon-type rustic appeal. Since Balthasar ran the business for 55 years, his spirit is rumored to still frequent the restaurant/bar area and stroll in the upstairs halls.

In 1981 the business was purchased by Rocco and Tara Sorrentino, who established its reputation for barbecue dishes and ribs. They operated Tony Rome's Globe Hotel until 2018 when they sold it to Molly Flynn. The Sorrentino family also ran Tony Rome's at 1537 Union Road in West Seneca until 1990.

Flynn closed the business at the end of 2022 and Balthasar's spirit is awaiting new ownership of this 200-year-old landmark.

Hamlin Village Farms
100 North Willow, East Aurora

Figure 191 The Judge's Stand

Cicero Hamlin moved to East Aurora in 1836 where he opened a general store. He moved to Buffalo in 1846, opening a dry goods store Wattles & Hamlin and a furniture/carpet store Hamlin & Mendsen.

He left the retail business in 1871 to concentrate on other businesses and real estate interests, including building the Hamlin Block where Hengerer's started their business. In 1868 he had purchased Buffalo Driving Park, where he created one of the premier American harness racing tracks, which also hosted other entertainment events. After it closed, in 1905 the land was purchased by developers to build a residential neighborhood marketed that is still called Hamlin Park.

In 1874 Cicero and his brother invested in the Buffalo Grape Sugar Company and developed it into The American Glucose Company. That company expanded to employing over 2,500 people and was sold to a glucose combine in 1897. Hamlin built homes at 435 Franklin Street, which became the American Legion Hamlin Post, and 1035 Delaware Avenue, which he sold to the Catholic Diocese to build St. Joseph's New Cathedral.

Hamlin remained part of East Aurora by starting Village Farms in 1855. Located on 66 acres north of Main Street, between Tanney Brook and Buffalo Road, the farm included over 800 stalls for horses and cattle. It became one of the premier trotting nurseries in the Western Hemisphere, breeding more world champions than any other farm. Hamlin's interest in good racing resulted in his origination of the rules for the National Trotting Association and organizing the Grand Circuit. Hamlin was inducted into the Harness Racing Hall of Fame in 1958.

In 1882 Hamlin purchase the 10-year-old Mambrino King for $25,000 (about $500,000 current dollars). Over 30,000 people came to see Mambrino King, who the East Aurora Advertiser called the "handsomest horse in the world". Breeders brought their mares for The King's stud service.

He is credited as the sire of 42 sons and 107 daughters that produced 360 trotters and 318 pacers that set standard records. Mambrino King died in 1899 and is buried on North Willow Street on what was part of Village Farms.

The Judge's Stand that presided over Hamlin's 5/8-mile track at Village Farm was restored by the Aurora Historical Society and moved to Absolut Care of Aurora Park at 292 Main Street in East Aurora.

KNOX FARM STATE PARK – KNOX FAMILY ESTATE
437 Buffalo Road, East Aurora

Knox Farm State Park, located in East Aurora, is a 633-acre property that was once the private estate of the prominent Knox family. With a remarkable collection of 21 different historic buildings and structures, the estate originated with Seymour H. Knox I, a successful businessman and philanthropist who gained his wealth from Woolworth's Five and Dime stores. Around 1900, he purchased a farm in East Aurora to breed and train racing standardbreds and carriage horses. He then bought several adjoining farms and called his property Ideal Stock Farm after his first stallion Prince Ideal, but it was soon nicknamed ESSKAY Farm, after his initials S.K.

Figure 192 Knox Farms Ess Kay Farm Fox Hunt PD

After Seymour I died in 1915, his descendants continued to transform the farm into an exquisite estate, complete with a grand mansion, carriage house, greenhouse, livestock barns, stables, and extensive gardens. The main house, a stunning Colonial Revival mansion, was completed in 1917 for Seymour Knox's daughter Dorothy and her husband Frank Goodyear. However, in 1929 Dorothy and Frank decided to move their homestead down the road to create a more elaborate English style estate, and named it Crag Burn (now a private golf club). The Knox summer estate was then handed down to her brother, Seymour II. Like his father, Seymour II had a passion for equine sports, especially polo. He was also passionate about modern art. The Albright-Knox Art Gallery (now the AKG Art Museum) bears the Knox name in honor of his many contributions to the museum.

Seymour II spent many summers with his wife Helen and their children at the estate until his death in 1990. His son, Seymour III, who co-owned the Buffalo Sabres with his brother Northrup, inherited the property and he and his wife Jean made it their year-round residence. Although Seymour III died in 1996, Jean continued to live in the home until 2000 when it was purchased by New York State and opened to the public as a state park. Ten years later, the mansion was in danger of being demolished. Thanks to its historic and architectural value, The Preservation League of New York State stepped in to save it. Today, Knox Farm State Park is a popular spot for outdoor recreation with several beautiful trails, picnic areas and a dog park. The park's charming landscape, historic buildings, and various programs make it a popular destination for visitors all year long.

By Doreen Regan

MILLARD FILLMORE HOUSE & MUSEUM
24 Shearer Avenue, East Aurora

Figure 193 Millard Fillmore House photo credit Marsha Falkowski

Millard Fillmore was born into poverty in the Finger Lakes region of Central New York and moved to East Aurora with his parents when he was 21 years old. He taught school in Buffalo while studying law at the offices of Asa Rice and Joseph Clary. Accepted to the bar at 23, was a lawyer and local politician in East Aurora before becoming the 13th president of the United States.

In 1826, Fillmore built his own house across the street from his East Aurora law office on Main Street. It was nicknamed The Honeymoon Cottage because it is where he lived with his new bride, Abigail. Two years later their son, Millard Powers Fillmore, was born in the home.

The Fillmore's only lived there for 4 years before moving to the city of Buffalo. He was elected as Zachary Taylor's vice president in 1849 and served as president from 1850-1853, following President Taylor's untimely death. Meanwhile, his humble little house in East Aurora changed owners several times and had numerous additions made. It was moved in 1915 to sit further back on the property so The Aurora Theatre could be constructed on its original spot.

Sadly, it was abandoned for the next 15 years and fell into disrepair. Margaret Price, one of the founders of The Fisher Price Toy Company, admired the quaint little house and its history, so she and her husband Irving purchased it in 1930 and moved the original structure to its current location at 24 Shearer Avenue. They had it completely renovated so it could be used as Margaret's art studio. Although Margaret and Irving resided in a different home nearby, she continued to use the Fillmore house as her studio for the next 43 years, until her death in 1973.

The house was designated as a National Historic Landmark in 1974 and was acquired by the Aurora Historical Society a year later. As one of the only remaining homes in America ever hand-built by a U.S. president, it is now a historic house museum that has been meticulously decorated to reflect its original 1826 era, with federal period furnishings and housewares. Several artifacts owned by Millard Fillmore and his family are proudly displayed within its walls.

Tours of the home are available from April to October by appointment only and last about an hour.

by Doreen Gallagher Regan

ROYCROFT CAMPUS
Main and South Grove Streets, East Aurora

The Roycroft Campus was one of the first Arts & Crafts communities in America. It was instituted in 1897 by Elbert Hubbard, a writer, speaker, and businessman who brought the semi-utopian artisan colony to East Aurora.

Elbert Hubbard was born in Illinois in 1856. Early in his career, he became a traveling salesman for the Larkin Soap Company, which eventually led him to Buffalo. In 1885, Hubbard and his first wife Bertha Crawford moved to rural East Aurora, due to his love of horses. After two decades with Larkin, Hubbard left the company in 1892 and journeyed to England where he visited William Morris's Kelmscott Press, a company renowned for its production of exquisite, handcrafted books. Morris is considered the founder of the Arts & Crafts movement in England. He believed in creating quality handmade items inspired by the beauty and simplicity of nature. These principles deeply resonated with Hubbard, who returned to America determined to spread Morris' philosophy.

Figure 194 Roycroft Campus Chapel Library 1973 photo National Register of Historic Places

Upon Hubbard's return to his hometown of East Aurora, the Roycroft Press was born, named in honor of 17th century London bookmakers Samuel and Thomas Roycroft. Hubbard was inspired by their last name, believing it was translated from "king's craft".

Hubbard was a prolific writer and quickly gained notoriety for his numerous pamphlets and books. In 1899, his essay "A Message to Garcia" became a global sensation. As interest in the Arts and Crafts movement spread, the community expanded to include potters, painters, coppersmiths, leather workers and furniture designers. The Roycroft Campus grew to become an impressive collection of artisan workshops, with fourteen buildings in total. At its height, over five hundred artisans and craftsmen worked there.

In 1915, Elbert Hubbard and his second wife, Alice, perished during a trip to Europe when the ship they were traveling on, the Lusitania, was torpedoed by a German U-boat. Hubbard's son assumed ownership of the campus, and the Roycrofters continued to produce goods throughout the 1920's. But their popularity began to wane, and the Roycroft Campus eventually shut down during the Great Depression.

A movement to revive the Roycroft campus emerged in the 1970's, and extensive restorations began. The campus became a National Historic Landmark in 1986 representing the largest, most well-preserved collection of guild era buildings in America from the late 19th century. Nine structures remain and the campus is open to the public with a museum, inn, restaurant, and artisan shops.

by Doreen Gallagher Regan

ROYCROFT INN
40 South Grove Street, East Aurora

Figure 195 Roycroft Inn in early 1900s photo courtesy Roycroft Archives

The Roycroft Inn opened in 1905 for visitors looking to experience the emerging lifestyle of the "Roycrofters". The Roycroft way of life began around 1897 with Elbert Hubbard, who founded the American Arts and Crafts movement in East Aurora and developed the Roycroft Campus, a center for entrepreneurship, creativity and learning.

In early 1985, after leaving his job at the Larkin Soap Company and touring England, Hubbard joined forces with Harry Taber and William Mackintosh at Pendennis Press in East Aurora, which was part of White & Wagoner Printing. Together they formed the Roycroft Printing Shop. After taking ownership of the business, Hubbard began building a Gothic style print shop on South Grove Street, fashioned after the structures he had admired overseas. The Roycroft Chapel, bearing the historic meaning for chapel as a place for printing, was completed in 1898.

A year later the success of the essay "A Message to Garcia" necessitated building a larger print shop. The original Roycroft Chapel became the Phalanstery Dining Room, and a few years later it served briefly as the Roycroft Bank. The Roycroft Inn officially opened in 1905, with the Chapel becoming the Reception Room. Later additions included the Oak Room, Library, Morris Room, and Ruskin Room. The Salon features restored murals by Alexis Jean Fournier, an original Roycroft artist. A three-story tower was added at the rear, topped with a cupola. By 1909, additions to the Inn were complete, with fifty guest rooms tastefully furnished with Roycroft pieces. A peristyle walkway connecting the public areas to the guest rooms is said to have a striking resemblance to the one Frank Lloyd Wright designed for The Larkin Administration building in Buffalo.

Kitty Turgeon, of the Turgeon Brothers Restaurants. started restoration of the property in 1976. Representative Jack Kemp (the Buffalo Bills stayed at the inn while training at Knox Farms), assisted in obtaining National Historic Landmark status in 1986. Over a nine-year period, with support from the Margaret L. Wendt Foundation, the Inn underwent an $8 million restoration to return it to its original splendor. It was reopened in 1995 as a restaurant and boutique hotel, featuring the skilled craftsmanship and unique style of the Roycrofters, with original artifacts throughout the entire facility. Developer and real estate investor Douglas Jamal purchased the property in April 2024, keeping the legendary Inn open to the public, with a promise to carry on its historic legacy.

by Doreen Gallagher Regan

Vidler's 5 & 10
676-694 Main Street, East Aurora

Vidler's was opened by Robert S. Vidler on June 21, 1930, eight months after the beginning of the Great Depression. For the first 15 years it was called "Fair 5c to $1.00 Store". Robert was not certain the store was going to make it, so he did not want to associate it with the family name.

The business started after Robert Vidler moved to East Aurora and his mother-in-law complained that she could not buy a spool of thread locally and had to travel to Buffalo (a half day trip at that time) to get anything. Robert thought he could do retail and manage a store, so he opened a variety dry goods store at 694 Main Street, a historic location that previously housed the original law office of President Millard Fillmore. Vidler's rented only part of the building, 900 square feet consisting of only two aisles.

Figure 196 Vidler's 1930 Center Store 2 aisles with 900 Sq. Ft. vidlers5and10.com

In 1946 Robert Sr. purchased the building and doubled the size of the store. His sons Bob and Ed started working full time at the store in 1949 and in 1953 the business was incorporated as Vidler's 5c, 10c, $1.00 and Up, Inc., finally using the Vidler name. A 28x30 foot addition and a basement "Toyland" were added the following year.

In the late 1960s the store was remodeled to give it a historic and nostalgic appearance. Other national chain 5 & 10 stores opened in East Aurora, but closed not being able to compete with Vidler's. Starting in the 1980s Vidler's gained national attention with TV commercials featuring Mission Impossible actor Peter Graves and the store became known for quirky commercials produced by Bob and Ed.

Vidler's continued to obtain national attention with articles about the store featured in Business Week and Martha Stewart's Living. In 2015 the store entered a contest with over 15,000 entries to win a free commercial on the Super Bowl. They made it to the top ten but ended up coming in second place. The store was even included as a location in made for TV Christmas movies.

Vidler's 5 & 10 now consists of four connected buildings, eleven rooms and almost 20,000 square feet of display space. It is run by third generation Vidler's, Ed's son Don and daughter Beverly. In June 2024 the store celebrated its 94th anniversary and was added to the NYS Historic Business Preservation Registry.

Marilla Country Store
1673 Two Rod Road, Marilla

Figure 197 G.C. Monchow & Co. Store photo Marilla Country Store Archives

Built in 1851 at the corner of Two Rod Road and Bullis Road, the Marilla Country Store is the oldest continuously operating store in New York State. The store is even two years older than Marilla, as the town was not formed until 1853.

A tragedy in a cornfield and a team of oxen lead to a trade that made Harrison T. Foster the first owner of this store. In 1848 Foster purchased 60 acres of land to start a logging business. His oxen broke into a cornfield and ate most of the corn. Foster decided to rid himself of the thieving oxen by trading his logging business and land for a shopkeeper's store. That site became and remained the location of the Marilla Country Store.

The store was opened as the first business to provide goods and services to the settlers who came to the Marilla area and started farms. In the horse and buggy days, the entire family would come to town on Saturday to do their shopping. They purchased everything from flour to clothing to tools. Saturday shopping became a social affair.

It was initially called HT & Foster Store, run by Harrison T. Foster and his partner Gustav Monchow. When Gustav took over ownership the name was changed to G.C. Monchow & Co. In 1916, Gustav's son Louis Monchow took over the store, running it until his death in 1943 and his wife Mildred ran the store until her retirement in 1977.

When the Gingerich family purchased the business in 1977, they established the Marilla Country Store Museum on the second floor. They filled old display cases with artifacts from the store's history, including the original safe. The walls are covered with old newspaper ads, clippings and copies of the customers' trade account ledgers. Tours are given to school groups and curious visitors from across the country.

When you enter the store, you are taken back in time by the creaking of the original wooden flooring and welcomed by a nostalgic candy department that features 500 types of old-fashioned varieties. Shelves are crowded with sundry items from spices to folk art to gifts and all you would expect to find in an old-fashioned country store.

Sandy and Paul Grunzweig purchased the store from Sandy's parents, the Gingerich's in 2000. They have retained and expanded upon the nostalgic charm and country store theme.

TOWN OF GRAND ISLAND

PROFILES

This section includes profiles of the Town of **Grand Island** and historic places on the Island.

Town of Grand Island

Grand Island, NY is located approximately halfway between Niagara Falls and Buffalo. Surrounded by the Niagara River that connects Lakes Erie and Ontario, Grand Island is about 8 miles long and 6 miles across at its widest. It was called "Owanungah" by the Neuters, "Ga-We-Not" by the Senecas and on an 1804 map the French made the first reference to the name it carries today, labeling it "La Grande Isle" because it is the largest island (over 17,000 acres) in the Niagara River.

Figure 198 Whitehaven Settlement
photo courtesy Grand Island Historical Society

Used for centuries for hunting and fishing and then by squatters for a few years in the early 1800s, the opening of the Erie Canal in 1825 brought the first complete survey of the Island. Mordecai Noah, thinking it would make a perfect refuge for the Jews, had an agent purchase 2,555 acres and commissioned a cornerstone. The idea died, but the cornerstone is displayed at the Buffalo History Museum. In 1834 Grand Island's first permanent settlement, Whitehaven, began harvesting and cutting the massive white oak trees covering the 16,000 acres of the island they had purchased. The world's largest steam powered sawmill operated there. A smokehouse and the Whitehaven Cemetery remain.

Whitehaven was bankrupt by 1840 but much of the island had been cleared, making way for farming. Prominent Buffalo businessman and experimental farmer Lewis Allen, who had been instrumental in the development of the Allentown area of Buffalo, needed more land for his farm and recognized the potential for resorts and summer homes for residents of the city. He purchased nearly 700 acres, the entire southern end of Grand Island, early in 1851.

When Allen's 18-year-old nephew Grover Cleveland visited in 1855, he stayed and established himself in Buffalo and went on to become the 22nd and 24th President of the United States. Much of Allen's farm is now Beaver Island State Park and the 1873 farmhouse, River Lea, houses the Grand Island Historical Society Museum.

After being part of Niagara County, the town of Buffalo in 1822 and the town of Tonawanda in 1836, the Tonawanda Board of Supervisors created the town of Grand Island in 1852. John Nice was elected the town's first supervisor in an election held in his home on March 1, 1853.

Buffalo, during the 1800s, was a growing city because of the Erie Canal, but this growth brought noise, pollution, and unpleasant living conditions. Wealthy businessmen wanted to provide their families a healthier environment. In 1859, Lewis Allen opened the Falconwood Club on the West River, one of many establishments on the Grand Island shoreline offering pleasant accommodation for Buffalo residents seeking relief from the heat and smells of city living in the summer.

Other resorts included the Beaver Island Club, of which Grover Cleveland was a charter member, the Oakfield Club, the Island Club and the Bedell House. The last was the Buffalo Launch Club, incorporated in 1902 and North America's oldest powerboat club. Organized for those who were interested in powerboats and competing in regattas, this club is on the East River of the island and is still in operation.

Access to Grand Island from the mainland was strictly by water until 1935. Ferry service began in 1825 from Buffalo and Black Rock, with service from Tonawanda and Niagara Falls added in the 1870s. A bill authorizing the building of a bridge was signed by President McKinley in 1898. The Niagara Frontier Bridge Commission was created in 1928. The south and north bridges were finally opened in July of 1935.

Figure 199 Grand Island Bridge photo credit Marsha Falkowski

With the opening of the bridges, development followed. First was Sandy Beach at the north end in 1937. The second, Grandyle Village, came at the south end in 1941-42, with kit homes designed by the Sears & Roebuck Company. Elementary schools were built near each area in the 1950s. Island population increased from 626 in 1930 to 3081 in 1950. Many residents commuted to work off Grand Island, to Buffalo, Niagara Falls and surrounding areas.

Grand Island was home to World War II Medal of Honor recipient Charles N. DeGlopper, who gave his life at age 22 on June 9, 1944 to save his platoon that had been separated and trapped by the enemy in LaFiere, France. He, along with the Island's 68 Civil War soldiers and those killed in action in military conflicts since WWI are honored at the DeGlopper Memorial on Grand Island Boulevard and Baseline Road.

With the residential developments came the need for stores and services for residents. The first car dealership was Alt Chevrolet on Whitehaven Road in 1948 on farmland in the family from the mid-1800s. The first plaza was opened on Love Road in 1952 in Grandyle Village. The Grand Island Plaza opened in 1957 in the center of the island, near Baseline Road and Grand Island Boulevard.

Biotechnology came to Grand Island as GIBCO, or Grand Island Biological Company, established in 1962. There are now more life science companies on Grand Island with almost 2000 total employees, the largest being Fresenius-Kabi and Thermo Fisher Scientific (originally GIBCO).

Being situated in the middle of the Niagara River, Grand Island is perfect for recreation and eco-tourism. There are three state parks, Beaver Island, Bix Six Marina and Buckhorn Island, all with canoe/kayak access to the river. There are bike and nature trails at the parks, along West River and at other interior locations.

by Mary Stang Cooke & June Crawford Grand Island Historical Society and Jodi Robinson Grand Island Town Historian

BEDELL HOUSE
1437 Ferry Road, Grand Island

Figure 200 Bedell House Annex when opened in 1877
photo courtesy Grand Island Historical Society

The Bedell House was opened in 1876 by Ossian Bedell who purchased land from the Allenton Farm owned by Lewis F. Allen. Ossian was born in Georgia Center, Vermont in 1832 and moved to Grand Island at the age of eight in 1840. He drove a team for his father on the Erie Canal at the age of 11 and by the age of 21 owned his first farm.

Bedell served as Grand Island town supervisor from 1862 to 1863 and built the Buffalo & Grand Island Ferry from the foot of Sheridan Drive to the site of The Bedell House in 1874. The original Bedell House burned down in a fire in 1877 and was rebuilt ten years later. It included beautiful grounds, featured a rose garden and a three-story hotel, a restaurant and meeting halls. Ferries brought hundreds of visitors to the hotel from the foot of Sheridan and the city of Buffalo. Grand Island was described as a very healthy place to visit, with the best health record in the U.S. and claimed to have no mosquitoes. "But what about those sand flies."

Members of the Bedell family served as Grand Island postmasters in the 1880s and 1890s. Ossian was a member of the delegation that traveled to Washington DC in 1896 to lobby the U.S. Government to approve a bridge across the Niagara River. In 1898 an event was held at the Bedell House to celebrate the passage of a bill to build a bridge to Grand Island. It was never built. Subsequent attempts in the early 20th century to influence Erie County and New York State to build a bridge were also unsuccessful. Representing the town was Ossian's son John V. Bedell, town supervisor in the early 1900s.

Finally in 1935 the Grand Island Bridges were completed. The opening of the bridges resulted in the discontinuance of ferry service to the Bedell House. Shortly after the bridges opened there was a fire at the Bedell House. Some of the first vehicles to cross the bridge were fire trucks from the Sheridan Fire Company, but they were not able to save the building.

A smaller Bedell House was rebuilt and remained popular until it burned down in 1988. Today part of the rose gardens remains at the property, along with a hot dog stand called Casey's Cabana.

GRAND ISLAND NIKE BASE
3278 Whitehaven Road, Grand Island

During the Cold War the Soviet Union began developing long range bombers capable of reaching large population centers in the U.S. In response the U.S. built an anti-aircraft defense system that included about 250 Nike missile bases. These were joint U.S. Army and Air Force bases.

Seven Nike-Ajax and Nike-Hercules missile launcher bases were created in the Buffalo – Niagara Falls area. They were BU-09 Ransom Creek/Millersport, BU-18 Lancaster/Millgrove, BU-34/35 Orchard Park, BU-52 Hamburg, NF-03 Model City, NF-16 Sanborn/Cambria and NF-41 Grand Island.

Figure 201 Grand Island Nike Base and Golden Age Center photo courtesy Grand Island Historical Society

Originally there were separate defensive zones for the Buffalo and Niagara Falls areas. Beginning in 1950 the Niagara Falls Defense Area was commanded from historic Fort Niagara until the Lockport Air Force Station on Route 31 – Saunders Settlement Road was established in 1951. The two commands merged in 1961 and the 763rd Air Defense squadron was inactivated in 1979.

There were three different defensive types of radar at the sites. Acquisition Radar (ACQR) would detect an incoming aircraft, Target Tracking Radar (TRR) would lock on to the aircraft and Missile Tracking Radar (MTR) would lock on to any deployed incoming missile. They were linked to a computer guidance system that would detonate a warhead to eliminate any threat. With the advent of more powerful Intercontinental Ballistic Missiles (ICBM) the Nike bases were phased out by the early 1970s.

The Grand Island base was a double site with the integrated fire control area on Whitehaven Road and launcher on Staley Road at West River Parkway. Barracks between Whitehaven and Staley Roads could accommodate 200 troops, both regular Army and National Guard. The base was activated in 1955 and housed 24 surface-to-air missiles, with additional missiles stored underground and able to be elevated in seconds. Missiles could reach a speed of 1,600 mph.

In 1969 the Grand Island base was decommissioned. The Staley Road area became a nature education center, Eco-Island, in 1974 and is managed by the Grand Island Schools. The 3278 Whitehaven Road area still includes the former Nike base military buildings. It became the Golden Age Center, housing a Senior Citizens Center that offers activities, meals and community events. It is also the administrative center for the Recreation Department and is Grand Island's second largest park. The park features a play unit with swings, 6 tennis courts, a lighted softball diamond, a free 9-hole Par 3 golf course and nature trails.

Lewis Allen Villa at River Lea
Beaver Island State Park, Grand Island

*Figure 202 Lewis Allen House on Grand Island
photo credit Rick Falkowski*

Lewis Allen owned the former General Peter Buell Porter home on Niagara Street and is known as the father of the Allentown neighborhood in Buffalo. However, he contributed much more to WNY including the development of Grand Island.

In 1834 Allen was one of the agents for the East Boston Timber Company, which purchased 16,000 acres of Grand Island at $6.00 per acre to harvest the white oak and other trees that grew on the island. This was the beginning of the lumber industry in the Tonawandas.

After the company completed cutting down the trees on Grand Island, in 1851 he purchased 658 acres of the company's land to establish Allenton Farms, one of the country's first experimental farms. Allen was a successful businessman, but he considered himself a farmer. He wrote about advances in agriculture and raising cattle. Allen introduced peach trees and northern spy apples to Grand Island and WNY and was one of the founders of the Erie County Agricultural Society which held the first Erie County Fair in Buffalo in 1841.

Allen built the Falconwood Resort, selling it in 1865 to club members that maintained it until the 1920s. He subdivided Allenton Farms, transforming Grand Island into a resort community. Future President Grover Cleveland, Allen's nephew, was a regular guest and worker at Allenton and Cleveland was one of the founders of the Jolly Reefers Sportsman's Club on Beaver Island. Other clubs built on former Allen property included the Oakfield Club and former Spaulding-Sidway estate, River Lawn.

In 1866 Allen gave his son William Cleveland Allen two parcels of the farmland, upon which the Villa or River Lea House was built. The home was based off a design in a farm architecture book Lewis Allen published in 1852. Allen sold off his Grand Island property by 1887 with River Lea remaining a summer home. It was ravaged by a fire in 1934 but rebuilt as a privately owned duplex.

During the 1930s New York State began purchasing land to create Beaver Island State Park. In 1962 the state bought River Lea and the surrounding property to build an 18-hole golf course. The project called for the demolition of William Cleveland Allen's Villa, but members of the Grand Island Historical Society and Grand Island community saved the property. The house is now the Grand Island Historical Society Building.

WBEN RADIO: Transmitter Building
1791 Bush Road, Grand Island

The origin of WBEN-AM radio dates back to WMAK, owned by Norton Laboratories in Lockport, that began broadcasting in September 1922. They moved their transmitter tower to Shawnee Road in the Martinsville section of North Tonawanda in 1927 and the station was acquired by Buffalo Broadcasting Company in 1929.

In June 1930 the FCC determined that Buffalo Broadcasting's ownership of WGR, WKBW, WMAK and WKEN was a virtual monopoly, so it granted a license for the Buffalo Evening News, owned by Edward Butler, Jr., to create a radio station at 900 kHz and build a new transmission site. All parties appealed this ruling but prior to an appeals court decision, Buffalo Broadcasting sold MWAK to the newspaper, the call letters were changed to WBEN, and WBEN agreed to upgrade the Shawnee Road transmitter site.

Figure 203 WBEN Transmitter Site photo credit Rick Falkowski

WBEN began broadcasting at 930 kHz on September 8, 1930, at the former WGR studios in the Statler Hotel, which became available after Buffalo Broadcasting moved WGR and WKBW and their transmitting tower to the Rand Building in 1929. The move to the Statler gave WBEN access to performances by the orchestras performing at the hotel.

In 1941 WBEN built their new transmitter site and two antennae towers at the Grand Island location. The station became an incubator for radio talent with Jack Parr, later the Tonight Show host, being the announcer for the morning program until he was drafted in 1943 to serve during WWII. His replacement was Clint Buehlman, who remained at the station until 1977 and is referred to as the King of Buffalo Broadcasting. Buffalo Bob Smith also left WGR and joined WBEN in 1943, later starting the Howdy Doody Show.

The Buffalo Evening News ownership of the station resulted in further advances in communications. Under the leadership of editor Alfred H. Kirchhofer they founded the first FM radio station in Buffalo and in 1948 started the first Buffalo television station. After the death of Katherine Butler, the Butler Family ownership of the *Buffalo News*, WBEN-AM, WBEN-FM and WBEN-TV was transferred to other companies - Warren Buffet's Blue Chips Stamps, Larry Levite's Algonquin Broadcasting and Robert Howard Publications.

The WBEN studios moved from the Statler to 2077 Elmwood Avenue, and they are currently located at 500 Corporate Parkway in Amherst. WBEN-AM remains one of the top-rated radio stations in WNY and their transmitter site is still located in Grand Island.

TOWN OF HAMBURG

VILLAGE OF HAMBURG

VILLAGE OF BLASDELL

HAMLET OF LAKE VIEW

PROFILES

This section includes profiles of the Town of **Hamburg** and historic places in the Village of **Hamburg**, the Village of **Blasdell** and the Hamlet of **Lake View**.

Town of Hamburg

The Town of Hamburg lies along the western edge of Erie County, with Lackawanna to the north, Orchard Park to the east and Evans to the south.

Figure 204 Hamburg Water Works 1913
Hamburg Historical Society PD

Hamburg was originally inhabited by the Erie and Kahquak Indian tribes, whose arrowheads have been discovered along Eighteen Mile Creek and near the Erie County Fairgrounds. Erie County and Lake Erie get their names from the Erie Indians. The town was first settled around 1804 by Nathaniel Titus and Dr. Ruth Belden, and by 1805, the settlement was known as "Barkerville," named after postmaster Zenas Barker. John Cummings, the first landowner, moved to the area around the same time and built the first grist mill south of Buffalo in 1806, at the Eighteen Mile Creek waterfalls near Old Lakeview and Smith Roads. Hamburg was officially established as a town on March 20, 1812, formed from a settlement previously known as Willink. The new town's name originated from the city of Hamburg, Germany and was coined by one of the early landowners. The first town meeting was held on April 7, 1812 at Jacob Wright's tavern, which was located in an area called Wright's Corners. It was later renamed Abbott's Corners and is now the hamlet of Armor. One of the first orders of business was to address the issue of wolves and panthers in the area. A reward of $5 would be issued to anyone who brought in a hide.

Early settlers from New England were followed by German immigrants in the 1830s, who significantly contributed to the agricultural development of the area. The town's size decreased around 1850 when the towns of East Hamburgh (which became Orchard Park) and West Seneca separated from the original boundaries of the Town of Hamburg. Transportation greatly influenced growth in the area with the addition of improved roadways, the construction of the Erie Railroad around 1852 and a trolley car system in the early 1900s.

Figure 205 Bank of Hamburgh
Hamburg Historical Society PD

Hamburg has gained international recognition for the Devonian fossils found along the banks of Eighteen Mile Creek. Visitors from around the world come to Penn Dixie Fossil Park to dig up fossilized treasures. Hamburg is also well-known for hosting the Erie County Fair, which has been in the town since 1868 and is one of the largest county fairs in the United States. It is said that it is here that the very first hamburger was served in 1885, by vendors Frank and Charles Menches. They named their new ground beef sandwich the hamburger in honor of the town in which it was invented.

Figure 206 Saints Peter & Paul Church Hamburg PD

The Village of Hamburg is located in the center of the town. It emerged as a settlement around 1820 known as "White's Corners", at the corner of what is now Buffalo and Main Streets, where Thomas T. White operated a shop. The area experienced rapid growth after the construction of the Buffalo and White's Corners Plank Road around 1850. By 1871, the local post office was named "Hamburgh". The Village of Hamburgh was officially incorporated three years later, and the Village of Blasdell was incorporated in 1898. In 1877, the final "h" from Hamburgh was dropped, and the community became known simply as the Village of Hamburg. Many historic buildings still exist throughout the village. Saints Peter and Paul Catholic Church was built in 1860 and remains an active parish. The Hamburg Palace Theatre, dating back to 1924, is also a significant landmark, as well as The Hamburg Grange Building, built in 1892 by John H. Salisbury who sold farm implements. Salisbury's sister was Lorinda Salisbury Colvin, a member of the Nineteenth Century Club which founded the Hamburg Free Library in 1897. The weekly news publication, The Erie County Independent, began in 1875 and is still in publication, now titled The Hamburg Sun. The Hamburg Main Street Historic District was listed on the National Register of Historic Places in 2012.

by Doreen Gallagher Regan

Figure 207 Hamburg Grange in 1930 Hamburg Historical Society PD

PENN DIXIE FOSSIL PARK & NATURE RESERVE
4050 North Street, Blasdell

For decades high school teachers and college professors brought their students to Penn Dixie, using it as an outdoor classroom to provide instruction and allow the students to dig for fossils.

Figure 208 Penn Dixie photo credit Marsha Falkowski

In 1990 residents in the area of Big Tree and Bay View Roads launched a campaign to preserve the 54-acre former quarry owned by the Penn Dixie Cement Company. Hamburg town officials and environmental geologists agreed the site needed be saved due to its wealth of fossils from the Devonian period.

An all-volunteer Hamburg Natural History Society (HNHS) was incorporated in 1993. They received nonprofit 501c3 status in 1994 and in 1995 the town agreed to purchase the quarry at a reduced price of $242,500. Members of the community cleaned out tires, junk cars, refrigerators and other trash from the grounds and in 1976 the property was deeded to the NHNS group.

Penn Dixie Fossil Park is one of the most popular fossil sites in the U.S. due to its extremely well-preserved, abundant, and diverse Devonian-aged marine fossils. Several species of coral and crinoids, over a dozen species of brachiopods, and multiple species of trilobites can be found in the layers of Middle Devonian Windom Shale.

It's a true slice of the Devonian period which flourished from about 360 to 420 million years ago. The earth has shifted on its axis and during that time the WNY area was located about 30 degrees south of the equator. This area was covered by water and the closest land was the peaks of the Adirondack Mountains. The trilobites, rugose and tabulate corals, brachiopods, and crinoids found at Penn Dixie were all sea animals and plant life from that period.

In 2011 Penn Dixie was ranked as the #1` fossil park in the U.S. by a scientific study and in 2018 Penn Dixie claimed the Guinness World Records title for the World's Largest Fossil Dig when 905 fossil hunters participated in a fossil dig.

Penn Dixie is open for people to dig for fossils, and you can keep any that you find. In addition, due to the lack of lighting in the area, the Town of Hamburg and Buffalo Astronomical Association offers Stargazing in Hamburg – where they map the night sky including stars, planets, constellations and deep space objects. Telescopes and specialized equipment are provided for stargazing, and tools are available for fossil digging.

Woodlawn Beach
S-3580 Lakeshore Road, Blasdell

Figure 209 Woodlawn Beach 1896 PD

In the 1800s there was an 800-foot-wide sand beach at the eastern terminus of Lake Erie extending for several miles from the Buffalo city line to Bayview. It was one of the most beautiful inland beaches in the U.S.

During the early 1890s the Woodlawn Beach and Cottage Company opened a combined swimming and amusement park in the Woodlawn area. Beginning in 1892, a steamer made four daily trips from Buffalo Harbor. It was advertised as the "American Resort for Americans," a campaign to compete with Crystal Beach in Canada. The park owners added more attractions and in 1894 it was promoted that the park was illuminated by electricity. Woodlawn Beach featured a hotel, restaurants, dance hall, bowling alley, billiard hall and a 30-acre picnic grove.

The park began to sell liquor at some of the concessions in 1896. Instead of bringing in additional revenue, attendance dropped. During 1898 boat service was discontinued and the company filed for bankruptcy in 1899.

Lackawanna Steel moved their operations from Scranton Pennsylvania to the shore of Lake Erie. In 1899 they purchased all the land south of Buffalo, west of the Lakeshore Turnpike, down to Hamburg. This included the entire holdings of the defunct Woodlawn Beach and Cottage Company.

Portions of the former Woodlawn Beach property away from the water remained in operation. During the 1920s you could take a 7-minute trolly ride from Buffalo to enjoy a roller coaster, carousel, Penny Arcade, dance halls, restaurants and refreshment stands.

When Bethlehem Steel bought Lackawanna Steel in 1922, they used Woodlawn Beach as a dumping ground for its waste products and slag. Swimmers continued to use the beach, and Bethlehem erected a 10-foot fence with barbed wire to keep them out.

Bethlehem Steel closed in 1982, leaving a slag polluted shoreline. It became Woodlawn Beach State Park in 1996 but the industrial waste, sewage overflows, urban runoff from Smokes, Rush and Blasdell Creeks, and algae made it one of the most polluted beaches in NYS, often closed after failing water quality safety tests. Ten years of improvements by the town of Hamburg and a return to NYS control in 2020 improved the property.

Ilio DiPaolo's Restaurant now operates Sole at Woodlawn Beach, with a nightclub on the upper level and tiki bar with concerts and events on the beach. It is again a destination and nature is reclaiming the natural beauty of the shoreline.

IDLEWOOD ASSOCIATION
West Arnold Drive, Lake View

The Idlewood Association was once a summer resort colony for wealthy Buffalonians seeking recreation and relaxation away from the city. Although the association disbanded sometime around the Great Depression, its exclusive, elegant lifestyle set the stage for future lakefront estates to be built in the area.

Figure 210 Bridge Over 18 Mile Creek Schoellkopf Tannery 1906

During the early 1800s, pioneers began to settle near the mouth of Eighteen Mile Creek in the hamlet later referred to as Lake View. A tannery and grist mill were built on the south bank of the creek, which Jacob Schoellkopf purchased in the mid 1800's. Schoellkopf owned the business for 20 years before establishing his hydroelectric power company in Niagara Falls.

Around 1880, a group of prominent lawyers chose a pristine parcel of waterfront land next to Schoelkopf's summer estate to establish the Idlewood Association. It became a gathering place where the great influencers of the time socialized and networked. Although the residents originally camped in tents, permanent summer cottages were built over time. The colony had its own rustic dance hall and central dining hall. Influential Buffalonians such as James N. Adam, George Pierce, Spencer Kellogg and John D. Larkin were among its earliest members. Larkin often brought his young business associate Darwin D. Martin to spend time there. Martin was so enchanted with the area that he had renowned architect Frank Lloyd Wright design his opulent summer estate Graycliff on the other side of the creek many years later.

At the beginning of each summer, the families would drive out to Idlewood with their horses and household goods. Although the New York Central and Pennsylvania Railroads offered service to the center of Lake View regularly, members of Idlewood convinced the railway to build another station on the bluff where the railroad crossed Eighteen Mile Creek, closer to their colony. It was named Idlewood Station. Later on, electric trolley tracks were added to transport residents back and forth to the city.

By the late 1930's, descendants of Idlewood's members failed to financially support the association, so it fell into bankruptcy and was taken over by Erie County Savings Bank. In 1945, the colony went to private ownership. Though the membership was discontinued and many of the original homes are gone, Idlewood remains a quiet little community by the lake.

by Doreen Gallagher Regan

LAKE VIEW HOTEL
1957 Lake View Road, Lake View

Figure 211 Lake View Hotel 1908 PD

In the heart of Lake View stands a significant landmark, the Lake View Hotel. It was built in 1880 by Catherine Walden Myer, daughter of former Buffalo mayor Ebenezer Walden and the wife of Civil War physician Albert James Myer, founder of the U.S. Weather Service. During the late 1800s, a constant flow of traveling salesmen nicknamed "drummers," would converge on Lake View numerous times a day after arriving by train to sell their wares in the surrounding countryside. The Lake View Hotel, conveniently located across from the train station, offered weary travelers a place to rest, and a horse and buggy to rent from the on-site livery stable. There was a tavern and dance hall on the first floor, and six bedrooms on the second.

By 1890, more railroad lines made stops in Lake View, greatly boosting the local economy. Soon thereafter, an electric trolley was built to transport the abundance of travelers back and forth to Buffalo. It was around this time Catherine decided to sell the Lake View Hotel to Daniel Hanley, who owned the adjoining farmland. Rather than managing the business himself, Hanley leased it to various tavern keepers, including John Bentley, John Murjahn, Maria Fritchie, and Art Thompson. John Bentley tragically hung himself in the hotel's barn. John Murjahn, who owned the nearby Bayview Hotel, ran the Lake View Hotel for a time until he moved to another location. Maria Fritchie was the innkeeper after him, until Art Thompson took ownership of the building and passed it on to his daughter Olive, wife of Charles Stadler. In turn, Fritchie was forced to give up her lease, which made her so angry that she opened another saloon down the road called The Red Onion. Her saloon quickly gained a reputation for serving a raucous clientele.

During prohibition, Charles and Olive Stadler transformed the Lake View hotel into an ice cream parlor and gas station. When Prohibition ended, they turned it back into a restaurant and bar. It was briefly owned by John Rockwood and Stan Kocic, who passed in on to Reginald Lombard in 1948. It was Lombard who transformed the hotel into a widely popular smorgasbord restaurant, which lasted into the 1990's.

The Lake View Hotel has endured numerous renovations over the years and now stands vacant, but the original structure still remains by the railroad tracks, barely visible above the modern one-story addition that surrounds it.

by Doreen Gallagher Regan

VILLAGE OF KENMORE

TOWN OF TONAWANDA

PROFILES

This section includes profiles of the Village of **Kenmore** and the Town of **Tonawanda** and a couple historic places in the Village and the Town.

Village of Kenmore

The Village of Kenmore, nestled within the borders of the Town of Tonawanda, and just north of the city of Buffalo's limit, was among the first planned suburbs in the United States. Louis P.A. Eberhardt is considered to be the "Father of Kenmore". In the 1890's he built the "twin sentinels" for himself and his brother Fred that were located on the southwest plot of land just inside the Village of Kenmore on Delaware Avenue.

The Tonawanda-Kenmore Historical Society (TKHS) was established by Dr. Frederick S. Parkhurst and other local prominent businessmen in 1929. For decades, the Society operated out of various locations within the Town of Tonawanda.

Figure 212 St. Peter's Evangelical Church built 1849
photo courtesy Tonawanda-Kenmore Historical Society

St. Peter's German Evangelical Church, located at 100 Knoche Road in the Town of Tonawanda, is the TKHS museum. It is the oldest public building in the Town of Tonawanda. St. Peter's was built in 1849 by settlers from Alsace Lorraine who were referred to as the "Mohawk Valley Settlement" or the "Military Road Settlers". The land for the church and cemetery was donated by Philip Knoche and a cemetery was established in 1847. Many pioneers of the Ken-Ton area are buried in the cemetery which surrounds the museum.

The church, with services spoken in German until the early 1920's, attracted German-speaking congregants from as far away as Williamsville and Lancaster. Attendance dwindled and the last service was held in June 1967, with the abandoned church deeded to the Town of Tonawanda. After many refurbishments to the interior and exterior, in 1976 in conjunction with the U.S. 200th Bicentennial year, the Town leased the former St. Peter's German Evangelical Church to TKHS for use as a history museum.

There are several other notable and historic places in the town and village. The Village of Kenmore/Town of Tonawanda Municipal Building at the south triangle of Delaware Ave. and Delaware Rd. is a distinctive Art Deco style building replete with new world corn and tobacco motifs despite its marker claiming "classical monumental" influence. It was designed by famous Buffalo architect E.B. Green in 1936 and replaced the former District School # 6 building from 1892, the first grammar school in the Village. The school building was reused as the municipal offices from 1911 until 1936.

Another Art Deco building is the nearby home and office at 69 Delaware Road designed by Buffalo architects Duane Lyman and Lawrence Bley in 1933 for Doctor Daniel Stedem and later occupied by famous watercolor artist Rita Argen Auerbach, as her home and studio. The oldest extant church building in the Village is the Kenmore Baptist Church from 1916, across from the Municipal Building.

The home now at 136 Warren was one of many moved from its original site to make way for public or commercial purposes. Home to the Birdwetzel family since the Civil War, it once stood on Delaware Avenue at the junction of Delaware Road and was moved around 1911 for the construction of the first Kenmore High School. Other homes moved off Delaware include the home of the pioneering Mang family which was divided in the 1920s to addresses on Mang, 72 and #111, still occupied by family descendants.

The world-famous Kenmore Stamp Company once thrived at the brick Tudor style building at Kinsey and Delaware from 1937 to 1948, started as a hobby for its founder Niagara Falls Smelting and Refinery owner Ernest Jarvis.

The Town has several historic markers and could support several more. The Zimmerman settlement on Delaware Rd. is comprised of several homes built by the settlers who arrived in the Town in 1813, including the homestead built in 1840 by Robert Zimmerman at #785. A former schoolhouse built by Zimmerman and his neighbor Richard Faling in 1829 was moved from the north triangle of Delaware Road and Delaware Avenue to #833 around 1907 for use as a bunkhouse.

Figure 213 Adam Zimmerman House at 785 Delaware Road photo courtesy Tonawanda-Kenmore Historical Society

Zimmerman and Faling donated parts of their adjoining lots on Delaware Road at Willowbreeze for a cemetery where a marker is located commemorating notable burials, including several War of 1812 combatants.

Another marker is found at the "Werkley" St. John's Cemetery on Eggert, where two veterans of the Mexican War are buried. The oldest road in the Town, completed around 1809, Military, is marked by a boulder at the junction with Sheridan Drive.

A marker commemorating the Erie Canal is at a site, on River Road, about ½ mile from the Grand Island bridge, where the Hamilton Cherry family built a farm alongside the Erie Canal in 1851, adjoining Nicholas Munch who had purchased his property in 1847.

Figure 214 St. John's RC North Bush Chapel photo courtesy Tonawanda-Kenmore Historical Society

Other markers can be found at the TKHS Museum, near the former Curtiss airport at Curtis Pkwy. and at the site of a church founded by a man later given sainthood, St. John Neuman, at Englewood.

By Judy Tucker & Margorie Murray, Tonawanda-Kenmore Historical Society

EBERHARDT MANSION
2746 Delaware Avenue, Kenmore

Figure 215 Eberhardt Mansions
photo courtesy Tonawanda-Kenmore Historical Society

Louis P.A. Eberhardt and Fred Eberhardt were the entrepreneurs that developed the village of Kenmore, considered the first suburb of Buffalo. In 1888 they began purchasing farmland just outside the city from the Ackerman and Mang families.

The first home built in Kenmore was at 2749 Delaware Avenue, the northeast corner of Delaware and Kenmore Avenue, in 1889. That was also the real estate office of L.P.A. and Fred Eberhardt. When that home burned down, L.P.A. acquired the site of the Winfred Mang store and tavern across the street.

In 1894 the brothers built twin homes of red Medina Sandstone, in Richardsonian Romanesque style at the northwest corner of Kenmore and Delaware Avenue. Both homes were designed by architect Cyrus Kinne Porter, a Victorian style architect who designed many churches, businesses and homes in the WNY area, including The Cyclorama Building, Trinity Church, Richmond Avenue Church of Christ and the William Hengerer Company. Each home cost $15,000 to build and the Eberhardt brothers hoped to create a series of mansions in Kenmore, similar to Millionaires Row on Delaware Avenue in the city of Buffalo.

The barn from the former 2749 Delaware Avenue property was salvaged and moved across the street behind L.P.A.'s new stone mansion. The barn initially housed the Eberhardt family horse buggy, a 3-seated, 3-span carriage similar to the one used by the Kings and Queens of England. The garage later stored Eberhardt's Stanley Steamer and Pierce-Arrow. The Kenmore speed limit was 5 miles per hour and it was strictly enforced, just like you do not exceed 30 mph in the village today.

The L.P.A. Eberhardt's home, at 2756 Delaware Avenue at W. Hazeltine, became the Kenmore YWCA in 1918. It remained the YWCA for most of the 20th century and was demolished in 1977.

In 1915 The Fred Eberhardt Home became the Wheel Chair Home for the Incurables, previously located at 93 17th Street and 344 Hudson Street in Buffalo. That organization built a new facility on Elmwood Avenue named The Schofield Residence and 2746 Delaware Avenue was listed for sale in 1980. Perkins Pancake House offered $350,000 for the building, planning to tear it down and build a new restaurant.

Fortunately, Jack Hunt Coins purchased the building in 1981, refurbished it to properly portray its historic appearance and is still operating their precious metals and property management businesses in the building.

Huntley Power Plant
3500 River Road, Tonawanda

The 1906 Burton Act and a 1910 treaty with Great Britian limited the amount of water that could be diverted above Niagara Falls. There was an increased demand for power during WWI and since no additional hydroelectric generated power could be obtained from the Falls, Buffalo General Electric began construction of coal steam generated power stations.

Figure 216 Huntley Power Plant photo credit Marsha Falkowski

In 1916 Buffalo General Electric built the 600-megawatt capacity coal fired Dunkirk Steam Station and in Tonawanda they built the 760-megawatt River Station. They were the largest steam generator plants in NYS. Upon the death of Buffalo General Electric President Charles R. Huntley, who was one of the individuals responsible for providing electricity to the Pan American Exposition, the River Station was renamed the Charles R. Huntley Station in 1923. For over 100 years columns of black smoke flowed from the plant's two large chimneys, providing additional electricity to the area but also polluting the air.

NRG purchased the Huntley Generation Station from Niagara Mohawk in 1999. Due to low natural gas prices, the coal fired Huntley Plant could not remain competitive and pre-tax revenues tumbled by $113 million between 2008 and 2012. Huntley retired half of the plant's capacity, with a corresponding drop in tax revenues. In 2016 the plant was shut down. NRG had been the largest taxpayer in Tonawanda and this resulted in an over $6 million annual reduction in town, county and local school district revenue. At this time NYS education funding was also being reduced and even with operation cost reductions, 140 teachers lost their jobs, and three elementary schools and one middle school closed.

Erie County lost its largest air and water polluter, but it also lost tax revenue and the employment of 80 workers at the plant. The Clean Air Coalition partnered with labor unions and community groups to form the Huntley Alliance that successfully lobbied the state to provide a temporary cash infusion to offset the revenue loss. However, that is not a long-term remedy.

It is estimated that $80 million will be required to clean up the property and remediate the ground. NRG has unsuccessfully tried to sell the property, and Tonawanda has initiated eminent domain to reclaim it. Tonawanda hopes that once the town obtains possession of the property it can be sold to investors that have expressed interest in redeveloping this valuable waterfront property and returning it to the tax rolls.

CITY OF LACKAWANNA PROFILES

This section includes profiles of the city of **Lackawanna** and a few historic places in the city.

City of Lackawanna

The land of what is now the city of Lackawanna was part of Buffalo Creek reservations. It was not available for settlement until the Seneca Nation relinquished the land in the Treaty of 1842. Lackawanna formed in 1909 when it seceded from the town of West Seneca.

In 1655 the Seneca eliminated other Indian tribes from the WNY area. They used the area for hunting and trapping, moving to the Buffalo Creek area after the American Revolution. A Seneca settlement was built along Smokes Creek, named after the local chief, known as Old Smoke. On the high ground that separated the watersheds of Buffalo Creek and Smokes Creek a road was built and came to be known as Ridge Road.

The 1842 Compromise Treaty of Buffalo Creek stipulated that the Seneca vacate Buffalo Creek reservation. The land was sold to the Ogden Company, and the Ebenezer Colonies of the Community of True Inspiration purchased 5,000 acres at $10.00 per acre in 1851. They formed the town of Seneca, in honor of the Senecas, which was changed to West Seneca when it was ascertained that a town of Seneca already existed in the Finger Lakes.

After West Seneca was established, the northeastern settlement was called Ebenezer, center settlement Limestone Hill, southern settlement Roland (owned by a Massachusetts' Wood Harmon land developers) and Stony Point settlement along the lake. The rest of the land was undeveloped or small farms.

A plank road between Buffalo and White Corners, now Hamburg, was called White's Corners Road, now known as South Park Avenue. At the intersection of Ridge Road, St. Patrick's Catholic Church was built in 1850, in what was called Limestone Hill because of the underlying limestone ridge. In 1857 St. Joseph's Orphan Boys Asylum opened and St. John's Protectory was built in 1864. Father Nelson H. Baker became the pastor and was given charge of the orphanage, renaming it Our Lady of Victory (OLV) Institutions and Basilica.

Figure 217 Limestone Hill late 1800s St. Patrick's Church and St. Joseph's Orphanage PD

At the end of the 1800s the U.S. Government erected a 7,500-foot breakwall that made that area of Lake Erie at Stony Point an ideal spot for industry. Lackawanna Steel moved their plant from Pennsylvania. In 1922 the plant was purchased by Bethlehem Steel and employment peaked at 20,000 workers. When the plant closed in 1983, the city of Lackawanna lost its largest business and taxpayer.

Figure 218 Early Photo of Lackawanna Steel PD

BETHLEHEM STEEL
Route 5, Lackawanna

Figure 219 Bethlehem Steel Plant during WWII showing Ships being built

The story of Bethlehem Steel began in the mid-1800s with two separate iron-making companies from Pennsylvania. The Bethlehem Iron Company was a successful iron manufacturer in Bethlehem, PA that transitioned to a steelmaking factory in 1899 called The Bethlehem Steel Company. Around the same time, another major iron forge was started by two brothers, George and Seldon Scranton. Their initial venture, located in the town that would later be called Scranton in their honor, became the second-largest iron producer in the United States. They named the business The Lackawanna Iron and Steel Company, after the Lackawanna River Valley in Pennsylvania where it was originally located, an area rich in iron and coal deposits.

By 1902, the company had evolved into the Lackawanna Steel Company. They decided to relocate to the outskirts of Buffalo to capitalize on lower labor costs and convenient access to Great Lakes shipping. They moved to a 1,300-acre lakefront site that was once part of West Seneca. Operations at the new mill began in 1903 with 6,000 workers and they soon saw rapid growth, quickly becoming a leading producer of rails and sheet piling. In 1909, the residents of West Seneca voted to be separated from the steel mill area, as the enormous influx of steelworkers began to wear greatly on the town's infrastructure and resources, nearly bankrupting them. The new municipality became the city of Lackawanna.

After some years of financial instability, Lackawanna Steel was purchased by Bethlehem Steel in 1922 for $60 million. A substantial investment of $40 million over the next decade was dedicated to modernizing the Lackawanna plant. It became one of the world's largest steel factories, providing employment to over 20,000 people. Famous structures such the Empire State Building and the Golden Gate Bridge were constructed from steel beams made in Lackawanna. During World War II, they shifted their production to military weaponry, making steel plates for warships and tanks. The company's prosperity continued into the early 1970s, but rising costs, foreign competition, newer technology and dwindling demand forced Bethlehem Steel to close most of the Lackawanna plant by 1983.

After the plant closed the land became a brownfield and was remediated. It is now known as the Renaissance Commerce Park and is managed by the Erie County Industrial Development Agency. The property is a mixed-use area with light manufacturing, warehousing and the potential for other industrial use.

by Doreen Gallagher Regan

HOLY CROSS CEMETERY
2900 South Park Avenue, Lackawanna

Holy Cross opened as a parish cemetery in 1849 but records show burials dating back to 1830. The original entrance was at 915 Ridge Road.

The first Catholic burials in Buffalo took place on land donated by Louis LeCouteulx at Main and Edward Streets in the 1820s and 1830s. After the 1832 cholera epidemic in Buffalo, burials took place in a cemetery at East North Street near Masten, consecrated by Bishop Timon in 1849. A larger cemetery space was required and in 1853 Bishop Timon borrowed $1,200 to purchase 40 acres of farmland which became Holy Cross Cemetery. It was originally called the "Bishops" cemetery because the title was in his name.

Figure 220 Holy Cross Cemetery Entrance photo courtesy Holy Cross Cemetery

Many of the Irish immigrants who dug the Erie Canal, built the railroads, worked on the Buffalo docks and Great Lakes steamboats, and labored at the grain elevators and steel plants are buried at Holy Cross. It is also the burial ground of the casualties of the 1880 Birge Wallpaper factory fire, nearly 700 victims of the 1918 Spanish Flu epidemic, Casmir Mazurek who was killed during the 1919 Lackawanna Steel Company strike and Lieutenant Edward R. Lonegrin who died during the Fenian 1866 Battle of Ridgeway, Ontario. It includes the graves of Mayor Jimmy Griffin, businessman William "Fingy" Conners, politician William Sheehan, boxer Jimmy Slattery and the McDonnell family monument.

Since Holy Cross Cemetery is adjacent to Our Lady of Victory Basilica, when Father Nelson Baker died in 1936, he was laid to rest in a portion of the cemetery in the shadow of the basilica. In July 1998 Father Baker's remains were transferred from the cemetery to a tomb within the Grotto Shrine to Our Lady of Lourdes inside the basilica. This was done at the recommendation of the Congregation for the Causes of Saints in Rome to help raise awareness of Father Baker for his canonization as a Saint.

Holy Cross is part of the Catholic Cemeteries of the Diocese of Buffalo. The other member cemeteries are Mount Olivet in Kenmore, Holy Sepulcher in Cheektowaga, Gate of Heaven in Lewiston, Assumption in Grand Island and Queen of Heaven in Lockport.

Holy Cross Cemetery is the largest Catholic Cemetery in the Diocese of Buffalo. It encompasses over 191 acres of land, over 130,000 internments and there remains about 60 acres of undeveloped land for future use.

JOHN B. WEBER MANSION
1619 Abbott Road, Lackawanna

Figure 221 John B Weber Mansion
photo credit Rick Falkowski

John Baptiste Weber was born in a cottage on Oak Street in Buffalo on September 21, 1842. He attended P.S. 15 and Central High School in Buffalo.

At the age of 14 he joined the 65th Regiment of the Militia as their color guard and enlisted as a private at the start of the Civil War. Based upon his performance in battles, Weber was promoted to the rank of Colonel, obtaining that rank two days before his 21st birthday, making him one of the youngest colonels in the military.

While serving in the militia Weber met fellow soldier Nelson Baker. They remained lifelong friends and after Nelson became a catholic priest and was assigned to St. Patrick's Church at Limestone Hill (later Our Lady of Victory Basilica and Orphanage) they worked together on projects in Lackawanna.

In 1868 Weber was engaged in the wholesale grocery business on the Central Wharf in Buffalo and established a 67-acre farm and vineyard at 1616 Abbott Road in Lackawanna. His brick colonial mansion is the oldest standing structure in Lackawanna, retaining its original woodwork and flooring. Land from the farm was donated to Lackawanna Schools and the mansion is currently the rectory for Our Lady of Bistrica Roman Catholic Church, the home church of the Croatian community

Weber assisted in forming the Republican Third Ward Club for the presidential election of General Grant. He ran for the office of Erie County Sheriff in 1870, losing by a small margin to Grover Cleveland. Weber was appointed assistant postmaster for Buffalo from 1871 to 1873 and again ran for Sheriff, winning the election and serving from 1874-1876. He was elected U.S. Congressman for the 33rd District from 1885 to 1889 and held the post of Grade-Crossing Commissioner of the city of Buffalo from 1888 to 1908.

Legislation was passed in 1888 that all immigration ports of entry were placed under Federal control. President Harrison appointed Weber the Commissioner of Immigration for the Port of New York. He reformed inefficient practices by enforcing the Civil Service rules for employees, closed Castle Island and opened Ellis Island as the main entry point to the U.S.

Weber was the commissioner general for the Pan American Exposition and during WWI he was chairman of the Erie County Home Defense Committee. In addition, Weber worked in founding Cazenovia Park, South Park and influencing Lackawanna Steel to locate along Lake Erie.

Our Lady of Victory Basilica
767 Ridge Road, Lackawanna

Our Lady of Victory Basilica began as a vision from a humble priest by the name of Nelson Baker. Born in Buffalo in 1842, he was baptized Lutheran but at the age of ten converted to Catholicism. Baker was ordained a Catholic priest in 1876 and assigned to St. Patrick's Church in Limestone Hill, now Lackawanna.

The church, which included an orphanage and reform school, was in serious debt, so Father Baker started the Association of Our Lady of Victory with a writing campaign asking charitable Catholic women across the country for donations. This campaign was so successful he was able to clear the church's debts and open an infant home for unwed mothers and their babies. Hoping to reduce heating costs, Baker hired a drilling company to find

Figure 222 Our Lady of Victory in 1920s photo courtesy Our Lady of Victory Charities

natural gas on the property. Encouraged by Baker's unwavering faith, the drillers hit a well that yielded enough gas to heat all their buildings, as well as fifty homes nearby.

In 1916, when Baker was 74 years old, a fire severely damaged St. Patrick's Church. At a parish meeting soon after, Baker announced his vision to replace the church with a shrine dedicated to Our Lady of Victory, inspired by the great basilicas of Europe. He began raising the necessary funds and assembled a team of highly skilled craftsmen and artisans to build the shrine. By December 1925, the basilica was completed and fully paid for.

Our Lady of Victory's exterior is made of pure white marble, topped with two tall spires and a massive copper dome adorned with trumpeting angels. This dome was the second largest in the U.S. at the time of its construction surpassed only by the Capitol's dome in Washington D.C. Inside, the magnificent shrine is embellished with gorgeous stained-glass windows, breathtaking murals, beautifully hand-carved marble statues and pews made of rare African mahogany. In 1926, The Vatican officially designated OLV as a Minor Basilica, which means it must always be ready to receive the pope. The main altar is flanked by an umbraculum, a red and gold umbrella to shield the pope, and a tintinnabulum, a bell on a pole used to announce the pope's arrival. Father Nelson Baker passed away in 1936. His Cause for Canonization was approved in 1987 and his remains were moved from Holy Cross Cemetery to a tomb within the basilica eleven years later.

by Doreen Gallagher Regan

VILLAGE OF LANCASTER

TOWN OF LANCASTER PROFILES

This section includes profiles of the Village & Town of **Lancaster** and some historic places found there.

Village & Town of Lancaster

After Clarence and Williamsville, the next area settled in WNY was the Bowmansville area of Lancaster. In 1803, land was purchased by Alanson Eggleston, Amos Woodward, James Woodward and William Sheldon. The next year Warren Hull, Joel Parmalee and Matthew Wing purchased property.

Most of the early settlers were native New Englanders or Hudson Valley New Yorkers who were referred to as Yankees. After clearing the land, they built what were called Yankee cabins and brought their livestock, tools and looms with them. They had to make everything else that was required to settle on the land. Most of the settlers did not have the cash to make an outright purchase of the lots so they took an "article" on the property, making a small downpayment and a promise to work at improving the land for a term of usually ten years. Due to the lack of currency, the Holland Land company often had to accept livestock or crops. Incentives were given to settlers who opened taverns, gristmills, sawmills and blacksmith shops, with land sold for as little as $2.00 an acre.

The first sawmill was built by David Robinson in 1810. It was purchased by Benjamin Bowman in 1811 and the location was called Bowman's Mills or Bowmansville. In 1811, Bartholomew Johnson built a sawmill a mile west of the Alden town line, with that area becoming known as Johnson's Corners. Ahaz Allen created a dam on Cayuga Creek and opened the first grist mill on the site of what is now the village of Lancaster. Prior to the opening of that grist mill settlers had to transport wheat and corn to either Ransom's mill in Clarence Hollow or Stephen's mill in Willink, now East Aurora.

When the grist mill opened, Joseph Carpenter erected a hotel and the village began to grow. The Johnson School, taught by Miss Freelove Johnson, opened in 1810, and Reverend William Waith gave the first Christian worship in 1811. James Clark opened the first tavern named the Pioneer House. The first post office was established in 1823 and the town was called Cayuga Creek. Several large farms with elegant homes were built along the road from the village to Alden.

Figure 223 Central Avenue in 1908 Lancaster Historical Society PD

The town of Lancaster was formed from Clarence in 1833 and extended to the Buffalo Creek Reservation. When the town of Elma was formed in 1857, Lancaster was reduced to its current size.

Hull House & Gipple Cabin
5976 Genesee Street, Lancaster

Figure 224 Hull House photo credit Rick Falkowski

Amos and James Woodward were the first settlers in the Clarence-Lancaster area of WNY in 1803. They built a Yankee log cabin known as Gipple Cabin, which for years was the oldest standing building in Erie County. It was located at what is now the southwest corner of Wehrle & Harris Hill in the hamlet of Bowmansville, town of Lancaster.

In 1804 Warren Hull and his cousin Joel Parmalee took articles (made a small downpayment and promised to work at cleaning and improving the land for a term of usually ten years) on lots to the west of Woodward on the north side of a new road called the Batavia Road (now Genesee) that Ellicott planned to build from Buffalo to Batavia. Hull built a permanent home in 1810 at 5976 Genesee Street. It is the oldest fully restored stone building in Erie County and is known as The Hull House.

Warren Hull was born in 1762 in Killingworth (later renamed Clinton), Connecticut. At the age of 17 in 1779 Warren began serving in the Continental Army during American Revolution with his father Lieutenant Peter Hull. In 1783 Hull married Polly Gillet and they headed westward., When they arrived in WNY, after living in several other New York counties, he and Polly already had ten children, two more were born after settling in Lancaster. Polly taught her children at home until a schoolhouse was built on Gunnville Road.

The Warren Hull House is a rare surviving Federal style stone structure, retaining a great deal of its original features and woodwork, along with the original stairways, floors and fireplaces. Being built in 1810, it survived while many WNY structures were destroyed during the War of 1812 and the burning of Buffalo. It was built into a hill, so it appears like a two-story home from the front, but all three floors are visible from the rear, with the basement at ground level. The basement includes the fully restored kitchen hearth and the original beehive oven. Curators of the Hull House salvaged the wood from the Gipple Cabin and plan to restore it on the Hull property.

In addition to tours and historical reenactments, when the Gipple Cabin is erected the Hull property will have the oldest stone house and oldest existing wooden house in Erie County.

Lancaster Opera House
21 Central Avenue, Lancaster

At the turn of the century, it was not uncommon to combine a music hall with a town's main government buildings. Such multi-functional buildings were called Opera Houses, even if they did not present operas. The Lancaster Opera House designed by George J. Metzger in 1897 is one of a few such Town Opera Houses remaining in the U.S.

Figure 225 Lancaster Opera House In 1906
Lancaster Historical Society PD

Buffalo architect and builder George J. Metzger designed and built the Schoellkopf Mansion at Delaware and Allen Streets, commercial buildings including the Masten Street Armory and several buildings at the UB South Campus. His construction company was a major contractor of Women's & Children's Hospital at 219 Bryant Street. Metzger designed the Lancaster Opera House for a variety of purposes. The town of Lancaster municipal offices were in the basement and first floor of the structure. On the second story, instead of installing a raked floor, he created a flat floor with removable seats so it could also be used for dancing and other events. The stage was built with a rake of ½ inch per foot, allowing the back to be higher than the front. This allowed the actors at the back of the stage to be seen by the audience. A suspended balcony, that did not require reinforcement by obtrusive columns to the floor, surrounded the main hall.

When the building opened it was used for dances, recitals, debates and social activities, as well as musicals and traveling shows. In the 1920s and 1930s, musicals and minstrel shows were presented. During the Depression the hall was used for food and clothing distribution to the poor, during WWII parachutes were prepared and packed, and the hall was later a Civil Defense Headquarters.

Restoration of the building began in 1975. After all the items that were being stored in the building were removed, the linoleum was stripped off the auditorium floor so the natural wood could be refinished. The walls and ceilings were repaired, the plaster frieze work of the proscenium was restored, period specific lighting fixtures were installed and the wainscoting and hardware from St. Mary's Elementary School was installed in the Opera House. A new stairwell and elevator were built to provide handicap access.

The Lancaster Opera House and its production company again presents plays, musicals and concerts. Their restoration work won an award from the Landmark Society of the Niagara Frontier for outstanding renovation of a historic venue.

TOWN OF LEWISTON PROFILES

This section includes profiles of the Town of **Lewiston** and several historic places in the Town.

Town of Lewiston

Lewiston is the birthplace of Niagara Falls. After the waters from Lake Tonawanda and Glacial Lake Iroquois receded over 12,000 years ago, the newly formed Niagara River went over the Niagara escarpment near the current location of Artpark. The erosion caused by the fast-moving water created the seven miles of the Niagara Gorge to the current falls site.

It was the first European settlement in Western New York, with French explorer Etienne Brule arriving in 1615. LaSalle landed in Lewiston on December 6, 1678, and after receiving permission from the Seneca, Chabert Joncaire built the first permanent structure in 1720 on what is now the grounds of Artpark. Lewiston was called the "carrying place" with merchandise delivered to the docks, carried up the steep incline from the river and transported along the portage route to a point above Niagara Falls where the Niagara River was navigable. Furs from the western Great Lakes followed the opposite route for shipment to the Eastern Coast and Europe.

In 1775 Joseph Brant (Thayendanegea) British Loyalist and chief of the Mohawk settled his tribe along current Route 104, with his home at the intersection of Ridge and Creek Roads. During and after the American Revolution British Loyalists came to Lewiston to cross into Canada. Governor Simcoe of Upper Canada started a ferry service between Lewiston and Queenston in 1791 and the line to cross the border was often three miles long.

The village was named Lewis Town in honor of Morgan Lewis, the 3rd Governor of NYS. In 1805 Lewiston was surveyed, with the streets from the river numbered one to nine and the crossing streets named after the tribes of the Six Nations, with Center Street in the middle. However, due to the War of 1812 the lots were not sold until 1815.

On October 13, 1812 the first major battle of the War of 1812 took place when American troops from Lewiston invaded Queenston in Canada. The Americans assembled behind the artillery battery on the property of Benjamin Barton. During the Battle of Queenston Heights, British Commander General Isaac Brock was killed.

When the town was burned by the British in 1813 only one building remained standing, Hustler's Tavern, which was in the current location of 800 Center Street. It was rumored that British officers saved the structure because they recalled the good times they had at the tavern enjoying a drink called a cocktail. Owner Catherine invented the gin drink when she stirred a gin mixture with the tail feather of a cockerel (a young male of the domestic fowl). Author James Fenimore Cooper visited the tavern in 1821 and immortalized the owners as the characters Sergeant Hollister and Betty Flanigan in his novel *The Spy*.

After the War of 1812, villagers returned and began the process of rebuilding Lewiston. Prior to the opening of the Erie Canal in 1825 Lewiston was called the Gateway to the West and had a population larger than the village of Buffalo. It was the Social Center of the Niagara Frontier and stagecoaches thundered through the village. The village was considered the center of the Great Overland Route across the Continent.

Figure 226 Kelsey Tavern at 625 Center Street in 1800s PD

In 1820, Thomas and Catherine Kelsey built the Kelsey Tavern at 625 Center Street. It was opened for upper class guests to the Lewiston area and featured ballrooms on both the first and second floors, making it the location for receptions. Each of the hotel bedrooms had their own fireplace. In 1825 Marquis DeLafayette reunited at the hotel with Nicholas Cusick, a Tuscarora Chief who saved his life during a battle during the American Revolution.

Benjamin Barton built the Frontier Hotel with his son Samuel and Josua Fairbanks during 1824/5. It was in operation before the opening of the Erie Canal and was called the finest hotel in the U.S. west of Albany. Many of the buildings along Center Street were built in the 1800s.

In the early to mid-1800s, thousands of former enslaved people arrived via the Underground Railroad and were smuggled into Canada. Lewiston tailor Josiah Tyron and other anti-slavery residents guided slaves from the First Presbyterian Church at 5th and Cayuga Streets, or from the Episcopal Church on Plain Street, across the river in row boats. The Freedom Crossing Monument (figure 227) commemorates this activity.

Figure 227 Freedom Crossing Monument photo credit Rick Falkowski

The Lewiston Council on the Arts sponsors several festivals and events during the year and Artpark provides a variety of entertainment, bringing thousands of visitors to the historic shops and restaurants in the village. Among the many restaurants are the Silo Restaurant, overlooking the gorge in the former coal silo that fueled the steamers docked at Lewiston.

The Historical Association of Lewiston maintains the Lewiston Museum in the former St. Paul's Episcopal Church, built in 1835 and located at 469 Plain Street.

ARTPARK
450 South 4th Street, Lewiston

The first location settled by French explorers in WNY was an area near the mouth of the Niagara River and Lake Ontario that is now called Lewiston.

LaSalle visited the eastern bank of the Niagara River in 1669 and docked there on December 6, 1678 when he returned with Father Hennepin on his journey to the Great Lakes. The land around Niagara Falls was known as the portage and Lewiston was called the carrying place. Seneca Indians were employed to carry goods from the lower landing at Lewiston up the Niagara escarpment.

Figure 228 Artpark Concert Stage with Niagara George

In 1720, Thomas Joncaire created the Lower Landing along the bank of the Niagara River, which in modern times is south of the first parking lot. He then built The Magazin Royale and Fort Joncaire a trading post that was located on the current Artpark site, between the lower and upper parking lots. The Lewiston Mound, an ancient Indian burial mound is near these sites, with historic markers identifying the locations.

French soldiers cut a narrow road from the lower landing to the top of the Niagara escarpment. A series of capstans and booms were installed to assist people and oxen to pull wagons up the zigzag road. After the British won the French & Indian War in 1763, they improved the portage trails.

Artpark has been transformed during Lewiston's history. In 1974, the Earl W. Brydges Artpark was funded by the Natural Heritage Trust as a 150-acre family-oriented setting for live theatrical performances, musical concerts, dance and the creation of visual performance. Artpark was created as a natural and cultural site committed to an unprecedented experiment in artist-public interaction, balancing a popularist mission of public access with a bold commitment to commission some of the most avant-garde investigational art of the day.

Formed in 1976, The Niagara Frontier Performing Arts Center, renamed Artpark & Company, is a 501c3 nonprofit created to provide programming, operational and financial support to the State Park in collaboration with the New York State Office of Parks, Recreation and Historic Preservation.

Events and installations take place throughout the park. Concerts, theater events and special performances are presented in the 4,000 capacity Mainstage Theatre. In 1999, the Tuesday in the Park series premiered, offering shows at the outdoor Amphitheatre that can accommodate over 10,000 people. The outdoor concerts were originally free but drew overflow crowds that necessitated charging a low admission price to regulate the attendance.

Benjamin Barton House
210 Center Street, Lewiston

Figure 229 Benjamin Barton House

In 1805 the Mile Reserve (a one-mile-wide strip of land along the Niagara River from Lake Erie to Lewiston) was offered for sale by New York State. That land was ceded to the State by the Seneca Nation in retribution for the Devils Hole Massacre, the killing of over 100 British teamsters and soldiers in 1763 along the Niagara Portage. In addition, at the 1805 sale, NYS was offering leases for the docks and portage facilities at Lewiston and Schlosser, located just above Niagara Falls.

Benjamin Barton and his relative Joseph Annin, who completed the survey of the Mile Reserve lands, attended the auction. At the sale Barton and Annin formed Porter, Barton & Company, with Augustus and Peter Buell Porter, to bid together on the lands and leases. They were successful in obtaining the Lewiston/Schlosses lease, and purchased the Mile Reserve land around Niagara Falls and on the upper Niagara River near Black Rock. After assisting Augustus Porter in building a gristmill above the falls, Barton moved his family to Lewiston. There he managed the portage in Lewiston and built a home on a hill above the Niagara River gorge.

During the War of 1812, the first major battle of the conflict was the Battle of Queenston Heights. An artillery battery was placed on Barton Hill, where the first cannon volleys of the war were fired on October 13, 1812. Barton's property was the staging area for American troops that invaded Canada by crossing the Niagara River at Lewiston.

After the British captured nearby Fort Niagara on December 19, 1813, the town of Lewiston was attacked by the British. Many civilians were killed, and the Barton House was burned. To assist the war effort, Benjamin Barton was appointed the quartermaster of the militia led by his business partner General Peter Buell Porter, with Barton being granted a commission as a major in the regular army.

In 1815 Barton returned to Lewiston. He rebuilt his home at the corner of Center and 3rd Streets and with the assistance of his son James, he reconstructed the Lewiston warehouses and resumed management of the Porter, Barton & Company operations. Benjamin served as Lewiston Supervisor from 1819 to 1827, built the Frontier House with his son Samuel and retired to his Barton Hill estate where he died at the age of 72 in 1842.

Frontier House
460 Center Street, Lewiston

After the burning of Lewiston in 1813, villagers began rebuilding their lives, homes and businesses. Due to the portage of goods processed through Lewiston before the opening of the Erie Canal and stagecoach activity from Lewiston being on the "Great Overland Route Across the Continent," the village became a social center of the Niagara Frontier.

Lewiston needed a hotel for the merchants and travelers in the village. In 1824-5 Joshua Fairbanks, Benjamin Barton and his son Samuel built the Frontier House. Constructed of stone from the Bay of Quinte at the Northeastern end of Lake Ontario, it required 18 men working 18 months laying up the solid stone 30-inch walls. Built in the Federal style of architecture, it featured oval windows, full-width porch and hipped roof. The first floor included Barton's office and a restaurant, the second floor featured a large ballroom, the third floor included 14 bedrooms with fireplaces and the fourth floor was used for meetings, famously for the Freemasons. Completed in 1825, The Frontier House was considered the finest hotel in the United States west of Albany and became Lewiston's premiere historic landmark.

Figure 230 Frontier House photo Library of Congress

The hotel gained a place in history when the Masonic traitor William Morgan was brought to the Frontier House by stagecoach in 1826. He changed coaches at the hotel and continued to Fort Niagara, never to be seen again. The Freemasons were suspected of kidnapping Morgan to prevent him from divulging their secrets. The stagecoach he arrived in remained behind at the Frontier House for years because people feared if they moved it, they might be implicated in the abduction plot.

Benjamin Barton owned the hotel until his death in 1842. It was purchased by Caleb Raymond in 1844 for $5,000 and future generations of his family operated the Frontier House until 1963. Ownership was then transferred among several people and from 1977 to 2004 when McDonald's leased the property for their fast-food franchise. Since it was the only McDonalds Restaurant inside a historic building, it never featured McDonald's trademark golden arches.

Due to its status as a quality hotel, historic guests at the Frontier House include Governor DeWitt Clinton, Edward the Prince of Wales, James Fenimore Cooper, Charles Dickens, Jenny Lind, Henry Clay, Samuel Clemens, Daniel Webster, Millard Fillmore and John L. Sullivan.

After a $5 million renovation, Frontier House reopened in 2025 as the Fairbanks Restaurant, five upscale apartments and six Airbnb rentals.

Our Lady of Fatima National Shrine
1023 Swann Road, Lewiston

Figure 231 Our Lady of Fatima Shrine photo credit Marsha Falkowski

The Basilica of The National Shrine of Our Lady of Fatima can be traced back to the Barnabite fathers being invited by the Catholic Diocese of Buffalo to teach in WNY Catholic Schools in 1953. They arrived from Italy and began to study English in Buffalo and Niagara Falls. Their goal was to build a seminary to house candidates for the priesthood and a devotional center in honor of Our Lady, where people could come and be refreshed.

Walter Ciurzak recovered from a stroke, through the intercession of the Blessed Mother. When approached by Reverend Gino Andreani, rector of the order, Ciurzak offered 16 acres of his farm for one dollar, with the stipulation that the Barnabite Fathers build a shrine to Our Lady of Fatima. Word of his gift spread, and donations poured in from across the country.

What began as a simple grotto with a humble statue of Our Lady of Fatima evolved into an outdoor shrine in the shape of a cross, including a glass domed worship site and a pool in the shape of the rosary, created by architect Joseph E. Fronczak. On top of the dome is a 13-foot-high granite statue of Our Lady of Fatima, weighing ten tons.

Following masses in the basilica, devotional processions slowly proceed through the grounds and along the avenue of the saints, which includes over one hundred life size marble statues of Saints, numerous grottos, a Chapel of Fatima, Shrine to St. Anthony Mary Zaccari (founder of the Barnabites) and a Shrine to Mother Cabrini (the first American Saint).

Professor Joseph Slawinski of Poland was hired to create an altar piece depicting the two outcomes for humanity. The aftermath of an atomic bomb detonation is on the left, a tranquil cosmic harmony on the right, with the potential of peace supported by the four races of humanity in the center. The Peace Mural is of Sgraffito style, a type of artwork that dates back to decorating Etruscan tombs and catacombs of ancient Rome.

Our Lady of Fatima Shrine is unique in that it is run by an Italian based religious order, dedicated to a Portuguese miracle, built on land donated by a Polish born laborer. Pope Paul IV declared the site a basilica in 1975 and it is annually visited by thousands of pilgrims from around the world.

CITY OF LOCKPORT

TOWN OF NEWFANE

HAMLET OF BURT

TOWN OF OLCOTT PROFILES

This section includes profiles of the city of **Lockport**, the town of **Newfane** and historic places in Lockport and the hamlet of **Burt** and the town of **Olcott**.

City of Lockport/ Town of Newfane

The city of Lockport is the county seat for Niagara County, and this town profile includes the city and the towns that are included along route 78 to Lake Ontario. This area will be covered in more detail in Volume II of Historic Places of Buffalo & WNY.

Adam Strouse built the first cabin in what became Lockport in 1802 in the Cold Springs area and in 1805 Charles Wilber built a tavern. Settlers arrived from the Lewiston and Cambria area over the toll road built by David Maxwell through Wrights Corners and Morton Corners. During the early 1800s, much of the present city of Lockport was purchased from the Holland Land Company by a group of Quakers, who built the first church at Main, Market and Elm Streets in 1819.

Figure 232 Erie Canal Locks at Lockport PD

In 1818 Nathan Haines mapped out the city, In 1820 David Thomas was named engineer for the Erie Canal west of the Genesee River. When he selected Lockport as the site for the locks, development began in the village, which only consisted of scattered cabins in the woods. Blacksmith Deacon Luther Crocker moved his blacksmith business to Lockport in 1821. Dr. Isaac Smith opened his medical office at 69 Main Street, the current location of the Bewley Building. A town meeting was held in 1821, where Smith proposed the name of Lockport for the village. Since **Bartimus Ferguson moved his printing press from Lewiston to Lockport, Lockport instead of Cambria became the county seat.** By the end of the year, there were 40 or 50 buildings in Lockport.

This led to land speculation by **Colonel William Bond and brought Erie Canal proponent Jesse Hawley to the village.** In 1823 Nathan Roberts came up with the idea of the Flight of Five locks to solve raising canal barges 60 feet up the Niagara escarpment. On 2/2/1924 Lockport was formally established and the Erie Canal opened in 1825.

James Van Horn moved to 2159 Lockport-Olcott Road in Burt in 1811 and built a grist mill and sawmill. They were burned by the English in the War of 1812. This brick home was built in 1823 and the first town meeting of the town of Newfane was held in the house in 1824. The home is now the Town of Newfane Historical Society.

Olcott was founded as Kempville by Burgoyne Kemp who purchased land at the mouth of Eighteen Mile Creek at Lake Ontario in 1805. The town name became Olcott in 1871 after Theodore Olcott invested in renovating the harbor. Extension of the IRC Trolly expanded the amusement parks and hotels of Olcott to a regional destination.

VAN HORN MANSION
2159 Lockport-Olcott Road, Burt

James Van Horn began construction of a grist mill on Eighteen Mile Creek in 1811. Since it provided flour to Fort Niagara it was burned by the British during the War of 1812 in 1813.

He and millwright Ira Tompkins returned after the war and rebuilt the mill, with the entire Van Horn family moving to the area in 1819, initially living in a log cabin. In 1823 the current mansion was built, with bricks made in the on-site brickyard and lumber from their new sawmill. A store and distillery were also opened by the family. The meeting to form the town of Newfane was held at the house in 1824 and town offices were originally in the home.

Figure 233 Van Horn Mansion photo Newfane Historical Society

James Van Horn, Jr. operated the family mill businesses and opened the Van Horn & Company wool factory about a mile south of the house in 1842. He served four terms as Newfane town supervisor. His brother Burt Van Horn converted the 643-acre family wheat farm to a fruit farm, that included over 1,000 apple trees. He was elected to the State Assembly and U.S. Congress, obtaining funding for Olcott Harbor. The hamlet of Burt was named after Burt Van Horn in 1901.

The Federal/Greek style mansion was remodeled by Burt Van Horn, Jr. in 1900, at which time he added a kitchen and dining room, along with the third floor, including a leaded glass skylight imported from France and protected by a glass dome. It was the first area home with electricity. Burt Jr. built the WNY trolly system with W. Carl Ely, including the Lockport-Olcott Trolly. He sold the mansion to Henry Winter Davis in 1910. Mary Wagner converted it to the Green Acres restaurant in 1949. After serving as a boarding house in the 1960s, Noury Chemical purchased the home and property around the estate in 1977.

The mansion has long been associated with spirits allegedly haunting the property. In 1838 James Van Horn, Jr. married Malinda Niles. She died a mysterious death within a year of their marriage and is said to continue haunting the grounds. Other sightings, noises, smells and occurrences have plagued the property for over 150 years.

These hauntings and eventual construction obstructions contributed to Noury Chemical donating the home to the town of Newfane. The building is now the Newfane Historical Society and tours are available at the property.

Colonel William Bond/Jesse Hawley House
143 Ontario Street, Lockport

Figure 234 Jesse Hawley House niagarafallsusa.com

In 1823, this home at 143 Ontario Street was built by William Bond. It was the first brick house built in Lockport. The bricks were manufactured on site by William Bond, who was born in 1780 in New Hampshire and earned the rank of Colonel during the War of 1812. He married Nancy Ralston in 1812 and they had seven children. During the time that Bond owned the home he was involved in land speculation, buying and selling properties along the Erie Canal. He donated the land for the building of the Niagara County Courthouse in Lockport.

Bond went bankrupt in 1831 and sold the home to his brother-in-law Jesse Hawley. Hawley wrote 14 essays promoting the idea of the Erie Canal that were published in the Genesee Messenger in 1807 and 1808. These articles inspired NYS Governor DeWitt Clinton to campaign for the passing of legislation to build the Erie Canal. Hawley is acknowledged as the first advocate for creating a canal across New York State.

When he owned the home at 143 Ontario Street, Hawley was the treasurer of the village of Lockport. He sold it to the Prudden family, who lived there from 1837 to 1887. They in turn sold the house to the Chase family, who were relatives of Solmon P. Chase, Abraham Lincoln's Secretary of the Treasury and later Chief Justice of the U.S. Supreme Court. Kate Chase Seymour, the great-granddaughter of Colonel Bond took possession of the home in 1913. She converted the three-story house into three apartments. Kate lived there until her death in 1955, when her son obtained ownership.

The Niagara County Historical Society purchased the home in 1968 and restored it back to its original floor plan. The 12 rooms of the home are decorated with early to mid-19th century Empire period furnishings, to depict the lifestyle of a middle-class family in Lockport during the busiest and most profitable years of the Erie Canal. It is available for tours by appointment.

OLCOTT BEACH AMUSEMENT PARK
5979 Main Street, Olcott

In the late 1800s and early 1900s Olcott Beach drew thousands of summer vacationers that arrived by train from inland towns and by steamers to Olcott Pier from American and Canadian ports on Lake Ontario. They came to play at the amusement parks, stay at the hotels, dance to the bands and enjoy the sandy beach.

Figure 235 The Rialto Amusement Park early 1900s PD

An advertisement in the 1853 *Buffalo Courier Times* promoted an Olcott picnic grove with a man-powered carousel. In 1889 the Electric Riding Gallery carousel was installed. The Rustic Theater concert venue opened in the 1890s and was located near the current location of Krull Park. In 1899 NYS Governor Teddy Roosevelt spoke there to a crowd of 20,000 spectators, on Pioneer Days held annually on the third Wednesday of August.

Luna Park opened in 1898, offering games, food, amusement rides and souvenirs. In 1902 the IRC Railroad & Trolly built Rialto Park, that featured The Figure 8 (a large wooden roller coaster), a carousel and other family activities. Over 100,000 people a year came to the parks in the early 1900s.

At one time there were eight hotels in Olcott. The largest was the Olcott Beach Hotel that overlooked the lake and had over 100 rooms. Top musical performers like Paul Whitman, the Dorsey Brothers and Artie Shaw performed at the Olcott Beach Hotel's 14,000 square foot ballroom, Luna Park's Dreamland Ballroom or the Rustic Theater.

When the automobile negated the need for staying overnight at hotels and the Depression affected entertainment spending, the hotels and amusement parks closed. There was a resurgence in the 1940s and the New Rialto and Olcott Amusement Park opened, but they closed in the 1980s.

In 1999 the Krull Olcott Development Committee was formed to restore the carousel roundhouse building in the former Olcott Amusement Park. After the building was restored, the committee began fundraising to purchase a replacement for the 1920s style Herschell carousel that was housed in the building from the 1940s to the 1980s. It premiered in 2003. That year the park also built a west pavilion and purchased three vintage kiddie rides, the Skyfighter, the Kiddie Car/Fire Truck and Boat Ride. In 2004 they added an east pavilion with Skee ball machines, the Rocket Swing and a 1931 Wurlitzer Band Organ. The kiddie Ferris wheel from the former Whistle Pig was repaired and installed in 2007. Rides remain a nostalgic 25 cents each.

CITY OF NIAGARA FALLS

PROFILES

This section includes profiles of the city of **Niagara Falls** and several historic places in the Falls.

City of Niagara Falls

After LaSalle landed in Lewiston on December 6, 1678, his men built a boat to sail the western Great Lakes. Due to Niagara Falls, the boat had to be built above the falls, and a site was selected at the mouth of Cayuga Creek, where Cayuga Island formed a natural harbor. In 1679, that was the first location settled by Europeans in what became the city of Niagara Falls.

Figure 236 Frozen Niagara Falls in 1903 PD

The French established the portage around Niagara Falls, along an existing Indian path, to transport furs from the western Great Lakes to Lewiston. Frenchman's Landing was erected in 1745 and in 1750 Chabert Joncaire built Little Fort Niagara above the rapids. Fur trading expanded, with furs valued at 200,000 livres passing through the portage, where over 200 Seneca served as porters.

When the British were victorious in the French & Indian War, in 1760 they took possession of Joncaire's fort. John Stedman became portage master in 1762 and he expanded Joncaire's warehouses and sawmill to include a store and tavern. Fort Schloesser was constructed to protect the portage trail, with the original chimney from Little Fort Niagara used as part of Fort Schloesser. This created the first settlement in Niagara Falls with English teamsters and Seneca members residing near the fort.

The U.S. victory in the American Revolution resulted in possession of Fort Niagara, which the English did not relinquish until 1796. In 1805 the Mile Reserve along the Niagara River was put up for sale and leases offered for Lewiston and Schlosser. A group led by Peter Buell Porter and Augustus Porter purchased much of the land and got the leases, forming Porter, Barton & Company with Benjamin Barton, a freight forwarding company from Lake Erie to Lake Ontario, via the Portage Road around Niagara Falls.

When the portage company was formed in 1805, there were not any buildings or improvements in the vicinity of the falls. Augustus Porter built a sawmill and blacksmith shop in 1805 and moved his family into the town in 1806. He also possessed the water rights to the Niagara rapids and gorge below Niagara Falls. Porter built a grist mill and tannery at Joncaire's original water channel at Willow Island above the falls. Benjamin Barton of the Portage Company assisted in building Augustus Porter's Niagara Falls properties before relocating to manage the portage business at Lewiston. Parkhurst Whitney also assisted Porter, rented his sawmill and had a farm four miles above the falls.

These few buildings were burned by the British during the War of 1812. Augustus rebuilt his house, mills and a general store, becoming the first postmaster and judge of the town that became known as Manchester. Whitney purchased the Porter's Eagle House log tavern and the block including Old Main Street and Falls Street. The Eagle House was expanded to the premier tourist accommodation near the falls, and Whitney purchased the Cataract House in 1831 to service his growing business.

Samuel DeVeaux began working for the Porters as a clerk in the commissary at Fort Niagara in 1807. He began purchasing land in the Niagara region before and after the War of 1812. DeVeaux opened a trading post in Manchester in 1817 and was one of the organizers of the company to build the suspension bridge. He was named the first school commissioner in 1819, Justice of the Peace in 1823 and wrote the first travel guide to Niagara Falls in 1839. He left his land holdings to the Episcopal Church which created Deveaux College for Orphans, later Deveaux School.

In 1816 the Porter Brothers purchased Goat Island, built a bridge to the island and began promoting the tourist industry. When the Erie Canal opened in 1825 the Porters' portage company closed, with the tourist industry and railroad transportation becoming more important.

The Village of Niagara Falls (originally called Schloesser and later Manchester) was incorporated in July 1848 and the village of Suspension Bridge (Bellevue) in June 1854. They were combined into the city of Niagara Falls on March 17, 1892.

Beginning in the 1860s, landscape architect Frederick Law Olmsted advocated for the preservation of Niagara Falls and with a group of early environmentalists founded the Free Niagara Movement. This was created to protect Niagara Falls from commercial interests and retain free access to the falls for the public. In 1879, Olmsted proposed increased public access by NYS purchasing the land surrounding the falls. A committee was formed, which included future President Theodore Roosevelt, to investigate the state buying and developing the land. In 1885, the Porter family sold Niagara Falls and much of the surrounding land (including Goat Island) to NYS to set up Niagara Reservation, the first State Park in the U.S..

Figure 237 Niagara Falls 1882 Map PD

Jacob Schoellkopf purchased the Niagara Falls Canal Company in 1877 and completed the first Schoellkopf Power Plant in 1881. George Westinghouse was given the contract in 1893, for a hydroelectric power station to utilize the natural power of Niagara Falls to provide electricity to local industries and beyond. The alternating current of Nikola Tesla reached a local factory in 1895 and on November 16, 1896 long distance transportation of AC electricity was delivered from Niagara Falls to Buffalo, NY.

Niagara Falls became known as the honeymoon capital of the U.S. The opening of the Seneca Niagara Casino on December 31, 2002 and revitalization of Olmstead's Niagara Parkways, has retained the importance of Niagara Falls, drawing over 8 million tourists annually.

Adams Power Plant Transformer House
1501 Buffalo Avenue, Niagara Falls

The Edward Dean Adams Power Plant was located beside the Niagara River on Buffalo Avenue near Portage Road. Most of the complex has been demolished but the transformer house building is the only surviving plant structure.

In 1886 engineer Thomas Evershed proposed a traditional mill-over-the-wheel-pit technology and a diversionary canal to expand the number of sites serviced by electricity.

Figure 238 Adams Power Plant photo Library of Congress

Charles Gaskill organized the Niagara River Hydraulic Tunnel, Power and Sewer Company, renamed the Niagara Falls Power Company. In 1889, New York City investors headed by J.P. Morgan, William K. Vanderbilt and John Jacob Astor bought out Gaskill. They formed the Cataract Construction Company with Edward Dean Adams as president and manager.

The investors revised Evershed's plans and proposed constructing a central station to supply nearby industrial users and reach distant customers. In 1890 they proceeded with the tunnel, but they were not certain what technology would be used to distribute electricity over an extended distance - Thomas Edison's direct current or George Westinghouse's alternating current.

From above the falls, they constructed an 18 x 21-foot brick lined tunnel under the city, discharging the water near the base of the Honeymoon Bridge. Construction took three years, used 16 million bricks and took the lives of 28 workers.

In 1891 construction began on the Power Plant designed by McKim, Mead & White. It was built from locally quarried limestone and the transformer house was originally flanked by two large power houses. Project engineer George Forbes chose Westinghouse to produce AC generators and Nikola Tesla supervised the installation of the generators, turbines and distribution of AC electricity.

The power plant went into operation in 1895, with their first customer being the Pittsburgh Reduction Company (ALCOA), who built a plant adjacent to the power plant. They used Hall's electrolytic refining process to produce aluminum, lowering its price from $1.00 an ounce to 35 cents a pound. Other early customers were the Carborundum Company and Union Carbide

The first long distance electricity transmission was on November 16, 1896 to Buffalo.

In 1927 the complex was named after Edward Dean Adams. It closed in 1961, replaced by the Robert Moses Niagara Power Plant and Lewiston Pump Generating Plant. The arch of the power plant was rebuilt on Goat Island and one generator is in the Smithsonian Institution.

Castellani Art Museum
5795 Lewiston Road, Niagara University, Niagara Falls

Figure 239 Castellani Art Museum
photo courtesy Castellani Art Museum of Niagara University

In 1956 Armand Castellani took a trip to Italy and visited the Sistine Chapel with his cousin who was an art professor. He pointed out a work by Giotto, a 14 century Florentine master, and Armand's reaction was, "I couldn't see what was so impressive about it."

Curiosity sparked his interest and Armand began studying art. He became an avid collector of art in the 1960s. His business partner Thomas Buscaglia died in 1967 and Castellani became the CEO of Niagara Frontier Services, the parent company of Tops Markets and other area companies. Castellani wanted to combine his interest in art with his dedication to community service, in a memorial to Buscaglia.

In 1964 Castellani received an Honorary Doctor of Commercial Science Degree from Niagara University and served as a member of the Niagara University Board of Trustees. After the University purchased the former DeVeaux School, a private preparatory school for boys on Lewiston Road, for use as a second campus, Armand established the Buscaglia-Castellani Art Gallery to honor his friend. In 1978, this 7,500 square foot building became the home to the more than 300 pieces of art that Armand and Eleanor Castellani accumulated.

The art collection expanded to over 3,000 pieces, outgrowing the DeVeaux Campus gallery. In 1990 the Castellani Art Museum opened on the main Niagara University Campus at 5795 Lewiston Road. Designed by Thomas Moscati, the 23,000 square foot building boasts eight different gallery spaces, including a huge cathedral-like central gallery, along with indoor and outdoor sculpture courts, a museum store, offices, storage and preparation spaces. It also serves educational purposes and is the home of the Niagara University Art History with Museum Studies program, with studio and classroom facilities for students.

In addition to developing this museum dedicated to the arts at Niagara University, Castellani occupied a seat on the Board of the Albright Knox Art Gallery. He and Seymour Knox II were considered two of the main art benefactors in the WNY area. Armand also donated artwork to the Brooklyn Museum, Ringling Museum, Burchfield-Penney Art Center and Niagara Arts Center, along with supporting Media Study Buffalo and Hallwalls.

The Castellani Art Museum currently has a permanent collection of over 5,700 art works, including paintings, prints, photographs, drawings and sculptures, concentrating upon 19th century, modern and contemporary movements.

Armand Castellani died in 2002 leaving a legacy of not only great business success but also great art and philanthropic contributions that have done much to enrich the WNY community.

Cayuga Island
Niagara Falls

Cayuga Island is located in the LaSalle Section of Niagara Falls. It is in the Niagara River and a stream known as Little Niagara River flows between it and the mainland.

In 1679, at the mouth of Cayuga Creek at the island near the current site of the 86th Street bridge the explorer LaSalle built Le Griffon, the first ship that sailed on the western Great Lakes, in 1679.

Cayuga Island was also the original planned location of the Pan American Exposition.

Figure 240 Mckinley Pan Am Stake Lasalle Island Buffalo Times PD

In 1897 the Pan American Exposition Company was formed. Niagara Falls businessmen William Caryl Ely and John M. Brinker, who had railroad interests in the Cataract City, invited a group of seven South American dignitaries to visit Niagara Falls, discuss the Exposition and tour Cayuga Island. It was chosen as the site due to its proximity to several rail and trolly lines, its access to steamers on the Niagara River and the abundance of vacant land where the Expo could be built.

On August 26, 1897, President William McKinley arrived at the Cayuga Island to drive the ceremonial stake marking what was to be the center of the Exposition. It was placed next to the D.N. Long home, which still stands not far from the 86th Street Bridge to the island. After the ceremony, the Presidential party boarded carriages for a tour of Cayuga Island and the adjacent village of LaSalle. McKinley returned to Buffalo where he was the guest of honor at the 31st annual Grand Army of the Republic encampment.

The Exposition was to take place in the summer of 1899, so work immediately began by grading land on the island for construction of the buildings and placing billboards along roads and rail lines. Elaborate plans were made for the construction of a bridge from Buffalo to Grand Island, building an electric railroad across the Grand Island to ferry lines, creating a new train station in LaSalle to accommodate the thousands of guests, and hiring architects to design the finest buildings constructed in the Western Hemisphere.

Unfortunately, the Spanish American War started on April 21, 1898 and plans for the Exposition were put on hold. When rescheduled the Expo was relocated to Buffalo.

DeVeaux College
3100 Lewiston Road, Niagara Falls

Figure 241 Schoellkopf Hall is the only building still standing in DeVeaux Woods State Park

Samuel DeVeaux began working in the commissary at Fort Niagara for the Porter family of Niagara Falls in 1807. Influenced by the Porters' purchase of property, he began buying land in the northern section of what became Niagara Falls.

Returning to the Niagara area after the War of 1812, DeVeaux opened a trading post in 1817 and was considered one of the areas' first merchants. He was named school commissioner in 1819 and Justice of the Peace in 1823, a title he retained for the rest of his life. DeVeaux served on the State Legislature and was one of the incorporators of the Village of Niagara Falls in 1847. Due to his land holdings, investments in railroads and promotion of Niagara as a tourist area, he became one of the wealthiest men in Niagara Falls.

Upon his death in 1852 he willed a 364-acre farm and an endowment of $262,000 to fund a school for fatherless and destitute boys. Administered by the Episcopal Church, DeVeaux College opened in 1857 with a curriculum designed to prepare students for entrance to universities, professions schools, the U.S. Military Academy, Naval Academy or business pursuits. From 1870 to 1950 it operated as a military school, with students wearing military uniforms. Tuition paying students were eventually accepted. Military uniforms were discontinued in 1950, replaced by a sport coat and tie.

Van Rensselaer Hall was a 3 ½ story stone building completed in 1857. It housed the classrooms, dormitory, offices, chapel, offices, library and dining facilities. In 1929 Schoellkopf Hall was the last structure added to the 12-building 51-acre campus. Due to the decline of prep school education, the Episcopal Diocese closed the school in 1971. It was used by various educational or government institutions until being purchased by Niagara University in 1977, as a second campus and for additional dormitory space. Beginning in 1978 it housed the Buscaglia-Castellani Art Gallery until the gallery was relocated to the main Niagara Campus in 1990. The dorms were closed in 1983 and most of the buildings, except Schoellkopf Hall, were demolished in 1994.

The property was acquired by the New York State Office of Parks, Recreation and Historic Preservation in 2001. It is designated DeVeaux Woods State Park and includes some of the oldest unaltered woodlands along the American Niagara Gorge, called Old Growth Woods. A nature trail crosses the Niagara Scenic Parkway to Whirlpool State Park.

DEVIL'S HOLE STATE PARK
3120 DeVeaux Woods Drive, Niagara Falls

Figure 242 Devil's Hole photo credit Ellen Mika Zelasko

Devils Hole State Park is one of the most scenic points along the Niagara Gorge. It is steeped in geological and legendary history.

Over 12,000 years ago, Niagara Falls carved its way through the Niagara Gorge and was located at the present location of Devils Hole. As the falls moved further south, an older waterfall from the drainage of glacial Lake Tonawanda assisted in creating Devils Hole topography.

Native American belief, particularly among the Seneca nation, associated the cave at Devils Hole with the Devil's Snake, a malevolent entity that inhabited the entrance to the underworld. It was an area of spiritual significance that was to be avoided or approached with extreme caution and respect.

The Neuter Nation, who preceded the Seneca used Devils Hole cave as a hiding place during times of war. If anyone other than a Neuter tribe member entered the gorge at this point, they were killed. Since no one returned alive from this area, outsiders considered the area evil and called it Devils Hole.

The trail along the rim of the gorge was the portage route for Native Americans, where they carried their canoes and supplies around Niagara Falls and the Niagara Rapids. That route was utilized by the French under direction of Joncaire to transport goods from Lewiston to Little Fort Niagara above the falls. After the British were victorious in the French & Indian War, they continued the Niagara Portage, under the direction of John Stedman.

During Pontiac's Rebellion, The Devil's Hole Massacre took place on September 14, 1763. The Seneca led by Farmers Brother attacked a portage wagon train. They forced the over 20 teamsters with their mules, horses and wagons into the gorge. When a British regiment came to their aid, the Seneca ambushed them. In total over 100 English were killed, while the Seneca only suffered one injury.

Currently, Devils Hole State Park is a day-use park for hiking and fishing, with snowshoeing and cross-country skiing during the winter. The park features a 400 stone step trail that descends 300 feet to the bottom of the Niagara Gorge, allowing hikers to get close to the rapids and offering a breathtaking view from the edge of the Niagara River. Along the top of the gorge, trails connect Devils Hole to Whirlpool State Park, closer to Niagara Falls.

FORT SCHLOSSER
Niagara Falls

Figure 243 Old Chimney & Falls photo credit Rick Falkowski

In 1750 David Joncaire assumed the post of Portage Master from his father. He built Little Fort Niagara at Frenchman's Landing where a storehouse and blockhouse had been erected in 1745. This was the southern land route portage location that the French created above Niagara Falls.

When Joncaire occupied the area, he dug a channel to divert water from the Niagara River to power mills he built between Little Fort Niagara and the brink of Niagara Falls, across from Goat Island. That was the first use of the Niagara River for waterpower. The diversion channel created the man-made Willow Island, which remained until the 1960s when the channel was filled in to build the Robert Moses Parkway.

The French abandoned Little Fort Niagara during the French & Indian War. After taking possession of the fort in 1760, the British rebuilt it about 650 feet upstream. It was renamed Fort Schlosser after British Captain John Schlosser, the commanding officer of the 60th Regiment of Foot that rebuilt the fort. It was located near the current location of the Upper Niagara Intake Observation Point. The British also built a shipyard across the Niagara River on Navy Island.

John Stedman was appointed Portage Master by the British in 1762 and took possession of the former Joncaire properties in Lewiston and above the falls. He rebuilt Joncaire's warehouses and sawmill. To protect his interests and the portage route, the British expanded Fort Schloesser to include a stockade with four bastions, a mess hall and barracks. Stedman additionally profited by providing a tavern for the soldiers, sold the British wood for their construction projects from his sawmill and established a store where he sold supplies to the soldiers and Seneca who worked as carriers on the portage route.

The British retained possession of Fort Schlosser during the American Revolution and ceded it to the U.S. in 1796. Occupied by U.S. troops, it was burned down by the British during the War of 1812.

The chimney from Little Fort Niagara was used when building Fort Schlosser and Stedman's properties. That chimney still remains and was rebuilt in two different locations, now standing between the road and the Niagara River just before the traffic circle at the end of Niagara Scenic Parkway.

GREAT BEAR MARKET
1801 Pine Avenue, Niagara Falls

Armand Castellani was three years old when his parents Ferrante and Elisa Guarino Castellani emigrated from Giuliano di Roma, near Rome Italy. In 1921 they settled in Utica but moved to Niagara Falls where his father opened a small food store at Garden and Highland Avenues, later at Highland and Centre Avenues. Armand began working for his father at 16.

After being discharged as a captain from the U.S. Army after WWII, he and his brother Alfred began formulating plans to follow their father's vocation. In 1949 Armand opened a Great Bear Market on Pine and 18th, which he moved up Pine Avenue and across the street, next to the Niagara Falls City Market.

Figure 244 Great Bear Market PD

Armand's plan was to expand beyond the small sized grocery stores. He envisioned creating larger stores, a concept that would become the supermarkets of the future. During the 1940s the typical store was only about 3,000 square feet and they felt this boutique style store was becoming obsolete. Consumers wanted to streamline their shopping and a larger store, with a larger variety of items, could fulfill that requirement.

While operating their stores, Armand became associated with Thomas Buscaglia of A & C Buscaglia. Tom expanded his wholesale grocery business to include selling equipment for the retail food businesses. After Alfred passed away in 1951, to service the growing larger retail store market, Castellani and Buscaglia formed T.A. Buscaglia Equipment in 1953, with Armand handling the food retailing and Thomas the construction and engineering for existing and new supermarkets.

After opening two Bells stores from 1954 to 1960, they were joined by the Great Bear Market meat department manager, Savino P. Nanula, and formed Niagara Frontier Services, Inc. They decided to open their own supermarkets and franchise their operations as Tops Markets, with the first 25,000 square foot Tops Markets opening in 1962. Smaller stores of 6.000 – 9,000 square feet were named B-Kwik Markets. Niagara Frontier Services supported supermarkets with all the services necessary to open and operate their business. Additional company owned and franchised stores were built and by the year 2000 Tops Friendly Markets became the largest supermarket chain in WNY. Their chain of Wilson Farms Convenience Stores also became the leading convenience store group in Erie and Niagara Counties.

What began at the Great Bear Market became one of the area's largest food shopping chains.

Love Canal
Niagara Falls

Figure 245 Children's protest at Love Canal photo courtesy Rob Neubauer

The Love Canal was proposed in 1890 as a link between Lake Erie and Lake Ontario but the project was abandoned after only one mile was dug. In the 1920s the canal became a dump site for municipal refuse of the city of Niagara Falls. The canal was purchased by Hooker Chemical Company in the 1940s to dump almost 20,000 tons of byproducts from the manufacturing of chemicals. Hooker buried the waste in drums at a depth of 25 feet and covered the canal with a clay seal to prevent leakage.

Due to increasing population, homes were built near the location. A school was needed for the children living in the area and the School District inquired about purchasing the land from Hooker Chemical. The company sold it to the school district for one dollar with the stipulation that since hazardous waste was buried, the land should not have any underground construction and the company was not responsible if the city did not follow their advised building restrictions. In 1954 workers building a school on the site discovered buried drums.

In 1957 developers began building homes adjacent to the Love Canal site. This was not above the land purchased from Hooker Chemical so residents were not advised of the potential dangers. When building the sewer beds, construction crews breached the canal walls. The city used part of the protective clay cap as dirt fill for the 93rd Street School. Holes were punched in the solid clay walls to build water lines. This allowed toxic waste to escape when rainwater washed through the removed cap and the buried chemicals seeped from the canal to the surrounding ground.

By 1976 high chemical levels were discovered. In 1977 the government started investigating the problem and it received national attention due to protests led by Lois Gibbs. In 1978 Love Canal was declared a federal health emergency by President Carter. Congress passed the Superfund Act taxing chemical and petroleum industries to assist in the cleanup of hazardous substances.

The federal government relocated 800 families and reimbursed them for the loss of their homes. In 1994, the government demolished several rings of homes and Hooker Chemical (now Occidental Petroleum) agreed to pay 120 million dollars in restitution.

The area of Love Canal remains fenced in with hazardous waste still buried beneath it, but the surrounding land was deemed remediated and redeveloped as Black Creek Village.

Niagara Falls State Park
332 Prospect Street, Niagara Falls

The world was introduced to Niagara Falls by Father Louis Hennepin, a Jesuit priest in explorer Rene-Robert de LaSalle's expedition, who wrote about viewing it on December 7, 1678. When Hennepin experienced the falls, twice as much water flowed over it as today because half the water is diverted to hydroelectric plants in the U.S. and Canada.

Figure 246 Niagara Falls photo credit Marsha Falkowski

In 1804, Napolean Bonaparte's brother Jerome is credited with starting the tradition of making Niagara Falls the Honeymoon Capital when he and his American bride enjoyed their honeymoon at the falls. The development of railroad transportation made Niagara Falls a destination for visitors from around the world.

Augustus and Peter Porter purchased the American Falls in 1805 at a New York State public auction. This included the land around Niagara Falls and water rights to the eastern rapids both above and below the falls. They rebuilt Daniel Joncaire's grist mill on the rapids, purchased Goat Island after the War of 1812 and started the tourist trade. The family built a wooden walkway to the brink of the falls at Terrapin Point (Porter's Bluff) in 1817 and even owned the iconic Cataract House hotel

Landscape architect Frederick Law Olmsted was part of a group of early environmentalists that in the 1860s founded the Free Niagara Movement advocating for the preservation of Niagara Falls. In 1879 Olmsted and State Surveyor James T. Gardner assisted in preparing a report arguing for increased public access and recommending that NYS purchase the lands surrounding Niagara Falls. New York State Governor Grover Cleveland signed a bill authorizing the purchase of lands to create the Niagara Reservation in 1885, recognized as the oldest state park in the U.S.

Theodore Roosevelt was a member of the committee to establish the park; the land was purchased from the Porter family and the grounds were designed by William Law Olmsted & Calvert Vaux.

In 1896 Nikola Tesla harnessed the power of Niagara Falls. 3,160 tons of water flow over Niagara Falls every second and 2.6 million kilowatts of electricity are produced annually.

There have been numerous improvements on the American side of the Falls, including making the nature walkways along the Niagara River more like Olmsted's vision for the park. Also, only on the American side can you experience the power of the rapids as the water rushes past along the shore.

Niagara University
5795 Lewiston Road, Niagara Falls

Figure 247 Seminary of Our Lady of Angels Niagara University niagara.edu

Niagara University was created on November 21, 1856, when two faculty members and six seminary students moved from the residence of Buffalo's first Catholic Bishop Timon to a vacant orphan home on Best Street in Buffalo. Vincentian Fathers John J. Lynch and John Monaghan began searching for a better location and while visiting Suspension Bridge (now Niagara Falls) found that the 100-acre Vedder farm on Monteagle Ridge was for sale. Father Lynch then purchased the neighboring 200-acre DeVeaux farm, complete with a barn and two-story tavern known as The Half-Way House.

In 1857 the newly formed College and Seminary of Our Lady of Angels moved to Niagara Falls. The barroom and bowling alley of the Half-Way House became the sacristy and chapel, while the attic of the building was the dormitory, later expanding to the barn. Enrollment increased to 24 in 1857 and to 60 in 1858. Father Lynch, considered the co-founder of the university with Bishop Timon, left the school when he was appointed coadjutor bishop of the Diocese of Toronto, Canada in 1859.

Due to the increasing number of students, construction of new buildings commenced in 1862 and in 1863 it was granted a charter by NYS to confer degrees to graduates. The school celebrated its 25th Anniversary in 1881 with Bishop Stephen V. Ryan, provincial supervisor of the Vincentian Congregation and second Bishop of Buffalo, congratulating the school and seminary for graduating 300 priests, 25 doctors, 47 lawyers, 40 professors and many members of the Legislature.

In 1883 NYS Governor Grover Cleveland signed the documents to rename the college Niagara University. Our Lady of Angels Seminary remained at the school until 1961 when it moved to Albany.

The university continued to expand, opening the four-story Gothic style St. Vincent's Hall in 1905. That building now houses the College of Hospitality and Tourism Management. An $80 million capital campaign was completed in 2012, that included the Thomas Golisano Center for Integrated Sciences. The Russell J. Salvatore Dining Commons was renovated in 2017 and Kiernan Recreation Center completed in 2023.

Niagara University offers over 50 professional and career-oriented programs to 2,700 undergraduate students and more than 900 graduate students, from the U.S. and Canada. In addition, the school competes in 19 Division I NCAA sports. Niagara University was the alma mater of NBA superstar Calvin Murphy, and the founder of the CIA William Donovan.

OAKWOOD CEMETERY
747 Portage Road, Niagara Falls

In 1852, Lavinia Porter, the daughter of Judge Augustus Porter, donated the land upon which Oakwood Cemetery was built. Augustus and Peter Porter were the founders and original landowners of much of Niagara Falls. Their property, including Goat Island, was sold to New York State in 1885 to establish the Niagara Falls Reservation, the first State Park in the U.S.

Figure 248 Oakwood Cemetery Mausoleum photo courtesy Oakwood Cemetery

Like Forest Lawn Cemetery in Buffalo, Oakwood was built in the style of the rural cemetery movement, with funerary art intertwined with the natural beauty of the landscape. The topography of curving roadways and planned landscaping was designed by noted civil engineer Theodore Dehone Judah, who was also responsible for the establishment and design of the first transcontinental railroad. In 1882, his plans were refined by Drake Whitney, nephew of the three Whitney Sisters for which Niagara Falls State Park's Three Sisters Islands are named. The cemetery contains outstanding examples of obelisks, sarcophagi and statuary in a landscape lush with mature plantings and trees, many dating back to the earliest time of the cemetery.

In 1913 the architectural firm of Green and Wicks designed the Oakwood Mausoleum, covered by hand cut gray Vermont marble and featuring soaring stone columns supporting a centered entrance portico. The interior is faced and floored in white marble, lit by clerestory windows and two stained glass windows, one created by Louis Comfort Tiffany. Huge bronze doors grace the entrance to the chapel centered in the mausoleum.

Among the over 22,000 people buried at Oakwood Cemetery, it is the final resting place for Annie Edson Taylor (the first person to survive going over the falls in a barrel), Homan Walsh (who flew a kite across the gorge to facilitate the building of the Suspension Bridge), the hermit of Goat Island, Underground Railroad porters at the Cataract Hotel, Charles Hyde, Charles Gaskill, Frank A. Jenss, Judge Augustus Porter, General Peter Buell Porter, a memorial to the Civil War "Comrades of the Grand Army of the Republic" and many of the families whose names are associated with the growth and development of Niagara Falls as an industrial city and tourist attraction.

The Oakwood Cemetery Heritage Foundation presents special events and gives popular tours including the Daredevils of Niagara, Tragic Tales, Phenomenal Females, Streets of Niagara Tour and historical tours featuring European founding families of Niagara Falls like the Schoellkopfs, Whitneys and Porters.

Peter Porter Mansion
6 4th Street, Niagara Falls

Figure 249 Peter Porter Mansion photo credit Rick Falkowski

The Peter A. Porter Mansion on 4th Street and Buffalo Avenue was built in 1876 by Peter A. Porter, who was born in 1853 in the home of his grandfather General Peter Buell Porter on Falls Street. The location of the Falls Street house became the site of the Strand and Cataract Theaters.

In 1877 Porter married Alice Adele Taylor at her family's home on Buffalo Avenue, later the site of the Niagara Club. Porter operated the Cataract House, owned the Niagara Falls Gazette, was president of Cataract Bank and a member of Congress. In 1885 his family sold Niagara Falls and much of the surrounding land to New York State to create the first State Park in the U.S. After his retirement Porter was active with the Buffalo Historical Society and was the founder and president of the Niagara Frontier Historical Society. He was one of the foremost writers of Niagara Falls History.

In 1921 the home was sold to Alexander Jeffrey Porter, chairman of the Natural Food Company (later known as the Shredded Wheat Company) and great grandson of Judge Augustus Porter. The Tatler Club was formed in 1925 by Gertrude W. Porter as a women's benevolent society where prominent women of the area met to discuss issues of interest, replicating the activities of Buffalo's Twentieth Century Club. They met in the 4th Street home until it was sold in 1935. At that time the Tatler Club relocated to the Schoellkopf house on Jefferson Avenue, until it was sold to the city of Niagara Falls. The Tatler's repurchased the Porter Mansion in 1957 and continue to refurbish it as an example of late 19th century mansions.

The Italianate design mansion features a large side porch that overlooks the Niagara River rapids. It includes many original details including 19th century flooring, doors, light fixtures, sinks and leaded glass windows. The mansion is filled with 19th century style furniture, some of which dates back to Porter family ownership.

This Niagara Falls landmark has received grants that will allow the Tatler Club to further restore the mansion, build a walking path to the river and allow the building to be open to visitors on a regular basis. They hope to expand upon the Porter family's role in the Underground Railroad and highlight their involvement with the city, including donating the land for Oakwood Cemetery.

SCHOELLKOPF POWER PLANT
Niagara Gorge, Niagara Falls

Jacob Schoellkopf purchased the property and land of the Niagara Falls Canal company at a bankruptcy auction in 1877 for $71,000. He improved the canal and in 1881 built Schoellkopf Power House Number 1, the first company to generate electricity from Niagara Falls.

Figure 250 Schoellkopf Power Plant PD

After his death in 1903, his sons took over the company becoming The Niagara Falls Hydraulic Power and Manufacturing Company and subsequently added Power Stations 2, 3A and 3B, making it the largest hydroelectric power station in the world. In addition to the turbine generator stations at the base, there were offices, gate houses and other buildings at the top of the gorge. They consolidated with Edward Dean Adams interests to form the Niagara Falls Power Company in 1918 and in 1950 became part of Niagara Mohawk – now National Grid.

On June 7, 1956, the plant collapsed, destroying 2/3 of the complex and the 6 generators that produced 300,000 horsepower, causing 100 million dollars of damage. The entire southern section of the plant fell into the gorge and the rest was soon afterwards demolished. This resulted in the loss of 400,000 kilowatts of power from the power grid.

After the collapse of the Schoellkopf Power Houses in 1956, the 4,600-foot canal that ran through the city to the plant was drained and the land was donated by Niagara Mohawk to the city of Niagara Falls. The canal was considered a safety hazard and was filled by the city during the late 1950s and early 1960s.

The destruction of the Schoellkopf Plant necessitated building the Niagara Power Project, 4.5 miles from the falls near Lewiston. Opened in 1961, it diverts 750,000 gallons of water per second from above the falls, through tunnels below the city to the plant. There, 25 turbines produce 2.6 million kilowatts of clean electricity per year. Free tours are available at the Robert Moses Niagara Power Plant.

In 2013 the Maid of the Mist constructed winter storage facilities and a maintenance area in the Schoellkopf area at the base of the falls. This construction project restored the original elevator shaft, that lowers you to where the plant stood. Access to the elevator is free. At the base, information is available about the plant, along with details of its collapse. In addition, there is access to hiking trails along the river that provide unique views of the gorge and Rainbow Bridge.

WHITNEY MANSION
335 Buffalo Avenue, Niagara Falls

Figure 251 Whitney Mansion photo Library of Congress

The Whitney Mansion at 335 Buffalo Avenue was built by Solon Whitney, the son of General Parkhurst Whitney who established the two most prestigious hotels in Niagara Falls – The Eagle House and Cataract House.

Parkhurst Whitney was one of the first settlers of Niagara Falls in 1805, moving to a farm four miles north of the falls and renting a sawmill from Augustus Porter. During the War of 1812 he served under General Winfield Scott and remained in the militia after the war, being promoted to the rank of Major General.

After Manchester (initial name of Niagara Falls) was burned by the British during the War of 1812, Whitney leased the Eagle House, a log tavern on Old Main Street near Falls Street. He purchased the entire block from Augustus and Peter Porter in 1817 and built the Eagle House into the premier tourist accommodation near the falls. In 1831 he bought the Cataract House to service his overflow hospitality business.

There were no bridges from the Cataract House across the river to Goat Island. Parkhurst Whitney's daughters crossed the water on an ice jam and were the first to explore the islands off Goat Island. Three Sisters Islands on Goat Island were named after Parkhurst's daughters, Asenath, Angeline and Celinda. A fourth smaller inaccessible island was named Little Brother Island for his son Solon.

Solon Whitney purchased land on a bluff overlooking the Niagara rapids and in 1851 built a Medina limestone Greek Revival mansion. It featured a front two-story porch supported by four heavy Iconic columns, first floor windows extending to the floor and a gabled roof with a wide dentil cornice.

In 1846 Solon Whitney assumed management of the Cataract House and married Frances Drake, the daughter of the owner of the United States Hotel and Congress Hall in Saratoga Springs. The Cataract House became the society hotel of Niagara Falls and legendary Underground Railroad station, with hotel porters leading enslaved people to freedom in Canada.

The Whitney family sold the mansion to A.H. Zimmerman of Moore Business Forms in 1931, who sold it to Edward Franchot, the brother-in-law of Carborundum founder Frank J. Tone. The Carborundum Company purchased it as the home for its president. After being the University Club's home for young executives, it became the Niagara Falls Preservation Society Museum and is possibly the oldest residence in Niagara Falls.

CITY OF NORTH TONAWANDA

PROFILES

This section includes profiles of the city of **North Tonawanda** and several historic places in N.T.

City of North Tonawanda

"The Lumber City"

Originally occupied by the Wenro Tribe and later by the Senaca Nation, present day North Tonawanda was heavily forested and not the home of any European immigrants until 1809. In that year George Burger built a roadhouse on the Military Road (now River Road) a little south of present-day Wheatfield Street. By 1811 Joshua Pettit and the Van Slyke families had also lived along Military Road. These buildings were all burned down by a British and Canadian force in December 1813 during the War of 1812.

Figure 252 Long Bridge Collapsed with Buildings

After 1815, settlers slowly returned, attracted by the fledgling lumber harvesting business. The mainland and Grand Island had large stands of White Oak trees which were cut and transported to the shipbuilding yards of New England and New York City. The lumber was carried from North Tonawanda and portaged down the Niagara Escarpment to the mouth of the Niagara River, then loaded onto barges and shipped to the Hudson River. Later White and Yellow Pines harvested from farther west in Canada and Minnesota were transported down the Great Lakes to North Tonawanda and followed the same route.

When the Erie Canal was opened in 1825 it cut the transportation time to Albany from over 2 weeks to less than 1 week. Land speculators started buying large sections and reselling into smaller farm lots and homestead plots. The Sweeney brothers and their nephew George Goundry are the most remembered. They campaigned to have the area known as the village of Niagara but by 1836 "Tonawanda" was formed. It was loosely described as the area north of Black Rock, north to past the canal.

In 1839, Henry P. Smith reduced the cost of lumber production by creating rafts and floating the logs to N.T. Soon a few lumber mills were built along the Niagara River and Tonawanda Creek to support the growing local need and also to ship finished products eastward. Land speculator Vandervoort sold 400 acres in the Martinsville area to German immigrants.

In 1854, the village of Tonawanda was formed, spanning two counties, with 3 wards south of the Erie Canal and 1 ward north of it. The next year the north ward withdrew from the village in disputes over taxes. The north ward became part of the Town of Wheatfield and in 1865 it was incorporated as the "Village of Wheatfield" with a population of 440 mostly concentrated where the canal branched to the Niagara River.

The 1870's saw a lot of industrial growth in the village. Armitage and Herschell moved their "Tonawanda Engine and Machine" works in, an Iron refining mill opened as did carriage and shingle manufacturers. Gratwick lumber, Gratwick shipping and Gratwick planning mills opened. The village name was changed to "North Tonawanda". By 1880 the population was 1,492.

In the 1880's continued growth in lumber, produce,

Figure 253 Tonawanda Paper Mill on Tonawanda Island
photo taken from River Road PD

and shipping attracted more worker with their families, creating the need for more housing and supportive businesses. Armitage and Herschell began building carousels, telephone service began, as did municipal water. Harbor improvements were made. More heavy industries opened dealing with iron steel, boilers and electricity delivery. By 1890 the population more than tripled to 4,793.

In 1897, North Tonawanda became a city comprised of the village and the Gratwick, Martinville and Sawyer's Station areas. More workers and families arrived, driving the increases in housing, businesses, and infrastructure. New industries continued to open – The Rand Ledger Co., De Kleist Barrel Organ Factory, and Buffalo Bolt are the most well-known. Lumber stacks lined the area between the river and River Road, the entire shoreline and all of Tonawanda Island. More board feet of lumber were shipped from North Tonawanda than anywhere else in the world. By 1900 the population was 9,069.

The next decade saw new factories. Among these were Herschell Spillman, Van Raalte Silk Mills, Riverside Chemical, Richardson Boat, Creo-Dipt Shingles, and Bennett Homes. Wurlitzer moved it's manufacturing from Ohio to North Tonawanda. By 1905 North Tonawanda was the largest lumber market in the world. There was a strong iron industry. 63 express trains and 92 passenger trains traveled through daily.

By the 1920's, new factories and businesses were opening: Durez plastics, Tonawanda Paper Mill, Remington Rand and National Grinding Wheel were the largest of these. The 1930 census counted 19,019 residents.

The 1930's Great Depression slowed industrial and business growth, but there was a slight increase in in population. During World War II, 6 companies earned the "E" for Excellence banner for meeting production goals – Bison Shipyards, Buffalo Bolt, Buffalo Pumps, Richardson Boat, Wurlitzer, and Wales-Strippit. By 1950 the population was 24,731.

The 1950's and 1960's witnessed many plant closings and industries being bought-out and moving to other areas. In some cases, newer technologies were the cause. For some others it was the opening of the Saint Lawrence Seaway (bypassing the Erie Canal) and the New York State Thruway (bypassing the city). The city's peak population was reached in 1970 with 36,012 residents. By 2020 it had declined to 30,433, and the city was redefining itself as a destination for recreation and tourism.

by Howard Roeske, Executive Director North Tonawanda History Museum

Cantilever Bridge
Erie Canal near Sweeney at Oliver Street, North Tonawanda

*Figure 254 Bascule Bridge in North Tonawanda
photo credit Marsha Falkowski*

The Cantilever Railroad Bridge is a bascule bridge across the Erie Canal and over Sweeney Street near Oliver Street in North Tonawanda and East Niagara Street near East Avenue in the city of Tonawanda.

It was built by the New York Central Railroad in 1919 to replace the railroad bridge adjacent to the Long Bridge that crossed the canal from Main Street in Tonawanda to Webster Street in North Tonawanda. The Long Bridge collapsed after a barge collided with it in 1916. It was proposed that a bascule bridge be built to replace the Long Bridge and railroad track bridge. The railroad refused to build a bascule bridge unless it had access for two sets of tracks. Since that could not be accommodated, the Cantilever Bridge was built further east down Tonawanda Creek.

The New York State transportation authority, upon the provisions of the expansion of the barge canal, wanted all bridges on the Erie Canal to be lift bridges so taller boats could use the canal. This required New York Central to build a bascule bridge instead of a fixed structure. A cantilever bridge is supported only at one end. A bascule bridge is a drawbridge, usually with a counterweight to balance its span and allow for lift at its supported end. The bridge was only lifted one time at its grand opening. NYS rescinded its higher bridge requirement after the bridge was built.

With the construction of this bridge and their 1917-1922 track re-alignment project, New York Central Railroad relocated their railway tracks in both cities. The reconfiguration removed train tracks from Main Street in Tonawanda and Webster Street in North Tonawanda. This improved the appearance of the downtown streets in both cities and resulted in safer downtown shopping districts.

After the Erie Canal was re-engineered to become the Erie Barge Canal, in 1918 the Tonawanda Dam was removed. The dam was built in 1823, in the current Gateway Harbor Park area, to raise the level of Tonawanda Creek by four feet, required to allow entrance to the water level of the Erie Canal that was built alongside the Niagara River to Buffalo. When the dam was removed the Erie Canal drained directly into the Niagara River, making the Tonawandas the western terminus of the canal. It also allowed the canal section built along the shore to covered and reclaimed as Niawanda and Isle View Parks.

The Cantilever Bridge continues to be the primary railway connection between Buffalo and Niagara Falls.

Carnegie Library
240 Goundry Street, North Tonawanda

According to Andrew Carnegie's "Gospel of Wealth" a man who accumulates great wealth has a duty to use his surplus wealth for the improvement of mankind in philanthropic causes. He believed in giving one's wealth away during their lifetime, and his most famous quote was "The man who dies thus rich dies disgraced."

Figure 255 Carnegie Library with NT Football Hall of Fame photo credit Dennis Reed Jr. nthistory.com

Born in 1835, Carnegie emigrated from Scotland to Allegheny, Pennsylvania and started working as a bobbin boy in a cotton factory at the age of 12. He educated himself by reading and writing and attending night school. At 14 he got a job as a telegraph messenger, at 18 became the private secretary and telegraph operator for the president of the Pennsylvania Railroad Company and was superintendent of the railroad's Pittsburgh division at 23. He invested in the Woodruff Sleeping Car Company (Pullman), built bridges, traded bonds, owned iron and steel companies and became the richest man in the world when he sold his steel interests to J.P. Morgan for $492 million dollars in 1901 (equivalent to over $18 billion current dollars).

Carnegie began donating money to benevolent causes at the age of 35. His first donation to a library was in 1881 to Dunfermline, Scotland, the town where he was born and the first commissioned in the U.S. was to his hometown of Allegheny. From 1886 to 1919 he donated over $40 million for 1,679 library buildings in the U.S. based on a formula of $2.00 per resident and the community's commitment to maintain the library.

In 1903, North Tonawanda received $20,000 from Carnegie to build the library at 240 Goundry Street, next to the Goundry Street School. The building features a beautiful rotunda, with two side galleries and yellow pine floors that were cut at one of the lumber mills in the city. The architect was Edgar E. Joralemon, who also designed the former Felton High School.

It was used as the North Tonawanda Library until 1975, when the new North Tonawanda Library opened on Meadow Drive. In 1976 the building became the Carnegie Art Center of the Tonawandas Council on the Arts. A non-profit art gallery and art school, it also provides children's workshops in visual, language and dance arts, literary presentations, dance performances and outdoor concerts.

Behind the Carnegie Art Center is the former caretaker's cottage for the Goundry Street School, which now houses the North Tonawanda Football Hall of Fame.

DeGraff Mansion
273 Goundry Street, North Tonawanda

*Figure 256 DeGraff Mansion in 1900
photo courtesy Maria Aurigema*

Built in 1883 for James and Mary Simson DeGraff, this Queen Ann style home at Goundry and Payne Avenue was one of the few brick residences built in North Tonawanda. Elevations of patterned brickwork were broken by Medina sandstone belt courses that divide the stories. It is crowned by a gable and hip roof, with massive chimneys that flare out at the top. The home contains mahogany woodwork, stained glass windows, glittering chandeliers and parquet floors.

It was one of the first houses in North Tonawanda to have running water. Before the city waterworks were completed, the home had a reservoir on the third floor, to which water was piped. That water flowed to the toilets, sinks and bathtubs on the lower floors. The home also had the first residential elevator, running from the basement to the third-floor billiard room.

James DeGraff moved to North Tonawanda in 1856 and became involved with the lumber industry. He was also a bank officer, Town of Tonawanda supervisor in 1875-1876 and Wheatfield supervisor from 1881-1882. John married Mary Simson, a descendant of the Long sisters, in 1859 and they had three children.

LeGrand Simson DeGraff inherited the home and carried on his father's lumber interests, serving as a partner in A. Weston & Son. He was president of State National Bank and served as a director when it became part of Marine Trust Company. DeGraff was also president of the Tonawanda Power Company and director of other power companies that merged to form Niagara Mohawk.

LeGrand and his wife VeNorma Crown did not have children, and both were involved in charitable endeavors and philanthropy in North Tonawanda. VeNorma was president of the local Red Cross and LeGrand was the major contributor in founding DeGraff Hospital. He lived at 273 Goundry until the 1950s. LeGrand died in 1960 at the institution he founded, DeGraff Hospital.

In the 1960s the house was purchased by Jay and Brigitte Aurigema who ran a pizza restaurant out of the basement. They hosted parties for the actors and crew of Melody Fair productions. A party of over 150 people was raided in 1972 and police found LSD and other narcotics on the premises. Charges were dropped due to a technicality in the search warrant.

The Dingman family has owned the DeGraff Mansion since 1978 and Dingman Property Management is in the process of restoring the building.

GATEWAY HARBOR PARK
Erie Canal between Tonawanda and North Tonawanda

Figure 257 Gateway Harbor Park Tonawanda/NT photo credit Dennis Reed Jr. nthistory.com

When the Erie Canal opened in 1825 its western terminus was the harbor at Buffalo. After the Erie Canal section along the Niagara River was filled in during 1918, Tonawanda Harbor became the western end of the canal.

To maintain the water level of the Erie Canal so the locks at Lockport would be the same height as the water at Lake Erie, a dam was built on Tonawanda Creek in Tonawanda Harbor by Judge Samuel Wilkeson and Dr. Ebenezer Johnson of Buffalo in 1823. It was placed west of the mouth of Ellicott Creek and east of the bridge crossing the canal between Main Street in Tonawanda and Webster Street in North Tonawanda.

Tonawanda Creek from Tonawanda to Pendleton was the longest section of natural waterways utilized in building the canal and the dam raised the level of the creek by 4 ½ feet. This allowed the barges, which required a depth of four feet, to navigate the canal without requiring additional dredging of Tonawanda Creek. However, this resulted in spring flooding, with canal ditches being dug (above the dam) through both Tonawanda and North Tonawanda in an attempt to alleviate the flooding.

A lock at the north end allowed passage of boats directly into the Niagara River. The canal was dug through the city of Tonawanda and continued along the current Niagara Street and through Niawanda and Isle View Park. This created Goose Island, a red-light district (similar to the brothels and taverns of Canal Street in Buffalo), along with industrial sites, in the current area of Tops Market and the Niagara Shores Condos.

The location of Tonawanda Harbor resulted in it becoming the lumber capital of the world. Lumber arrived initially from Grand Island and later from the western Great Lakes. It was processed at sawmills, planing mills and lumber yards on Tonawanda Island and North Tonawanda. In Gateway Harbor the lumber was prepared for shipment to the east Coast. Lumber was stacked to a height of 14 feet along seven miles of the Niagara River from Niagara Park to Gratwick Park and almost 100 companies were involved in the lumber industry.

In addition to the lumber business, grain mills, paper factories, livestock yards and later iron and steel industries were built in the Tonawandas for shipment along the Erie Canal.

Gateway Harbor Park is now a recreation area, featuring boating, concerts and the annual Canal Fest.

HERSCHELL CARROUSEL FACTORY
180 Thompson Street, North Tonawanda

Figure 258 Allan Herschell Factory in 1919 photo courtesy Allan Herschell Carrousel Museum

North Tonawanda is called the "Lumber City" and the "Home of the Carousel". Allan Herschell and the Herschell Carrousel Factory Museum are responsible for the carousel moniker.

The Allen Herschell Carrousel Company began when Herschell and partners formed the Armitage Herschell Company in 1873, a machine shop that started making carousels. That was followed by the North Tonawanda Barrel Organ Factory with Eugene DeKleist in 1888 and Herschell Spillman Company in 1901. Herschell Spillman was located at 162-196 Sweeney Street. Herschell left that company in 1911 and in 1919 it was renamed Spillman Engineering. In 1924 Spillman Engineering moved to the corner of Oliver and Goundry Street, where they began making carousels in competition with Herschell. They remained in operation until 1945 when they were purchased and absorbed by the Allan Herschell Company. The Carousel Park Apartments were built at their Oliver and Goundry location.

After parting ways with Spillman in 1915, Herschell opened the Allen Herschell Company on Thompson Street with John Wendler and Fred Fritchie. Herschell retired in 1923 and died in 1927 but the company was continued under his name. The company became the most prolific manufacturer of carousels, specializing in making portable merry go rounds that could be used by traveling carnivals and featuring elaborately hand carved wooden carousel horses. They produced over 3,000 hand carved wooden carousels that were shipped across the world. The company also manufactured roller coasters, thrill rides, miniature trains and assorted kiddie rides.

Manufacturing continued at the Thompson Street plant until 1953 when the Allan Herschell Company was sold to Weisner/Rapp Company at 1165 Clinton Street in Buffalo. They continued manufacturing carousels and amusement park rides until the company was sold to Chance Manufacturing in Wichita Kansas.

In 1979, a community group, including Allan Herschell (grandson of the company founder) was formed to purchase the Thompson Street factory and bring an original Herschell Carousel back to North Tonawanda. The museum obtained one of the first carousels that was shipped from the factory in 1916, and opened the Allan Herschel Factory Museum in July 1983, the first day of the first Canal Fest, a week-long event sponsored by the museum.

The Carousel Society of the Niagara Frontier purchased the assets of Chance Rides and operates the museum where they provide exhibits of band organs and mechanical music machines, the only operating Wurlitzer paper roll perforating machine, tours, demonstrations, classes and rides on the historic 1916 carousel.

Niagara Falls Power Transfer Station
Twin City Highway & Robinson Street, North Tonawanda

The National Grid Niagara Falls Power Transfer Station, also referred to as the North Tonawanda Transformer Building, is regarded as one of the most important buildings in the worldwide history of electricity.

In 1895 the Niagara Falls Power Company started building the first long distance power line along the Old Mile Reserve right of way from Niagara Falls to Buffalo. Working with George Westinghouse's General Electric Company, they transmitted electricity using Nikola Tesla's breakthrough alternating current that could travel long distances with minimal loss. On November 15, 1896 the first long distance transmission of electricity traveled 23 miles from Niagara Falls to Buffalo through this transformer building. The service initially powered the Buffalo streetcars and provided electricity to the 1901 Pan-American Exposition.

Figure 259 Niagara Falls Power Transfer Station photo credit Dennis Reed Jr. nthistory.com

The transformer house stepped down the high voltage transmission for local distribution which resulted in North Tonawanda being one of the first industrial areas to receive AC power. This substation continued high voltage transmission to Buffalo, Lockport and other destinations. In the early 1900s an adjacent two-story switching tower, which directed the long-distance transmission, was connected to the transformer house. On October 31, 1920 a horrific explosion at the tower killed 13 employees.

Interest in preserving the legacy of Nikola Tesla was spurred by former Buffalo State professor Dr. Francis Lestingi. His efforts resulted in a seven-foot-tall statue of Tesla being erected in Tesla Park at the corner of North Division and Main Street in Buffalo in September 2020. This monument points to the Ellicott Square Building where the "Electric Banquet" was attended by 400 dignitaries on January 12, 1897 to honor Tesla's accomplishment. A statue of Tesla that was gifted in 1976 by the Yugoslavian government overlooks Niagara Falls on Goat Island, and includes an informational panel donated by Lestingi in 2021. In addition, Lestingi designed a Telsa Coil that stands in North Tonawanda's Gratwick Park, creating the Tesla Legacy Corridor running from Niagara Falls through North Tonawanda to Buffalo.

National Grid at one time applied for a permit to raze the Transfer Station but it was denied. After the building was designated as a historic landmark, National Grid decided to refurbish it and once again utilize it as a transfer station. The renovated building now features photos of Westinghouse, Tesla and the history of electricity, an informational panel about the building and it is illuminated by LED lighting to show the features of the structure.

Niagara Power Building
2-6 Webster Street, North Tonawanda

Figure 260 Scanlon House State Bank Sweeney Building

The first building after you crossed the Erie Canal, on the western side of Webster Street in North Tonawanda was the Scanlon House. It was built for politician Matthew Scanlon but was eventually owned by Philip Perew who operated the White Star Hotel behind it at the corner of Manhattan and Tremont Streets.

Perew also owned most of Goose Island on the Tonawanda side of the Canal, created when the Erie Canal was dug. Goose Island was bounded by Tonawanda Creek, the Erie Canal and the Niagara River. It became known for drunkenness, brawling and bawdy displays at its cheap boarding houses, hotels, bars and brothels. After the Erie Canal was filled in from Tonawanda to Buffalo in 1918, it was no longer an island. More area was devoted to the Tonawanda Board & Paper Company but through the 1920s and 1930s the taverns and red-light district remained. After urban renewal and gentrification in the 1970s, the paper company and remaining buildings were demolished, replaced by Tops Market, a condominium development and the new Tonawanda Police Station/Town Hall.

In 1919 The Bascule Bridge was constructed across the Erie Canal, replacing the Long Bridge which was damaged by a barge and collapsed in 1916. The Bascule Bridge could be raised for boat traffic and was permanently replaced by the Renaissance Bridge in 1979.

After a devastating fire, in 1929 the Scanlon House was torn down and replaced by the Niagara Power Building, the first building constructed in the U.S. in which the steel skeleton was welded rather than riveted. The Niagara Power Company was on the south side of the building and State Trust Bank on the north side of the structure. It was designed by prominent Buffalo architect E.B. Green. The Niagara Power Company was originally across Webster Street in the Sweeney Building at 15 Webster Street, while State Trust Bank was across Sweeney Street at 8 Webster Street. Several other businesses were also located in the Niagara Power Building.

In 2002 the Niagara Power Building was purchased by the Buffalo Suzuki Strings Musical Art Center, a non-profit organization started locally by Nary Cay Neal in Kenmore in 1969. The organization provides musical instruction using the Suzuki method and utilizes the entire building, including the Wutz Concert Hall on the first floor.

NORTH TONAWANDA ERIE RAILROAD STATION
111 Oliver Street, North Tonawanda

During the late 1800s and early 1900s there were 16 different railroad lines and four main trolley lines operating in North Tonawanda. This resulted in dangerous roadways with railroad crossings guarded by gates, as well as watchmen at some corners. Added to that were the trolleys on Webster, Tremont, Main, Goundry, Vandervoort, Robinson, Oliver, Payne, Sweeney and Ward, plus the High-Speed Line along Division. Between 1900 and 1930 about 100 people were injured and three people killed every year on the streets of North Tonawanda.

Figure 261 Erie Railway North Tonawanda Station 1910 PD photo Library of Congress

The Erie Railroad was chartered in 1832 and was the first railway in the U.S. to use the telegraph for its operations, along with being the first U.S. railroad over 400 miles in length. It started operating in the Tonawandas in the 1850s and in 1922 built the Erie Railroad freight depot at 111 Oliver Street, near Goundry Street. This was midway between Buffalo and Niagara Falls, and with the industry in North Tonawanda it became a busy freight artery. For a period of time a regular schedule of passenger trains was routed through the terminal and the International Railway Company also ran its trolley on the Erie Railroad right-of-way. The New York Central passenger terminal was located about a block away on Main Street near Goundry.

Until 1960 the Oliver Street Erie Terminal served trains, and the Railway Historical Society purchased the terminal from Conrail in 1986. The museum displays two bay window cabooses, one from the Erie Railroad and one from New York Central. It also has a gasoline powered Plymouth 20-Tonner locomotive and Witcomb 50-Ton Diesel-Hydraulic centercab switcher, along with a worker's hand car that you can ride.

The Niagara Frontier Chapter of the National Railway Historical Society (NRHS) received its charter on February 1, 1942 and is one of the oldest in the country. Its original members were associated with the Buffalo Division of the Railroad Enthusiasts. They changed their name to the Niagara Frontier NRHS Inc. in 1988 and on June 1, 2003, opened their Railroad Museum in the historic Erie Freight Terminal.

This museum sits along the Erie-Lackawanna tracks, displaying items in the former freight depot and ticket office. An abandoned New York Central railroad tower is across the street, reminding people of the heritage of the railroads in the Tonawandas.

REMINGTON RAND BUILDING
162-184 Sweeney Street, North Tonawanda

Figure 262 Remington Building 2008 photo credit Dennis Reed Jr. nthistory.com

This building is an example of the early 20th century daylight factory building. The front facing gable building (184 Sweeney) was constructed in 1895 as a Power House for the Buffalo & Niagara Electric Railway Company. The reinforced concrete frame and brick factory buildings were added in 1913, 1917, 1919 and 1921 for the Herschell Spillman Motor Company.

The powerhouse building at 184 Sweeney became the trolley barn for the International Railway Corp. and was the original section occupied by Herschell Spillman.

Allan Herschell left the Armitage Herschell Company in 1900 and formed the Herschell Spillman Company with his brother-in-law Edward O. Spillman, who was an early developer of the internal combustion engine. They purchased 162-196 Sweeney Street and started making engines and cars. The company only manufactured a few cars but their engines were used by numerous automobile manufacturers, including Daniels Motor Company and Peerless. They also made engines for the Curtis Aeroplane Company and continued the carousel manufacturing that Allan Herschell developed after they purchased the assets of the Armitage Herschell Company in 1903.

Herschell Spillman continued making engines and carousels at the building until 1924 when they sold it to Rand Kardex Inc. in 1925. Rand Kardex was created from the merger of Rand Ledger Company (owned by James Rand, Sr.) and American Kardex (owned by his son James Rand, Jr.). They combined the Rand Company factory facilities at 95-111 Goundry Street and a Payne Avenue plant at the Junction in North Tonawanda with the American Kardex plant at 532 Main Street in Tonawanda in the Sweeney Street complex.

In 1927, Rand Kardex merged with the Remington Typewriter Company, Dalton and several other office machine companies to form the Remington Rand Company. The typewriter and office machine manufacturing were consolidated at the Sweeney Street Company. In 1951 the company released the UNIVAC I computer, the first mainframe computer for the U.S. Census Bureau. The computer was so large it was housed in the Sweeney Street building and companies came there to process information. The company was acquired by Sperry Corp. in 1955, becoming known as Sperry Rand. The North Tonawanda plant was utilized until the 1960s.

The building was converted to the Remington Lofts with commercial space on the first floor and apartments on the upper three floors in 2012. The 1895 former trolley power house at 184 Sweeney is now the Remington Tavern.

RIVIERA THEATRE
67 Webster Street, North Tonawanda

On December 30, 1926 the 1140 seat capacity Twin Cities Rivera opened at the Webster Street building patterned in the Italian Renaissance style by architects Leon H. Lampart & Sons. Financing of the new theater was arranged by Max Yellow, president of Loew's Buffalo Theatre Company. The construction was managed by Henry Henschel, President of the Owners Corporation of the theatre and it was managed by James J. Kelly. In addition to silent films accompanied by organist Fred Meyer on the Mighty Wurlitzer, the stage featured vaudeville and music events, as well as magic shows.

Figure 263 Riviera Theatre with remodeled lobby & ticket office 2025 photo credit Rick Falkowski

Henry Henschel was a real estate developer who owned other properties on Main, Tremont, Webster and Goundry Streets. He was head of the Tonawanda Apartments, owner of Brown's Hotel and real estate on the city of Tonawanda's Main Street. It was the intention that the Rivera would become the cornerstone of the Webster Street business district.

The Depression resulted in difficult times for the theater. In 1930 although Max Yellon still owned the property, management was assumed by Michael Shea of Paramount Publix Corp. and the name was changed to Shea's Riviera. In 1939 Dipson and Basil Theaters took over operations of the theater.

When movies with sound replaced silent films, the Wurlitzer organ was not used to accompany the movies and the organ was not utilized for special concerts. The organ fell into disrepair and Carlton Finch was hired to restore the Wurlitzer. On D-Day June 6, 1944 Fisk gave the first concert on the organ in over 10 years. It again fell silent until the Niagara Frontier Theatre Organ Enthusiasts presented Fisk in a concert in March 1962.

Under various owners the building deteriorated and the Niagara Frontier Organ Society pitched in to clean it up. They restored the Wurlitzer using parts from the organ removed from the Kensington Theatre, purchased the chandelier from the Genesee Theater for the main theater and a chandelier from the Park Lane Restaurant for the lobby. Eventually they purchased the building in 1988.

The Society just completed another major renovation that expanded the lobby, added backstage facilities, additional bathrooms and other amenities. It is now known for its shows by major recording artists, Friday night tribute concerts and Wurlitzer Organ events. It is once again a major feature of the downtown North Tonawanda Webster Street business district.

Wurlitzer Building

908 Niagara Falls Boulevard, North Tonawanda

Figure 264 *Wurlitzer Events Center 2025 photo credit Rick Falkowski*

Eugene DeKleist developed the fairground barrel for use in carousels while working for the French company Limonaire Freres. He moved to London in the 1880s and started doing business with the Armitage Herschell Company in North Tonawanda. The U.S. passed a tariff on organs in 1892 and Allen Herschell convinced DeKleist to move to WNY.

Arriving in the U.S., DeKleist worked for the Armitage-Herschell Company factory at Goundry and Oliver Street (current site of the Carousel Park Apartments). In 1893 he formed the North Tonawanda Barrel Organ factory and opened a production facility in the Martinville section of North Tonawanda.

The Wurlitzer family began making musical instruments in the 17th century. Rudolph Wurlitzer immigrated to the U.S. and formed the Rudolph Wurlitzer Company in Cincinnati Ohio in 1853. He sold instruments imported from his family in Germany, built the first Wurlitzer piano in 1880 and in 1896 began selling a coin operated player piano called the Tonophone that was made by DeKleist. Their relationship was so fruitful that in 1897 Wurlitzer invested in the company and it was renamed the DeKleist Musical Instrument Mfg. Co.

In 1909 Wurlitzer purchased DeKleist's company and moved the Wurlitzer operations to North Tonawanda. Always looking to expand, they hired Robert Hope Jones in 1910 and began making the Wurlitzer Theater Organ that Jones designed. It became the industry standard and Mighty Wurlitzer organs were installed in theaters and concerts halls worldwide.

Rudolph's son Farney Wurlitzer purchased a patented jukebox mechanism in 1933 and hired staff to design and market the product. By the late 1930s Wurlitzer produced over 45,000 jukeboxes a year. Manufacturing pianos, organs, other musical instruments, music rolls, radios and jukeboxes, employment at the North Tonawanda factory peaked at 3,000 workers. It was the largest musical instruments manufacturing plant in the world.

The Wurlitzer plant was considered a modern and innovative factory. Manufacturing, sales and administrative divisions were all operated out of the building. When Seeburg Corp, became the jukebox industry leader, the jukebox portion of Wurlitzer was sold to a German company. The musical instrument side of the business was sold to the Baldwin Piano Company and eventually to Gibson Guitars.

Jukebox and organ production were phased out in 1972 and by 1976 Wurlitzer operations were moved to other locations. 908 Niagara Falls Boulevard is now the Wurlitzer Industrial Complex, an events center and home to over 40 different businesses.

TOWN OF ORCHARD PARK

PROFILES

This section includes profiles of the Town of **Orchard Park** and historic places in Orchard Park and the Town of **Sardinia**

 # Town of Orchard Park

In 1797, the Holland Land Company (HLC) acquired Western New York, with Joseph Ellicott leading the survey. The region that is now Orchard Park was promoted as having fertile soil, abundant water, and generous timber. Ellicott offered land at an average of $2 per acre—significantly less than the $20 per acre in eastern New York. The HLC's generous credit terms allowed many families to homestead with minimal initial expenditure. The allure of this lush area resonated with Quaker communities from Vermont, eastern New York and Pennsylvania, who sought quiet communities away from the big cities. In 1803, Didymus C. Kinney and his family were the first recorded settlers in Orchard Park, followed the next year by Ezekiel Smith, Amos Colvin, and David Eddy, a Quaker who purchased nearly 600 acres. The Eddy family became central figures during the early years of the settlement. In 1804, The Middle Road (later Big Tree Road) was completed, which connected Lake Erie to Orchard Park and Hamburg, greatly contributing to the area's growth and development.

Figure 265 Lincoln Street in Orchard Park 1908 PD

In December 1811, the Quaker's Society of Friends purchased land at the Four Corners (today's Village Center) to build a meeting house. The log house they built is considered the first church structure of any denomination in present-day Erie County. The Four Corners area was originally part of the Town of Hamburgh and named "Potter's Corners" in honor of the prominent Quaker family by that name. In 1812, Daniel Sumner became the first settler on the highest land in the region, now known as Chestnut Ridge.

The first documented common school, District #5 School House, was constructed in the southwest part of the township in 1820. By then, over 25 Quaker families had settled in the community. They coexisted peacefully with non-Quaker settlers, though their lifestyle was much more reserved and restrictive than their counterparts. They established the first lending library in 1823, and their own log schoolhouse in early 1826. Later, in 1866, Quaker John Allen built a boarding academy, which became the East Hamburgh Friends Institute a few years later. It operated until 1881 when a portion was sold to the public school district, and the remainder burned in 1882. Hamburgh's eastern half separated and became East Hamburgh in 1850.

The Seneca Native Americans ceded their Buffalo Creek Reservation in 1851, opening land north of Webster Road to settlers. This resulted in the arrival of German immigrants, who established a significant community in the northeastern part of Orchard Park and on farms to the south. The informal name Orchard Park emerged around 1882, reflecting the community's resemblance to a park of orchards, and was officially incorporated as a village in 1921. The entire township officially became Orchard Park in 1934. Infrastructure improvements were made, including the upgrade of dirt roads to plank, and eventually stone and brick. The railroad extended to Orchard Park in 1883, and an electric trolley line connected Buffalo to Orchard Park in 1900 which operated until 1932. In turn, the early 1900s saw a growing number of city residents moving southward, particularly a large number of Irish families from South Buffalo.

Figure 266 Friends Meeting House Orchard Park 1911 PD

Figure 267 Orchard Park Country Club in 1920s PD

Orchard Park's development was significantly impacted by businessman and philanthropist Harry Yates, an individual who significantly contributed to the community. Beginning in the early 1900s, Yates purchased thousands of acres and made substantial donations to the town, including the site of the railroad depot and library (1911), Green Lake (1912), the Girl Scout Camp (1920), Yates Park (1942), two churches and a cemetery.

Today, Orchard Park is a vibrant, flourishing community with elegant neighborhoods, upscale shops and high-end restaurants. Yet, it has maintained its unique rural charm by retaining miles of open landscape, rolling hills and pristine countryside.

by Doreen Gallagher Regan

Chestnut Ridge Park
6121 Chestnut Ridge Road, Orchard Park

Figure 268 Original Casino Building (late 1920's) before it burned

One of the most popular destinations in Western New York is Chestnut Ridge Park. Founded in the spring of 1925 and named after the line of chestnut trees that once stood along the hilltops, it was one of the first parks established in Erie County. It is also the biggest county park in the area, with 1,200 acres of rugged terrain, mature woodlands, open meadows, beautiful nature trails and easily accessible picnic areas.

The park also includes several structures dating back to the Works Progress Administration (WPA) era of the 1930's, which was responsible for a significant portion of the park's infrastructure and development, including several vintage buildings that have stood the test of time.

A favorite spot among visitors is the large grassy hillside that offers breathtaking panoramic views of downtown Buffalo and the Canadian shoreline. During the snowy winter months, it becomes a beloved destination for sledding, skiing, snowboarding and tobogganing. Sitting at the top of the hill is a set of historic toboggan chutes dating back to the 1930's. The four chutes stand as one of the last remaining sets of toboggan runs in the United States. They are located next to the "Casino" building, where sledders can warm up inside by an enormous stone hearth.

The Casino itself has an interesting history. Originally built in 1925, it served as a versatile meeting space for both public and private gatherings. Its design included a large fireplace, a concession counter, and an observation platform on the upper level, all contributing to the visitor experience. The original structure burned in a fire in 1932 and was replaced with a larger timber and stone casino in 1938. The builders recycled the stone from streets in the area during a repaving project, and sections of the Erie Canal that were being backfilled around that time. Most of the wood came from the park forest directly. Unfortunately, a fungal blight destroyed the chestnut trees by mid-century.

The southwestern portion of the park, sometimes referred to as the Shale Creek Preserve, has a remarkable natural wonder called the "Eternal Flame" that burns under a waterfall. Chestnut Ridge Park and the Casino Building remain open year-round for visitors to enjoy.

by Doreen Gallagher Regan

Figure 269 Eternal Flame
Chestnut Ridge Conservancy

JOHNSON-JOLLS HOUSE
4287 South Buffalo St., Orchard Park

The long-time residence of Dr. Willard B. Jolls, a prominent country physician who served his community throughout much of the 20th century, is a historic centerpiece in the heart of Orchard Park. It was originally built for a merchant named Ambrose Johnson and his wife Mary Abbey, who moved to Orchard Park around 1855 and later co-founded a successful dry goods store on the corner of South Buffalo Street and East Quaker Road. Their appreciation for Italianate style homes led them to build this elegant brick structure in 1870, where they lived for the remainder of their lives.

Figure 270 Johnson Jolls House
photo courtesy Orchard Park Historical Society

After Ambrose and Mary passed away, their daughter Ava rented the house to Dr. Jolls and his wife Ida. Dr. Jolls, a graduate of the University at Buffalo Medical School, established his practice in Orchard Park, which had only 350 residents at the time. In 1902, he purchased the Johnson house and used the front rooms as his waiting room and office before creating a designated medical space at the rear. Over his 65-year career as the town's beloved doctor, he provided medical care to countless residents and delivered over 1,200 babies, often making house calls by horse and buggy prior to owning a car. His practice included dentistry as well as ophthalmology and he grew his own medicinal herbs in the backyard. For a time, Dr. Jolls served as the Orchard Park Health Officer and was an advocate for better sanitary conditions, leading to the implementation of a more modern sanitation system. Dr. Jolls also wrote a weekly health column for the Orchard Park Press. He donated a portion of his land for the town's municipal building, which was dedicated in 1949 and lived in the house with Ida and their housekeeper, Millie M. Michelfelder, until his passing in 1963.

Having no children, the Jolls left their home to Millie. After she passed away, her estate sold the property to the Town of Orchard Park in 1979, and the home was listed on the National Register of Historic Places a year later. It was rented until 1996, and then became the Johnson-Jolls House Museum, thanks to a partnership between the town and the Orchard Park Historical Society, who continue to support its preservation. The house, featuring Dr. Jolls' original three-room medical office, has been carefully restored to reflect its appearance during his years of occupancy.

by Doreen Gallagher Regan

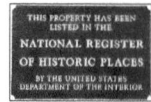

ORCHARD PARK BUFFALO, ROCHESTER, PITTSBURGH STATION

395 South Lincoln Avenue, Orchard Park

*Figure 271 Orchard Park BR&P Train Depot
photo courtesy Western New York Railway Historical Society*

The Buffalo, Rochester and Pittsburgh (BR&P) Railway Station in Orchard Park is a beautifully preserved historical structure that was built in 1911 and opened to the public in 1912. The station was made possible by Harry Yates, a wealthy businessman of the coal mining, hotel and railroad industries. Yates lived on East Quaker Road in an area then known as East Hamburg (renamed Orchard Park in 1932), where he owned several farms and used the local train depot to ship cattle and dairy products to Buffalo. Yates often traveled to Auburndale, Massachusetts to golf, and was enamored by its Romanesque style train station built by renowned architect H.H. Richardson. He decided to build a nearly identical replica in Orchard Park, donating land on South Lincoln Avenue and using Richardson's design plans to create an extravagant depot certain to impress visitors. Constructed of brick rather than stone and influenced by the popular Arts and Crafts movement of the time, it was designed with an arched porte-cochere and 160 foot-long canopied platform. The interior, adorned with wood wainscoting, exposed ceiling beams and oak benches, had separate waiting rooms for men and women, with a ticket counter in between. The surrounding gardens were inspired by Frederick Law Olmsted and required two full-time gardeners. The station also had a freight house, a windmill, sewer system and water well.

The Orchard Park BR&P station offered several daily commutes to Buffalo, leading Orchard Park to become one of the largest suburbs in Western New York. It also connected the area to a broader network of rail systems that extended into Pittsburgh, the Pennsylvania coalmines and beyond. The station was a vibrant hub of activity for over 40 years, but passenger service slowly began to decline and finally ended in 1955, while freight service continued until 1979. The depot and freight house were purchased in 1971 by local developers Mr. and Mrs. Edmund F. Burke. They initially considered converting the depot into a restaurant, but in 1983 donated the property to the Western New York Railway Historical Society (WNYRHS), who then embarked on an ambitious project to restore it to its original 1912 grandeur.

Now named the WNYRHS museum, it is listed on state and national historic registers of historic places. In 2016, several scenes from the movie *Marshall*, and in 2019, a small part in *A Quiet Place Part Two* were filmed at the depot.

by Doreen Gallagher Regan

OLMSTED CAMP
12820 Benton Road, Sardinia

Figure 272 Olmsted Camp

The Olmsted Camp was founded in the late 1800s when John Bartow Olmsted, an attorney from Buffalo, went on a fishing trip to Cattaraugus Creek near Chaffee, NY. While hiking along the creek, he noticed a beautiful red brick Greek Revival farmhouse on top of the bank. The house was part of the 188-acre Rider-Hopkins Farm. Olmsted was so enamored by the beauty of the location that he asked the owner if he could come back with his family. Over the next few years, Olmsted, his wife Clara, and their six sons rented out a section of the farmhouse from Mrs. Hopkins during their summer vacation until 1898, when Olmsted leased five acres of the land to establish a family campsite. Each summer, the family would arrive by train from Buffalo and be transported to the farm by a horse-drawn cart. They initially stayed in canvas tents with wooden platforms equipped with sleeping cots and furniture.

In 1909, the Hopkins family gave the Olmsteds permission to build a six-bedroom lodge on their leased property. John Olmsted's fourth son, Harold LeRoy Olmsted, had just graduated from Harvard University with a B.F.A. in architecture, so John commissioned him to design the structure. Harold drew up plans for an Adirondack style lodge that reflected the Arts and Crafts movement popular at the time. A one-story barn/garage was also built that year, which had a second-floor dormitory added in 1921. Two small sleeping cabins were constructed later on, along with a tennis court made of clay excavated from the banks of the Cattaraugus Creek.

In 1944, Harold's daughter Emily Roderick and her husband purchased the camp buildings as well as the entire Rider-Hopkins farm, keeping the entire compound intact. From 1991 to 1997, the newly established Western New York Land Conservancy utilized the farmhouse as its headquarters, and often hosted musical events on the campgrounds to raise funds for their organization. Then, in 1998, the Rider-Hopkins Farm and Olmsted Camp were officially listed on the National Register of Historic Places by the United States Department of the Interior. The Olmsted Camp is a prime example of how land shifted from farming to recreation at the turn of the century as American cities became overcrowded, and the middle-class urbanites wanted an escape to peaceful countryside retreats.

by Doreen Gallagher Regan

VILLAGE OF SPRINGVILLE

TOWN OF COLDEN PROFILES

This section includes profiles of the Village of **Springville** and historic places in the Town of **Colden** and in the Village of Springville.

Village of Springville

The Village of Springville in the Town of Concord was first settled in 1807. Its proximity to Cattaraugus Creek created opportunities for early factory, trade and service businesses.

Christopher Stone was the first non-native American settler, purchasing 787 acres of land for $1,575 in 1807. Springville got its name from the many freshwater springs in the area and was first known as Fiddlers Green. The village of Springville was incorporated in 1834.

The town of Concord was established in 1812 and originally included the neighboring towns of Sardinia, Collins and North Collins, taking its present form in 1822. An early settler was Jeremiah Richardson who established Woodside Farms in the Morton Corners section of town. His family built a recreation hall known as the Woodside Dance Hall, popular until it burned down in 1958.

By 1860 Springville began to emerge as a regional trade center with several small businesses including a woolen factory, two planing mills, turning shop, sawmill, two grist mills, tannery, stone sawing mill, foundry and machine shop. The area around town was agricultural and railroad services started in 1878.

In the Colden area, Richard Buffum and his employee James Bloomfield built roads to new farmhouses, assisting in developing the community. Mary Eddy taught at the first school and Silas Lewis was elected the first supervisor when the town was organized in 1828. E.P Hatch opened the first store (1831) and the first tannery opened (1833). Dr. Philo Baker was the first physician (1838), John Hedges opened a hotel (1850), the Livingstone Lodge #255 was organized (1852), Joslyn M. Carbin built a shingle mill that became a cheese factory (1857) and Richard Shelley opened a brick store (1858).

The Buffalo, Rochester & Pittsburgh Railroad built a 540-foot-long and 145-foot-high bridge in 1882 over Cattaraugus Creek Gorge. That was replaced in 1898 by the current 780 foot long and 190-foot-high bridge. In 1899 the railroad purchased a 150-acre farm on the west banks of the creek and opened Cascade Park. For a 15-cent ride on the railroad you could enjoy the park's walkways, swimming, dining hall and ballroom. In 1922 the park was sold to members that created the Springville Country Club.

Figure 273 Springville Railroad Depot 1910 postcard PD

For info about Springville visit the Concorde Historical Society Campus at 17 Franklin Street, Lucy Bensley Research Center at 23 N. Buffalo Street or the Springville Railroad Depot at 227 W. Main.

Buffum Inn
8335 Boston-Colden Road, Colden

Figure 274 Buffum Inn PD

The Buffum Inn was built by Richard Buffum, a wealthy mill owner from New England. He left Rhode Island in 1810 with his wife and children to start a new settlement in a section of Holland that is now Colden. He purchased 2000 acres from the Holland Land Company and became the first settler to take up residence there. The elevation and water supply of Cazenovia Creek made it an ideal location for his new homestead. Buffum built a grist mill in 1814 along the creek and named his new town Buffum's Mills. In 1828, the township was organized and The Buffum Inn was built. The inn was constructed with sawed planks rather than logs, modeled after Buffum's house back in Rhode Island. It was the first of its kind to be built in the new settlement, as sawed planks were just becoming more accessible and highly desirable for construction. The inn provided the locals with a tavern and a large second-story room that became a well-known destination for town hall meetings and local dances. In addition to being an inn the building was the meeting place for Livingstone Masonic Lodge #255 F. & A.M.

When the first post office was established in 1830, it was located in the home of Leander Robert. Robert named his post office Colden, after Cadwalder D. Colden, a state senator. The mail service was then moved to the Buffum Inn when Robert Buffum became the postmaster three years later, as the population increased to about 400 residents. The post office was still referred to as the Colden post, so Buffum's Mills eventually got renamed Colden.

Richard Buffum passed away in 1847 and the inn was sold by his son in 1855. From 1906 to the 1960s it was owned by the Hun family who then gifted it to their servant, Addy Wrest. Ownership then returned to the Buffums after they purchased it in 1968. The family created the Buffum Family Association to pay for its upkeep and placed a historical marker on the structure in 1970. A subsequent historical marker for the Buffum Homestead was erected a few feet away by the Erie County Sesquicentennial Committee in 1971.

The building is now the Buffum Museum and is available for tours by appointment.

by Doreen Gallagher Regan

Springville-Griffith Institute
290 North Buffalo Street, Springville

The Springville Academy was the first high school formed in Erie County. The original subscription for raising funds to build the school was passed in 1825. The construction of the school began in 1827 and the first students were admitted in 1830. Only one school academy in the area of the Holland Purchase or Western New York is older and that is the Fredonia Academy, which was incorporated in 1824.

Figure 275 Griffith Institute old postcard PD

Archibald Griffin arrived in Springville in 1815 and was an early supporter of establishing a school in the village. He even taught classes at the log schoolhouse which preceded the founding of the Academy. In 1865 Archibald Griffith donated $10,000 to the Academy, to be used mainly for the education of orphaned and indigent children of the Town of Concord. In consideration of his donation, the name of the school was changed from the Academy to Griffith Institute.

The school gained a reputation for excellent academic education, stressing discipline and good citizenship. Students were drawn from surrounding communities and boarded at local homes to attend the Institute.

Graduates of the school include a future governor, two senators, two mayors of Buffalo, six congressmen, Ralph B. Waite (pioneer of dental anesthesia), Edwin Walker (inventor with 50 patents including the ice cream scooper), Truman C. White (Judge who pronounced the death sentence for Leon Czolgosz, the assassin of President William McKinley) and Glenn "Pop" Warner (football coach who gave his name to youth football and donated the funds to start Springville's Warner Museum).

An 1885 addition to the Griffith Institute was designed by the first female architect in the U.S., Louise Blanchard Bethune of Buffalo. That addition doubled the size of the school.

The school district was initially centralized in 1941 to include students from Springville, Concord, Eden, Collins, Boston and Ashford. In 1953, it combined 33 separate schools into what is now four buildings, two elementary schools (grades K-5), a middle school (grades 6-8) and a high school (grades 9-12).

Final classes were held at the original Academy Street location of the school in 1970. The reorganization and centralization have made the Springville-Griffith Institute School District the largest geographical school district in New York state, servicing an area of nearly 141 square miles.

Waite Building
25 East Main Street, Springville

Figure 276 Waite Building Springville photo credit Paige Miller

Dental anesthetics, mouthwash, and toothpaste were manufactured by Dr. Ralph B. Waite's Antidolar Company in the Waite Building Springville. Construction of the Waite Building was completed in 1910. Prior to that, Waite developed and manufactured dental anesthetics in his home at 367 East Main Street. The Post Office was conveniently located on the first floor until 1937. The Antidolar Company shipped worldwide over 50,000 circulars per month. Currently, the Waite Building is home to a half dozen small businesses. The only change to the exterior of the building was to replace the original arch at the peak with a triangular-shaped gable. Red brick was almost substituted for the striking yellow-bricked exterior. However, Waite ordered the red brick, which was delivered by mistake, to be installed on his home until yellow brick arrived.

Ralph B. Waite was the son of Carlos Waite, who in 1868 established a dental practice in Springville. Ralph was literally born into the dental business in his father's office which was located across the street from the Waite Building. By the time Ralph was sixteen years old he was already assisting his father through which he became acutely aware of the pain associated with extracting teeth. After graduating from Griffith Institute in 1889, Ralph attended the Philadelphia Dental College (now Temple University). It was here that Waite learned of the first use in 1884 of cocaine as a local dental anesthetic. Prior to then, a slug of whiskey was commonly used. Before Waite graduated in 1891, he had developed and was marketing a safer formulation. It was the first local anesthetic manufactured with cocaine for general dental use. In 1898 Dr. Waite toured Europe introducing his discoveries. When procaine (trade name Novocain) was introduced in 1914, Dr. Waite shifted from using cocaine to procaine, which was not addictive.

The Antidolar company was the largest employer in Springville, employing between 100-200 people until the business was moved to West Virginia in 1948.

Dr. R.B Waite was also a philanthropist that believed in giving back to his local community. He and his lifetime friend, Glenn "Pop" Warner were founders of the Springville Country Club, which celebrated its 100th anniversary in 2002. He recommended that Warner purchase a home at 98 East Main Street to display Warner's collection of football memorabilia. Dr. Waite headed the first fund drive to construct the Bertrand Chaffee Hospital in Springville.

by Dave Ploetz

Warner Museum and Dygert Farm
98 East Main Street and 206 Elk Street, Springville

The Warner Museum was originally a house built in 1847 by George Crandall and was occupied by his descendants until 1953. The Concord Historical Society (CHS) purchased the Crandall house with funds donated by Glenn "Pop" Warner, based on a recommendation from his best friend, Dr. Ralph B. Waite.

Figure 277 Warner Museum photo credit Dave Ploetz

The Warner Museum contains displays from Pop's collection of football and sports memorabilia, Native American crafts, and original paintings, as well as articles of local historical significance which were previously stored in CHS founder Anna Brooks' home and Springville postmaster Monti Yost's barn loft. The CHS has since expanded its museum campus to four buildings: the Mercantile (2010) and Heritage Building (2018) and the original Warner Museum and Carriage House.

Pop Warner (1871-1954) was the one of the winningest coaches in college football history. Among coaches with at least ten seasons in NCAA Division I and its predecessors, Pop Warner is in fifth place based on total wins (319). He coached football at Iowa State, Georgia, Cornell, Carlisle, Pittsburgh, Stanford, Temple, and San Jose State, winning four national championships. Although Pop's name is used to endorse little league football (i.e., Pop Warner Little Scholars, Inc.) across the country, he never coached kids.

Pop's coaching career required him to travel around the country, but he frequently returned to Springville. He maintained a summer home which belonged to his parents at 292 East Main Street in addition to a residence in Palo Alto, California.

In addition to coaching football, Pop also coached track, including 1912 Olympic gold medalist Jim Thorpe, who was the first Native American to win a gold medal for the United States. In 1911 & 1912, Thorpe trained at the half-mile harness horse race track at the Dygert Farm, which was one of the earliest half-mile racetracks in New York. According to the farm's previous owner, Pete Dygert, Thorpe would run and keep pace with a horse and sulky travelling at slower speeds. This racetrack complete with grandstand was also the site of the Erie County Fair in 1866 & 1867. Abraham Dygert purchased this property in 1812 and built a farm owned by his descendants until 2024. The original farmhouse is still standing. The current barn was erected in 1933 on the same foundation as the original barn after it was lost in a fire that was intentionally set by a disgruntled farmhand.

by Dave Ploetz

CITY OF TONAWANDA PROFILES

This section includes profiles of the city of **Tonawanda** and historic places in the city.

City of Tonawanda

In the very early years of the 19th century, only a handful of buildings and individuals could be found at the mouth of Tonawanda Creek at the Niagara River. The land just south of the creek is today the city of Tonawanda.

Incorporated as a city in 1903, Tonawanda, like many places in New York, got its initial population and economic growth due to the opening of the Erie Canal. Tonawanda had an interesting position on the route of the canal in 1825. The original Erie Canal was incorporated into Tonawanda Creek until the canal neared the mouth of the creek. At that point a separate channel was dug through Tonawanda and on its way to Buffalo. The cutting of the canal through Tonawanda produced "Goose Island," an area north of the canal and south Tonawanda Harbor and the Niagara River. Goose Island was initially a residential area with store fronts along the canal. It later obtained the infamous reputation as where canal boatmen found their nighttime recreation. Industry, such as Tonawanda Board and Paper (later becoming the Robert Gair Company and Continental Can) was established on Goose Island in the 20th century.

Key to the importance of the Erie Canal to the growth and development of Tonawanda was a transition lock that allowed ships to move between the canal and Tonawanda Harbor. The lock and businesses supplying the canal trade made Canal Street (later Niagara Street) a booming economic hub.

Figure 278 Transition Lock from Erie Canal to Tonawanda Harbor photo courtesy Historical Society of the Tonawandas

In 1836, the railroad first came through Tonawanda and with the canal and Niagara River helped to establish commercial lines of transportation that spurred the economic growth of the area. Besides the many businesses needed to outfit and supply the canal trade and the people who ran it, lumber yards were established along the canal and the adjoining Ellicott Creek.

In 1854, what was known as the Village of Tonawanda was formally organized as a political entity. Initially, the Village comprised a north side in Niagara County and a south side in Erie County. Disagreements regarding taxation and the expenditure of funds led the north side of the village to sever its political connection to the rest of the Village in 1857.

Figure 279 Kibler High School photo courtesy Historical Society of the Tonawandas

By the mid-1800s, the population of the Village of Tonawanda was growing with individuals finding employment along the canal and the businesses it fostered. The need for lumber workers helped German immigration in the 1800s. German could be heard in many places as much as English.

In 1903, the population and economic importance of the Village had grown to such an extent that the Village was incorporated as the city of Tonawanda, with Frank Alliger as its first mayor. Tonawanda was only the second city incorporated in Erie County.

In 1905, New York State began changes to the Erie Canal that created the New York State Barge Canal. Chief among the changes was the decision to terminate the canal at Tonawanda. By the early 1920s, the canal from Tonawanda to Buffalo was closed and Tonawanda began to fill in the old canal bed. At the same time, Tonawanda saw the rerouting of trains that once cut through the very center of the city. These changes opened prime property for development and many businesses took advantage at a time when the lumber trade began to wane. Other industries stepped in to fill the void.

Besides the Robert Gair plant on Goose Island, large factories were built in Tonawanda, bringing Buffalo Steel and Columbus McKinnon to the city's Gastown area. In the south of the city, Spaulding Fibre was established in 1911. The Kardex Company, operated by James Rand, Jr., opened in 1920 and later became part of Remington Rand.

Figure 280 Niagara/Main/Young Traffic Circle before Urban Renewal
photo courtesy Historical Society of the Tonawandas

In the first part of the 20th century, the city of Tonawanda successfully transitioned from an economy built around the canal to one of industry. Interestingly, this was the same time that Tonawanda became known as the sea lion training capital of the world. People such as Thomas Webb, Roland Tiebor, and Harry Pickard established sea lion troupes trained in Tonawanda that traveled the world in circuses and later appeared in Hollywood movies and on such nation-wide television shows as The Ed Sullivan Show.

As with most places, when WWII started, the people and businesses of Tonawanda turned their attention to the war effort. Businesses were converted to war products production while hundreds of men and women of the city joined the armed forces. The service and sacrifice of the Niland brothers of Tonawanda became the basis for the film Saving Private Ryan.

By the 1960s, the large factories of Tonawanda started to close, and another period of economic transition began. The beginning of the 21st century has witnessed the city of Tonawanda embracing its history and location as it fosters tourism, examines its old canal days, and becomes a waterfront destination with such places as Niawanda Park, Gateway Harbor, and Ellicott Creek.

by James Williams, Historical Society of the Tonawandas

Benjamin Long Homestead
24 East Niagara Street, Tonawanda

The Benjamin Long Homestead was built in 1829 by Benjamin and Mary Hershey Long along the bank of the Erie Canal on part of 200 acres that Mary's father Christian Hershey purchased in 1815.

Benjamin and Mary Long arrived in Tonawanda from Lancaster County, Pennsylvania during December 1828, after traveling 330 miles in a covered wagon drawn by oxen. They were accompanied by their five daughters, aged 6 months to 16 years old. (The Longs later added another daughter and a son to the family.) After the spring thaw, they built a three story, 10 room house on a foundation of Medina red sandstone and hand-hewn logs cut from trees on the property. For the construction of the home, they used white oak for the supports and black walnut for the walls. Upon completion, the Long Homestead was one of 14 buildings that comprised the settlement of Tonawanda, with all the buildings clustered along the canal. The first Sunday school classes in the Tonawandas were held in the Long Homestead.

Figure 281 Long Homestead in 1920
photo courtesy Historical Society of the Tonawandas

The Erie Canal had been completed in 1825 and the house was at the mouth of Ellicott Creek where it meets Tonawanda Creek and the Erie Canal. The towpath on the south side of the canal was directly in front of the house. Rafts and barges of lumber passed on the water of the canal, making the Tonawandas the Lumber Capital of the World. One of these lumbermen was Henry P. Smith who married Long's daughter Christiana, after whom Christiana Street in North Tonawanda is named. The Long daughters and their descendants married into many of the prominent families of the Tonawandas, including the Rand, Simson, Leonard, Fassett, Kinsey, Harrington, Thomas and Hathaway families.

The house later became a livery stable and in 1941 opened as a restaurant called Jay's Log Cabin. It closed after a fire in 1971 and in 1975 the Long Homestead was purchased by the Historical Society of the Tonawandas and was restored as a museum. It was furnished with period pieces and furniture dating back to 1790, from families associated with Tonawanda and many items connected directly with the house. The home retains much of its original construction, including the fireplaces and stairways. It also displays artifacts and historic documents, including the Bible of Colonel John Sweeney dated 1816, the handwritten will of Benjamin Long and an 1824 poster offering land for sale in North Tonawanda, requesting those interested to contact George Goundry, James Sweeney or John Sweeney.

Tours are available through the Historical Society.

Tonawanda Armory
79 Delaware Street, Tonawanda

Figure 282 Tonawanda Armory museum.dmna.ny.gov PD

The Tonawanda Armory was built for the 25th Separate Company of the New York State Army National Guard, with construction completed in only six months, from the winter of 1896 to the summer of 1897. Designed by architect Isaac G. Perry, it is a fortress-like, castellated style edifice that reflects the influence of medieval architecture in the Late Victorian Richardsonian Romanesque style.

This building has a foundation of Warsaw blue granite and deep red brick walls, a two-story hipped roof administration building and a one and a half story eight bay gabled roof drill shed, divided by brick and granite buttresses with granite caps, with a five-story octagonal engaged tower at the southwest corner. The enclosed area is over 38,000 square feet.

Interior features of the administrative building include original oak staircases, elegant oak and tile mantels, white oak wainscoting and pressed metal ceilings with decorative cove moldings.

About 120 armories were built by New York State between 1700 and 1940. The Tonawanda Armory was one of nineteen armories designed by Isaac Perry and the most expensive, it cost about $85,000 or equivalent to approximately $6.8 million current value dollars. Perry was considered the "first state architect of New York" and he is best known for his design of the State Capital Building in Albany. Locally he also designed the Connecticut Street Armory and Niagara Falls Armory. Currently fewer than 24 armories remain in NYS as government buildings.

A Grand Ball attended by over 1,000 guests was held in 1897 to celebrate the inauguration of the armory. During the World Wars the 100-foot tower was used as an observation post to monitor the sky and the drill hall was filled to capacity during the 1930s for basketball games between Niagara University and St. Bonaventure College, along with other sporting and community events.

The armory became a community center in 1986 but it was vacant from 1996 to 2003. It was in such disrepair that the city of Tonawanda refused to purchase it for $1.00. The building was sold at an auction in 2004 and purchased for $70,000 by Mostafa Tanbakuchi, who refurbished the property into an events center with personal not public money. It is now known as Tonawanda Castle.

Tonawanda Railroad Station
113 Main Street, Tonawanda

In 1834 the Buffalo and Niagara Falls Railroad Company was incorporated to take over the Buffalo and Black Rock Company, that began as a horse pulled railway. The company was empowered to build a one or two track railroad between the city of Buffalo and Village of Niagara Falls.

The first railroad between Buffalo and Niagara Falls was completed and began running a regular schedule by November 1836, quite early in terms of railroad construction. It took about three hours for the wood stoked steam locomotive to complete the 28-mile journey. The Albany to Buffalo route was merged into one railway in 1853 and in 1869 it was consolidated into New York Central Railroad by Cornelius Vanderbilt.

Figure 283 New York Central Railroad Station in 1920 photo courtesy Historical Society of the Tonawandas

The railroad went through Tonawanda and North Tonawanda but the first railroad station was not built in Tonawanda until 1886. This building on a triangular piece of land bounded by Main, Fletcher and Grove Streets was built in what was considered the Steamboat Gothic style. The intricate details of the wooden gingerbread gables, along with hand carved animals and people were completed by wood workers from the carousel works of Alan Herschell. For over 50 years the wooden benches of the waiting room, heated by a pot-bellied stove, served the community. The passenger doors facing Main Street have been bricked over and the baggage door was on the north side of the depot.

At this time the railroad had a right of way on the east side Main Street in Tonawanda over the canal to Webster Street in North Tonawanda. More than 80 trains a day traveled this route, with passenger trains and long freight trains clogging the many intersections that the tracks crossed. The trains were dirty, noisy and dangerous to pedestrians, horse & buggy and later motorists. These trains went through town at high speeds because they had schedules to keep.

In 1917 plans were made to reroute the trains, benefiting the downtown areas and allowing the trains to increase the number of tracks. After the relocation was completed, passenger service was discontinued to the station in 1922. The building served as an American Legion Post, temporary schoolhouse and was the city library for 34 years. In 1964 the new Tonawanda City Library opened at 333 Main Street and the building was turned over to the Historical Society of the Tonawandas as a museum.

TOWN OF WEST SENECA

PROFILES

This section includes profiles of the Town of **West Seneca** and many historic places in the Town.

Town of West Seneca

The history of West Seneca, New York, follows an interesting path from Native American occupied wilderness to growth as one of the largest townships in Western New York.

The earliest inhabitants of the woodland area that was to become West Seneca were the Neutral (Neuter) and Wenroe Indians. Although few pictorial images exist of these people, 1000-year-old artifacts have been recovered at various sites. The Neutrals and Wenroes were followed by people of the Erie tribe of Indians. The powerful Seneca Indians eventually pushed out these early peoples and left their mark on the area.

Figure 284 Ebenezer Home now West Seneca Historical Society photo courtesy West Seneca Historical Society

Living on what would become the Buffalo Creek Indian Reservation in the late 1700s, the Senecas were, and continue to be, a part of the Iroquois Confederacy or Haudenosaunee. The Senecas gave the town its earliest substantial history as well as its eventual name. After the so-called Compromise Treaty of 1846, the Senecas left this area for the Cattaraugus and Allegany Reservations in the southern tier of Western New York State. The Buffalo Creek Reservation lands, including what would become West Seneca, were then opened up for sale and settlement by the first large group of Europeans in the area – the Ebenezers or "The Community of True Inspiration". Led by Christian Metz, this religious sect with their communal way of life left Germany to avoid persecution. From the late 1840s until the mid-1860s they transformed the area into several growing and prosperous communities including Upper Ebenezer (Blossom), Middle Ebenezer (Gardenville), Lower Ebenezer (Ebenezer,) and New Ebenezer (a small area on Clinton Street). Comprised of farmers, craftsmen, and tradesmen, the Ebenezers first occupied many of the Indian cabins and logging mills, etc., left by the Senecas before building their own homes and shops. A number of their sturdy structures still exist. Eventually numbering over two thousand people, they officially incorporated the town in 1851. Due to overcrowding, as well as the tempting proximity of the city of Buffalo, the Ebenezers left the area for Amana, Iowa by the mid-1860s.

With the formal establishment of the Town of Seneca in 1851 - renamed West Seneca to avoid confusion with a similarly named town in central New York State - and with the departure of the Ebenezer Society, the town began its next period of growth lasting almost one hundred years. Waves of immigrants – primarily from central Europe – as well as other area settlers populated the town and continued the agricultural and commercial development of the Ebenezer Society. Farms, shops, homes and factories popped up throughout the town. Some of the interesting and

Figure 285 Leydecker Covered Bridge
photo courtesy West Seneca Historical Society

notable places of this period were the Leydecker Road covered bridge, Wendling's Roadhouse Tavern, St. John's Orphanage, The Buffalo Gardenville and Ebenezer Railway, and the Ebenezer Glass Factory. Many of these places existed well into the twentieth century. Agriculture was the main occupation, however, and the town's many farms were known especially for their dairy products and vegetables like the Ebenezer onion. Schools and churches grew and flourished along with the growing population.

Some, like Fourteen Holy Helpers Roman Catholic Church, converted Ebenezer Society buildings for their own use.

Beginning about the time of the town's centennial celebration in 1951, and especially with the building of the Southgate Plaza in 1955, West Seneca started a period of tremendous growth as it changed into a true suburban community. Farms and grist mills were replaced by housing subdivisions and retail businesses – a process that continues. The centralization of the town's school districts in the late 1940s saw the old school districts merge into the West Seneca Central Schools with new buildings like the West Seneca Senior High School being built on Main Street, and old ones, like the Ebenezer High School on Mill Road, converted to elementary schools or closed. In the 1960s, the building by New York State of the huge West Seneca Developmental Center for Disabilities and Mental Health on East and West Road dramatically changed the landscape and employment opportunities. And the thousands of houses built for new residents looking to own their own homes increased the town's population to almost 46,000, making West Seneca the fourth largest town in the county. Construction in the 1950s of the New York State Thruway and the Aurora Expressway in the 1960s helped speed the town's development along.

Throughout its history, West Seneca was home to a number of interesting individuals, starting with some of the early Seneca Indian residents. Red Jacket or Sa-go-ye-wat-ha (circa 1758-1830) was a prominent chief who assisted the United States of America in negotiations with Midwest Indian tribes. Christian Ulrich (1839-1906) was a Civil War cavalryman involved in hunting down the assassin of President Abraham Lincoln, John Wilkes Booth. And one cannot leave out Old Shep (? – 1933) - the "Hermit of Leydecker Road". In more recent times, West Seneca has produced such luminaries as artist Charles Burchfield, Wilson Greatbatch, developer of the pacemaker, and rock musician Robby Takac, of the Goo Goo Dolls.

Add to this mix the so called "haunted" Ebenezer graveyard, Lein's Park and the Ebenezer cyclone of 1923 and you get the part of story of West Seneca, New York.

by Jim Pace, West Seneca Historian & West Seneca Historical Society

CHARLES E. BURCHFIELD NATURE & ART CENTER
2001 Union Road, West Seneca

In 1921, Charles Burchfield moved to Buffalo to accept the position of assistant designer for M.H. Birge & Sons, a prestigious wallpaper design company located at 390 Niagara Street. He lived at several apartments in the city before moving to 3574 Clinton Street in West Seneca.

Burchfield moved to West Seneca because he loved the country and the Seneca Street residence was on the bus line, only 20 minutes from the wallpaper factory. He enjoyed designing wallpaper but when he was promoted to department head in 1927, Burchfield did not like the added management responsibilities. Burchfield continued to sell his watercolor paintings and in August 1929 he decided to leave the wallpaper company to devote full attention to his artwork.

Figure 286 Charles Burchfield Home photo credit Mike Buckley

Across the street from Burchfield's Seneca Street home was land identified as Lots 94 & 95. That land has a rich history dating back to settlement by the Algonkian tribe or an offshoot of an Eskimo tribe. They were followed by the Mound Builders and the Erie Indians. The Seneca Indians of the Iroquois Five Nations Confederacy, also known as the Haudenosaunee, conquered the Erie and obtained the land. It was part of the Buffalo Creek Reservation and purchased by the Community of True Inspiration or Ebenezers in 1843. The Ebenezers built two millraces to support their sawmill, gristmill and tannery, turning the lot into an island

After the Ebenezers relocated to Iowa, much of the Ebenezer land was sold to German immigrants. Lot 94 and 95 became known as the Island Park or Ebenezer Park, with a hotel, dance hall, restaurant, picnic areas, boat house and canoeing in the millraces. The Island Park Hotel burned down in 1974.

To honor Charles Burchfield, in 1998 the town of West Seneca purchased the land across the street from his home. The Burchfield Nature and Art Center opened in 2000 and included a youth center and AmeriCorps offices. The 29-acre park now includes an amphitheater, playground, picnic areas, art installations and an education building. In addition, it has nature trails with boardwalks that highlight 12 placards of Burchfield's paintings, along with informational signage about the mill races and Middle Ebenezer Cemetery.

Burchfield created several of his nature and watercolor landscapes on what became the park site, including Rain and Wind Through the Tree. His home is directly across Clinton Street from the park and is identified as his former residence.

CHRISTIAN METZ HOUSE
12 School Street, West Seneca

*Figure 287 Christian Metz House 1903
photo courtesy West Seneca Historical Society*

This house was originally built around 1840 as the home of George Stanart, who operated the Indian sawmill on what is now Indian Church Road. When built the home was on the property of the Seneca Nation Buffalo Creek reservation.

After the property was purchased from the Ogden Land Company by the Community of True Inspiration, the home was occupied by the congregation's spiritual leader and prophet Christian Metz. The settlement was named Ebenezer in 1843 and in 1851 was incorporated by the Ebenezer Society as the town of Seneca, changed to West Seneca when it was discovered there was already a New York State town called Seneca in the Finger Lakes region, about 100 miles to the east.

Ebenezer was a communal self-sufficient community where the members of the Community of True Inspiration, a division from the Lutheran Church, lived a life of humility, dignity, self-denial, brotherly love and isolation from the temptations of society. Their life revolved around eleven weekly church services, with the assets from farming, their mills and craftwork shared among the congregants.

The Ebenezer community grew and by 1854 they required more land for their residents, activities and enterprises. The cost of land increased, the temptation of the city of Buffalo was encroaching upon the community, there was resentment from neighbors and grievances from dissatisfied former members, so Christian Metz relocated the community to larger, more isolated land in Iowa. There they formed the Amana Colonies, and their craftsmen created the Amana Corporation, manufacturers of household appliances.

After the Ebenezer lands were subdivided and sold to predominantly German immigrants, the area became known as the Gardenville District of West Seneca. The home had several different owners and served divergent purposes, including being a speakeasy during Prohibition. The building was not neglected but cosmetic changes like vinyl siding and modern windows upset the historic features of the property. In 2000 the state Parks, Recreation and Historic Preservation Department gave AmeriCorps, who occupied the building, a $200,000 grant. However, they used the funds to update rather than restore the building.

In 2012 the town of West Seneca took possession of the property. Restoration continues and the house is now maintained by the West Seneca Historical Society. Across from the Burchfield Nature and Arts Center, it is open to the public and available for historic tours.

LEIN'S PARK
810 Union Road, West Seneca

When Henry Lein opened Lein's Park in the early 1900s, he called it "The Greatest Summer Resort in Western New York." Admission was free and the park featured rustic themed buildings like a casino, hotel, bandstand, dance hall, bowling alley and numerous amusements.

Herny Lein was a successful businessman who owned Lein's Livestock Sales Stables in the Gardenville Section of West Seneca. He purchased lot 329, located on high ground, with abundant trees, south of Cazenovia Creek. He based the park off Starin's Glen Island Park, located in New Rochelle, Westchester County, just outside of New York City.

Figure 288 Lein's Park Welcome Arch PD

In 1895, Union Road ended at Seneca Street. Lein had to build a private road from Seneca Street south to Cazenovia Creek. To cross the creek, he built a wooden bridge, at a cost of $8,000, that led directly into the park. The bridge was used by the Buffalo, Gardenville & Ebenezer Railways, horse and carriage traffic and later automobiles. For a five-cent fare, electric trolly cars brought park visitors from the city line to the trolly station inside the park. After the bridge was destroyed by extreme ice flows during the severe winter of 1909/10, a temporary bridge was erected for people to walk across the creek. In 1911 the Town of West Seneca built a steel bridge, but the trolly only traveled to the north side of the creek.

Lein started building the park in 1896 and it held its grand opening in 1903. A 25' high and 25' wide Great Arch of Welcome greeted the patrons, and all the buildings had a rustic appearance. A 12-piece brass band performed in the bar, outside in the park and in the dance hall, which accommodated several hundred dancers. The Herschell built electric merry-go-round, with rocking horses, was a major attraction. Animal exhibits included a bear pit, with four black bears.

The opening of county parks and the advent of the automobile resulted in Lein Park closing in 1922. It was replaced by the Evangelical Association which opened Evangelical Park. It demolished all the Lein Park buildings except one and built a 1,000-person auditorium and two dormitories, changing its name to Buffalo Bible Conference.

Buffalo Bible Institute merged with Houghton College in 1969 to create a West Seneca Campus of Houghton College. When the West Seneca campus closed, Young Development converted 810 Union Road into the Park Lane Villas apartment complex.

Malecki Mansion

2544 Clinton Street, West Seneca

Figure 289 Malecki Mansion photo credit Rick Falkowski

This 24,000 square foot building on 12 acres of land is on Clinton Street, east of Harlem Road. It was built in 1890 and there is a pending proposal to convert the property into a housing development.

In the early 1900s the home was owned by the Catholic Diocese of Buffalo and housed nuns that worked at parochial schools. Horses were stabled in barns at the back of the property and the nuns would be driven by horse and carriage to St. Bernard's.

Joseph Malecki arrived in Buffalo in 1913 from Poland, where he was trained in the meat business. He set up a meat market on Broadway and expanded his business by opening a smokehouse on Person Street and packing house on Howard Street. Malecki's business expanded beyond the East Side and in 1948 Malecki's became the hot dog vendor for Ted's Hot Dogs.

During the 1930s Joseph Malecki purchased the home at 2544 Clinton Street, where he raised his six children on the white fenced lot where horses roamed the estate. The white mansion was a landmark in the eastern suburbs, was known to everyone as the Malecki Mansion and the name Malecki was synonymous with hot dogs, polish sausage and lunch meat. In 1965 the Malecki brand relocated to a $1.5 million processing plant at 2320 Clinton Street but Joseph Malecki passed away in 1964 and the house was too large for a family member to maintain it.

Ronald Malecki continued to expand the company after his father's death and the Polka Brand was introduced, with a logo of colorful polka dots. The brand was promoted as "Authentic Polish Sausage – made the delicious, Old-World way." However, the declining WNY market resulted in Malecki's closing in 1988. When Ted's Hot Dogs served the final Malecki's before switching to Sahlen's in 1988, people lined up at all Ted's locations to get their last Malecki's hot dog.

The home was sold in 1970 to Paul Snyder's Freezer Queen Company, with the mansion being expanded and transformed into office space. Freezer Queen maintained their headquarters at the mansion until the company closed. Buffalo Crushed Stone purchased the property and several other businesses operated at the address. It is currently owned by Rosen Publishing Group.

The proposed 2025 development would convert the former mansion and offices into apartments. Several other buildings would be constructed for a total of 88 units.

MAYER BROTHERS
1540 Seneca Creek Road, West Seneca

Mayer Brothers is one of the oldest family-owned businesses in New York State, founded in 1852 in West Seneca, NY. In addition, the company is one of the oldest cider mills in NYS, one of the largest processors of apple cider in North America and one of the oldest stores in WNY.

They offer brand-name apple beverages and bottled water, including contract and co-packing manufacturing to nationwide clients.

Figure 290 Mayer Brother Cider Mill 1900s photo from Company Archives

Jacob Mayer founded the company when he purchased a locally operated cider mill for farmers and families to bring apples from their orchards to be pressed into cider. Customers would supply their own barrels or jugs to fill with juice, before allowing it to ferment into hard cider. In the 1920s the Mayer family added baked goods, maple cider and other food items, to their own brand of apple cider. After Prohibition they even began making hard cider in 1936.

The company acquired the former Gerber Baby Foods facility in Barker, NY, which added hot filled juices, other drinks and additional apple cider processing capacity. They also introduced bottled water when the company located sources of mineral rich spring water in the foothills of the Allegheny Mountains.

To accommodate the increased product line and capacity, Mayer Brothers purchased storage space in Barker and Medina. At the Medina location they constructed a state-of-the-art controlled climate apple storage facility in the heart of New York State's apple growing area.

Every autumn they open their historic cider mill to the public and over 10,000 people a week visit to purchase the delicious cider and sample homestyle baked goods. To make your journey more than just a shopping trip, you can visit their pumpkin patch and enjoy free horse-drawn hayrides.

Although some of their products are seasonal by nature, their online shop is open year-round offering Mayer Brothers label apple butters, BBQ sauces, dips, jams, jellies, preserves, maple syrup, salad dressings, salsas and gift packs. In addition, you can find their products at area supermarkets and stores.

In business for over 170 years, the company is now being run by the 5th generation of the Mayer family and members of the 6th generation are already helping out at the store.

Schwabl's

789 Center Road, West Seneca

Figure 291 Semlitsch Tavern 1940 photo courtesy Schwabl's Restaurant

Schwabl's, one of the oldest restaurant businesses still operating in Erie County, is most famous for its traditional roast beef on kummelweck sandwiches, better known as "beef on weck". In 1837 Sebastian Schwabl, a German immigrant, began serving food in the Broadway neighborhood of Buffalo a few years after the city was officially incorporated. At that time, many European immigrants, including a large influx of Germans, were relocating to America in search of a better life.

As the population of Buffalo grew, so did the demand for Schwabl's, as their reputation for serving excellent quality food spread throughout the area. Soon, Sebastian Schwabl's four sons were opening restaurants in other locations around the city. One of the most popular spots was at the Parade House, a huge structure built in 1871 that stood at the entrance of Parade Park, now known as Martin Luther King, Jr. Park, in the Humboldt Parkway neighborhood. It was a lavish center for parties and entertainment frequented by the German-born community that lived nearby. Unfortunately, the Parade House burned to the ground in 1898. The Schwabl family then opened a restaurant near Pine Ridge and Genesee called Klein Deutschland. It was housed in a large entertainment complex that included a dance hall, bowling alley, merry-go-round, animal menagerie and botanical garden.

When the Pan American Exposition came to Buffalo in 1901, Schwabl's was there to serve food to the multitude of visitors. Right around that time, Schwabl's opened another restaurant in the small hamlet of Ebenezer, in a section of what is now West Seneca. In 1942, they opened their establishment on Center Road, where they still remain and continue to be widely popular.

In the early 2000s, after six generations of ownership, the Schwabl family sold the business to their employees, Cheryl and Gene Staychock, who retained many of the workers who had been with the restaurant for 10 to 40 years. The Staychocks have remained dedicated to Schwabl's proud tradition of using the finest quality ingredients for their traditional dishes such as German-style coleslaw, homemade

Figure 292 Schwabl's Restaurant 2025 photo credit Rick Falkowski

pickled beets, German potato salad, fresh homemade soups, cocktails prepared the "old-fashioned" way and of course beef on weck. Customers can still watch the roast beef being carved by the butcher behind the bar, and enjoy the Schwabl family recipes that have been handed down for almost 200 years.

by Doreen Gallegher Regan

TOWN OF WHEATFIELD PROFILES

This section includes profiles of the Town of **Wheatfield** and historic places in the Town.

Town of Wheatfield

The Town of Wheatfield lies in the southern section of Niagara County between the city of Niagara Falls to the west and Pendleton on its east. Most of the community was part of the Towns of Niagara and Cambria until 1836-1838, when the first Town Board meeting was held in schoolhouse No. 7 under Supervisor N.M. Ward.

Wheatfield was the last municipality to be formed in Niagara County. It began chiefly as a farming community and as a series of way-stops for those traveling to and from Niagara Falls or Lockport/Lake Ontario and the Tonawandas. A later three-time Supervisor, Lewis S. Payne, was a famous colonel in the American Civil War.

An early settler was George Burger who settled along the Niagara River in 1810, followed by Harvey Miller, who moved to Lockport and Niagara Falls Road in 1824. Established later by German immigrants was the hamlet of 'Neu Bergholz' in 1843, honoring their original community of Bergholz in the Ukermark area of north-eastern Germany. They then spread out to form the other hamlets of Martinsville, Walmore, Gratwick and St. Johnsburg.

Figure 293 6230 Baer Road
photo courtesy Justin Higner

The Baer House at 6230 Baer Road is an example of the early homes built in this area. It is the second oldest home in Wheatfield, built in 1824 and owned by the Baer family until 1984. The house has a hand-hewn wooden frame, built on a hand laid stone foundation. Beams are over eight inches in thickness and stones weigh as much as 300 pounds. When the walls were opened during remodeling, some of the vertical timbers still had bark on them.

The Kohler Homestead was built in 1860 at 16 Ward Road. It is rumored that it or a previous home at the location contained a tunnel that was a station on the Underground Railroad.

Wheatfield originally held North Tonawanda as an incorporated village within its borders along with the Martinsville, and Gratwick hamlets, but all were incorporated into the city of North Tonawanda by local referendum in 1894.

Figure 294 Kohler Homestead
photo courtesy Wheatfield Facebook page

Principle industries and contractors included Bell Aircraft (later Bell Aerospace) Corporation, the Carborundum Co.'s Coated Abrasive Products Division, Wheatfield Farms on River Road (later Demler Cider and Vinegar Mill), Voss Manufacturing Co. and Stoelting Machine Inc. among other historic names. A unique mid-20th century modern building was constructed in 1958 at 7227 Williams Road, when the street was still a farmers' dirt road. The Summit Park Mall on Williams Road, opened in 1973 but declined by the late 1990s and early 2000s. Today, it is under redevelopment.

The Sanborn Telephone Company was located on the corner of Lockport and Ward Roads, opposite from a present-day home that was the Shultz corner general store and farm. At the corner of Ward Road and Niagara Falls Boulevard was another general store, inn and stables that later installed gas pumps on the Ward Road side of the property. It was remodeled in 1912 and eventually became Janik's Steak House, a restaurant and country western music club. It was again rebuilt, utilizing part of the original building, as J.T. Wheatfields and Jack's Restaurant and Bar.

During the 1800s several taverns were built along Niagara Falls Boulevard at major crossroads to service the farmers, suppliers and travelers. Krull's Tavern dating to the late 1840s, Moeller's Tavern and store from the mid-1870s and across from the later-day Wurlitzer Factory was a tavern that became the Crystal Bar. The Sawyer Creek Inn, bar and restaurant built in the 1890s, was located on Nash Road and Niagara Falls Boulevard Another historic bar and restaurant establishment is the Walmore Inn, on Lockport Rd., built circa 1830. In 1896 William Voetsch, owner of the Edgewater Amusement Park on Grand Island, built the Edgewater Landing Hotel directly across the Niagara River on River Road. That later became the Wa-Ha-Kie Hotel. Another popular entertainment venue was the 1960s Peppermint Stick Teen Club, created in a former roller-skating rink on Ward Road.

Figure 295 Wa-ha-kie Hotel on River Road Wheatfield photo courtesy Town of Wheatfield

are schools located at each of the four Lutheran churches: Holy Ghost, and St. James's in Bergholz, St. John's in St. Johnsburg, and St. Peters on Walmore Road. Former schools include the smaller Bergholz, Nash Rd., and River Road early grade schools. Niagara Community College, originally founded in 1962 in Niagara Falls, is located immediately north in Cambria. Consolidation in the late 1950s created the Niagara-Wheatfield CSD out of our original nine districts of early-to-mid-1800s-era one-room schoolhouses.

The Shrine of the Infant Jesus was established in 1958 in a former one-room schoolhouse. It moved to a location on Niagara Falls Boulevard in 1978 and is operated by the Order if the Palatine Fathers.

Niagara Falls Air Base, partially located in Wheatfield, is Niagara County's largest employer, working alongside the newer Niagara Falls Airport.

Wheatfield has several parks and green spaces, most notably Oppenhiem County Park and Fairmont Park, located on Stieg and Nash Roads. The former, in part operating as the Oppenheim Zoo until the late 1980s, is known for its great spaces and annual 4th of July Fireworks show. The latter was originally a farm and a private community cemetery.

Volunteer Fire Companies include: Bergholz (formed in 1918), St. Johnsburg (1926), Adams (1924), Shawnee (1947) and Frontier (1938). American Legion Post 1451 on Ward Rd. was founded in about 1952.

by Justin Higner, Town of Wheatfield Historian, Mike Buckley & Rick Falkowski

BELL AIRCRAFT
Niagara Falls Boulevard, Wheatfield

Figure 296 Bell Aircraft photo courtesy Justin Higner

Larry Bell came to Buffalo in 1928 to work for Consolidated Aircraft. When Consolidated relocated to San Diego California in 1935 he remained in WNY and formed Bell Aircraft. Its initial location was in the former Consolidated plant at 2050 Elmwood Avenue, but when Bell received a contract to build 2,000 P-39 Airacobra fighter planes for use in WWII by the U.S. and Soviet Air Forces, the U.S. government assisted the company in building the Wheatfield Plant next to Niagara Falls Airport.

The Wheatfield plant employed as many as 28,000 employees, including many women wartime workers who received the "Rosie-the-Riveter" moniker. At the Wheatfield plant Bell manufactured the P-39 and P-63 aircraft. Between Curtis-Wright and Bell Aircraft, during 1940-1942 more aircraft were built in Buffalo than the rest or the entire aircraft industry combined and almost 33% of all U.S. aircraft flown during WWII were manufactured in Buffalo.

Bell developed the first commercial helicopter, the Model 30 designed by Arthur Young at the Bell Gardenville location in 1943. Helicopter manufacturing was based in Wheatfield and the Model 47 was the helicopter used during the Korean War, immortalized in the M*A*S*H movie and TV series. That evolved into the Huey Cobra during the Vietnam War.

After WWII Bell Aircraft consolidated all its operations at the Wheatfield plant. Bell built the first jet aircraft, the P-59, in the top-secret confines of the former Ford Motor plant at 2495 Main Street in Buffalo during 1942. It was at the Wheatfield location that Bell developed and performed the first test flights of the rocket powered X-1, the first aircraft to break the sound barrier on October 14, 1947. The X-2 attained speeds of 2,148 mph and an altitude of 126,000 feet in 1955 and helped pave the way for the founding of NASA in 1958.

Bell Aircraft in Wheatfield continued to make advancements in the aerospace industry with the development of Bell X-5, X-15, X-20 (Dyna-Soar – predecessor to the Space Shuttle), X-22 (vertical take-off), Bell Rocket Belt, Lunar Landing Training Vehicle, Agena rocket engine and amphibious hovercraft. In 1960 the helicopter division moved to Texas and in 1976 the company became Bell Aerospace Textron.

In 2025 portions of the Bell Wheatfield plant were demolished but Wheatfield Business Park LLC leases existing structures, and the Niagara Aerospace Museum displays and houses the archival, artifact and research inventory of the Bell company's long and storied legacy.

by Justin Higner & Rick Falkowski

Das Haus – German Heritage Museum
2549 Niagara Road, Wheatfield

In 1843, 800 Prussians left their homes, occupations, and families in Germany to make the 5,000-mile journey to a land they knew virtually nothing about. Their primary reason for leaving was to worship as they pleased and avoid government persecution for their religious beliefs.

These hardy farmers and craftsmen were the people that America needed. They landed in New York City and came to Western New York via the Erie Canal. Although the land in some other locations was more favorable, it was more expensive and these frugal settlers chose land that is currently in the villages of Bergholz, Walmore, Martinville and surrounding communities in the Town of Wheatfield.

Figure 297 Das Haus photo courtesy Justin Higner

Das Haus was originally a 19X27 ft. hand-hewn, Garrison type log cabin built in 1843. It was provided to the settlers by Wahington Hunt, a land agent for the Holland Land Company and later the governor of New York State. It is known as the Witwe (Widow) Mehwaldt Haus as it was sold to Justine Mehwaldt, wife of the community potter, in 1857 by the original owner Johann Hellert. Contributing to the authenticity of the museum, the house is located on the original site where it was built.

Einhaus was relocated from the Haseley Farm, less than a mile from its current location, where it was constructed in 1844. The structure is a hand-hewn oak timber framed house/barn combination that housed both the family and their animals. It was dismantled and reconstructed on the museum property in 2015 and displays the farming implements and artifacts that depict the life of the settlers in the 19th century.

There are not any metal fasteners in the structure. It was put together using hand cut mortise and tenon joints secured with pegs. This is a "Fachwerk" design, clay and straw filler in hand hewn timber 3–4-foot squares, a wood economy saving method that was prevalent in the Germanic states and imported with the immigrants.

Der Stall is a replica of the barn buildings found in the 19th century. This building serves as a library where the archives, artifacts and documents of the original community are preserved.

In the Bergholz area German remained the primary language until after WWI, when residents left the farms to obtain factory jobs and began learning English at work or school.

by Justin Higner & Rick Falkowski

Sawyer Creek Hotel

3264 Niagara Falls Boulevard, Wheatfield

Figure 298 Sawyer Creek Hotel photo courtesy Justin Higner

The Sawyer Creek Hotel and restaurant, was built in 1888 in Wheatfield at the intersection of Niagara Falls Boulevard and Nash Road. In September 1915, John Wiegand purchased the property from Jacob Knoell, after which nearby Knoll Road is named.

The main building has a hand-laid stone foundation and hand-hewn wooden beams that likely include a number of reused beams from much older buildings in the area. The town of Wheatfield paid $7.00 yearly for Mr. Wiegand to maintain a water pump and trough for horses.

While their horses were refreshed and rested, farmers caught up on the local news and gossip, played a game of cards or shopped in the store located in half of the present barroom. The store featured items including plug tobacco, cigarettes, candy, sardines, crackers, kerosene oil and seasonal items. To satisfy the farmers thirst, cold beer refrigerated in the ice house from ice the Wiegand's cut every winter at a pond in Sawyer Creek. The Weigand family lived in rooms now occupied by the current dining room and the second floor had eight rooms, seven bedrooms and a shared bathroom. In the 1920s two gasoline pumps were added where the water pump now stands on the property.

During prohibition Mr. Wiegand made his own home brew and supposed near beer to keep the business operating. The back kitchen section was added in 1935 and offered a limited menu. Some of the underpinnings for this and an enclosed breezeway side addition were made up of older paver bricks pulled up from the boulevard after it was repaved in asphalt.

To accommodate shift workers at Bell Aircraft and other related facilities during World War II, the tavern opened at 8:30 most mornings. The menu consisted of soup, ham and cheese sandwiches, limburger cheese and onion sandwiches and western-style sandwiches along with "Keg birch beer". No full dinners were served until the Cassatas took over the business.

John Wiegand passed away in April 1943. His sons Bill, John Jr., Adolph, Joe and Fritz continued the business. The hotel portion was shut down and Fritz managed it until 1981 as a bar and filling station.

In 1984, the building was taken over by former CFL Quarterback and Grey Cup champion Rick Cassata, along with his children Dana, Justin and Brett. The Cassata family still operates this business.

by Justin Higner and Rick Falkowski

VILLAGE OF WILLIAMSVILLE

TOWN OF AMHERST PROFILES

This section includes profiles of the Village of **Williamsville** and several historic places in the Town of **Amherst** and in the Village.

Village of Williamsville/ Town of Amherst

A Native American path called the Great Central Trail or the Great Iroquois Trail existed roughly on the same alignment as the current Main Street (NY Route 5). It was surveyed by the Holland Land Company in 1798 and became known as the Buffalo Road, serving as the principal route between Buffalo and settlements to the east.

The Holland Land Company offered lots at $2.00 per acre to anyone who would build a tavern along the Buffalo Road. Asa Ransom accepted that offer in 1799 when he purchased land in what became Clarence. In 1805, his brother Elias Ransom also accepted this offer and built a log tavern two miles west of what became Williamsville, on Buffalo Road near what became Bailey Avenue.

Due to Asa's purchase, Clarence was the first area settled on the route to Buffalo. The next area along Buffalo Road where land was purchased was at 11 Mile Creek. In 1799, Benjamin Ellicott, a surveyor and brother of Joseph Ellicott, and John Thompson purchased 300 acres of land which became the village of Williamsville. In return for Ellicott's service to the Holland Land Company, this land was sold at $2.00 an acre.

The land Ellicott purchased included the falls, which were called Ga-sko-sa-da-ne-o or "many falls" by the Seneca. It is now known as Glen Falls. The original name of the creek was Eleven Mile Creek, renamed Ellicott Creek in honor of Joseph Ellicott. Thompson built a mill near the falls, which he either never opened or just operated for just a short time. He built his home above the falls at what is now Main and Oakgrove Streets (in front of current Ed Young's Hardware). It was the first permanent residence built in Williamsville and was known as the Evans House, until it was torn down in 1955.

Figure 299 Glen Falls early 1900s photo Eastern Mill & Tannery edyoungs.com PD

In 1804, most of the Ellicott/ Thompson land and Thompson's abandoned mill was purchased by Jonas Williams, a clerk with the Holland Land Company and David Evans, a nephew of Joseph Ellicott. David Evans returned to Philadelphia but Williams remained to develop the property. In 1811, Williams built a mill (later referred to as the Dodge Mill) on the east side of Ellicott Creek. With sufficient water available from the falls for an overshot wheel powered without the construction of a dam or raceway, in front of that grist mill, he built a tannery. The mill on the west side was abandoned and replaced by the mill on Spring Street, known as the Williamsville Water Mill. This restored historic red building now houses Sweet Jenny's Ice Cream.

With the waterpower in the Williamsville area, other mills were opened. In 1806, William Maltby built a sawmill and gristmill north of the Williams property on Ellicott Creek, in Skinnerville near the current location of Millersport and North Forest Road. John Long opened a sawmill in 1808 on Buffalo Road (Main Street) near Union Road, behind the current McDonald's location. In 1808 John Reist purchased 196 acres extending from Mill Street to Reist Street, where he and his brother-in-law Abraham Long build a grist mill, flour mill, hemp mill and sawmill in what is now Amherst State Park, Sisters of St. Francis, Fredonia Place and Park Country Club. In addition to their limestone quarry, the John Fogelsonger family built a cider mill and grist mill in the Morningside development area behind North Presbyterian Church. John Batt built a mill between 560-564 North Forest Road and John Getz operated a sawmill on North Forest Road where it crosses Ellicott Creek.

Timothy S. Hopkins was a half-brother of Asa and Elias Ransom. He moved to Clarence in 1800, settling near Asa Ransom's property. In 1804 Hopkins moved near the farm of Elias Ransom and assisted in building Elias's frame house and barn, along with planting the orchards in this area. This made Eilas Ransom and Timothy Hopkins the first residents of the western portion of Clarence, now called Snyder/Amherst.

Hopkin's original log home, replaced by a stone home, was near the current location of Amherst High School. There he and his southern-born wife Nancy Kerr raised nine children and lived for 50 years. On April 28, 1804, their marriage was the first recorded in Erie County, and it took place in the Evans House. When Amherst was formed in 1818, Hopkins was elected the first town supervisor in 1819.

Other early landowners from 1804 to 1809 include Caleb Rogers, Stephen Colvin, Jacob Vanatta, Joel Chamberlain, James Hershey, John Drake, Samuel Fackler, Gamaliel St. John, James S. Youngs and John Frick. Additional landholders before the War of 1812 were Adam Vollner, Isaac F. Bowman, John Bieser, Eli Herr, John Herr, John Reid, Jacob Hershey, Thomas Coe, Darius Ayers, John Reist, John Fogelsonger, Daniel Frey and Dr. David S. Conkey.

The area that would become Amherst was first considered part of the town of Northampton. In 1802 it became part of Batavia, in 1804 the town of Erie, in 1808 the town of Clarence and in 1810 all land west of Transit Road was considered part of Buffalo. The first town meeting for the town of Clarence was held at Elias Ransom's Tavern, electing Jonas Williams as supervisor and Timothy S. Hopkins as one of the assessors.

During the War of 1812, American troops were stationed between Garrison Road and Ellicott Creek. A hospital was built on Garrison Road, with a cemetery on Aero Drive along the creek. General Winfield Scott used the Evans house as his headquarters in 1813 and his entire army of 5,000 to 6,000 men were in the village. When Buffalo was burned on December 30, 1813, the residents fled to the Williamsville area and beyond.

Amherst was named after Sir Jeffery Amherst, an English Lord who was commander of British Troops in America from 1758 to 1763, before the American Revolution. He was given 20,000 acres in New York State by King George for his service, but Amherst never visited the area. When the town of Amherst was formed on April 10, 1818 the town included all of current day Amherst and Cheektowaga, and part of West Seneca. In 1839, the southern portion of the town became Cheektowaga and the present boundaries of Amherst were established.

After the War of 1812, Jonas Williams retained ownership of the tanning company but sold the rest of his property to Juba Storrs & Company. When Storrs business failed, the mills were purchased by a company operated by James Roosevelt, of the NYC Roosevelt family. Upon the death of Jonas Williams in 1920, John Hutchinson purchased the tannery which he operated for the next 50 years.

In 1827, Oziel Smith purchased the mills and built the Eagle House in 1832. It was the stagecoach stop, hotel and restaurant in Williamsville. The business district of the village grew from the Eagle House to other businesses owned by John Lehn, A.M. Dunn, Benjamin Miller and E.H. Herr.

The grist mill became the flour mills of J. Wayne Dodge. The hydraulic lime works of King & Company were sold to T.A. Hopkins and later to Benjamin Miller. A brewery in a stone building next to Ellicott Creek was opened by Urban & Blocher and sold to John Daul.

The first private school in Williamsville was built in 1812 by Caleb Rogers at Main and Garrison Roads. A public school opened in 1817 at Main and Grove Streets, moving to 70 Eagle Street. A one room schoolhouse opened in 1940 at 72 South Cayuga on land donated by Timothy S. Hopkins. It later became the first Amherst Senior Center and first home for the Amherst Museum.

Figure 300 Williamsville One Room Schoolhouse 72 South Cayuga PD

In 1836, the Buffalo Macadam Company was incorporated to build a toll road between Williamsville and Buffalo. A road made with crushed stones that were paved into the roadway was created by the company. Toll booths were located every 9 miles, with the Getzville toll gate located on Main at Getzville Road, near the current location of Daemen College. Tolls were posted for vehicles and bicycles, with farmers transporting livestock to market being charged on a per head basis. The company was owned by the Hopkins, Eggert and Hutchinson families and the Getzville toll collected funds for maintenance and security until 1899.

Figure 301 Amherst Toll Gate at Getzville Road managed by the Fry Family in 1880 PD

The village of Williamsville was incorporated in 1850. The Amherst Bee was started by A.L. Reinwalt in 1870, and in 1882, a stone bridge was finally built across Ellicott Creek. Beginning in 1866, the Buffalo, Williamsville and Clarence Omnibus Line operated four horse coaches between the towns. In 1893, the Buffalo & Williamsville Electric Railway Company began operation, opening up regular transportation from Williamsville to the city of Buffalo.

Figure 302 Buffalo Williamsville Electric Glen Falls PD

Buffalo Niagara Heritage Village
3755 Tonawanda Creek Road, Amherst

Figure 303 Bigelow Farmhouse
photo courtesy Buffalo Niagara Heritage Village

Buffalo Niagara Heritage Village (BNHV), formerly the Amherst Museum, was established in 1972 by the Town of Amherst at New and Smith Roads. As a department of the Town of Amherst, the Museum focused on the history of the Town and its impact on the Buffalo Niagara region. Three buildings were moved to the site: Hoover House, Bigelow House, and the Williamsville Schoolhouse. In 1975, when their previous location was acquired to create the Ransom Oaks community, the Amherst Museum moved to the intersection of New and Tonawanda Creek Roads, the site of the former Amherst Nike Missile Base. This new location provided 35 acres to grow the footprint of the museum, which was chartered as an educational institution. In 2011 the name was changed to Buffalo Niagara Heritage Village and their 501c3 non-profit status was established. In 2019, their mission was updated to preserving the agricultural history and rural heritage of the Buffalo Niagara region.

The indoor museum space, located within the Shaw Exhibition Building, offers rotating exhibits of over 60,000 artifacts and archives. BNHV carries out its educational mission through interpretation of agricultural and rural life practices within the Historic Village and demonstration farmstead. They provide tours, programs, workshops, community events, and access to a variety of artifacts and historic resources retained within their collections. The museum also serves as the co-Town Historian in collaboration with the Williamsville Historical Society.

Ten historic 19th century buildings were relocated from locations in Amherst, where they were threatened with demolition due to growth and development. These relocated buildings are the Lavocat House (circa 1840), Williamsville School (1880), Sweet Home School (1847), Elliott House (1851), Doctor's Office (1888), Hoover House (1856), Schmitt Log House (circa 1840), Rubeck House (circa 1840), Bigelow House (circa 1840s) and Trinity Evangelical Lutheran Church (1854). The museum built a replica of a blacksmith shop in 1997. The campus also features the Steffen Educational Building and Amherst Library and Reading Room.

Buffalo Niagara Heritage Village is open for general admission from May to September. In the village, you can explore how agriculture and the Erie Canal affected farming, architecture, and day-to-day life. Outside general admission hours, guests can experience even more through educational and fun programs like Beekeeping Classes, Scout Programs, Maple Festival, Agriculture Fair, Halloween Trick or Treat, News and Brews: Trivia with a Twist, and much more.

COUNTRY CLUB OF BUFFALO
250 Youngs Road, Williamsville

Figure 304 Country Club of Buffalo Entrance
photo credit Rick Falkowski

The Country Club of Buffalo has been in three locations over the past 135 years.

Formed in 1889, the Country Club of Buffalo was created as a social and recreational club near the intersection of Elmwood and Nottingham Terrace. Built on land owned by Bronson Rumsey, the low-slung Shingle style clubhouse was designed by E.B. Green. It was originally a polo club and it absorbed the Buffalo Polo Club, founded by the Rumseys, Carys and Scatcherds. Golf was added in 1894 when the first hole was created by inserting a tomato can in the ground for a cup. Five holes were built on Rumsey land and the club received permission to expand the course on Delaware Park land to 18 holes.

In 1899 the club was told they had to vacate their clubhouse because all the Rumsey property between Elmwood and Delaware and north to Hertel Avenue was to be occupied by the Pan American Exposition. Their clubhouse was leased by the Pan Am and utilized as the Women's Building. The County Club moved to a temporary building at 1396 Amherst Street (Park Side Sanitarium) and used the Delaware Park golf course.

After the Pam Am, the club members split into two distinct younger and older groups. The older group led by John Milburn wanted to stay in the city close to their homes, remained at the site and changed their name to the Park Club. They physically moved the clubhouse to Lincoln Parkway and Nottingham Terrace, where they remained until moving to a new Park Club built on Sheridan Drive in Williamsville in 1928.

The younger group of members retained the Country Club of Buffalo name and in 1903 moved to a 70-acre golf course on Main Street near the city line with Amherst, with a clubhouse designed by George Cary. In 1912 the Men's U.S. Open Championship was held at the course and after the club moved to its current location, the course at Bailey and Main became the Grover Cleveland Public Golf Course.

In 1926 the Country Club of Buffalo moved to Youngs Road at Sheridan. They hosted the 1931 USGA Women's Championship and the Donald Ross designed course, making full use of the limestone escarpment, is considered one of the top 100 golf courses in the country.

EAGLE HOUSE
5578 Main Street, Williamsville

Figure 305 Eagle House PD

The Eagle House was built by Oziel Smith in 1827, who purchased all the land and mills around Ellicott Creek and Glen Falls, including the land where he built the tavern. After he completed construction of the Eagle House he had to travel to Buffalo, where he owned other businesses. While he was in Buffalo the tavern burned down. He immediately rebuilt, using limestone from his quarries and lumber from his wooded land, which was cut in his sawmill. Oziel Smith became a village leader, was elected one of the first town supervisors and to the New York State Assembly.

In 1832 the Eagle House was a stage coach stop for the Conestoga Wagon Line and an overnight stop for passengers traveling from Buffalo to Batavia. Horses were tied up on the dirt road in front of the tavern. The Williamsville stop was decreed "Bird, Beef and a Bottle with a bed for the weary traveler" with the Eagle House offering a hot meal for 25 cents and a bed for the night priced at 10 cents.

After Smith's death his wife and daughter ran the business until Timothy Hopkins took an interest in the property in 1844 and purchased it in 1857. During Hopkin's ownership the stone bridge on Main Street was built over Ellicott Creek in 1880. To celebrate the construction an Oyster Social was held in 1882, which became an annual political and social event.

When the future St. John Neumann was pastor of St. Peter & Paul Church on Main Street in 1836, before the rectory was completed, he rented a room on the second floor of The Eagle House. It is believed that the tunnels under the Eagle House were a stop on the Underground Railroad for enslaved people fleeing to Canada.

In 1909 the Eagle House was purchased by John Wooster, in 1923 by Fred Beck and in 1945 Louis Clare. It is now owned by the Hanny family that boasts five generations in the restaurant and hospitality business, dating back to Hanny's on Canal Street in 1880.

The Eagle House holds the oldest continuous liquor license in Erie County and New York State, with the liquor stamps displayed in the hallway of the restaurant.

GLEN PARK
5565 Main Street, Williamsville

In 1911 Louis M. Conshafter purchased the land surrounding Glen Falls and opened Conshafter's Picnic Grounds. He was followed by the Cardina brothers who went bankrupt in the Wallstreet Crash of 1929. Harry Altman bought the grounds from the bankruptcy court afterwards for $200.00.

Altman had a diner serving dime sandwiches and quarter pitchers of beer on the property. He owned several different nightclubs in downtown Buffalo and based upon that experience, tried various things to promote the grounds. In 1934 he opened a small nightclub called the Glen Barn, which burned in 1936 and was replaced by the 1,200 seat Glen Casino.

Figure 306 Glen Park Amusement Rides photo courtesy Susan Fenster

In the late 1940s Altman expanded the park from picnic grounds with swings, see saws, sand boxes and concessionaire offerings to an amusement park that included rides, games (like Skee Ball), entertainment and refreshment stands

Near the end of WWII, Altman and Harry Wallens opened a downtown nightclub called the Town Barn that burned down in 1945 and reopened as the Town Casino. The Glen Casino and Town Casino alternated between the summer and winter, featuring the top names in entertainment.

The amusement park was expanded to include a Ferris wheel, roller coaster, merry-go-round, cars, boats, enclosed cages and other rides. Tickets were a nickel each or a roll of 22 for a dollar.

Along with Clyde Urban, Superintendent of Glen Amusement Park & Casino, Altman added a petting zoo in the mid-1950s that featured mountain goats, sheep, rams, lambs, llamas, deer, peacocks and pony rides. They even had a monkey house.

When Altman died in 1966 and the Glen Casino was sold, promoter Kevin Elliot encouraged Altman's son-in-law David Goldman to change the entertainment format to rock music. The two men leased the Casino and renamed it "The Inferno" featuring the top national rock bands of the early and mid-1960s.

The Inferno became the most popular venue for early rock bands in WNY, but it burned down on September 23, 1968. A second fire destroyed other buildings on September 8, 1973 and the park closed.

In 1976 it was purchased by the town of Amherst and village of Williamsville. It is now known as Glen Park, one of the best locations in WNY for wedding photos and acclaimed for its annual Williamsville Art Show and picturesque Glen Falls.

by Susan Fenster & Rick Falkowski

Park Country Club
4949 Sheridan Drive, Williamsville

Figure 307 Park Country Club photo credit Rick Falkowski

The history of the Park Country Club can be traced back to the original Country Club of Buffalo that was formed in 1889. When the land where their clubhouse stood was allocated to the Pan American Exposition, the club moved to a temporary building at 1396 Amherst Street. After the Pan Am the club split into two factions. Younger members retained the Country Club of Buffalo name and relocated to Main and Bailey, while the older members wanted to stay in the city. They became the Park Club in 1903, built a new clubhouse at Lincoln Parkway and Nottingham Terrace and continued to play golf on the Delaware Park course.

In 1927, architect Clifford C. Wendehack, who designed the clubhouse for the iconic Winged Foot Country Club in Mamaroneck, Westchester County, New York created an elegant new clubhouse for the Park Club in Williamsville. The 50,000 plus square foot English Gothic Tudor tower edifice is like a castle relocated along suburban Sheridan Drive. In addition to the imposing exterior, the interior which resembles an English Manor, house experienced a multi-million-dollar renovation that retained its historic appearance but incorporated ultra high-end modern amenities. Facilities were expanded and blended with the coarse plaster walls and ceilings, hand-hewn wood timber and roof trusses, and oak furnishings of the structure. All overlooking the manicured golf course and flowing onto the outdoor bluestone terrace with stone fire pits.

The Park Country Club golf course was designed by Colt & Alison, considered the preeminent golf course architects of the early to mid-20th century. Its course incorporates Ellicott Creek on its grounds, manicured greens and has been lengthened to nearly 7,000 yards from the back tees. The 1934 PGA Championship was held at Park Country Club, along with numerous prestigious amateur events.

Park Country Club is a private club, with membership available on an invitation only basis, with a wait list to join. In addition to golf, the club provides aquatics in its large pool and a Racquet Club including tennis and pickleball courts, operated in partnership with the Village Glen Tennis & Pickleball Club. The social events calendar is filled with regular activities, meetings, dinners, clubs, membership incentives and special events for holidays year-round. Private parties, catered events and wedding receptions often include professional fireworks displays on the fairways, making them occasions that will be charismatically remembered.

Reformed Mennonite Church
5178 Main Street, Williamsville

The Mennonites arrived in Williamsville in 1805 from the Lancaster PA area. John Reist arrived in 1808 and purchased a 196-acre farm extending from Mill Street to near Reist Street. His brother-in-law John Long purchased the property facing Reist Street and in 1821 they built the Reist Milling Company on their two properties.

Figure 308 Reformed Mennonite Church PD

In 1828 the Amherst Mennonites were organized under John Herr. in 1830 John Reist became a minister of the Reformed Mennonite Church in 1830 and in 1834 their Meeting House was built at the corner of Main Street and North Forest Road. The building is one of the oldest extant religious buildings in Erie County.

Reist was a successful businessman and expanded his milling company to include a grist mill, flour mill, hemp mill, sawmill, copper shop and a number of mill buildings. Most of the mill property was sold to the Sisters of St. Francis in 1903 and a portion extended into the current Park Country Club. He served as pastor of the Church from 1836 to 1879.

The Reformed Mennonite Church served the Anabaptist community, which was one of the largest congregations in the area and counted many of the founding families of the Amherst area among its members including the Longs, Reists, Hersheys and Fogelsongers. Their austere one-room edifice was constructed with a wood shingled roof and walls of Onondaga Limestone from the nearby Fogelsonger Quarry. It was a Greek Revival design with quoins on the corners of the façade; cornice returns on the front gable and splayed lintels crowning the narrow windows.

After the congregation disbanded in 1981, the building served different purposes for the town of Amherst, including housing the Town Archives from 1985 to 2009. In 2012 the building was purchased by Evans Bank and restorations were undertaken in a historically sensitive manner. Evans Bank continues to operate a branch at the location, with the integrity of the early 1800s building retained.

Figure 309 Reformed Mennonite - Evans Bank

Saints Peter & Paul Church
5480 Main Street, Williamsville

*Figure 310 Saints Peter & Paul
photo credit Ellen Mika Zelasko*

As early as 1832, there were Catholic settlers in the Williamsville area in need of a German speaking priest. They had been forced to travel to Lamb of God Church (now St. Louis) in Buffalo, no easy feat in 1832. The settlers received permission from the pastor of Lamb of God Church to build a log chapel to be used when the priest could make it out to the village to celebrate mass.

In 1834, Oziel Smith a non-Catholic settler donated a plot of land to be used for a community church, provided it was to be built with stone. The plan was approved by the Catholic Church, and construction began.

When Father John Neumann arrived at the mission in July of 1836, there were roughly 40 families worshiping in the area, though not all lived in the village. The church was in use but was still unfinished. The walls were for the most part completed, but the structure had no roof or floor. Fr. Neumann started out living in the Village of Williamsville but was also assigned to mission chapels in Tonawanda and Lancaster.

In the winter of 1837, Fr. Neumann, while still assigned to all three missions, moved his residence to Tonawanda. Over the next three years, Neumann continued to minister to the three mission churches including the teaching of the children. Because travel was difficult, it was physically exhausting, and his health suffered. After a long illness, Neumann ended up joining the Redemptorist Society, a much less physically taxing priestly vocation.

He eventually became the fourth bishop of Philadelphia in 1852. Neumann was also credited with having founded the first Catholic diocesan school system in the country. Bishop John Neumann was canonized a saint by Pope Paul VI in 1977.

After Father Neumann left Buffalo, several priests moved through Saints Peter & Paul Parish. The area continued to grow and the need for a larger church became obvious.

Property was acquired where the current church now stands at the corner of Main Street and Grove. A home on the site was moved and served as the schoolhouse. This new church, built of stone from a quarry at the corner of Main Street and Kensington Avenue, was dedicated in 1866. Saints Peter & Paul Roman Catholic Church continues to serve the faithful of Williamsville to this day.

by Ellen Mika Zelasko

WILLIAMSVILLE MEETING HOUSE
5658 Main Street, Williamsville

The Society for the Disciples of Christ was formed in the 1830s and they held services at members' homes and various buildings. In 1853 the congregation founded Williamsville Classical Institute at 39 Academy Street, now the site of Christian Central Academy. It was the first school above the elementary level in Amherst. In 1871 they built the Williamsville Meeting House at Main and Mill Street, which they continually expanded and improved.

The red brick Italianate building features rose windows facing Main Street and twelve arched and arcaded windows. There are three types of glass in the windows, the original stenciled glass, pebble glass and the newer leaded glass.

This building fell into disrepair and in 1948 the bell tower was removed. The Society for the Disciples of Christ disbanded their congregation and in 1976 sold the building to the Village of Williamsville Historical Society for $1.00. The village made significant renovations to the building funded through grants from federal, state and other organizations. Improvements included installing a replica of the original bell tower and restoring the stained glass.

Figure 311 Williamsville Meeting House PD

Williamsville proposed selling The Meeting House to a private developer. Led by Susan Fenster, a campaign and online petition "Stop the Sale of the Williamsville Meeting House" was circulated that collected over 1,100 signatures. The proposed sale also led to offers of volunteer assistance for marketing and potential new uses. In addition, the village discovered that if they sold the property the municipality would have to pay back over $200,000 in Community Development Block Grant funds to the federal office of Housing & Urban Development. In 2021 the Village Board voted to cease the exploration of selling the building.

Currently the building is managed by the Williamsville Meeting House Events Committee. The Village of Williamsville Historical Society Museum has a display of historical artifacts in the former choir loft on the second Sunday of the month. The ground floor level is rented out for weddings, special events, concerts, Buffalo Friends of Folk Music productions and community theater by Rocking Horse Productions, along with youth and senior programming by the Williamsville Youth & Recreation Department.

VILLAGE OF WILSON PROFILES

This section includes profiles of the Village of **Wilson** and historic places in Wilson and the Town of **Youngstown**.

Village of Wilson

The town of Wilson is located at the mouth of Twelve Mile Creek, 12 miles east of where the Niagara River enters Lake Ontario.

In 1808 Henry Lockwood arrived from Canada, purchased 100 acres from the Holland Land Company in the northeast portion of the town and is considered the first settler. Later that year Robert Waterhouse from Connecticut settled in the southern part of the town and in 1809 Stephen Sheldon relocated from Jefferson County, purchasing 720 acres west of Twelve Mile Creek. Ruben Wilson, the namesake of the town, arrived in 1810 with Gilbert Purdy and the John Eastman family.

During the War of 1812, George Ash alerted town residents that the British were advancing from the west at Fort Niagara. Many fled eastwards. 15-year-old Luther Wilson drove a herd of 25 cattle to the east concealing the departure by stuffing straw in their cowbells. He had to move the cattle past the Van Horn property in Newfane, as the British had orders to destroy their grain mill that was supplying the U.S. troops. Reuben Wilson was taken by the British invaders as a prisoner to Fort Niagara but the hospitality of Mrs. Wilson, who fed the hostile British soldiers, allowed their home to be spared.

In 1818 Justice Reuben Wilson was the presiding officer at the inaugural town meeting, and his son Orrin Wilson was the first child born in the settlement in 1811. The 1821 marriage of Luther Wilson and Sarah Stevens was the first wedding in the town. Reuben purchased a sawmill built by Daniel Sheldon near the mouth of the creek in 1816 and constructed a grist mill. The Wilson home was relocated near the mills and the original logs of that home still exist in a house on Young Street. The Wilsons purchased the remaining land near the harbor, with Reuben and Luther credited with establishing the town.

When the construction of the Erie Canal was announced in 1821, most of northern Niagara County was unbroken wilderness. Ridge Road (Route 104) was a natural path on the high point of the forests, with swamps on either side. Since the road was just over 150 feet above lake level, the swamps were drained, creating fertile farmland for the growing of fruit trees, wheat and other crops. Until the reclamation of the land, Wilson was more accessible by water than over land routes, receiving supplies from Ontario and New York State towns on Lake Ontario.

The town includes many cobblestone homes and in the mid-1800s became known as a resort town with fine hotels, boating, fishing and other recreational activities. The harbor was designated an official Port of Entry by the U.S. government from 1851 to 1907. Several Yacht Clubs are located in Wilson Harbor, along with Sunset Island, which includes summer homes and does not allow vehicular traffic. The Wilson Boat House, built around 1900, is a restaurant that overlooks the harbor and the Wilson Pier remains a popular fishing location.

Wilson House

300 Lake Street, Wilson

Figure 312 Wilson House Inn

The Wilson House was built by Luther Wilson in 1844 on the site of the original schoolhouse in Wilson.

Luther Wilson was the oldest son of Reuben Wilson, who settled near the mouth of Twelve Mile Creek in 1810. The Wilson family arrived from York (Toronto) and first lived under their overturned rowboat while their log cabin was being built.

In 1816 Reuben purchased a sawmill from Daniel Sheldon on the east bank of Twelve Mile Creek and added a grist mill. Due to fluctuating water levels of the creek, the mill was unreliable until Luther Wilson later upgraded it to a steam powered mill.

The first marriage performed in Wilson was that of Sara Stephens and Luther Wilson in 1821. They moved into his father Reuben's home on Young Street in 1825, with that Wilson home becoming the post office, a store, a tavern and the center of Wilson social activity. A home was constructed, expanding upon the original log home, and a historic marker identifies the location of this dwelling.

Luther is credited with starting the hamlet of Wilson by laying out a single tier of lots along the north side of Young Street from Lake Street to the creek. He started most of the public improvements and the town was named after him.

In 1844 Luther built the large cobblestone house at the corner of Young and Lake Streets, in the location of the first school in Wilson, where Luther previously taught classes. In addition to assisting his father with his many business enterprises, Luther was elected to the State Assembly, built the first piers at Wilson Harbor, dredged the harbor, established a shipyard and built a warehouse for trading fruit and grain. He was elected the first mayor of Wilson in 1858, served as a Captain in the State Militia, and donated land for several churches and the Greenwood Cemetery. A joint funeral was held in the parlor of this home for Luther and his son Reuben, who died five days apart in 1890. Luther was interred at the age of 92 in the cemetery he donated to the town.

The Lake Street home was purchased in the 1920s by a group of businessmen who established the Wilsonian Club at the property, featuring dances and a bowling alley. In 1947 the building was converted into a public restaurant and inn, currently a restaurant with seven short-term rentals.

Fort Niagara & the French Castle
102 Morrow Plaza, Youngstown

Figure 313 French Castle at Fort Niagara
photo credit Marsha Falkowski

French explorer LaSalle built the first fortified structure called Fort Conti at the mouth of the Niagara River at Lake Ontario in 1678. The Governor of New France, Marquis de Denonville, replaced it with a new fort that he named Fort Denonville in 1687. He posted 100 men at the fort, but due to severe weather that resulted in the death of all but 12 soldiers, the fort was abandoned.

Thomas Joncaire was adopted by the Seneca and given permission to build a trading post at the former location of the forts. The building named the House of Peace (later called The French Castle) was built in 1726 and it is the oldest stone structure on the Great Lakes. In 1755, the French expanded the fort to its current size in response to armed conflict with the British that began as the Seven Years' War in Europe and was called the French & Indian War in America.

The British captured the fort during the Battle of Fort Niagara in July 1759 and during the American Revolution Fort Niagara was a Loyalist base, with John Butler of Butler's Rangers stationed at the fort. Although the British ceded Fort Niagara to the Americans at the Treaty of Paris in 1783, they continued to occupy Fort Niagara until 1796. Due to it being a British Loyalist stronghold, U.S. citizens did not begin settling the Niagara Frontier until after the fort was transferred to the U.S.

During the War of 1812, Fort Niagara and Fort George, that the British built across the Niagara River in Canada, were at the center of much of the armed engagements. The Americans captured Fort George and burned the adjacent town of Newark (Niagara-on-the-Lake) when they abandoned it. In retaliation, the British captured Fort Niagara and burned the towns of Youngstown, Lewiston, Manchester (Niagara Falls), Black Rock and Buffalo in 1813.

During the American Civil War, Fort Niagara was fortified by the Americans to prevent an attack by confederates that had operation in Toronto. It was a training center during the Spanish American War, an officers training center during WWI, and during WWII it housed German prisoners of war.

Fort Niagara is now operated by the Old Fort Niagara Association, a non-profit organization that educates the public about the fort by holding military reenactments and operating exhibits that are annually visited by about 100,000 people.

Source Notes

The name of the author for each Place or Municipality profile is listed at the end of the profile. If no author is listed, the profile was written by Rick Falkowski.

Akron-Newstead

Town of Newstead Profile

The Town of Newstead Sesquicentennial 1823 – 1998, buffaloah.com
History of the Town of Newstead, NY Genealogy, newyorkgenealogy.org
History of Akron and Vicinity, NY Genealogy, newyorkgenealogy.org
Village of Akron, NY, erie.gov/akron/about-akron
Destroyer Park Gold, destroyerparkgolf.com
Information from Newstead Historical Society's Pat Rodrigues (Knight-Sutton Museum Director) and Kate Stapleton Parzych (Rich-Twinn Octagon House Director).

Perry's Ice Cream

https://www.perrysicecream.com
https://en.wikipedia.org/wiki/Perry%27s_Ice_Cream
https://www.findagrave.com/memorial/257632500/harrison_morton_perry
https://oukosher.org/companies/generations-of-excellence-at-perrys-ice-cream/
New Ice Cream Plant will help Akron Firm Lick the Competition by Bob Buyer, *Buffalo News* 4/27/1982
The Town of Newstead Bicentennial 1823-2023 by the town of Newstead Historian's Office and Newstead Historical Society, 2023
Perry's Ice cream completes expansionwgrz.com 6/6/2024
Conversation with Brian Perry

Rich Twinn Octagon House

Rich-Twinn Octagon Home, buffaloah.com
Rich-Twinn Octagon House, Newstead Historical Society, newsteadhistoricalsociety.org
Rich-Twinn Octagon House, Visit Buffalo Niagara, visitbuffaloniagara.com
Information from Newstead Historical Society's Pat Rodrigues (Knight-Sutton Museum Director) and Kate Stapleton Parzych (Rich-Twinn Octagon House Director).

Angola/ Derby/ Evans

Town of Evans Profile

https://townofevansny.gov/history/
Evans, NY: Interesting Facts, Famous Things & History Information | What Is Evans Known For?
https://purple.niagara.edu/library-old/buffhist/1-571-583.pdf

Cradle Beach Camp

https://cradlebeach.org/did-you-know/#:~:text=History,from%20the%20city%20of%20Buffalo.
https://www.fmi.org/get-involved/community-uplift/nominees/view/cradle-beach-camp
https://nyshistoricnewspapers.org/?a=d&d=ben19030703-01.1.19&e=-------en-20--1--txt-txIN
https://www.wivb.com/news/you-get-a-new-view-of-the-world-1-million-goal-set-to-help-local-camp-thats-been-here-130-years/

https://buffalonews.com/news/cradle-beach-camp-moving-to-new-lakeshore-location-in-1995/article_3b6e0119-3b8b-551a-9753-2df5aa7b94f2.html#tncms-source=login

Emblem Cycling Company

https://midlifecycling.blogspot.com/2023/09/an-emblem-of-bicycle-history.html
https://buffalonews.com/news/local/fire-at-former-bicycle-factory-in-angola-under-investigation/article_056107de-5f91-11ee-b8ef-dba83c0361f4.html
https://thecabe.com/forum/threads/emblem-manufacturing-info.125531/
https://www.yesterdays.nl/product/emblem-1917-model-106-single-speed-2712/#:~:text=The%20company%20is%20founded%20in,involvement%20and%20attention%20to%20quality

White City

Images of America: Evans and Angola by Cheryl Delano Arcadia Publishing copyright 2009 pp. 37-38
100 Years of Grandview: Centennial Celebration of Grandview Bay 1922-2022, compiled by the Grandview Bay Community Association
https://www.hmdb.org/m.asp?m=105702

Graycliff

https://experiencegraycliff.org/
https://franklloydwright.org/site/graycliff/
https://www.visitbuffaloniagara.com/businesses/frank-lloyd-wrights-graycliff/
https://en.wikipedia.org/wiki/Graycliff

Lochevan

Conversation with Brian Kellogg, May 2025
Buffalo Courier Express- Sunday, April 2, 1933 edition
https://www.buffaloah.com/h/KellSpen/index.html
https://wnyhistory.com/portfolios/war/WW1/steam_yachts/steam_yachts.html
http://files.usgwarchives.net/ny/erie/bios/lewis/kellogg-howard.txt
https://www.wikitree.com/wiki/Larkin-2735

Sturgeon Point Marina

https://nyfalls.com/lakes/erie/sturgeon-point-marina/
https://pierce-arrow.org/pierce-arrow-history/294771-2/
https://www.findagrave.com/memorial/19547107/george_norman_pierce
https://townofevansny.gov/docs/legal-public-notices/archives/2022/sturgeon-point-master-plan-pre-proposal-meeting-slides-11-7-22/?layout=file
https://townofevansny.gov/departments/parks-department/sturgeon-point-marina/
https://buffaloah.com/a/mich/263/11_prce/prce.html
https://ancestors.familysearch.org/en/LVXS-WMZ/percival-peironnet-pierce-1878-1940

Suncliff Manor

https://buffaloah.com/a/DERBY/oldlake/6892/bn.html
https://sunclifffonthelake.com/new-about-us/
https://www.niagara-gazette.com/opinion/glynn-new-owner-to-convert-big-house/article_324b11a8-c7d6-11e7-8703-73a1ba1fcd5c.htm
https://columban.org/100points/100-points-light-1949
https://en.wikipedia.org/wiki/Jacob_F._Schoellkopf

Wendt Beach Park

https://commons.wikimedia.org/wiki/File:Henry_W._Wendt_Summer_House,_Wendt_Beach_County_Park,_Evans,_New_York_-_20210726.jpg
https://buffalonews.com/erie-county-seeks-developer-for-the-historic-wendt-mansion/article_391df2d6-1c39-54f7-a245-acdd84cbfcea.htm
https://en.wikipedia.org/wiki/Wendt_Beach_Park
"Henry W. Wendt Dies: Ex Foundry Executive" *Buffalo Courier-Express* August 24, 1966

Buffalo

City of Buffalo Profile

The First Settlers of Buffalo: 1790s by John Fagant, The Buffalo Downtowner April 2010
The Village of Buffalo – 1800 to 1832 by Wilma Laux, behsed.nylearns.org
How did Buffalo Get Its Name? by Cynthia Van Ness, Buffalo History Museum 6/22/2022
Historic & Influential People from Buffalo & WNY – the 1880s by Rick Falkowski

800 West Ferry

https://800westferry.org/
https://buffaloah.com/a/wferry/800/index.html
https://findingaids.lib.buffalo.edu/agents/people/1156
Historic & Influential People from Buffalo & WNY – the Early 1900s by Rick Falkowski

A&P Warehouse

AP Lofts at Larkinville, aploftsatlarkinville.com
Great Atlantic & Pacific Tea Company National Register of Historic Places registration form by Kimberly Konrad Alvarez of Landmark Consulting LLC, 7/6/2015

Adam Mickiewicz Library & Dramatic Circle

Adam Mickiewicz Library & Dramatic Circle, Polonia Trail, polonialtrail.com
Adam Mickiewicz Library & Dramatic Circle, Welcome to Forgotten Buffalo & Tours, forgottenbuffalo.com
Mickiewicz Music Fest is Part of a Triptych Cultural Showcase by Queenseye, buffalorising.com 5/15/2023
Torn Space, Capital Project, tornspacetheater.com
Conversations with Patra Mangus

Adult Learning Center

https://buffaloah.com/a/va/389/index.html
https://sah-archipedia.org/buildings/NY-01-029-0098
https://www.buffaloschools.org/o/dept-adult-ed/page/bpsadulted
https://www.wnyheritage.org/content/louis_le_couteulx_gentleman/index.html

Albright-Knox Art Gallery

Lackawanna Steel Company and Buffalo & Susquehanna Iron Company, buffaloah.com
Buffaloakg.org
Albright-Knox receives massive donation, changing name, wkbw.com
Profiles Volume I: Historic & Influential People from Buffalo & WNY – the 1800s by Rick Falkowski

AM&A's – JN Adam's Department Store

Profiles Volume I: Historic & Influential People from Buffalo & WNY – the 1800s by Rick Falkowski

J.N. Adam & Co./AM&A's Department Store, buffaloah.com
Bon-Ton stores to close by August 31, wkbw.com

American Radiator Company

American Radiator HVAC age. The Building Intelligence Center, building-center.org
American Radiator/ARCO Lofts. Preservation Ready Sites – Buffalo, preservationready.org
American Radiator Company Factory Complex. New York State Parks, Recreation & Historic Preservation, parks.ny.gov
American Radiator/American Standard. Lipsitz, Ponterio and Comerford, lipsitzponterio.com
Looking Backward: Institute for Thermal Research, dailypublic.com 8/15/2015
The ARCO, thebuffalolofts.com

Anchor Bar

Anchor Bar History – The Story of a Buffalo Classic, anchorbar.com
The Spirit of Buffalo Women, Teressa Bellissimo by Rick Falkowski.
The History of Buffalo Music & Entertainment by Rick Falkowski.

Anna Katharine Green House

Historic & Influential People from Buffalo & WNY – the 1800s by Rick Falkowski
New York's mother of detective fiction is still inspiring authors a century later by Viktoria Hallikaar, Spectrum News 3/20/2023.
The Mother of American Mystery: Anna Katharine Green by Michael Mallory, mysteryscenemag.com
Buffaloah.com

Asbury Delaware Avenue Methodist Church

Asbury Delaware Avenue Methodist Church, buffaloah.com
Houses of Worship: A Guide to Religious Architecture in Buffalo, New York by James Napora
Buffalo's Delaware Avenue Mansions & Families by Edward T. Dunn
Congregation of Buffalo's First Church Building Celebrates 200 Years by queenseyes, Buffalo Rising 2019
Babeville Buffalo, History & Architecture, babevillebuffalo.com

Belt Line Railroad

The Belt Line Railroad: Its Influence on the Development of Buffalo's Neighborhoods by Daniel Zornick
Buffalo Belt Line, Discovering Buffalo, One Street at a Time
Belt Line, preservationready.org

Blocher Mausoleum

Blocher Mausoleum by Douglas Keister, mausoleums.com
Blocher Monument Forest Lawn Cemetery Buffalo NY by Mary McCall, Love and Forest Lawn Cemetery Sesquicentennial, hmdb.org
Historic & Influential People from Buffalo & WNY – the 1800s by Rick Falkowski

Brisbane Building

Brisbane Building, thebrisbanebuilding.com
Mooney & Brisbane Building, buffaloah.com
Historic & Influential People from Buffalo & WNY by Rick Falkowski

Broadway Arsenal/Armory/Auditorium/Barn

Buffalo: Broadway Arsenal/Armory – 65th Regiment, museum.dman.ny.gov
Broadway Arsenal/Auditorium/Garage. Preservations-Ready, preservationreadt.org
Application for Landmark Site, Buffalo Preservation Board, preservationbuffaloniagara.org
Buffalo's First Armory is laden in Rich Memories. It later Became the City's First Auditorium, now a Streets Department Garage by Marge Thielman Hastreiter, *Buffalo News*, 6/21/1989
Broadway Barn will transform into sports complex, affordable housing, wgrz.com, 5/24/2023

Broadway Market

https://www.esd.ny.gov/sites/default/files/rfp/Bway-Mkt-RFP-Appendix-A.pdf
https://broadwaymarket.org/about/
https://www.buffalorising.com/2023/04/design-firm-sought-for-broadway-market-makeover

Buffalo & Erie County Botanical Gardens

Buffalo & Erie County Botanical Gardens, buffalogardens.com
Lord and Burnham, libguides.nybg.org
Botanical Gardens expansion by Jacob Tierney, Business First 12/4/2023

Buffalo & Erie County Public Library

The Buffalo & Erie County Public Library: A History, presentation by Susan Buttaccio on Imagine: Buffalo hosted by Dennis Galucki, buffalolib.com
History of the B&ECPL. Buffalolib.org
Grosvenor Library, buffaloah.com
Buffalo & Erie County Public Library, wnyheritage.com

Buffalo Athletic Club

Buffalo's Delaware Avenue Mansions and Families by Edward T. Dunn
A Gold Wynn for Buffalo – The Athletic Club Building by queenseyes, buffalorising.com 8/16/2018
Gold Wynn, goldwynn.com

Buffalo Central Terminal

Buffalo Central Terminal, buffalocentralterminal.org
Buffalo Central Terminal, Wikipedia.org
Research by Patra Mangus for Explore Buffalo tours

Buffalo City Hall

Buffalo City Hall: History, Architecture, and Facts (buildingsdb.com)
City Hall History - Buffalo, NY (buffalony.gov)

Buffalo Club

Watson House/Buffalo Club, buffaloah.com
Buffalo's Delaware Avenue Mansions and Families by Edward T. Dunn.

Buffalo Electric Vehicle Company

Buffalo Electric Vehicle Company, Buffalo NY in historic-structures.com
Buffaloah.com, Buffalo Auto Industry Early History
Western New York Heritage, Electric Automobiles
Artspace Buffalo Lofts, belmonthousingwny.org

Why She Wanted an Automobile by Jennette Lee, Lippincott's Magazine, *Buffalo News* 12/22/1902

Buffalo Gas Light Company

Up with the new: Recent and Current Projects. Health Now by Barry A. Muskat, Buffalo Spree July/August 2006.
Buffalo Gas Company/Health Now, buffaloah.com
Buffalo Gas Works, Forgotten Buffalo, forgottenbuffalo.com
Elbridge Gerry Spaulding: Life and Accomplishments, buffaloah.com
Last Look: Buffalo Gas Works by Judy Pellegrino, WNY Heritage Spring 2002
Highmark BCBSWNY announces move to Seneca One Tower, highmark.com 4/25/2023
Ingram Micro to move to former Highmark building in downtown Buffalo by Jonathan D. Epstein, *Buffalo News*, 3/17/2025

Buffalo History Museum

The Buffalo History Museum, buffalohistory.org
Buffalo History Museum, nyheritage.org
Young Men's Association of the City of Buffalo, University at Buffalofindingaids.lib.buffalo.edu

Buffalo Main Lighthouse

Buffalo Main Lighthouse, lighthousefriends.com
History of the Buffalo Main Lighthouse by Bryan Penberthy, buffaloah.com
Buffalo Lighthouse, buffaloah.com
The Saga and Legend of the Great Lakes First American Lighthouse by Eugene Ware, goerie.com

Buffalo Meter Company – Bethune Lofts

Obituary for George Barcley Bassett of Buffalo, New York, Buffalo Evening News 4/15/1955
Bethunelofts.com
Buffaloah.com

Buffalo Milk Company

Buffalo Milk Company Building, theclio.com
Buffalo Milk Company Building, Historic Structures, historic-structures.com
Niagara Gateway Apartments, regandevelopment.com
Niagara Gateway Apartments, HHL Architects, hhlarchitects.com
The Hollywood Sign, LA Conservancy, laconservancy.org

Buffalo Seminary

Buffalo Seminary, History & Traditions, buffaloseminary.org
History of Buffalo Seminary, buffaloah.com
Buffalo Seminary History 2018 by Harry Schooley
Buffalo Seminary, Niche, niche.com

Buffalo State College

Buffalo State University, suny.buffalostate.edu/history
State Normal School/Grover Cleveland High School, buffaloah.com
Burchfield Penney Art Center, burchfieldpenney.org
Historic & Influential People from Buffalo & WNY – the Early 1900s by Rick Falkowski

Buffalo Veterans Administration Hospital

About VA Western New York Healthcare System, U.S. Department of Veterans Affairs, va.gov

With plans for new downtown hospital off the table for new, VA is revamping its aging Buffalo Medical Center by Jon Harriss, *Buffalo News*, 5/24/2024

Grover Cleveland Golf Course. erie.gov

Buffalo Water Intake

Water Treatment Process, buffalowater.org

Cobwebs can't hide Intake Beauty by Bob Dearing, Courier Express

A touch of lonely awe amid beauty and spiders at Buffalo's Water Intake by Sean Kirts, *Buffalo News*, 10/11/2019

Buffalo Zoological Gardens

An Overview of the Buffalo Zoo, buffalozoo.org

Historic & Influential People from Buffalo & WNY – the 1800s by Rick Falkowski

New York State Announces opening of new $3.7 million Reptile House, 5/23/2019, parks.ny.gov

Donna Frenandes announces retirement from Buffalo Zoo by Mark Sommer, *Buffalo News* 10/20/2016

C.W. Miller Livery Stable

Charlie Miller's Livery Business by Susan J. Eck, wnyhistory.org

C.W. Miller Livery Stable, buffaloah.com

Williams Lansing, buffaloah.com

Ribbon cutting for the Buffalo school of culinary arts and hospitality management, buffalorising.com 3/5/2020

C.W. Miller Livery Stable, preservationready.org

Calumet Building

Green Light District Mark Goldman has a Child's Soul and a Life that doesn't always make sense by Mary Kunz, *Buffalo News* 10/15/1995.

Historic & Influential People from Buffalo & WNY – the Early 1900s by Rick Falkowski

Calumet Building, buffaloah.com

The Calumet: Making old elements appear new again, buffalorising.com 11/2/2012

Campanile Apartments

https://buffaloah.com/a/del/925/index.html

Classic Buffalo: A Heritage of Distinguished Architecture: https://archive.org/details/classicbuffalohe0000olen/page/76/mode/2up by Andy Olenick & Richard O. Reisem

Canalside

https://buffalowaterfront.com/

https://en.wikipedia.org/wiki/Canalside

https://www.visitbuffaloniagara.com/businesses/canalside/

Canisius College

About Canisius, Canisius University, catalog.canisius.edu

Houses of Worship: A Guide to the Religious Architecture of Buffalo, New York by James Napora

Canisius College, buffaloah.com

Canisius University, Wikipedia.org
Canisius College Montante Cultural Center, projects.archiexpo.com

Canisius High School - Rand Mansion

https://hellobuffalohikes.com/city-living-around-the-block-at-agassiz-circle/
https://hellobuffalohikes.com/the-rand-building-no-respect/
https://buffalonews.com/opinion/columnists/sean-kirst-how-gregg-allman-and-cher-stunned-canisius-high-assembly-in-1976/article_60499905-a2a9-5e42-ae81-35b884c7c8bd.html#link_time=1496578066
https://buffalonews.com/entertainment/gregg-allman-had-a-therapeutic-buffalo-connection/article_31de0fe6-a886-5f8a-9d44-aa73ddbf0e03.html
https://www.canisiushigh.org/news/post/~board/news/post/history-of-the-aud
https://buffaloah.com/a/del/1180/index.html

Coit House

Hello Buffalo: https://hellobuffalohikes.com/coit-house-buffalos-oldest-home-and-the-man-who-built-it/
The Picture Book of Earlier Buffalo by Frank H. Severance
Allentown Association: https://www.allentown.org/
Buffalo Architecture & History: https://buffaloah.com/h/coit/coit.html

Colored Musicians Club

The Historic Colored Musicians Club by Rick Falkowski, Forever Young Magazine, November 2019
The Historic Colored Musicians Club & Jazz Museum, thecoloredmusiciansclub.com
History of Buffalo Music & Entertainment by Rick Falkowski

Connecticut Street Armory

Buffalo: Connecticut Street Armory, museum.dmna.ny.gov
The Story of the 74th Regimental Armory in Buffalo, NY by Warren R. Bates, buffaloah.com
Exterior – Connecticut Street Armory, buffaloah.com
Explore Buffalo Building Profile: Tales of Two Armories by Susan Ernst, Buffalo Rising 5/29/2020
History of Buffalo Music & Entertainment by Rick Falkowski

Cornell Mansion

Buffalo's Delaware Avenue Mansions & Families by Edward T. Dunn
Historic & Influential People from Buffalo & WNY - the 1800s by Rick Falkowski
S. Douglas Cornell House, buffaloah.com

Curtiss Aircraft – Consolidated – Bell – M Wile

A Piece of History about to be History by Peter Gallivan, wrgz.com 12/27/2018
Curtis A-2 Triad, San Diego Air Space Museum, sandiegoairandspace.org
Historic & Influential People from Buffalo & WNY – the early 1900s by Rick Falkowski
Demolition crew moving in on century old M. Wile warehouse by Al Vaughters, wivb.com 11/30/2018

Curtiss Building – Curtiss Hotel

Harlow C. Curtiss Building, National Register of Historic Places Registration Form
The Curtiss Hotel: Buffalo's New 5-Star Retreat by Bruce Haydon, Buffalo Rising 3/19/2015

Curtiss Hotel: History. Elegance. Luxury by Amanda Dudek, Home Magazine 6/28/2022
Curtiss Hotel, curtisshotel.com

Cyclorama Building – Grosvenor Library

Cyclorama Building, preservationready.org
The Cyclorama Building by Meg Healy, buffaloah.com
The Buffalo Cyclorama Building by David Steele, buffalorising.com 2/17/2008
History of the Cyclorama Building, Lumsden McCormick CPA, lumsdencpa.com

D'Youville College

D'Youville University, dyu.edu
Houses of Worship: A Guide to the Religious Architecture of Buffalo NY by James Napora.
D'Youville University, Wikipedia.org

Darwin Martin House

Frank Lloyd Wright's Martin House, martinhouse.org
Frank Lloyd Wright Foundation, franklloydwright.org
Historic & Influential People from Buffalo & WNY – the early 1900s by Rick Falkowski

Delaware Midway Rowhouses

Hello Buffalo: https://hellobuffalohikes.com/?s=Rowhouses
https://buffalophotoblog.com/the-midway-rowhouses
https://buffaloah.com/a/del/midway/index.html

DL&W terminal & Train Sheds

Preservation by Dale Anderson, *Buffalo News* Gusto cover story, 2/1/1980
Delaware, Lackawanna & Western Terminal, *Buffalo News* 2/1/1917
DL&W Train Shed/NFTA Depot & Repair Center, buffaloah.com
Delaware, Lackawanna & Western Terminal, WNY Heritage, wnyheritage.org
DL&W Railroad Station, guide.in.ua
DL&W Buffalo Terminal, dlandwbuffalo.com

The Dun Building

https://hellobuffalohikes.com/the-dun-building-tall-and-strong/
https://www.priamllc.com/properties/the-dun-building/
https://buffaloah.com/a/pearl/110/int/index.html
http://blog.buffalostories.com/what-it-looked-like-wednesday-dun-building-buffalos-first-high-rise/

E. & B. Holmes Machinery Company Building,

The E. & B. Holmes Machinery Company Building, National Register of Historic Places Registration Form by Jennifer Walkowski 0f Clinton Brown Company Architecture in buffaloah.com
History – E. & B. Holmes Machinery Company – The Cooperage" buffaloah.com
River Lofts Buffalo, The Cooperage, riverloftsbuffalo.com
Cooperage Apartments, ellicottdevelopment.com
The Spirit of Buffalo Women by Rick Falkowski

E.M. Hager & Sons Company

E.M. Hager & Sons Company/Spaghetti Warehouse, preservationready.org
Latest National Register Landmark, 141 Elm Street by Newell Nussbaumer, Buffalo Rising 6/12/2013

E.M. Hager & Sons Company Building, National Register of Historic Places Registration Form by Caitlin T. Boyle, Preservation Studios 2/12/2013
The Planing Mill Buffalo, tmmontante.com

Edward M. Cotter Fireboat & Icebreaker

https://hellobuffalohikes.com/whats-happening-at-the-edward-m-cotter/
https://www.buffalohistorygazette.net/2010/09/today-in-buffalo-history-september-2.html
https://en.wikipedia.org/wiki/Edward_M._Cotter_(fireboat)
https://www.wivb.com/news/local-news/buffalo/an-inside-look-at-the-worlds-oldest-fireboat-the-edward-m-cotter/
https://stepoutbuffalo.com/188863-2/

Ellicott Square Building

Ellicott Square Building, Ellicott Development, ellicottdevelopment.com
Ellicott Square Building – History, buffaloah.com
Ellicott Square Building – Courtyard, buffaloah.com
120 years ago, city celebrated 'weird electric genius' Tesla by Maki Becker, *Buffalo News* 1/12/2017
Nikola Tesla Park: Innovation, Power, Place by queenseye, buffalorising.com 10/27/2020
Historic & Influential People from Buffalo & WNY – the 1800s by Rick Falkowski

F.N. Burt Company Factory

F.N. Burt Company Factory, Buffalo NY, Historic Structures, historic-structures.com
F.N. Burt Building, 500 Seneca Street, Preservation Ready sites, preservationready.org
F.N. Burt was World's Largest Paper Box Manufacturer by Chris Hawley, The Hydraulics Press 3/16/2009
Historic & Influential People from Buffalo & WNY – the early 1900s by Rick Falkowski
Five Hundred Seneca, Savarino, savarinocompanies.com

Forest Lawn Cemetery

Forest Lawn History, forest-lawn.com
Historic & Influential People from Buffalo & WNY – the 1800s by Rick Falkowski
Blue Sky Mausoleum at Forest Lawn Cemetery, franklloydwright.org

Fosdick-Maston Park High School – City Honors

City Honors School at Fosdick-Maston Park, cityhonors.org
The Fosdick Field Restoration Project, restoreourfield.org
Historic & Influential People from Buffalo & WNY – the 1800s by Rick Falkowski
City Honors/Masten Park High School. Preservationready.org

Foster Mansion

Orin Foster, Find a Grave, findagrave.com
Paul F. Mann from Curtiss Building Nomination for Listing on the State & National Registers of Historic Place's by Francis R. Kowsky and Martin Wachadio
Inside Buffalo's most expensive home listing in a decade by Liam Bunny, Buffalo Business First 6/10/2024
Gurney Becker & Bourne book created for listing of the property
Conversations with Kristan Anderson of Gurney Becker & Bourne
Big Deal: 50 Tudor Place sell for Record Price, buffalorising.com 3/25/2025
Historic Mansion sets record for most expensive home sale in Buffalo by Liam Bunny, Buffalo Business First 3/27/2025

Foster Mansion – DeRose Foods

Orin Foster, Find A Grave, findagrave.com
Orin Foster House, buffaloah.com
Orin Foster Mansion, commons.wikimedia.org
Foster-Milburn Company, preservationready.org
Foster, Milburn & Company, Kook Science, hatch.kookscience.com
Buffalo History Buff, Dr. Thomas' Eclectic Oil, buffalohistorybuff.com
Inside Look (and Sonocine Open House): OWM Integrative Wellness. buffalorising.com, 6/15/2023
OWM, owmintegrativewellness.com

Francis Fronczak House

Archives & Special Collections: Dr. Francis E. Fronczak Collection, E.H. Butler Library, library.buffalostate.edu
The Monumental Accomplishments of Dr. Francis Fronczak, 10/27/24, Canisius.edu
Historic & Influential People from Buffalo & WNY – the Early 1900s by Rick Falkowski
Patra Mangus research for Explore Buffalo tours of Broadway-Fillmore

Garret Club

Olmsted's Elmwood by Clinton E. Brown and Ramona Pando Whitaker
The Garret Club: Since 1902 – A Tradition of Learning and Friendship. Garretclub.com
The Garret Club – Buffalo, NY waymarking.com
Women in Buffalo History, Selected Sources in the Grosvenor Room, buffalolib.org
The Garret Club 1902-2022 A History – Jane Kwiatkowski & Martin Wachadlo
Recommendations by Catherine Schweitzer.

General Electric Tower

Buffalo General Electric Company History, written for the Pan-American Exposition, buffaloah.com
Niagara Mohawk Power Corp., Buffalo: Lake City on Niagara Land by Richard C. Brown & Bob Watson
Plugging into the History of the Iskalo Electric Tower by Paula D'Amico, WKBW 12/28/2023
Explore Buffalo Building Profile: Electric Tower, 4/30/2020, buffalorising.com

Goodyear Mansion

https://hellobuffalohikes.com/the-life-times-of-888-delaware-ave/
https://goodyearmansion.com/
https://buffaloah.com/a/del/888/index.html

Great Lakes & Paramount Theaters, Nemmer Furniture and the City Centre Condos

Then and Now: Massive Change by Steel, Buffalo Rising 3/28/2008
Great Lakes, Cinema Treasures, cinematreasurers.org
What it looked like Wednesday: City Centre/Nemmer Furniture by Steve Cichon, published in the *Buffalo News* and posted online in buffaloah.com in 2016.

Guaranty Building

https://hellobuffalohikes.com/the-guaranty-building-buffalos-first-skyscraper/
https://www.hodgsonruss.com/Louis-Sullivans-Guaranty-Building
https://archeyes.com/louis-sullivans-masterpiece-the-guaranty-building/
https://buffaloah.com/a/church/28/02ext/

Holy Angels Church

Holy Angels Catholic Church, holyangelsbuffalo.com
Houses of Worship: A Guide to the Religious Architecture of Buffalo New York by James Napora
D'Youville Finalizes Purchase of Former Holy Angels Church, dyu.edu
Torn-Down Tuesday: Bishop Fallon High School by Steve Cichon, *Buffalo News* 12.18.2018

Hotel Lafayette

Hello Buffalo: https://hellobuffalohikes.com/the-hotel-lafayette/
Louise Blanchard Bethune: Every Woman Her Own Architect: Kelly Hayes McAlonie
Buffalo Architecture & History: https://www.buffaloah.com/a/washngtn/391/index.html

Hotel Lenox

Lenox Hotel, Western New York Heritage, 2004
Lenox Hotel and Suites, lenoxhotelandsuites.com
a
The Picture Book of Earlier Buffalo, Buffalo Historical Society, 1912
Historic & Influential People from Buffalo & WNY – the 1800s by Rick Falkowski

Japanese Garden of Buffalo

Japanese Gardens of Buffalo, buffaloniagara.com
Blossomfestival.org
Friends of the Japanese Garden of Buffalo, Facebook Group
Your Specialty Gardens, Buffalo Olmsted Park System, bfloparks.org
History of the Japanese Garden, 2010 National Buffalo Garden Festival, buffaloah.com

Kleinhans Music Hall

History of Buffalo Music & Entertainment by Rick Falkowski
https://kleinhansbuffalo.org/
https://bpo.org/
https://buffaloah.com/a/sym/klein/index.html

Knox Mansion

Buffalo Delaware Avenue Mansions and Families by Edward T. Dunn
Grace Knox Mansion, American Aristocracy, americanaristocracy.com
Knox House, buffaloah.com
Historic & Influential People from Buffalo & WNY – the Early 1900s by Rick Falkowski
Historical tours of the Knox Mansion, Cellino Law, cellinolaw.com

Lafayette High School

Lafayette International Community High School of Buffalo. lafayetteinternationalbuffalo@weebly.com
Lafayette's problems lead to '11 closing and restructuring by Mary B. Pasciak, *Buffalo News* 7/8/2010
Lafayette High School, buffaloah.com
Central High School, buffaloah.com
Historic & Influential People from Buffalo & WNY – the 1900s by Rick Falkowski

Lafayette Square

Old County Court House, buffaloah.com
Lafayette Square, Visit Buffalo Niagara, visitbuffaloniagara.com
The Free-Soil Party Convention in Buffalo – August 9 & 10, 1848 by John Fagant

History of the B&ECPL, buffalolib.org
Buffalo – Lake City in Niagara Land by Richard C. Brown and Bob Watson
Where Did All the Cannons Go? by Jim Mendola, Buffalo Rising 7/13/2017
Soldiers & Sailors Monument in Lafayette Square by Benjamin R. Maryniak, Lancaster Historical Society

Linde Air Products Factory

National Register of Historic Places Registration form by Preservations Studios 2017.
National Resources of the Black Rock Planning Neighborhood by Jennifer Walkowski, Clinton Brown Company Architects 2010
Information from William Butler, director Black Rock Historical Society

Margaret Wendt House

William F. Wendt House – Margaret L. Wendt House, buffaloah.com
Margaret L. Wendt. Buffaloah.com
The Margaret L. Wendt Foundation, themlwendtfoundation.org
Historic & Influential People from Buffalo & WNY – the Early 1900s by Rick Falkowski

Market Arcade

Hello Buffalo: https://hellobuffalohikes.com/the-market-arcade/
Buffalo Spree Magazine: https://www.buffalospree.com/features/a-look-back-at-the-washington-market/article_ce426f4f-e3e1-550b-9056-072f377ec28b.html

Mayfair Lane

https://www.themayfaircastle.com/
https://buffaloah.com/a/archs/ebg/assoc/index.html
https://studiosky.co/blog/2014/the-mayfair-lane.html
https://www.realtor.com/realestateandhomes-detail/21-Mayfair-Ln_Buffalo_NY_14201_M45514-35914
Historic & Influential People from Buffalo & WNY – the early 1900s by Rick Falkowski

McDonnell & Sons – Granite Works

The Story of a Monumental Women by Timothy Bohen in WNY Heritage magazine Spring 2015
The Old Curiosity Shop: McDonnell & Sons Monument Company by Cynthia Van Ness in BuffaloResearch.com
McDonnell & Sons/Stone Art Memorial Company in buffaloah.com

Mentholatum Company

Historic & Influential People from Buffalo & WNY – the early 1900s by Rick Falkowski
Buffalo Lake City in Niagara Land by Richard C. Brown & Bob Watson
Mentholatum Company, buffaloah.com
us.mentholatum.com

Michigan Avenue Baptist Church

Historic Michigan Street Baptist Church, michiganstreetbaptistchurch.org
Houses of Worship: A Guide to the Religious Architecture of Buffalo NY by James Napora
Origins of the Michigan street Baptist Church Buffalo New York by Monroe Fordham
Historic & Influential People from Buffalo & WNY – the early 1900s by Rick Falkowski

Monroe Building

Monroe Building/Record theatre, preservationready.com
Architects in Buffalo, G. Morton Wolfe, buffaloah.com

Leonard "Lenny" Silver, music mogul, founder of Record Theatre chain dies, *Buffalo News* 3/12/2017
The Final Days of Record Theatre, newyorkglobalmarketingsolutions.com
Development Partners Announce the Grand Opening and Transformation of the Monroe Building in Buffalo NY. Community Development Coro. Community.com

Nash House Museum

Nash House Museum by Monroe Fordham, nashhousemuseum.com
Historic & Influential People from Buffalo & WNY – the Early 1900s by Rick Falkowski

Niagara Square

Niagara Square, Links to Buildings – Past and Present, buffaloah.com
A Brief History of Niagara Square, buffaloah.com

Nietzsche's, Mulligan's Brick Bar, The Old Pink

Buffalo in the 90s: Music at Nietzsche's by Steve Cichon, Buffalo Stories.
Nietzsche's, longtime hub of Buffalo live music scene is for sale by Jeff Miers, *Buffalo News* 1/17/2023
The Rebirth of Nietzsche's by queenseyes, Buffalo Rising 1/6/2025
Forgotten Buffalo 1/7/2025 Facebook post about Mulligan's fire
At Mulligan's Brick Bar, countless legacies extend beyond the fire by Sean Kirst, *Buffalo News* 1/11/2025
The "Old Pink" and the Aftermath as the Dust Settles by Matthew Nash, Buffalo Rising 7/3/2024

North Park Theatre,

North Park Theatre, northparktheatre.org
North Park Theatre, Cinema Treasures, cinematreasures.org
North Park Theatre, buffaloah.com
History of Buffalo Music & Entertainment by Rick Falkowski 2017

Old County Hall

Hello Buffalo: https://hellobuffalohikes.com/old-county-hall/
The Picture Book of Earlier Buffalo by Frank H. Severance
Buffalo Architecture & History: https://www.buffaloah.com/a/franklin/92/index.html

Oscar Meyer Motor Corp – Coles Restaurant

AAA Glidden Tour, exchange.aaa.com
Coles a spirited part of Buffalo since 1934 by Jane Kwiatkowski, *Buffalo News* 11/4/2014

Packard Motor Care Showroom

Packard Motor Care Showroom & Storage Facility, Historic Structures, historic-structures.com
Packard Apartments, regandevelopment.com
Packard Building, buffaloah.com
Dealership List, packardinfo.com
Franklin Automobile, wikipedia

Palace Burlesk, Studio Arena, Shea's 710 Theatre

Torn-Down Tuesday: The Palace Burlesk by Steve Cichon, buffalostories.com
The End of Royalty by George Kunz, *Buffalo News* 8/1/1993
Shea's 710 Theatre, Cinema Treasures, cinematreasures.org

Shea's kicks off renovation of 710 Theatre for MusicalFare with new cabaret and lounge by Jonathan D. Epstein, *Buffalo News* 3/6/2025

Parade/Humboldt/Martin Luther King, Jr. Park

Picture Book of Earlier Buffalo by Frank Severance
Dr. Martin Luther King, Jr. Park, Buffalo Olmsted Parks Conservancy, bfloparks.org
Country Park & City: The Architecture & Life of Calbert Vaux by Francis R. Kowsky, Oxford Press, 1998
The Parade House Illustrated History, buffaloah.com
Historic & Influential People from Buffalo & WNY – the 1800s by Rick Falkowski

Parkside Candy

Parkside Candy – A Buffalo Tradition since 1927, The Parkside Story, parksidecandy.com
It's Time: Parkside Candy looking for new buyer as owner plans to retire by Jaurdyn, wkbw.com
Forgotten Buffalo featuring locations of the Natural – film, forgottenbuffalo.com

Peace Bridge

The Peace Bridge: Buffalo and Fort Erie, Western New York Heritage, wnyheritage.org
The Peace Bridge, Niagara Falls Info, niagarafallsinfo.com
The Peace Bridge, peacebridge.com
Historic & Influential People from Buffalo & WNY – the Early 1900s by Rick Falkowski

Pierce Arrow Factory

Great Arrow News, The Pierce Arrow Museum Newsletter, the Building Edition, January 2022
Thepiercearrowlofts.com
Profiles Volume II: Historic & Influential People from Buffalo & WNY – the early 1900s by Rick Falkowski

Pierce Arrow Showrooms – Verner Building

Vernor Building, buffaloah.com
Packard Royalty Comes to Buffalo by Elizabeth Licata, Buffalo Spree, January 2022
Second Pierce-Arrow Showroom, buffaloah.com
Profiles Volume II: Historic & Influential People from Buffalo & WNY – the 1900s by Rick Falkowski
Architecture Around Buffalo: The Pierce Arrow Showroom, The Griffin, March 2023
Braun Cadillac Showroom, watercolor by Dr. V. Roger Lalli, narrative by David M. Rote

Rand Building

Hello Buffalo: https://hellobuffalohikes.com/the-rand-building-no-respect/
https://www.priamllc.com/properties/the-rand-building/
https://www.wnyhistory.org/portfolios/businessindustry/rand_building/rand_building.htm
https://buffaloah.com/a/lafsq/14/ext/index.html

Richardson Olmsted Campus – Buffalo State Hospital

Richardson Olmsted Campus, Richardson-olmsted.com
Richardson Olmsted Campus, Buffaloah.com
Richardson Complex, buffaloah.com

Richmond – Lockwood House

Richmond-Lockwood House, buffaloah.com
Buffalo's Delaware Avenue Mansions and Families by Edward T. Dunn

Robert T. Coles House & Studio

Architecture + Advocacy. Robert Traynham Coles, edited by William H. Steiner with Sylvia Coles. Buffalo Arts Publishing, Tonawanda, 2016.
Robert Traynham Coles, Burchfield Penney Art Center, burchfieldpenney.org
Robert T. Coles House & Studio, National Register of Historic Paces Registration Form by Jennifer Walkowski, Clinton Brown Company Architecture
Erie County Has Always Been Home to Black Excellence – Robert T. Coles by Charles Skowronski, Buffalo Rising 2/22/2022

Roswell Park Comprehensive Cancer Center

Roswell Park Comprehensive Cancer Center, roswellpark.org
National Cancer Institute, cancer.gov
Roswell Park Cancer Center: Scott Bieler Clinical Sciences Center, buffaloah.com
Additional research by Ida Goeckel, Female Musicians Fighting Breast Cancer

Saturn Club

Buffalo's Delaware Avenue Mansions & Families by Edward T. Dunn
Saturn Club, saturnclub.org
Saturn Club, buffaloah.com

Schenck House

EC200 Bicentennial Heritage Projects to Include Schenk House Marker, The German Citizen June-May 2002
Schenck House 1823 by Tara Mancini, buffaloah.com
Schenck House Restoration, Erie County Parks, Recreation & Forestry, erie.gov
Saving the Schenck House, Buffalo Rising 9/3/2017

Seneca Indian Cemetery

The Re-internment of Red Jacket and Mary Jemeson by Brian Kellogg
The Graves of Red Jacket, Western Ner York Heritage Magazine
On this day, June 19,1912, Dedication of a Cemetery (Once Removed) Buffalo Rising
Mary Jemison: White Woman of the Genesee, HMdb.org

Shea's Buffalo Theatre

1975 Application for the National Register of Historic Places for Shea's Buffalo Theatre, buffaloah.com
Shea's Buffalo Theatre, preservationready.org
Shea's O'Connell Preservation Guild, Interior Theatre Restoration, regionalcouncils.ny.gov
History of Buffalo Music & Entertainment by Rick Falkowski

Shea's Seneca

Shea's Seneca Theater, Cinema Treasures, cinematreasures.org
(Not quite) Torn-Down Tuesday: The remnants of the Shea's Empire by Steve Cichon, Buffalo Stories, buffalostories.com 11/27/2018
Preservation Ready/Shea's Seneca: A former movie palace still has possibilities by Elizabeth Licata, Buffalo Spree 4/6/2012
History of Buffalo Music & Entertainment by Rick Falkowski 2017
Shea's Seneca LLC, Schneider Development Services, schneiderdevelopmentservices.com
The Caz, thecazbuffalo.com

St. Joseph's Cathedral

https://hellobuffalohikes.com/st-josephs-cathedral-the-old-one/

https://www.buffalodiocese.org/st-joseph-cathedral/
https://buffaloah.com/how/1/1.3/stjos.html

St. Louis Church

St. Louis Roman Catholic Church, stlouischurch.org
Bishop John Timon, buffaloah.com
Catholic Encyclopedia: Buffalo, newadvent.org

St. Paul's Episcopal Cathedral

hellobuffalohikes.com/st-pauls-episcopal-cathedral/
St. Paul's Episcopal Cathedral, spcbuffalo.org/
St. Paul's Episcopal Cathedral, buffaloah.com

St. Stanislaus Roman Catholic Church

https://hellobuffalohikes.com/seven-churches-st-stanislaus-church/
http://ststansbuffalo.com/
http://ststansbuffalo.com/
https://poloniatrail.com/location/st-stanislaus-church/

Statler Hotel

Statler Buffalo, thestatlerbuffalo.com
Millard Fillmore House, buffaloah.com
Statler: America's Extraordinary Hotelman by Floyd Miller
Profiles Volume II: Historic & Influential People from Buffalo & WNY – the Early 1900s by Rick Falkowski
From social Center to Civic Center, The Historical Marker database, hmdb.org

Swannie House

Buffalo's Waterfront: A Guidebook, edited by Timothy Tielman, Partners' Press 1990
The Original Swanneys of the Swannie House by Steve Cichon, *Buffalo News* 12/11/2023
History of Buffalo Music & Entertainment by Rick Falkowski
It's been a great ride: Tears and memories flow as Swannie House closes following owner Tim Wiles' death by Francesco Bond, *Buffalo News* 11/7/2024
Former Swannie House bartender opens new downtown bar: McCormick's Pub by Tracy Drury, Business First 3/13/2025
9 Amazing Buffalo Bars that are over 75 Years Old by Nik Rivers, wbuf.com

Temple Beth Zion

May-June 2025 Jewish Journal
Temple Beth Zion 175th Anniversary Exhibit
Temple Beth Zion Cofeld Judaic Museum
Interviews with Temple Beth Zion staff

Thomas Motors/Curtis Aeroplane/Rich Products

E.R. Thomas Motor Company, buffaloah.com
E.R. Thomas Motor Company/Curtiss Aeroplane/Rich Products, preservationready.com
Profiles Volume II: Historic & Influential People from Buffalo & WNY – the Early 1900s by Rick Falkowski

Ticor Title Building – Unitarian Church

Ticor Title Building, Visit Buffalo Niagara, visitbuffaloniagara.com
First Unitarian Church – 1833 by James Napora in buffaloah.com.

Historic Lincoln Building Transforms into Erie County Pandemic Response Hub, erie.gov, 1/8/2021

Tifft Nature Preserve

https://www.tifft.org/about-us/
https://en.wikipedia.org/wiki/Tifft_Nature_Preserve
https://www.buffalorising.com/2007/09/tifft-nature-preserve-an-urban-sanctuary/

Times Beach

The Dream of Times Beach by Susan J. Eck, 2016, wnyhistory.com
History of Times Beach, The Friends of Times Beach Nature Preserve, friendsoftkimesbeachnp.org
Times Beach Cottages, Buffalo Stage Digital Commons, digitalcommons.buffalostate.edu
Times Beach Nature Preserve, Our Outer Harbor, ourouterharbor.org

Town Casino

Hello Buffalo: https://hellobuffalohikes.com/the-town-ballroom-the-town-casino/
https://townballroom.com/
https://stepoutbuffalo.com/business/location-town-ballroom/
https://buffaloah.com/a/main/681/town.html
History of Buffalo Music & Entertainment by Rick Falkowski

Tri-Main Center

trimaincenter.com/history
Bell P-59B Airacomet, National Museum of the USAFnationalmuseum.af.mil

Trico Plant #1

Preservation Ready: Trico Plant #1 by Elizabeth Licata, Buffalo Spree 3/2/2-12
Trico Building Apartments, tricobuildingapartments.com
Historic & Influential People from Buffalo & WNY – the Early 1900s by Rick Falkowski
Look Inside: Trico Building Apartments by WCPerspective, buffalorising.com 12/12/2024

Trinity Church

Trinity Episcopal Church, trinitybuffalo.org
Watson House/Buffalo club, buffaloah.com
Buffalo Architecture: A Guide by Kowsky, Goldman, Fox, Randall, Quinan and Lasher
Buffalo's Delaware Avenue Mansions & Families by Edward T. Dunn

Twentieth Century Club of Buffalo

Twentiethcenturyclubbuffalo.com
Twentieth Century Club (Buffalo, New York) on Wikipedia.org

Union Ship Canal

https://www.hmdb.org/m.asp?m=86097
https://www.buffalorising.com/2011/11/ship-canal-commons-opens-on-outer-harbor/
https://buffaloah.com/h/unionship/index.html
https://extapps.dec.ny.gov/data/DecDocs/B00164/Report.ERP.B00164.2002-06-01.Historical_Summary_Union_Ship_Canal_Hanna_Furnace.pdf
https://www.facebook.com/SteelPlantMuseumWNY/posts/happy-throwbackthursday-this-photograph-shows-the-hanna-furnace-corporation-alon/2916984365002079/

Unitarian Universalist Church

Unitarian Universalist Church of Buffalo, buffaloah.com

The UU Church of Buffalo - A short History, buffalouu.org
Unitarian Universalist Church of Buffalo, buffalouu.org
From 1880 to Today: Church of the Messiah, Fountain Plaza by Steve Cichon, *Buffalo News* 7/9/2018

University of Buffalo – South Campus

Edward Michael: 101 Year of Buffalo Life. Part 2: UB- Michael's Baby by Susan Eck, wnyhistory.org
Historic & Influential People from Buffalo & WNY – the Early 1900s by Rick Falkowski

Ulrich's Tavern

Ulrich's – Buffalo Oldest tavern, ulrichs1868tavern.com
Ulrich's Tavern Facebook page
Ulrich's Tavern – Buffalo's Oldest Bar is Back in Business, buffalorising.com
Conversations with the owner at the bar and saw the basement lift.

War Memorial Stadium

Johnnie B. Wiley Pavilion, Our Humble Beginnings, johnniewiley.org
Discovering Buffalo One Street at a Time by Angela Kepple, buffalostreets.com
The Jubilee Water Works, buffaloah.com
War Memorial Stadium, wikipedia.org

Weed Block Building

https://hellobuffalohikes.com/the-fidelity-trust-building-swan-tower/
http://blog.buffalostories.com/tag/weed-block/
http://blog.buffalostories.com/tag/weed-co/
https://archive.org/details/FromOxCartToAeroplaneWeedCoHistory18181918/page/n5/mode/2up

Werner Photography Building

The Werner Photography Building, by Clinton Brown Company, 1/11/2011
History of the Genesee Black: The Werner Building, Buffalo Rising 2/1/2011
Photography of Buffalo NY – the Genesee Gateway, buffalophotoblog.com

Wilcox Mansion – Theodore Roosevelt Inaugural Site

Buffalo Delaware Avenue; Mansions & Families by Edward T. Dunn
Historic & Influential People from Buffalo & WNY – the 1800s by Rick Falkowski
Second Looks: A Pictorial History of Buffalo & Erie County by Scott Eberle and Joseph E. Grande
The Caroline Incident during the Patriot War, buffaloah.com
T.R. Inaugural Site, trsite.org
How the Wilcox Mansion came to be and how it was almost lost, Buffalo Stories by Steve Cichon

William Conners Mansion

The *Courier-Express* Newspaper, E.H. Butler Library, library.buffalostate.edu
Conners House/Gilda's Clubhouse, buffaloah.com
Buffalo's Delaware Avenue Mansions & Families by Edward T. Dunn
Hospice to place former Gilda's Club Mansion at 1140 Delaware on Market, hispicebuffalo.com
Canisius to start renovations at Conners Mansion by James Fink, Buffalo Business First 6/6/2017

Meet the Mansions: A Stroll along Buffalo's historic Delaware Avenue by Susan Martin, *Buffalo News* 1/8/2021

William Dorsheimer House

The William Dorsheimer House: A Reflection of French Suburban Architecture in the Early Works of H.H. Richardson by Francis R. Kowsky
William Dorsheimer House, buffaloah.com
Buffalo Architecture: A Guide by Francis R. Kowsky
Buffalo's Delaware Avenue Mansions & Families by Edward T. Dunn
Historic & Influential People from Buffalo & WNY - the early 1900s by Rick Falkowski

Williams-Butler Mansion

https://buffaloah.com
https://library.buffalostate.edu/archives/ehbutler
https://edwinmellen.com/book/Life-and-Times-of-Edward-H-Butler-Founder-of-the-Buffalo-News-1850-1914/5632/
https://www.youtube.com/watch?v=NK7vT8_Ene8
https://www.pyramidbrokerage.com/markets/pyramid-brokerage-buffalo/

Wurlitzer – Tent City Building

Wurlitzer Building/Tent City, buffaloah.com
The Wurlitzer Store – Tent City, preservationready.org
Wurlitzer Flats, wurlitzerflats.com

YMCA Building – Olympic Towers

Young Men's Christian Association Building by Francis R. Kowsky, 1983
Young Men's Christian Association Building, buffaloah.com
YMCA Building/Olympic Towers, preservationready.org
On this day in 1884, The Original YMCA Building is Dedicated, You Tube - Born Buffalo
Olympic towers sold for $2.5 Million by Jonathan D. Epstein, *Buffalo News* 1/24/2012
YMCA Heritage Sites of Buffalo, thecompletepilgrim.com

CATTARAUGUS/ CHAUTAUQUA County Profiles

Counties of Cattaraugus & Chautauqua Profile

History of Chautauqua County, New York, Chautauqua.nygenweb.net
History of Cattaraugus County, cattco.gov
Major Adam Hoops, findagrave.com
The Chautauqua Movement, Chautauqua.com
Brief History of Olean, cityofolean.org

Athenaeum Hotel

https://www.christinesmyczynski.com/athenaeum-hotel.html
https://npgallery.nps.gov/GetAsset/73101c6c-c1ab-4716-b6fb-e4d288b6c889
https://picryl.com/media/athenaeumhotel-2b9294
https://www.post-journal.com/news/local-news/2021/08/athenaeum-hotel-the-grande-dame-of-chautauqua-institution/
https://npgallery.nps.gov/GetAsset/73101c6c-c1ab-4716-b6fb-e4d288b6c889

Chautauqua Institution

https://www.chautauqua.com/2021/chautauqua-movement-history/#:~:text=In%201874%2C%20John%20Heyl%20Vincent,in%20the%20professionalization%20of%20teaching.

https://chautauqua.pastperfectonline.com/bysearchterm?keyword=Seaver%20Gymnasium
https://en.wikipedia.org/wiki/Chautauqua_Institution

Lewis Miller Cottage

https://chqdaily.com/2016/08/one-familys-140-years-with-the-miller-cottage/
https://www.chq.org/event/miller-cottage-tours-7/
https://en.wikipedia.org/wiki/Lewis_Miller_Cottage

Fredonia Gas Light & Water Company

A Brief History of Natural Gas, American Public Gas Association, apga.org
Fredonia Gas Light and Waterworks Company by Lois Banas, chqgov.com
Early History of the Natural gas Industry by Gary G. Lash & Eileen P. Lash, Geosciences SUNY Fredonia 8/29/2014
The U.S. natural gas industry was born in 1821 in Fredonia NY by Frances Yeager, 9/10/2024, habhegger.com
First Gas Well in the U.S. was 1825 in New York by Gregory DL Morriss, hartenergy.com

Sunset Bay Beach Club

Silver Creek First Settlers Page, from Major G.L. Heaton, silvercreekny.com
Sunset Bay Beach Club, sunsetbayusa.com
Sunset Bay Beach Club, tourchautauqua.com
Sunset Bay USA on Facebook
Conversations with and information from Sam Bova
Borrello finds hospitality rewarding work by Jo Ward, Observer 6/18/2025, observertoday.com

Thomas Indian School

Landmark of Indian Days to Pass from Scene by Walter McCausland, *Buffalo Courier-Express* 10/13/1940
The Thomas Indian School and the "Irredeemable" Children of New York by Keith R. Burich, Syracuse University Press, 2016.
The Thomas Indian School: A Forgotten Tragedy by Terry Belke, wgrz.com 11/24/2016
Thomas Indian School: Social Experiment Resulting in Traumatic Effects by Lori V. Quigley, Mohican.com
Asher Wright, Wikipedia information

Lily Dale Assembly

Lily Dale Assembly Inc., lilydaleassembly.org
Lily Dale Assembly 2025 Program Book
Lily Dale: New York's Town that talks to Spirits by Chris Clemens, exploringupstate.com 8/1/2013
What is Mesmerism – Is it the same as Hypnosis by Jacqui Dornan, salillehypmosis.com

J.N. Adams Memorial Hospital,

"J.N. Adams Memorial Hospital, once a state-of-the-art facility for treatment of TB patients, now in ruins" Springville Journal October 18, 2023 by Jolene Hawkins
    https://www.springvillejournal.com/articles/j-n-adams-memorial-hospital-once-a-state-of-the-art-facility-for-treatment-of-tb-patients-now-in-ruins/#:~:text=In%20the%20year%201910%2C%20over,own%20money%20for%20this%20purpose
https://en.wikipedia.org/wiki/James_N._Adam
https://www.atlasobscura.com/places/j-n-adam-memorial-hospital

https://www.dictionary.com/browse/heliotherapy
https://web.archive.org/web/20080517212717/http://www.buffalonian.com/history/industry/mayors/Walden.htm
Profiles Volume I: Historic & Influential People from Buffalo & WNY - the 1800s by Rick Falkowski

Barcelona Lighthouse: First of Its Kind

https://www.us-lighthouses.com/barcelona-lighthouse
https://parks.ny.gov/parks/barcelonalighthouse
https://www.lighthousedigest.com/digest/StoryPage.cfm?StoryKey=416
https://www.lighthousefriends.com/light.asp?ID=293
https://www.cchsmcclurg.org/news/barcelona-lighthouse

Welch Grape Juice Factory

https://westfieldny.com/living-here/history#:~:text=In%201897%20Dr.,20%2C000%20acres%20devoted%20to%20vineyards
https://www.welchs.com/our-story/
https://www.tourchautauqua.com/media/blog/historical-marker-tour-of-chautauqua-county
http://www.concordgrape.org/bodyhistory.html
https://www.columbiadental.com/tales-from-the-operatory-part-vii-thomas-charles-welch-the-unfermented-grape-juice/

Cheektowaga

Town of Cheektowaga Profile

Town of Cheektowaga History by Gary Parks, Town Historian, tocny.org
A history of the Town of Cheektowaga by Julia Boyer Reinstein, Buffalo & Erie County Historical Society 1971, cheektowagachronical.com
Bellevue – Cheektowaga Historic Rails to Trails, hmdb.org
Cheektowaga Historical Association archives
Information from Maureen Gleason and Mike McDonough of the Cheektowaga Historical Museum
Historic & Influential People from Buffalo & WNY - the 1800s by Rick Falkowski

Buffalo Niagara International Airport

Aero Club of Buffalo – Our History, About the Aero Club of Buffalo, aeroclubofbuffalo.org
John Satterfield: Father of the Buffalo Airport by Susan J. Eck, wnyhistory.com
Buffalo Niagara International Airport, Airport History, buffaloairport.com
Buffalo History Gazette post on Facebook
Becker Flying Service, Cheektowaga Historical Museum, cheektowagahistorydotorg.wordpress.com

Chapel of Our Lady Help of Christians

The Chapel: A Comprehensive History of the Chapel and Pilgrimage of Our Lady Help of Christians Cheektowaga, NY and of the Alsatian Immigrant community at Williamsville NY by Glenn R. Atwell and Ronald Elmer Batt. Published by the Town of Cheektowaga in 1979.
Our Lady Help of Christians, cheektowagacatholicfamily.org
Profiles Volume I: Historic & Influential People from Buffalo & WNY: the 1800s – Second Edition by Rick Falkowski, 2024

George Urban Mansion

Cheektowaga's Historical Site – The urban-Winspear Estate – Pine Ridge Road, Town of Cheektowaga, tocny.org

Junior, Buffalo Architecture and History, buffaloah.com

Mansion selected as 2025 Decorators Show House, buffalorising.com, 10/3/2024

Historic & Influential People from Buffalo & WNY – the 1800s by Rick Falkowski

Reinstein Woods Nature Preserve

Friends of Reinstein Woods, reinsteinwoods.org

Reinstein Woods Nature Preserve & Environmental Education Center, dec.ny.gov

Historic & Influential People from Buffalo & WNY – the early 1900s by Rick Falkowski

St. Stephen's Evangelical Lutheran Home

St. Stephen's Evangelical Lutheran Home/Music Mall, preservationready.org

Evangelical Church Home, Cheektowaga cheektowagahistorydororg.wordpress.com

CK Historical Association purchase to preserve History by Caitlyn Stair, Cheektowaga Bee, 4/25/2024

Cheektowaga Historical Association buys long sought after Building, wearebuffalo.net

Conversations with Keith Gregor and Julie Roland

War of 1812 Cemetery

War of 1812 Cemetery, Cheektowaga Historical Association, cheektowagahistorydotorg.wordpress.com

The Creek Road Graveyard by J.A. Buscaglia, warof1812cemetery.com

Profiles Volume I: Historic & Influential People from Buffalo & WNY – the 1800s by Rick Falkowski

Clarence

Town of Clarence Profile

Clarence Historical Society archives

History of the Town of Clarence by Oneta M. Baker

The League of the Haudenosaunee or Iroquois by Lewis Henry Morgan

Asa Ransom House

Historic & Influential People from Buffalo & WNY – the 1800s – Second Edition by Rick Falkowski

The Mystery of Ransom's Tavern by Heath J. Szymczak. Erie.gov/clarence

The New Old Duke of Clarence by Nancy Blumenstalk Mingus, Buffalo Spree, 10/23/2022

The Duke of Clarence website, dukeofclarence.com

Clarence Town Park Club House

Clarence: Images of The Hollow, a Publication of Clarence Historical Society Press by C. Douglas Kohler.

The History of Clarence, Past and Present, July 4, 1924

Clarence Bee

Buffaloah.com

Historical Society of Clarence & Goodrich-Landow Cabin

Historical Society of the Town of Clarence

Historic Preservation Commission, erie.gov/clarence

Goodrich-Landow Log Cabin, hmdb.org

Discussions with Sara Larkin

Spaulding Lake

Clarence: Images of The Hollow – A Publication of Clarence Historical Society Press by C. Douglas Kohler
When Spaulding Lake in Clarence NY was a quarry, answers.com
Spaulding Lake – Julius Blum Builders, juliusblumbuilders.com
Discussions with Clarance and Town of Newstead Historical Societies

East Aurora/ Marilla

Village of East Aurora Profile

About the Village, eastaurora.gov
History of the City of Buffalo & Erie County by Henry Perry Smith
Town of Aurora, NY -About Us, townofaurora.com
All Christmas movies filmed in eat Aurora by Don Vidler, vidlers5and10.com
Historic & Influential People from Buffalo & WNY – the 1800s and the Early 1900s by Rick Falkowski

Fisher-Price Toy Company

https://www.theguardian.com/lifeandstyle/2020/jun/13/ninety-and-still-into-toys-how-fisher-price-pulled-a-town-out-of-depression-and-may-do-so-again
https://www.toysnplaythings.media/fisher-price-looks-back-at-its-90-year-history/
https://www.eastaurorany.com/wp-content/uploads/2021/01/Answers_to_Scavenger_Hunt.pdf
https://www.nndb.com/people/228/000178691/
https://en.wikipedia.org/wiki/Fisher-Price
https://corporate.mattel.com/brand-portfolio/fisher-price
Historic & Influential People from Buffalo & WNY – the early 1900s by Rick Falkowski

Globe Hotel

Obituary for Victor H. Balthasar, newspapers.com
Historian's Office offers rate view inside Globe Hotel Guest Registers by Robert Goller, East Aurora Advertiser, 10/29/2024
The View from Right Filed: Spinning the Globe by Rick Ohler, East Aurora Advertiser, 1/25/23
    Historic East Aurora Restaurant by Christine A. Smyczynski, cityseeker.com
New York: The Globe Restaurant, spookeats.com, 5/27/2019

Hamlin Village Farms

The Judges Stand, aurorahistoricalsociety.com
Historic & Influential People from Buffalo & WNY – the 1800s by Rick Falkowski
Buffalo's Historic Neighborhoods: Hamlin Park by Mark Goldman, Buffalo Spree 7&8/2000
Horsing Around in Buffalo – Long Live the King, Buffalo History gazette. 3/7/2011

Knox Farm State Park

Images Of America: Knox Farm State Park by Gerald L. Halligan and Renee M Oubre
The Knox Summer Estate Saturday, April 27th to Sunday May 19, 2013 Junior League of Buffalo Show House History Jane C. Hamilton, Show House Historian Marie-Cecile O. Tidwell, PhD, Historian Committee Mary Falzone, Historian Committee
https://buffaloah.com/a/EastAur/knox/hamilton.pdf

Millard Fillmore House & Museum

https://buffaloah.com/h/presdts/scho4/scho4.html
https://www.aurorahistoricalsociety.com/pages/millard-fillmore-presidential-site
https://en.wikipedia.org/wiki/Fillmore_House
Historic & Influential People from Buffalo & WNY by Rick Falkowski

Roycroft Campus

https://en.wikipedia.org/wiki/Elbert_Hubbard
https://www.roycroftcampuscorporation.com/
https://www.crookedlakereview.com/newsocietygenesee/visits/0602roycroft.html
https://web.archive.org/web/20090911042746/http://tps.cr.nps.gov/nhl/detail.cfm?ResourceId=1460&ResourceType=District
https://buffaloah.com/a/archsty/a-c/roy/royinn/index.html
https://www.thecraftsmanbungalow.com/elbert-hubbard-roycroft-campus/
http://www.roycrofter.com/
https://www.museumaacm.org/exhibitions/love_labor_art.php
https://npgallery.nps.gov/NRHP/GetAsset/NHLS/74001236_photos

Roycroft Inn

https://en.wikipedia.org/wiki/Elbert_Hubbard
https://www.crookedlakereview.com/books/saints_sinners/martin15.html
https://www.roycroftcampuscorporation.com/
https://buffaloah.com/a/archsty/a-c/roy/royinn/index.html
https://roycroftinn.com/our-history/
Kitty Turgeon, 81, dies; preservationist was devoted to Roycroft by Michelle Kearns, *Buffalo News* 11/5/2014

Vidler's 5 & 10

Vidlers5and10.com
Just look for the red & white awning: Vidler's 5&10 received state attention by Hope Winter, wivb.com

Marilla Country Store

Marilla Country Store, marillacountrystore.com
Marilla Country Store, Retail Council of New York State, retailcouncilnys.com
Marilla Country Store, iloveny.com

Grand Island

Town of Grand Island Profile

Grand Island Historical Society, Isledegrande.com
Cinderella Island by Rob Roy Macleod, 1950
Images of America by Gerald Carpenter & June Justice Crawford, 2015

Bedell House

The History of Grand Island – 1952 Grand Island Centennial Bood, isledegrande.com
Grand Island's Lost & Forgotten Guiled Age by Alice E. Gerand, 2/10/2018, wnypapers.com

Grand Island Nike Base

Buffalo/Niagara Defense Area, astronautix.com
Hamburg Nike Missile Base, Hamburg Historical Society, hamburghistoricalsociety.org

Niagara Falls – Buffalo Defense Nike Battery, U.S. Army Corps of Engineers, Nn.uaXW.rmy.mil
Lockport Air Force Station, fortwiki.com
Nike Base Park, Grand Island Recreation Dept., grandislandny.myrec.com
Grand Island Historical Society, Mary Stang-Cooke

Lewis Allen Villa at River Lea

Allenton farm/Creating Beaver Island State Park, hmbd.org
Grover Cleveland & Grand Island/Lewis F. Allen & WNY, hmbd.org
Grand Island Historical Society, isledegrande.com
Historic & Influential People from Buffalo & WNY by Rick Falkowski

WBEN Radio: Transmitter Building

History of Buffalo Music & Entertainment by Rick Falkowski
Forgotten Buffalo
Buffalo Broadcasters Association
Buffalostories.com

Hamburg/Blasdell/Lake View

Town of Hamburg Profile

https://www.hmdb.org/m.asp?m=82421
https://purple.niagara.edu/library-old/buffhist/1-511-524.pdf
Hamburg town, NY: Interesting Facts, Famous Things & History Information | What Is Hamburg town Known For?
https://www.townofhamburgny.gov/485/History

Penn Dixie Fossil Park & Nature Reserve

Penn Dixie Fossil Park & Nature Reserve, penndixie.org
Penn Dixie Fossil Park & Nature Preserve, ancientodysseys.com
Penn Dixie Site – Middle Devonian, nautloid.net
Drive Seeks to preserve fossil site Hamburg Quarry considered valuable by Matt Gryta & Tom Ernst *Buffalo News* 3/5/1990
Hamburg OKs buying fossil quarry site by Gene Warner & Tom Ernst, *Buffalo News* 2/27/1995
Volunteer Cleanup set May 11 at Penn Dixie Quarry Site by Barbara O'Brien, *Buffalo News* 5/1/1996

Woodlawn Beach

Woodlawn Beach: A Shadow of its former Glory by Eugene Covelli, Buffalo Evening News 9/15/1996
Town of Hamburg looks to shed surplus properties by Dave McKinley, wgrz.com 10/17/2019
Woodlawn Beach state Park, Wikipedia.org
The Spacious Lake Erie Beach in New York with Beautiful Folling Sand Sunes and Trails, explore.com
Sole at Woodlawn Beach, soleatwoodlawnbeach.com

Idlewood Association

Except from the *Buffalo Courier Express* Sunday April 2 1933
https://chrisandrle.wordpress.com/2016/03/01/the-great-gatling-land-boom-hamburg-new-york/

https://web.archive.org/web/20080517212717/http://www.buffalonian.com/history/industry/mayors/Walden.htm
http://seiz2day.com/lakeviewny/TOC-FormativeYears.pdf
https://www.hodgsonruss.com/media/news/1578_Hodgson%20Russ%20Article%20WNY%20Heritage%20Spring.pdf

Lake View Hotel

"Out of the Past, The Lake View Hotel, Home of Smorgasbord, 1960: The Hamburg Sun, Oct. 5 2000 p.8
http://seiz2day.com/lakeviewny/lakeviewphotos.htm
https://en.wikipedia.org/wiki/Lake_View,_New_York#cite_note-7

Kenmore/Tonawanda Town

Village of Kenmore Profile

Tonawanda-Kenmore Historical Society archives

Eberhardt Mansion

Eberhardt History, buffaloah.com
Belt Line Railroad in Buffalo by Mark Goldman, High Hopes: The Rise and Decline of Buffalo New York
In Eberhardt Mansion, Buffalo's Wheel Chair Home for Incurables by Steve Cichon *Buffalo News* 6/17/2021

Huntley Power Plant

Rising from the ashes, a Buffalo suburb ends its dependence on coal by Elizabeth McGowan, grist.org 7/11/2017
Court upholds Tonawanda's right to take over long-shuttered Huntley Power Plant Stephen T. Watson, *Buffalo News* 6/23/2023
Tonawanda moving forward in restoring Huntley Plant property by Aidan Joly, *Buffalo News* 2/7/2025
Historic & Influential People from Buffalo & WNY – the Early 1900s by Rick Falkowski

Lackawanna

City of Lackawanna Profile

City of Lackawanna, lackawannany.gov
EC200: A Brief History of Lackawanna by Charles Skowronski, Buffalo Rising 10/28/2021
Historic & Influential People from Buffalo & WNY – the 1800s and Early 1900s by Rick Falkowski

Bethlehem Steel:

https://www.abandonedamerica.us/lackawanna-steel
https://lipsitzponterio.com/asbestos-job-site/bethlehem-steel/history-of-bethlehem-steel-lackawanna-plant/
https://www.buffalotales.net/post/when-steel-was-king
https://en.wikipedia.org/wiki/Lackawanna_Steel_Company

Holy Cross Cemetery

Holy ross Cemetery, Catholic Cemeteries Diocese of Buffalo, buffalocatholiccemeteries.org
Holy Cross Cemetery, buffaloah.com
Father Baker's Tomb, Our Lady of Victory National Shrine & Basilica, olvbasillica.org

John B. Weber Mansion

Colonel John B. Weber, buffaloah.com
Colonel John B. Weber, William G. Pomeroy Foundation, wgpfoundation.org
Information for William Tojek, Lackawanna City Historian and assistance from Andrea Haxton

Our Lady of Victory Basilica

https://www.olvbasilica.org/history-of-the-shrine
https://hellobuffalohikes.com/our-lady-of-victory-basilica-the-man-who-built-it/
https://en.wikipedia.org/wiki/Nelson_Baker
https://en.wikipedia.org/wiki/Our_Lady_of_Victory_Basilica_(Lackawanna,_New_York)

Lancaster

Town of Lancaster Profile

Holland Land Company Purchase NS ITS EARLY Settlement, nyheritage.org
History of the City of Buffalo and Erie County by Henry Perry Smith
Historic & Influential People from Buffalo & WNY – the 1800 by Rick Falkowski

Hull House & Gipple Cabin

Hullfamilyhome.com
Hull Family Home and Farmstead, buffaloah.com

Lancaster Opera House

Lancaster Opera House, Info, lancasteropera.org
George J. Metzger, buffaloah.com
Lancaster Opera House, Theatre Alliance of Buffalo, thetheatreallianceofbuffalo.com

Lewiston

City of Lewiston Profile

Historiclewiston.org
Lewiston Area Historical society, lewistonhisoricalsociety.com
Village of Lewiston, villageoflewiston.net
Counting down to Lewiston's bicentennial: Kelsey Tavern a magnificent marvel, Niagara Frontier Publications, 6/17/2022

Artpark

The Historical Marker database. HMdb.org
Artpark.net
Profiles Volume I: Historic & Influential People from Buffalo & WNY – the 1800s by Rick Falkowski

Benjamin Barton House

History of Lewiston, historiclewiston.org
Historic & Influential People from Buffalo & WNY – the 1800s by Rick Falkowski
Historic Marker Database, HMdb.org

Frontier House

Historiclewiston.org
The Frontier House: Lewiston's Crown Jewel
U.S. Register of Historic Places on waymarketing.com

Our Lady of Fatima National Shrine
Basilica of the National Shrine of Our Lady of Fatima, barnaabites.com
Basilica of the National Shrine of Our Lady of Fatima, Polonia Trail, poloniatrail.com

Lockport/ Burt/ Olcott/ Newfane

City of Lockport Profile
City of Lockport Resources Survey by The Clinton Brown Company, April 2011
History of Newfane, newfanehistoricalsociety.com
Historic & Influential People of Buffalo & WNY – the 1800s by Rick Falkowski

Van Horn Mansion
The Niagara Historic Trail by North Tonawanda History Museum 2008-9.
Haunted History Trail of New York State, hauntedhistorytrail.com
Van Horn Mansion, newfanehistoricalsociety.com

Colonel William Bond/Jesse Hawley House
William Bond/Jesse Hawley House, Niagara History Center, niagarahistory.org
Colonel William Bond House – Jesse Hawley House, iloveny.com
Jesse Hawley, findagrave.com

Olcott Beach Amusement Park
Olcott Beach: A Lakeside Resort, HMdb.org
New York's Olcott Beach – Then and Now by Karen Roberts, travelthruhistory.com
Olcott Beach Carousel Park, olcottbeachcarouselpark.org
History of Buffalo Music & Entertainment by Rick Falkowski

Niagara Falls

City of Niagara Falls Profile
History of Niagara Falls New York, niagarafallsusa.org
The French Settlement in Niagara, niagarafallsinfo.com
Telsa and Niagara Falls, discoverniagara.org
Historic & Influential People from Buffalo & WNY – the 1800s by Rick Falkowski

Adams Power Plant Transformer House
National Register of Historic Places, U.S. Dept. of the Interior, npgallery.nps.gov
Adams Power Plant Transformer House, Society of Architectural Historians, sah-archipedia.org
Edward Dean Adams Power Plant by Allison Meier, Atlas Obscura, atlasobscura.com

Castellani Art Museum
Armand Castellani: From Apples to Art by Ann Podd, *Courier Express* 12/9/1979
A Sackfull of Dreams by Alice P. Stern, *Buffalo News*, Buffalo Magazine 10/30/1988
How Armand Castellani learned about art and shared the wealth by Richard Huntington, *Buffalo News* 2/7/1999.
Conversations with and information from Bob Castellani
The Armand & Eleanor Castellani Collection: Art for the Public Eye by Castellani Art Museum

Cayuga Island
Cayuga Island had, then lost, the Pan American Exposition by Ann Marie Linnabery, Lockport Journal 2/27/2016

The Pan American Exposition by Isabe; Vaughan James, bechsed.nylearns.org
Cayuga Island, Wikipedia

DeVeaux College

DeVeaux College Niagara Falls NY 1857-1971, lostcolleges.com
DeVeaux School – Niagara Falls, Big Daddy Dave, blogger.com 9/16/2019
Desolation at DeVeaux Woods, sheepieniagara.com
DeVeus Woods State Park, parks.ny.gov
Historic & Influential People from Buffalo & WNY – the 1800s Second Edition by Rick Falkowski 2024

Devils Hole State Park

Devils Hole State Park, parks.ny.gov/parks
Devils Hole State Park, The Historical Marker Database, HMdb.org
Devils Hole Ravine, niagarafallsinfo.com
Devils Hole Cave by Scott A. Ensminger, falzguy.com

Fort Schlosser

Fort Schlosser, Historical Marker Database, hmdb.org
Fort Schlosser, New York State Military Museum and Veterans Research Center, museum.dmna.ny.gov/forts
Profiles Volume I: Historic & Influential People from Buffalo & WNY – the 1800s by Rick Falkowski

Great Bear Market

Armand J. Castellani, Western New Yorker of the Year by Maia B. Scrivani, WNY January 1988
Tops co-founder Castellani Dies by Karen Brady & Tom Buckham, Buffalo News 2/1/2002
Castellani dies at 84 by Susan Mikula Campbell & Don Glynn, Niagara Gazette 2/1/2002
A Sackful of Dreams by Alice P. Stern, Buffalo Magazine 10/30/1988
Information from Bob and Larry Castellani

Love Canal

Love Canal: A Brief History by Dr. Jordan Kleiman, Geneseo.edu/history
Love Canal: Timeline and photos, University Archives, University at Buffalo, SUNY
Love Canal, Wikipedia
Superfund: The Waste Left Behind by Tommy Delp, Rochester Institute of Technology 3/3/2022

Niagara Falls State Park

Niagara Falls History, niagarafallsstatepark.com
Augustus and Peter Porter, niagarafallsinfo.com
Porter Clan had Great Impact by Clarence Adams, *Buffalo News* 6/14/1998
Historic & Influential People from Buffalo & WNY – the 1800s by Rick Falkowski
The Hydropower of Niagara Falls, niagarafallsusa.com
Terrapin Point, niagarafrontier.com

Niagara University

Niagara University, Niagara.edu/nu-history
Niagara University in Ontario, niagarau.ca

Oakwood Cemetery

Oakwood is where Niagara's history resides, oakwoodniagara.org

Oakwood Cemetery, Niagara National Heritage Area, discoverniagara.org

Peter Porter Mansion

Preservation Award Winner: Porter Mansion, by Sarah Maurer, Buffalo Rising, 5/8/2011
A Closer Look: The Peter A. Porter Mansion in Niagara Falls by Mark Mulville, *Buffalo News*, 5/11/2022
Greenway Funding helps preserve historic Niagara Falls mansion by Thomas J. Prohaska, *Buffalo News* 3/15/2022.
Oakwood Cemetery, oakwoodniagara.org

Schoellkopf Power Plant

Schoellkopf Power Station Ruins Site, niagarafallsstatepark.com
Schoellkopf Power Station, tripadvisor.com
The Niagara Falls Hydraulic Power and Manufacturing Company, nyheritage.org
Niagara Falls Power Project, discoverniagara.org

Whitney Mansion

Solon Whitney Mansion, Niagara Falls Historic Prevention Society, nfhps.org
Historic & Influential People from Buffalo & WNY – the 1800s by Rick Falkowski
Parkhurst Whitney, Find a Grave, findagrave.com

North Tonawanda

City of North Tonawanda Profile

Executive Director North Tonawanda History Museum Archives

Cantilever Bridge

Bascule Bridge at North Tonawanda, theniagarabanch.wordpress.com
North Tonawanda: The Lumber City edited by Donna Zellner Neal
North Tonawanda: Historic Treasures. Presented by The North Tonawanda History Museum and edited by Donna Zellmer Neal

Carnegie Library

Andrew Carnegie by David Nasaw
Carnegie Libraries, National Park Service, nps.org
The Gospel of Wealth, carnegie.org
Anderw Carnegie: American industrialist and philanthropist, Britannica.com
North Tonawanda: Historic Treasures, NT History Museum edited by Donnal Zellner Neal

DeGraff Mansion

North Tonawanda Historic Treasurers, North Tonawanda Historical Society edited by Donna Zellner Neal
DeGraff Mansion (273 Goundry Street), North Tonawanda History, nthistory.com
DeGraff Mansion Memoirs page on Facebook and conversations with Maria Aurigema
DeGraff Mansion Restoration page on Facebook and info from David Dingman

Gateway Harbor Park

The Erie Canal: From Lockport to Buffalo by John W. Percy, Partner's Press 1979
North Tonawanda: The Lumber City, edited by Donna Zellner Neal for the NT History Museum.
Gateway Harbor North Tonawanda, gatewayharbornt.com
Tonawandas Gateway Harbor Park, tonawandasgatewayharbor.net
Canal Fest of the Tonawandas, canalfest.org

Herschell Carrousel Factory

Herschell Carrousel Factory Museum, carrouselmuseum.org
Historic & Influential People from Buffalo & WNY – the Early 1900s by Rick Falkowski
Herschell-Spillman Motor Company Complex, National Register, flickr.com
Information from Ian K. Seppala and Ward Bray

Niagara Falls Power Transfer Station

The Birthplace of Electricity by David Bertola, nationalgridus.com, 12/21/2022
Renovations Complete at Historic Transformer Building by David Bertola, nationalgridus.com, 10/9/2023
National Grid Transformer Building Restoration Project, Buffalo Rising, 10/7/2023
History of Electricity Preserved in North Tonawanda by Nancy A. Fischer, Buffalo News, 6/22/2014
Profiles Volume I: Historic & Influential People from Buffalo & WNY – the 1800s by Rick Falkowski

Niagara Power Building

North Tonawanda: The Lumber City edited by Donna Zellner Neal
North Tonawanda: Historic Treasures. Presented by The North Tonawanda History Museum and edited by Donna Zellmer Neal

North Tonawanda Erie Railroad Station

Railroad Museum of the Niagara Frontier, nfcnrhs.org
North Tonawanda: The Lumber City by N.T. History Museum, edited by Donna Zellner Neal
North Tonawanda: Historic Treasures by N.T. History Museum, edited by Donna Zellner Neal
Railroad Museum of the Niagara Frontier, Which Museum, whichmuseum.com

Remington Rand Building

Herschell-Spillman Motor Company Complex, National Register, flickr.com
Herschell-Spillman – General Discussion, Antique Automobile Club of America, forums.aaca.org
North Tonawanda Momentum, Lumber City Development, ntmomentum.com/nowthen/
Remington Rand, National Museum of American History, americanhistory.si.edu
North Tonawanda: The Lumber City, North Tonawanda History Museum edited by Donna Zeller Neal
Historic & Influential People from Buffalo & WNY – the early 1900s by Rick Falkowski

Riviera Theatre

West Herr Riviera Theatre, rivieratheatre.org
North Tonawanda: The Lumber City, North Tonawanda History Museum edited by Donna Zellner Neal
The Riviera Story by Diane Meholick
History of Buffalo Music & Entertainment by Rick Falkowski

Wurlitzer Building

History of the Wurlitzer Building, thewurlitzerbuilding.com
History of Buffalo Music & Entertainment by Rick Falkowski
Wurlitzer Industrial Park, thewurlitzerbuilding.com

Orchard Park

Town of Orchard Park Profile

https://purple.niagara.edu/library-old/buffhist/1-524-534.pdf
https://en.wikipedia.org/wiki/Orchard_Park,_New_York
https://www.orchardparkny.gov/about/orchard-park-history/

Chestnut Ridge Park

https://www3.erie.gov/parks/chestnut-ridge
https://commons.wikimedia.org/wiki/File:Chestnut_Ridge_Park_casino,_Orchard_Park,_New_York_-_20210703.jpg
https://chestnutridgeconservancy.org/nostalgic-chestnut-ridge/
https://hellobuffalohikes.com/chestnut-ridge-park/
https://chestnutridgeconservancy.org/nostalgic-chestnut-ridge/

Johnson-Jolls House:

https://www.hmdb.org/m.asp?m=80749
https://ophistoricalsociety.wordpress.com/

Orchard Park Buffalo, Rochester, Pittsburgh Station

http://www.trainweb.org/wnyrhs/opdepotFrame1Source1.htm
https://en.wikipedia.org/wiki/Orchard_Park_station
https://www.hmdb.org/m.asp?m=80566
https://www.buffalospree.com/wny_life/harry-yates-orchard-park-legacy/article_4024c280-5c37-11eb-a63a-57e8d7a6aa2a.html
https://www.optraindepot.org
Orchard Park BR&P Depot Facebook page

Olmsted Camp

https://olmstedcamp.com/history/
https://en.wikipedia.org/wiki/Rider–Hopkins_Farm_and_Olmsted_Camp
https://buffaloah.com/a/kowsky/camp/hp/hp.html

Springville/Colden

Village of Springville Profile

Village of Springville – History, villageofspringvilleny.org
Town of Colden – History, townofcolden.com
History of the Town of Concorde and Village of Springville by Jolene Hawkins, springvillejournal.com
100th Anniversary of the Springville Country Club, buffalogolfer.com

Buffum Inn:

https://www.hmdb.org/m.asp?m=104177
https://buffalonews.com/news/buffum-inn/article_fd91b8e8-331a-5199-b9c4-5184ed23b839.html
https://www.archivaria.com/GdDhistory/GdDhistory48.html
https://purple.niagara.edu/library-old/buffhist/1-601-607.pdf
Buffum Museum, buffumfamilyassociation.com

Springville-Griffith Institute

Springville-Griffith Celebrates Storied Past by Janice L. Habuda & Elmer Ploetz, *Buffalo News* 5/17/2005

Springville-Griffith Institute, springvillegi.org
Springville-Griffith Institute, Facebook
History of the City of Buffalo and Erie County by Henry Perry Smith, 1884

Waite Building

Springville Journal archives at Lucy Bensley Center
A Brief History of Local Anesthesia by John Nathan & Lynda Asadourian, International Journal of Head and Neck Surgery, January-March 2016
Museum Donations find Purpose in Springville Heritage Building by Robin Comeau, UB Dentist, Spring 2018
Waite of Springville Still Experimenting *Buffalo Courier-Express*, March 1, 1953
Dr, Ralph B. Waite, Pioneer in Painless Dentistry, Dies, Buffalo Evening News
Dr. Ralph B. Waite, Springville History Souvenir 1939, published by the Springville Fire Department

Warner Museum and Dygert Farm

Handout from the official opening of Warner Museum, May 22, 1954 courtesy Concord Historical Society archives
A Historical Documentary and Memoirs of the Springville Dygert Family, Farm, Racetrack and Horse-Racing Exploits [from] 1812-2012 by J. Peter Dygert
Pop Warner A life on the Gridiron by Jeffrey J. Miller, 2015
Springville Journal, May 3, 1945 & January 4,1951

Tonawanda, City of

City of Tonawanda Profile

Historical Society of the Tonawandas archives

Benjamin Long Homestead

North Tonawanda: The Lumber City by Donna Zeller Neal
Pieces of the Past: Benjamin Long Homestead by Jill Keppeler, wnynewspapers.com
The Long Homestead, hmdb.org

Tonawanda Armory

National Register of Historic Places Registration form complied by Nancy L. Todd in December 1993
Tonawanda Castle, A Building Brought Back to Life, tonawandacastle.com
Explore Buffalo Building Profile: Tales of Two Armories by Explore Buffalo, buffalorising.com 5/29/2020

Tonawanda Railroad Station

Great Railroad Stations – Tonawanda NY by John C. Dahl, trainweb.org
North Tonawanda History – Trains and Trolleys, nthistory.com
The Railroad, The Historical Marker database, hmdb.org

West Seneca

Town of West Seneca Profile

West Seneca Historian & West Seneca Historical Society Archives

Charles E. Burchfield Nature & Art Center

History of Burchfield "Lots 94 & 95" by James E. Manley, westseneca.gov
Burchfield Nature & Art Center, burchfieldnac.org

Historic & Influential People from Buffalo & WNY – the Early 1900s by Rick Falkowski

Christian Metz House

Christian Metz House, The Historic Marker Database, hmdb.org

Metz House, West Seneca "jewel" is target of rehabilitation effort by T.J. Pignataro, *Buffalo News* 4/22/2012

Christian Metz House, westsenecahistory.com

Lein's Park

Lein's Park, westsenecahistory.com

Leinsny.html, freepages.rootsweb.com

Young Development pursues projects in West Seneca, Cheektowaga by Jonathan D. Epstein, *Buffalo News* 10/5/2023

Malecki Mansion

Rochester firm plans affordable housing at former West Seneca mansion by Jonathan D. Epstein, *Buffalo News* 7/19/2024

West Seneca proposal would turn mansion into apartments by Jacob Tierney, Business First 6/18/2024

Malecki conversations

Malecki's Meats promotional item brings back memories by Gregory Witul, ampoleagle.com 1/8/2013

Joseph Malecki Family History, myheritage.com

Historic & Influential People from Buffalo & WNY by Rick Falkowski

Mayer Brothers

Mayer Brothers, mayerbrothers.com

Mayer Brothers Cider Mill, Visit Buffalo Niagara, visitbuffaloniagara.com

Buffalo Behind the Scenes: Mayer Brothers by Marlee Tuskes, 8/31/2022, wivb.com

Schwabl's

https://www.schwabls.com/history/

https://www.yumpu.com/en/document/read/3331994/a-short-history-of-schwabls

https://buffaloah.com/a/archs/vaux/parade/index.html#:~:text=For%20the%20new%20Buffalo%20parks,activities%20on%20the%20parade%20fieldSt. Joseph's Cathedral

https://hellobuffalohikes.com/st-josephs-cathedral-the-old-one/

https://www.buffalodiocese.org/st-joseph-cathedral/

https://buffaloah.com/how/1/1.3/stjos.html

Wheatfield

Town of Wheatfield Profile

Wheatfield History section of Niagara County profiles 1897

Chuck Cedarman's Wheatfield town history from 2006

Wheatfield Town Historian's office archives and tax assessment records

Eugene Camann History of Wheatfield 1986

Town of Wheatfield – Our History - Facebook

Bell Aircraft

Wheatfield Town Historian records

Niagara Falls Aerospace Museum

Bell Aircraft Plant, preservationready.org

Bell Aerospace office will be demolished in Niagara Falls by Alexandra Rios-Malviya, Channel 2 3/14/2025, wgrz.com
Historic & Influential People from Buffalo & WNY – the Early 1900s by Rick Falkowski
Larry Bell's Legacy: Aerospace Pioneering by Hugh Neeson

Das Haus – German Heritage Museum

Das Haus, EinHaus und Der Stall booklet
Das Haus, EinHaus und Der Stall – German Heritage Museum, dashausmuseum.org
Das Haus Museum and its collection, whichmuseum.com
Niagara Historic Trail, A self-guided tour by the County of Niagara, North Tonawanda History Museum 2008-2009.

Sawyer Creek Hotel

Sawyer Creek Hotel, history, sawyercreekhotel.com
Discussions with the Cassata family
Wheatfield Town Historians archives and tax records

Williamsville

Town of Williamsville Profile

History of the City of Buffalo and Erie County by Henry Perry Smith
Images of America by Joseph A. Grande
A History of the Town of Amherst by Sue Miller Young
Buffaloah.com
Historic & Influential People from Buffalo & WNY – the 1800s by Rick Falkowski

Buffalo Niagara Heritage Village

Bigelow House c.1860s, HMdb.org
Buffalo Niagara Heritage Village 1975 – 2025, bnhv.org
Buffalo Niagara Heritage Village, theclio.com
Get to know Buffalo Niagara Heritage Village: The Village Store (circa 1888) by Queenseyes, Buffalo Rising 8/3/2021, buffalorising.com
Input from Carrie Stiver (BNHV Executive Director) and Rachel Ravago (BNHV Deputy Director & Curator)

Country Club of Buffalo

ccofbuffalo.org
The Clubhouse with Three Lives by Susan J. Eck in Western New York History in 2016, wnyhistory.org
Country Club of Buffalo, top100golfcourses.com

Eagle House

The Eagle House Restaurant – About Us, eaglehouseonline.com
Profiles Volume I: Historic & Influential People from Buffalo & WNY – the 1800s by Rick Falkowski.
Explore Buffalo: The Williamsville Tour by Explore Buffalo in Buffalo Rising 8/12/2020

Glen Park

The Zoo and Amusement Park in Williamsville that will take you back in time, Interview with Ron Globe, by Kadie Daye, wyrk.com 8/3/2021
Glen Park, buffaloah.com

Park Country Club

The Clubhouse with Three Lives by Susan J. Eck, Western New York History, 2016.
Park Country Club, parkclub.org
How Park CC Builds on its Grand tradition by Joe Banks, Club Resort Living 4/26/2018, clubandresortbusiness.com

Reformed Mennonite Church

Early History of Reist Mill at Amherst State Park, amherststatepark.org
Evans Bank- former Mennonite church of Williamsville, Amherst Town Archives by Andre Carrotflower, commons.wikipedia.org
Intensive Level Survey of Historic Resources, Amherst.ny.us

Saints Peter & Paul Church

The Chapel: A Comprehensive History of the Chapel and Pilgrimage of Our Lady Help of Christians, Cheektowaga, New York and of the Alsatian Immigrant Community at Williamsville, New York by Glenn R. Atwell and Ronald Elmer Batt
https://en.wikipedia.org/wiki/John_Neumann
https://ssppchurch.com/our-church/parish-history/

Williamsville Meeting House

The Meeting House, visitbuffaloniagara.com
The Meeting House, walkablewilliamsville.com
Williamsville won't sell Meeting House, eyes new uses for historic venue by Stephen T. Watson, *Buffalo News* 5/13/2021
Illustrated Williamsville Chronology, buffaloah.com
Discussions with Susan Fenster (Fenster)

Wilson

Town of Wilson Profile

Village of Wilson, villagewilson.digitaltowpath.org
Luther Wilson, Find A Grave, findagrave.com
Reuben Wilson, The Historical Database, HMdb.org
Niagara Historic Trail, North Tonawanda History Museum, 2008/9.

Wilson House

Village of Wilson, villagewilson.digitaltowpath.org
Luther Wilson, Find A Grave, findagrave.com
Reuben Wilson, The Historical Database, HMdb.org
Niagara Historic Trail, North Tonawanda History Museum, 2008/9.
The Reuben Wilson Home, wilsonnewyork.com
The Wilson House Restaurant, thewilsonhouserestaurant.com

Youngstown

Fort Niagara & the French Castle Profile

Oldfortniagara.org
Profiles Volume I: Historic & Influential People from Buffalo & WNY – the 1800s by Rick Falkowski
Fort Niagara – The Amazing Story of One of America's Oldest Military Fortifications, militaryhistorynow.com

Bibliography

Books

Atwell, Glen R. & Batt, Ronald Elmer. *The Chapel: A Comprehensive History of the Chapel and Pilgrimage of Our Lady Help of Christians Cheektowaga NY and of the Alsatian Immigrant Community at Williamsville NY*. Cheektowaga: Town of Cheektowaga, 1979.

Baker, Oneta M. *History of the Town of Clarence*. Clarence Center: Diane C. Baker, 1983.

Brown, Clifton E. and Whitaker, Ramona Pando. *Olmsted's Elmwood: The Rise, Decline and Renewal of Buffalo's Parkway Neighborhood*. Buffalo: Buffalo Heritage Press, 2022.

Brown, Richard C. and Watson, Bob. *Buffalo Lake City in Niagara Land*. Sponsored by Buffalo & Erie County Historical Society: Windsor Publications, 1981.

Crawford, June Justice & Carpenter, Gerald. *Images of America: Grand Island*. Charleston SC: Arcadia Press, 2015.

Delano, Cheryl. *Images of America: Evans and Angola*. Charleston SC: Arcadia Publishing, 2009.

Dunn, Edward T. *Buffalo's Delaware Avenue: Mansions and Families*. Buffalo: Canisius College Press, 2003.

Eberle, Scott & Grande, Joseph E. *Second Looks: A Pictorial History of Buffalo & Erie County*. Virginia Beach VA: Donning Company, 1987.

Falkowski, Rick. *History of Buffalo Music & Entertainment*. Williamsville: BuffaloHistoryBooks, 2017.

Falkowski, Rick. *Profiles Volume I: Historic & Influential People from Buffalo & WNY – the 1800s*. Williamsville: BuffaloHistoryBooks, 2019.

Falkowski, Rick. *Profiles Volume I: Historic & Influential People from Buffalo & WNY – the Early 1900s*. Williamsville: BuffaloHistoryBooks, 2021.

Falkowski, Rick. *The Spirit of Buffalo Women*. Williamsville: BuffaloHistoryBooks, 2023.

Goldman, Mark. *High Hopes: The Rise and Decline of Buffalo, New York*. Albany: State University of New York Press, 1984.

Grande, Joseph A. *Images of America: Amherst*. Mount Pleasant SC: Arcadia Publishing, 2004.

Halligan, Gerald L. & Oubre, Renee M. *Images of America: Knox Farms State Park*. Mount Pleasant SC: Arcadia Publishing, 2013.

Holmes, Donald. *The Town of Newstead: Bicentennial 1823-2023*. Town of Newstead, 2023

Kohler, C. Douglas. *Clarence: Images of the Hollow* – A publication by the Clarence Historical Society Press

Kowsky, Francis R. et al. *Buffalo Architecture: A Guide*, Cambridge: MIT Press, 1981.

Kowsky, Francis R. *County, Park & City: The Architecture and Life of Calvert Vaux*. New York: Oxford University Press, 1998.

Lalli, V. Roger. *The Buffalo Architectural Watercolors*. Hamburg: Boncraft Arts Publications, 2002.

Laux, Wilma. *The Village of Buffalo, 1800-1832*. Buffalo: Buffalo and Erie County Historical Society, 1960.

McAlonie, Kelly Hayes. *Louise Blanchard Bethune: Every Woman Her Own Architect.* Buffalo: State University of New York Press, 2023.

MacLeod, Rob Roy. *Cinderella Island.* Hassell Street Press, 1950.

Miller, Floyd. *Statler: America's Extraordinary Hotelman.* Buffalo: Statler Foundation, 1968.

Miller, Jeffrey J. *POP Warner: A Life on the Gridiron.* Jefferson NC: McFarland & Co. 2015..

Morgan, Lewis Henry. *The League of the Haudenosaunee or Iroquois.* North Dighton, MA: JG Press, 1852 & 1995.

Napora, James. *Houses of Worship: A Guide to the Religious Architecture of Buffalo New York.* Buffalo: State University of New York at Buffalo, 1995.

Nasaw, David. *Andrew Carnegie.* New York: Penguin Press, 2006.

Neal, Donna Zellner (ed.). *Niagara Historic Trail: A Self-Guided Historic Tour of Niagara County.* North Tonawanda: North Tonawanda History Museum, 2008.

Neal, Donna Zellner (ed.). *North Tonawanda: Historic Treasures, Vol 1 & 2.* North Tonawanda: North Tonawanda History Museum, 2011.

Neal, Donna Zellner (ed.). *North Tonawanda: The Lumber City.* North Tonawanda: North Tonawanda History Museum, 2007.

Neeson, Hugh. *Larry Bell's Legacy: Aerospace Pioneering.* Buffalo: BuffaloHistoryBooks, 2022.

Olenick, Andy and Reisem, Richard O. *Classic Buffalo: A Heritage of Distinguished Architecture.* Buffalo: Canisius College Press, 1999.

Olsen, Dr. Sandra. *The Armand & Eleanor Castellani Collection: Art for the Public Eye.* Lewiston: Castellani Art Museum of Niagara County, 2015.

Percy, John W. *The Erie Canal: From Lockport to Buffalo.* Buffalo: Partner's Press, 1979

Severance, Frank H. (ed.). *Picture Book of Earlier Buffalo.* Buffalo: Buffalo Historical Society, 1912.

Smith, Henry Perry. *History of the City of Buffalo and Erie County.* Syracuse: D. Mason Publishers, 1884.

Steiner, William H. and Coles, Sylvia. *Architecture + Advocacy: Robert Traynham Coles.* Tonawanda: Buffalo Arts Publishing, 2016.

Tielman, Timothy. *Buffalo's Waterfront: A Guidebook.* Buffalo: Partner's Press Inc., 1990.

Young, Sue Miller. *A History of the Town of Amherst, New York, 1818-1965.* Amherst: 1965.

Zornick, Daniel. *The Belt Line Railroad: Its Influence on the Development of Buffalo's Neighborhoods.* Buffalo: 2002

Publications

Information was gathered from the following newspapers, magazines and other publications to prepare this book. The article and author are listed in the source notes of the profile.

Buffalo Courier Express	*Home Magazine*
Buffalo History Gazette	*International Journal of Head and Neck Surgery*
Buffalo Magazine	*Jewish Journal*
Buffalo News	*Lockport Journal*
Buffalo Rising	*Niagara Frontier Publications*
Buffalo Spree	*Niagara Gazette*
Business First	*Springville Journal*
Cheektowaga Bee	*The German Citizen*
Clarence Bee	*The Griffin*
East Aurora Advertiser	*UB Dentist*
Forever Young Magazine	*Western New York (WNY) Heritage*
Hamburg Sun	

Websites

Information was reviewed in the following websites to prepare this book. The website and if applicable, the article and author, are listed in the source notes of the profile.

800westferry.org	belmonthousingwny.org
abaandonedamerica.us	bechsed.nylearns.org
aeroclubofbuffalo.org	bethunelofts.com
allentown.org	bfloparks.org
americanaristocracy.com	blogger.com
americanhistory.si.edu	blossomfestival.org
amherst.ny.us	bnhv.org
amherststatepark.org	bpo.org
ampoleagle.com	britannica.com
ancestors.familysearch.org	broadwaymarket.com
anchorbar.com	buffaloah.com
ancientodysseys.com	buffaloairport.com
answers.com	buffalocatholiccemeteries.org
apga.org	buffalocentralterminal.org
aploftsatlarkinville.com	buffalodiocese.org
archivaria.com	buffalogardens.com
archive.org	buffalogolfer.com
artpark.net	buffalohistory.org
atlasobscura.com	buffalohistorybuff.com
astronautix.com	buffalolib.org
aurorahistoricalsociety.com	buffalonews.com
babevillebuffalo.com	buffalonian.com
barnaabites.com	buffalony.gov

buffalophotoblog.com
buffaloresearch.com
buffalorising.com
buffaloseminary.org
buffaloschools.org
buffalospree.com
buffalostreets.com
buffalostories.com
buffalotales.net
buffalouu.org
buffalowater.org
buffalowaterfront.com
buffalozoo.org
buffumfamilyassociation.com
building-center.org
buildingsdb.com
burchfieldnac.org
burchfieldpenney.org
canalfest.org
cancer.gov
canisius.edu
carrouselmuseum.org
canisiushigh.org
carnegie.org
cattco.gov
cchsmcclurg.org
ccofbuffalo.org
cellinolaw.com
chautauqua.com
chautauqua.nygenweb.net
chautauqua.pastperfectonline.com
cheektowagacatholicfamily.org
cheektowagachronical.com
cheektowagahistorydotorg.wordpress.com
chestnutridgeconservancy.org
chq.gov
chq.org
chqdaily.com
chrisandle.wordpress.com
christinesmycaynski.com
cinematreasurers.org
cityhonors.org
cityofolean.org
cityseeker.com
clubandresortbusiness.com
columban.org
columgiadental.com
concordgrape.org
corporate.mattel.com
cradlebeach.org
crookedlakereview.com

curtisshotel.com
dailypublic.com
dashausmuseum.org
dec.ny.gov
destroyerparkgolf.com
dianemeholick.com
dictionary.com
digitalcommons.buffalostate.edu
discoverniagara.org
dlandwbuffalo.com
dukeofclarence.com
dyu.edu
eaglehouseonline.com
eastaurora.gov
eastaurorany.com
ellicottdevelopment.com
erie.gov
esd.ny.gov
exchange.aaa.com
experiencegraycliff.org
explore.com
exploringupstate.com
extapps.dec.ny.gov
falzguy.com
findagrave.com
findingaids.lib.buffalo.edu
flickr.com
fmi.org
forest-lawn.com
forgottenbuffalo.com
fortwiki.com
forums.aaca.org
franklloydwright.org
freepages.rootsweb.com
friendsoftimesbeachnp.org
garretclub.com
gatewayharbornt.com
geneseo.edu
goerie.com
goldwynn.com
goodyearmansion.com
grandislandny.myree.com
grist.org
guide.in.ua
habheegger.com
hamburghistoricalsociety.org
hartenergy.com
hatch.kookscience.com
hauntedhistorytrail.com
hellobuffalohikes.com
hhlarchitects.com

highmark.com
historiclewiston.org
historic-structures.com
hmdb.org
hodgsonruss.com
holyangelsbuffalo.com
hospicebuffalo.com
hullfamilyhome.com
iloveny.com
isledegrande.com
johnniewiley.org
juliusblembuilders.com
kleinhansbuffalo.org
lackawannany.gov
laconservancy.org
lancasteropera.org
lenoxhotelandsuites.com
lewistonhistoricalsociety.com
libguides.nybg.org
library.buffalostate.edu
lighthousefriends.com
lilydaleassembly.org
lipsitzpontario.com
lostcolleges.com
lumsdencpa.commartinhouse.org
marillacountrystore.com
mausoleums.com
mayerbrothers.com
michiganstreetbaptistchurch.org
midlifecycling.blogspot.com
militaryhistorynow.com
mohican.com
museum.dman.ny.gov
myheritage.com
mysteryscenemag.com
nashhousemuseum.com
nationalgridus.com
nationalmuseum.af.mil
nautoid.net
newadvent.org
newfanehistoricalsociety.com
newspapers.com
newyorkgenealogy.org
newyorkglobalmarketingsolutions.com
nfcnrhs.org
nfhps.org
niagara.edu
niagarafallsinfo.com
niagarafallsstatepark.com
niagarafrontier.com
niagarafallsusa.org

niagara-gazette.com
niagarahistory.org
niagarau.ca
niche.com
northparktheatre.org
npgallery.nps.gov
nthistory.com
ntmomentum.com
nyfalls.com
nyheritage.org
nyshistoricnewspaperrs.org
oakwoodniagara.org
observertoday.com
olcottbeachcarouselpark.org
oldfortniagara.org
olmstedcamp.com
olvbasillica.org
ophistoricalsociety.wordpress.com
optraindepot.org
orchardparkny.gov
ourouterharbor.org
owmintegrativewellness.com
packardinfo.com
parks.ny.gov
parkclub.org
parksidecandy.com
peacebridge.com
penndixie.org
perrysicecream.com
picryl.com
pierce-arrow.org
poloniatrail.com
postjournal.com
preservationbuffaloniagara.org
preservationready.org
primllc.com
projects.archiexpo.com
purpleeagle.edu
purpleniagara.edu
pyramidbrokerage.com
regandevelopment.com
regionalcouncils.ny.gov
reinsteinwoods.org
reporter.rit.edu
restoreourfield.org
retailcouncilnys.com
richardson-olmsted.com
riverloftsbuffalo.com
rivieratheatre.org
roswellpark.org
roycroftcampuscorporation.com

roycrofter.com
roycroftinn.com
salillehypmosis.com
sandiegoairandspace.org
sah-archipedia.org
saturnclub.org
sawyercreekhotel.com
schneiderdevelopmentservices.com
schwabls.com
seiz2day.com
sheepieniagara.com
silvercreekny.com
soleatwoodlawnbeach.com
spookeats.com
spcbuffalo.org
springvillegi.org
springvillejournal.com
ssppchurch.com
stlouischurch.org
stepoutbuffalo.com
ststansbuffalo.com
suncliffonthelake.com
sunsetbayusa.com
suny.buffalostate.edu
thebrisbanebuilding.com
thebuffalolofts.com
thecabe.com
thecazbuffalo.com
theclio.com
thecoloremusiciansclub.com
thecompletepilgrim.com
theguardian.com
thehydraulics.com
themayfaircastle.com
themlwendtfoundation.org
theniagarabranch.wordpress.com
thepiercearrowlofts.com
thestatlerbuffalo.com
thetheatreallianceofbuffalo.com
thewilsonhouserestaurant.com
thewurlitzerbuilding.com
tifft.org
tmmontante.com
tocny.org
tonawandacastle.com
tonawandasgatewayharbor.net
top100golfcourses.com
tornspacetheater.com

tourchautauqua.com
townballroom.com
townofaurora.com
townofcolden.com
townofevans.gov
townofhamburgny.gov
trainweb.org
travelthruhistory.com
trimaincenter.com
trinitybuffalo.org
tripadvisor.com
trsite.org
twentiethcenturyclcubbuffalo.com
ulrichs1868tavern.com
us-lighthouses.com
us.mentholatum.com
usgwarchives.net
va.gov
vidlers5and10.com
villageoflewiston.net
villageofspringvilleny.org
villagewilson.digitaltowpath.org
visitbuffaloniagara.com
walkablewilliamwville.com
warof1812cemetery.com
waymarketing.com
wearebuffalo.net
welchs.com
westfieldny.com
westseneca.gov
westsenecahistory.com
wgpfoundation.org
wgrz.com
whichmuseum.com
wibv.com
wikitree.com
wikipedia.org
wilsonnewyork.com
wkbw.com
wny.org
wnyheritage.org
wnyhistory.com
wnynewspapers.com
wnypapers.com
wurlitzerflats.com
wyrk.com
yumpu.com

Organizations

The following organizations were consulted to obtain information for the preparation of this book. Reference to the organization will be listed in the source notes of the profile.

Black Rock Historical Society

Buffalo Broadcasters Association

Buffalo History Museum

Cheektowaga Historical Association

Cheektowaga Historical Museum

Cheektowaga Historical Society

Clarence Historical Society

Concord Historical Society

Explore Buffalo

Grand Island Historical Society

Historical Society of the Tonawandas

Lackawanna Historical Association

Lancaster Historical Society

Lucy Bensley Center

National Register of Historic Places

Newstead Historians Office

Newstead Historical Society

Niagara Falls Aerospace Museum

North Tonawanda History Museum

Pierce Arrow Museum

Rich Twinn Octagon House

Spectrum News

Temple Beth Zion

Tonawanda-Kenmore Historical Society

West Seneca Historical Society

Wheatfield Town Historians' Office

Staff Photo

Figure 314 Mike Buckley (Editor), Ellen Mika Zelasko (Author), Nancy Wise-Reid (Interior Design), Doreen Gallagher Regan (Author) and Rick Falkowski (Author)
photo credit Mike Reid

Michael Buckley was a Computer Science and Engineering professor for 30 years, and is the author of numerous technical publications. He is currently a researcher at the University at Buffalo Medical School in communicative disorders and technologies for the disabled. He is a long-time unapologetic supporter of the wonderful life that is WNY.

Ellen Mika Zelasko is a (mostly) retired Buffalo history nerd of the highest level, is crazy about Buffalo architecture and homes, and especially the stories of the people behind them. There's always a story in there somewhere. Ellen is convinced she was born a century too late and sometimes wishes she could time travel to really experience Buffalo's gilded age. But then she'd miss her husband, her kids and grandkids. Wife, Mother and Nana are her favorite roles, after child of God, of course. Find Ellen at hellobuffalohikes.com.

Nancy Wise Reid, owner of WiseBookDesigns, is the expert behind beautifully formatted print books for authors. Her expertise in Microsoft Word, combined with a background in computer programming, allows her to precisely design and format every aspect of a book, delivering the high-quality PDF needed for printing. In addition to her book design work, Nancy empowers others through WiseClasses, teaching essential computer and smartphone skills. When she's not immersed in book design or computer use education, Nancy enjoys Origami the Japanese art of paperfolding.

Doreen Gallagher Regan was born and raised on the West Side of Buffalo. Her family owned Gallagher Printing and the Buffalo Rocket/ West Side Times weekly newspapers, which meant Doreen was exposed to print media at a very early age. She started writing stories and illustrating her own handmade children's books by the age of 7. After graduating from SUNY Geneseo and several years working in sales, she began volunteering as a literacy tutor and quickly realized her love for teaching. This led to a Masters in TESOL (Teaching English to Speakers of Other Languages) from The University of Buffalo, followed by a 35-year career as an educator. She has taught at colleges, universities, public schools and adult education programs around the country, often infusing local history lessons into her English classes. Doreen and her husband Daniel currently reside in the lovely hamlet of Derby, NY.

Rick Falkowski has been involved in all aspects of WNY entertainment during the past 60 years. He is the founder of the Buffalo Music Hall of Fame and Buffalo Music Awards, former publisher of Buffalo Backstage Magazine, coordinator of Tonawanda's Gateway Harbor Concerts, a UB graduate, USAF veteran and a Time Warner retiree. He presents classes on the History of Buffalo Music and Buffalo History at community centers, senior living centers, libraries, organizations and private/public clubs. In addition, Rick is the author of four books about the history of people from Buffalo and WNY, with several additional books in various stages of completion.

Books by Rick Falkowski

- *History of Buffalo Music & Entertainment* – published September 2017
- *Profiles Volume I: Historic & Influential People from Buffalo & WNY – the 1800s* – published October 2019
- *Profiles Volume II: Historic & Influential People from Buffalo & WNY – the Early 1900s* – published November 2021
- *The Spirit of Buffalo Women – Prominent Women who called WNY their Home* – published November 2023

Future books that will be published by Buffalo History Books

- *Profiles Volume III: Historic & Influential People from Buffalo & WNY – the Late 1900s*
- *Profiles Volume IV: Historic & Influential People from Buffalo & WNY – the 2000s*
- *Historical Places of Buffalo and WNY – Information about Historic Locations, Buildings, Homes & Places Volume II*

Several Area History Books by other Authors are also being considered for publication.

Books available at book stores, gift shops, museums and other locations across WNY

Available on-line at Amazon.com and store web sites.

History & Music Presentations available from Rick Falkowski

Figure 315 Buffalo History Museum Presentation photo credit Nancy Wise-Reid

- Early Buffalo Music & Entertainment
- Rock N Roll Buffalo
- Historic & Influential People from Buffalo & WNY – the early 1800s
- Town Founders
- Late 1800s Industry, Business & Culture
- Early 1900s Society & Culture
- Early 1900s Industry & Manufacturing
- Early 1900s Combo
- Spirit of Buffalo Women – Arts & Entertainment
- Spirit of Buffalo Women – Society & Business
- Philanthropists & Social Benefactors of WNY
- Historic Places of Buffalo & WNY – Niagara County
- Historic Places of Buffalo & WNY – Northtowns
- Historic Places of Buffalo & WNY – Southtowns
- Historic Places of Buffalo & WNY – Buffalo

To inquire about scheduling a presentation or having books sold at your business contact rickfalkowski@aol.com

Index

A

Adirondack style, 14, 271
Albright, John, 24, 77, 142, 145
Alfred A. Berrick, 41
American Institute of Architects, 45, 86
architect
  Albert Kahn, 107, 136
  Andrew Jackson Warner, 105
  Arthur Gillman, 138
  August Esenwein, 178
  B. Frank Kelly, 54
  Burton and Ellicott, 137
  Carmina Wood Morris, 21
  Clifford C. Wendehack, 308
  Clinton Brown, 70
  Colt & Alison, 308
  Cyrus K. Porter & Sons, 64
  Cyrus Kinne Porter, 210
  Daniel H. Burnham, 73
  Dietel, Wade & Jones, 39
  E.B. Green, 24, 26, 81, 116, 208, 260
  Edgar E Joralemon, 255
  Edward Austin Kent, 61
  Edward Kent, 142, 151
  Eliel & Eero Saarinen, 89
  Esenwein & Johnson, 53, 76, 116
  F.J. & W.A. Kidd, 89
  F.W. Caulkins, 132, 146
  first professional woman, 86
  first woman, 45
  Flynn Battaglia, 29
  Frank Henry Chappelle, 78
  Frank Lloyd Wright, 205
  Franklyn J. & William A. Kidd, 57
  Frederick Law Olmsted, 236
  George Cary, 43, 112
  George F. Newton, 47
  George J. Metzger, 221
  George Morton Wolfe, 100
  George Townsend, 98
  H.H. Little, 23
  H.H. Richardson, 102, 270
  Harold E. Plummer, 137
  Henry Hobson Richardson, 115
  Henry Spann, 104
  Isaac G. Perry, 282
  James A. Johnson, 81
  James B. McCreary, 93
  James Johnson, 178
  John H. Selkirk, 29
  Joseph E. Fronczak, 228
  Joseph Fronczak, 79
  Kenneth M. Murchison, 68
  Leon H. Lampert, 83
  Louise Blanchard Bethune, 89, 275
  Max Abramovitz, 130
  Milton E. Beebe & Son, 32
  Morton Wolf, 110
  Patrick Keely, 124
  Paul F. Mann, 77, 137
  Paul Mann, 63
  Richard A. Waite, 146
  Richard Upjohn, 126
  Robert North, 80
  Sebastian J. Tauriello, 66
  Sidney H. Woodruff, 131
  Sidney Hawks Woodruff, 46
  Stanford White, 150
  Theodore A. Biggie, 108
  Thomas Tilden, 147
  W.W. Carlin, 155
  William T. Spann, 123
  Williams Lansing, 52
architectural firm, 117
  Architectual Resources, 137
  Bethune, Bethune & Fuchs, 86
  Bley and Lyman, 20
  Dankmar Adler & Louis Sullivan, 84
  E.B. Green, 132
  E.B. Green & Son, 37, 143
  Esenwein & Johnson, 91, 93
  Fellheimer & Wagner, 38
  Fred Henry Loverin and Frederick A. Whelan, 87
  Green & Wicks, 95, 139, 145, 152, 247
  HHL, 46
  Leon H. Lampart & Sons, 263
  Lockwood, Green & Company, 45
  Richard Waite & F.W. Caulkins, 86
architectural gem, 29, 66
architectural masterpiece, 12, 96, 130
Architectural Resources, 29, 137
architectural style
  Art Deco, 114, 208
  Arts and Crafts, 178
  Beaux Arts, 90
  Brutalist, 130
  Colonial Revival, 94
  Daylight Factory Industrial, 112
  English, 187
  English Gothic, 126
  English-Flemish, 152
  Federal, 220, 227
  Georgian Revival, 150

Gothic, 190
Louis XIII, 149
Mid-Century Modern, 117
Neoclassical, 107
Richardsonian Romanesque, 115, 210
Romanesque, 105
Swiss Chalet, 157
Tudor, 96, 209
Tudor Revival, 119
Victorian Gothic, 152
architectural style
   Adirondack, 14
   Art Deco, 38
   Art Nouveau, 53
   Arts and Crafts, 78
   Beaux-Arts Classical, 81
   Chicago, 63
   Colonial Revival, 16, 37
   Craftsman, 28, 78
   Daylight Factory, 21
   Federal, 58
   French Renaissance, 82
   French Renaissance Revival, 61
   Gardenesque, 26
   Gothic and Collegiate Gothic, 47
   Gothic Revival, 29, 33
   Greek Revival, 5
   International, 89
   Italian Renaissance, 73
   Italian Renaissance Revival, 54
   Mediterranean Revival or Spanish Colonial Revival, 78
   Mission, 28
   Neoclassical, 57, 69
   Organic, 12
   Prairie, 26
   Renaissance Revival, 46
   Richardsonian Romanesque style, 60
   Romanesque Revival, 23, 52
   Rowhouses, 67
   Scottish, 13
   Traditional, 77
   Tudor Revival and Jacobean Revival, 57
architectural treasures, 67
Art Deco style, 20, 37, 38, 39, 81, 104, 113, 114, 168, 208
Art Nouveau style, 53
Arts and Crafts movement, 189, 190, 270, 271
Arts and Crafts style, 78, 178
Asa Ransom, 2, 175, 177, 178, 179, 300, 301, 338

B

Beaux Arts style, 90

Beaux-Arts Classical style, 81
Bellissimo
   Frank and Theresa, 27
Bethune, Louise Blanchard, 45, 60, 86, 275, 327, 354
Bishop Timon, 56, 65, 85, 125, 169, 215, 246
Brisbane
   Albert and George, 32
Brutalist style, 130
Buffalo Creek, 2, 18, 19, 44, 55, 81, 121, 160, 173, 177, 213, 219, 267, 285, 287, 288
Buffum Museum, 274, 348

C

Calvin N. Otis, 33
Cary, George, 43, 67, 112, 305
Charles Rich, 5
Chicago style, 63
Coit, George, 19, 58
Colonial Revival style, 16, 37, 48, 78, 94, 187
contemporary European architecture, 117
Cornell, S. Douglas, 61, 323
Cornell, Samuel G., 61
Craftsman style, 28, 78
Cyclorama Building, 36, 64, 210, 324

D

Darwin D. Martin, 8, 12, 20, 54, 75, 205
Darwin D. Martin House, 12
Darwin Martin House, 20, 66, 94
David F. Day, 35
daylight factory, 45, 262
Daylight Factory Industrial style, 112
Daylight Factory style, 21, 137
Delaware Midway Rowhouses, 67, 324
Depression, 3, 20, 22, 54, 57, 64, 89, 100, 112, 221, 233, 263
Depression, 339
Dietel, Wade & Jones, 39

E

E.B. Green, 24, 26, 69, 80, 81, 82, 96, 116, 208, 260, 305
E.B. Green & Company, 37
E.B. Green & Son, 37, 143
early 20th century Daylight Factory style, 137

early 20th century design style, 39
early American architecture, 163
Edward J. Meyer, 41
Ellicott, Joseph, 8, 18, 69, 73, 92, 102, 175, 177, 182, 266, 300, 301
English Country Gothic, 142
English Gothic style, 126
English style, 187
English style gardens, 13
English-Flemish style, 152
Esenwein & Johnson, 53, 76, 81, 93, 116

F

Father Nelson Baker, 169, 215, 217
Federal style, 58, 220, 227
Federal/Greek style, 231
Fellhemier & Wagner, 38
first
   African-American owned architecture firm in NYS, 117
   aircraft to break the sound barrier, 296
   aircraft to cross the Atlantic Ocean, 62
   area home with electricity, 231
   Buffalo's...bishop, 124
   business in Buffalo to have a telephone, 52
   chancellor of UB, 143
   child born ...in 1811, 313
   club run by women for women, 139
   clubhouse owned by women in the U.S., 47
   commercial installation of AC in the U.S., 81
   commissioner of Peace Bridge Authority Frank B. Baird, 111
   concert at ...Kleinhans Music Hall, 89
   consolidated banking system, 57
   curator of the Buffalo Zoo, 51
   designing...state park in the U.S., 149
   electrified block in the world, 130
   European settlement in WNY, 18
   female member of the American Institute of Archtects, 86
   Health Commissioner of Buffalo, 79
   high-rise building, 69
   hospital, 124
   Indian orphanage, 160
   integrated clubs in WNY, 59
   jet-powered airplane built, 136
   Judaic Museum in Buffalo, 130
   male saint from the U.S., 125
   mayor of Buffalo, 47
   mixed use redevelopment, 97
   modern air conditioning, 16
   Native American to win a gold medal for the United States, 277
   natural gas lighthouse in the world, 163
   not-for-profit organization to manage a public parks system in the country, 109
   oxygen extraction facility in America, 93
   pastor of Buffalo, 125
   plane to launch from an aircraft carrier, 62
   prefabricated homes in America, 157
   production of motorcycles in the U.S., 131
   professional woman architect, 86
   public high school in Buffalo, 91
   railroad between Buffalo and Niagara Falls, 283
   skyscraper in Buffalo, 84
   space built specifically as a motion picture theatre in the U.S., 73
   State Park in the U.S., 248
   suburb in WNY, 30
   suburb of Buffalo, 210
   tri-engine commercial passenger aircraft, 62
   unfermented grape juice ...in the U.S., 164
   use of the Niagara River for waterpower, 242
   woman architect, 45
   woman architect in the country, 89
   woman Fellow of the AIA, 86
   women's college in WNY, 65
Frank Lloyd Wright, 12, 20, 66, 75, 178, 190, 205
Frederick Law Olmsted, 24, 35, 51, 76, 88, 102, 109, 115, 117, 149, 245, 270
French & Indian War, 18, 225, 235, 241, 242, 315
French Renaissance Revival, 61, 91
French Renaissance style, 82
Fresh Air Mission, 9

G

Gardenesque style, 26
George Crandall, 277
George N. Pierce, 14, 112
Georgian Neoclassical, 15
Georgian Revival style, 48, 150
Gothic Revival and Collegiate Gothic style, 47
Gothic Revival style, 29, 33
Gothic style, 190, 246
Great Depression, 10, 38, 189, 191, 205, 253
Greek Revival, 5, 132, 179, 250, 271, 309
Green & Wicks, 67, 69, 82, 95, 115, 132, 139, 145

Grover Cleveland, 40, 48, 49, 63, 82, 92, 105, 116, 120, 144, 145, 147, 149, 170, 185, 194, 198, 216, 245, 246, 305, 321, 322, 341

H

H. Morton Perry, 3, 4
H.H. Richardson, xv, 36, 102, 149, 270
Hans Schmidt, 15
High Victorian Romanesque or Norman Romanesque, 105
Historical Society, xv, 5, 36, 43, 93, 121, 171, 173, 179, 186, 188, 194, 195, 198, 208, 209, 230, 231, 232, 248, 261, 269, 270, 273, 277, 280, 281, 283, 286, 288, 304, 311, 316, 327, 328, 337, 338, 339, 340, 341, 342, 346, 349, 353, 354, 361
Hoelscher Building Company, 63
Holland Land Company, 2, 7, 8, 11, 18, 87, 92, 102, 147, 154, 159, 163, 166, 173, 177, 178, 182, 230, 266, 274, 297, 300, 301, 313, 343

I

International style, 89
Isaac G. Perry, 60, 282
Italian Renaissance Revival style, 54
Italian Renaissance style, 73, 263
Italianate style, 269

J

J.N. Adam, 25, 319
Jacob Frederick Schoellkopf, 15
James C. Twinn, 5
James N. Adam, 25, 205
Jeffery Gundlach, 24
John B. Pierce, 26
John Blocher, 31, 97
John H. Selkirk, 29
    considered Buffalo's first architect, 42
John W. Cowper, 21
Johnson, Ebenezer, 19, 47, 257
Johnson-Jolls House Museum, 269
Jonathan Russell, 2, 5
Joseph Bond, 26

L

landscape architect
    Ellen Biddle Shipman, 12, 157
    Frederick Law Olmstead, 115, 149, 245

Lansing, Bley and Lyman, 70
Late Victorian Richardsonian Romanesque style, 282
Letchworth State Park, 94, 121
Letchworth, William, 160
Lewis Allen, 131, 194, 198, 341
Louis Le Couteulx, 23
Louis XIII style, 149
Louise Blanchard Bethune, 45, 89
Lyman, Duane, 56, 119, 208

M

mansion, 13, 15, 16, 31, 39, 61, 67, 77, 78, 90, 116, 128, 147, 148, 187, 210, 216, 231, 248, 250, 290, 318, 346, 350
    William Hengerer and William Gratwick, Jr., 20
Marling & Johnson, 67
Martin, Darwin R., 20, 54
McKim, Mead and White Architects, 150
Mediterranean Revival style, 78
Metz Brothers Construction Company, 63
Metz, Christian, 288, 350
Mid-Century Modern style, 117
Millard Fillmore, xv, 40, 43, 75, 102, 126, 128, 132, 142, 143, 145, 149, 182, 185, 188, 191, 227, 332, 340
Mission style, 28
modern-Tudor style, 20

N

National Historic Landmark, 72, 89, 115, 157, 188, 189, 190
Neoclassical, 46
Neoclassical style, 57, 69, 104, 107, 151
Neo-Gothic style, 20
Newton, George F., 47

O

oldest, 22, 23, 24, 33, 44, 47, 51, 58, 68, 70, 72, 84, 91, 120, 129, 132, 139, 140, 151, 156, 157, 168, 169, 171, 172, 182, 185, 192, 195, 208, 209, 216, 220, 240, 245, 250, 261, 291, 292, 294, 306, 309, 314, 315, 323, 325
Olmsted, 35, 88, 109, 115, 149, 236, 245
Olmsted Camp, 271
Olmsted, John, 271
Organic style, 12

P

Pan-American Exposition, 24, 28, 30, 40, 63, 71, 101, 112, 113, 178, 259, 326
Pierce Arrow Motor Company, 14
Pierce, George, 8, 14, 112, 113, 205
Pierce, George N., 14
Prairie style, 26
Pratt, Samuel, 18, 43
Pratt, Samuel Fletcher, 40

Q

Queen Ann style, 256

R

railroad architecture, 38
Red Jacket, 2, 43, 75, 109, 121, 286, 331
Regan Development Company, 46
Renaissance Revival style, 46
Richardsonian Romanesque style, 60, 115, 210, 282
Robert Borthwick Adam, 25, 162
Robert J. Reidpath, 33
Romanesque Revival style, 23, 52
Romanesque style, 270
Rowhouses, 67, 324

S

Samuel F. Pratt, 42, 47
Savarino Companies, 68, 74
Scottish style, 13
Seth Grosvenor, 36
Seymour Knox II, 24
Sgraffito style, 228
Shingle style, 305
Shipman, Ellen Biddle, 12, 157
skyscraper, 69, 84, 114, 326
Spanish Colonial Revival style, 78
Spencer Kellogg, 8, 13, 14, 205
Steamboat Gothic style, 283
stock market crash, 10
Swiss chalet style, 157

T

Traditional style, 77
Tudor Revival and Jacobean Revival styles, 57
Tudor Revival style, 119
Tudor style, 96, 209
Twentieth Century Club, 47, 71, 80, 139, 248, 333

U

Underground Railroad, 99, 224, 247, 248, 250, 294, 306
Urban, Jr., George, 168, 170

V

Victorian Gothic style, 152
Victorian style, 210

W

War Memorial Stadium, 60, 110, 144, 334
Welch, Leroy H., 56
Wendt Jr., Henry, 8, 16
William F. Felton, 33
William Heil, 10
William J. Conners, 11, 149
William McKinley, 40, 102, 105, 147, 150, 239, 275
William Schack, 10
William Wicks, 69
Williams Lansing, 52, 60, 322
Woodruff, Sidney Hawks, 46